AUSTRIAN ECONOMICS

CLASSICS
IN
AUSTRIAN ECONOMICS

A Sampling in the History of a Tradition

Edited by
ISRAEL M. KIRZNER

VOLUME I

THE FOUNDING ERA

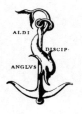

LONDON
WILLIAM PICKERING
1994

Published by Pickering & Chatto (Publishers) Limited
17 Pall Mall, London, SW1Y 5NB

© Pickering & Chatto (Publishers) Limited
Introduction © Israel M. Kirzner

British Library Cataloguing in Publication Data
Classics in Austrian Economics: A Sampling
in the History of a Tradition. – Vol. I: The
Founding Era
I. Kirzner, Israel M.
330.9436
Set ISBN 1 85196 138 0
This volume ISBN 1 85196 155 0

Printed and bound in Great Britain by
Antony Rowe Limited
Chippenham

VOLUME I

CONTENTS

v

VOLUME II

CONTENTS

CONTENTS

B13

IX — XXX

BK Title

ed.

INTRODUCTION

The three volumes making up this collection of papers in Austrian Economics cover a one-hundred-year span of modern intellectual history, from approximately 1870 to 1970. In the history of economics, the Austrian School is recognized as an important component in the development of contemporary economic thought. The purpose of these volumes is to provide a sampling of the contributions of the major writers in the Austrian tradition, in order to illustrate the nature of that tradition, its development and maturation during its history, and its relation to other contemporaneous varieties of economics. A major focus is thus upon the modifications and changes in Austrian thinking which have occurred over the decades, and consequently upon the changing character of what has constituted the essential characteristics of Austrian thought, at different periods throughout this century of Austrian economic thought. The time period covered commences, naturally enough, with the beginning of the school's existence, as marked by the 1871 publication of Menger's *Grundsätze*. It concludes at about 1970, by which time all the important contributions to economics of both Mises and Hayek had already been made.

It has proved convenient to divide this collection into three chronologically separate volumes. The first volume contains contributions by the early Austrians up until the outbreak of World War I. The founding period between 1871 and 1914 is generally recognized as constituting a single continuous stage of intellectual development in Austrian Economics. The papers selected for this volume express the major contributions of the founders of Austrian Economics, and cover the gamut of topics, from methodology to utility theory, to the theory of value, the theory of capital, the theory of money, and to an exercise in applied economics.

Volume II consists of papers taken from books and journals of the interwar period. This period saw a vigorous spurt of development in Austrian thought, propelling the school to the forefront of professional attention, and also marking its closest agreement with mainstream economic doctrine. In a narrow sense, it was the period of greatest professional success – but the close of this period also represented the beginning of a long period of eclipse for Austrian Economics.

This period of eclipse beginning in the late 1930s left only two major economists whose on-going work was clearly identified by the profession as being in the Austrian tradition. These economists were, of course, Ludwig von Mises and Friedrich von Hayek. Their work continued vigorously, for each in his own separate mode, for several decades; and, as we shall argue, that work, taken together, represented a decisively important new stage in the history of Austrian Economics. The work of Mises and Hayek (*including* a sampling of their contributions during the interwar years) make up the contents of Volume III. For a variety of reasons this collection of papers does *not* cover the period since 1970, which has been marked by a remarkable rebirth of interest and work in the Austrian tradition (largely building upon the work of Mises and Hayek).

Both Volume II and Volume III open with introductory essays by the editor, providing overviews of the character and significance of the respective periods covered by these volumes. This present introductory essay will, besides providing a similar overview of the contents of Volume I, offer a somewhat idiosyncratic bird's-eye view of the entire history of Austrian Economics, and comment on a variety of fascinating *dogmengeschichtliche* puzzles and ironies that characterise that history.

*   *   *

The Distinctiveness of the Austrian School: Puzzle and Paradox

The founding period in Austrian Economics began with the 1871 publication of Carl Menger's *Grundsätze* (see in this volume, papers 2 and 3). The notion of any such entity as an Austrian *School*, however, certainly had no factual relevance before the 1980s (see Mises, 1969, p. 10). It was in the 1980s that a series of important works by Eugen von Böhm-Bawerk and Friedrich von Wieser reinforced the central innovative doctrines introduced by Menger. Several students of Menger published their books in this period. In addition Menger's 1883 work on methodology, together with Gustav Schmoller's contemptuous review of it (on this see further in this volume, paper 5), ushered in the *Methodenstreit*, the famous (or notorious) dispute over method which raged between the Austrians and the dominant German Historical School. All this focused professional attention on the work of Menger and his younger colleagues, so that by the early 1890s, Menger, Böhm-Bawerk, and Wieser, were writing articles for British and American scholarly journals, for foreign audiences apparently eager to learn about the newly emerging school of thought in Austria (see, in this volume, papers 4, 5, 9). By the turn of the century, such overseas attention to the Austrians had generated translations of their books into

English, and (particularly for Böhm-Bawerk) extensive polemical discussion with foreign critics (see e.g. in this volume, paper 6).

Paradoxically, the features of Austrianism which set it apart from other contemporary schools of economics were eventually to undermine its distinctiveness in the eyes of the profession. In these formative, founding decades of the Austrian School, this distinctiveness was perceived (both by its own members and by economists elsewhere) as consisting in two significant features. First, it was identified as the *subjectivist* school (sometimes, for example by Wieser, see in this volume, paper 11, this was expressed by reference to the 'psychological method'), in that its theories placed prime emphasis upon the subjective preferences of consumers (rather than upon the objective conditions governing production). Second, the Austrian School was identified as a *theoretical* school, impatient with the narrowly descriptive studies of the Historical School, and eager to demonstrate the validity of economic laws which transcend the particularities of time, place, and institutional circumstance. The first of these two features came, for later historians of economic thought, to mean that the Austrians were perceived as hardly distinctive at all, being seen as merely one element in the marginalist revolution which introduced neoclassical economics and pushed Ricardianism (and classical economics generally) from centre stage in post-1870 economics. The second of the above two features was, again, to mean (especially with the decline of the German Historical School after 1914) that the Austrian methodological stance was seen as basically identical with that adopted by economists generally. To insist on the vindication of pure economic theory, however controversial this may have been in the latter decades of the nineteenth century, was, in the early twentieth century, to push against an open door. So it is not surprising to discover that, by 1930, it was widely held among Austrians and other economists alike, that while the emergence of the Austrian School was indeed an important and benign historical element in the advance of modern economics, there was nonetheless no continuing basis for emphasizing any uniquely distinctive characteristics of Austrian economic thought (as compared to the neoclassical consensus which had crystallized within the profession by that date). When Lionel (later Lord) Robbins wrote his hugely influential 1932 book, *The Nature and Significance of Economic Science*, he did so after having thoroughly absorbed the Austrian ideas of the interwar period, in the works of such Austrians as Mises, Mayer, Schams, Strigl, Schönfeld, Hayek and Morgenstern, but he saw these Austrian ideas as throwing a fresh light on the true character of a commonly-shared *mainstream* economics, rather than as representing an alternative theoretical structure. What was valid and important in Austrian economic theory had, by the time Robbins wrote, already been successfully absorbed into the mainstream itself. Or so, at least, ran the conventional wisdom.

And here we have before us the essential puzzle which suffuses the history of the Austrian School – and to the exploration of which much of this *Introduction* will be directed: the subsequent history of Austrian Economics (particularly that reflected in the papers in the third volume of the present collection) would prove this conventional wisdom, which seemed so plausible around 1930, to be quite false. It would become apparent that the Mengerian legacy would generate developments in the theory of the market process which would be thoroughly inconsistent with the central content of the neoclassical orthodoxy (as that orthodoxy developed organically from the mainstream economics of the pre-Keynesian era). These developments would mature in the decades *after* the close of the Mises-Hayek era represented here in the third and final volume of this collection. It is in the contemporary *post*-Misesian revival of Austrian Economics that the distinctiveness of the Austrian tradition has emerged as a natural extension of – or perhaps more accurately, the explicit unpacking of the ideas implicit in – the theoretical contributions pioneered by Menger in his 1871 *Grundsätze*.

A Thesis Asserted

In this section we concisely present, as a thesis to be developed and defended in the subsequent sections of this Introduction, an interpretation of the overall history of the Austrian tradition capable, we claim, of accounting for the changes over time in the perception of the distinctiveness (or lack of it) of Austrian Economics.

This thesis is that Menger, already in 1871, glimpsed a radically subjectivist way of understanding the determination of economic phenomena in market economies, which diverged sharply, of course, from that of classical economics. It was a vision, however, which really did differ sharply, in its radical subjectivism, also from the broad understandings of the economic process which came to be encapsulated in Marshallian and in Walrasian economics. Menger, however, was not able to articulate the full implications of what he glimpsed. Nor did his immediate associates and followers fully grasp the complete perspective which their master had, at least in outline, perceived. They proceeded, therefore, to develop certain parts or aspects of Menger's explicitly stated economic doctrines *without* placing their contributions in the context of Menger's wider (but incompletely articulated) subjectivist vision of the economic process. Because the early developments in Austrian economics (certainly up until about

1930) were direct extensions of the work of Böhm-Bawerk and Wieser, rather than of Menger himself, it is not surprising that the Austrian economics of the interwar period failed to reflect those aspects of the Mengerian subjectivist vision which, as stated, really did differ sharply from the understandings of Marshallian and of Walrasian economics. It is for this reason that the economics of the interwar Austrians (represented in this collection in the papers on Volume II) seemed, and still seems, by and large to be closest to the economics of the mainstream of the profession.

Our thesis further maintains that the debate concerning the possibility of rational economic calculation under central planning, a debate which raged in the interwar period and in which Mises and Hayek were the prominent exponents of what came to be seen as the 'Austrian' position had, as an unintended side effect, an important influence on the thought of both Mises and Hayek (but not necessarily upon that of other Austrians). The debate forced Mises and Hayek separately to come to grips with aspects of the economic process which called for precisely those radically subjectivist insights which had been implicit, at the very least, in Menger's broad vision. It was their articulation of these newly discovered or rediscovered insights (see e.g. papers 22, 26, 30, 31) which definitively came to mark the Austrian economics of the era of Mises and Hayek as in no way to be considered congruent with mainstream economics. It was, further, these newly articulated insights which inspired the revival of Austrian Economics which we have witnessed in the post-Misesian period. And it is, accordingly, by no means surprising that it has been in the course of this revival (and of reactions to it) that there has occurred in recent years a remarkable volume of fresh research into the economics of Menger and its relation to the economics of his contemporary marginal utility pioneers in other schools. See for example Smith and Grassl (1986), Caldwell (1990), Alter (1990), Streissler (1990), Hayek (1972).

What was it that Menger saw? How did his followers, pursuing Menger's insights, fail to see what Menger had seen? And how did these lost insights come to be rediscovered in the work of Mises, Hayek, and of the subsequent Austrians who were themselves inspired by Mises, or by Hayek, or by both? Let us start from the beginning.

The Mengerian Vision

In order to understand what constituted the essence of Menger's vision, we have to appreciate the revolution which that vision implied in regard to the Ricardian view of the world, which Menger was concerned to displace.

In the Ricardian view of the world, the economic phenomena which economic theory can account for (and which therefore mark out the boundaries within which attempts by economists to account for real world observables must be confined) are those rigidly determined, at least in the long run, by objective, physical realities. It is the set of such realities which inexorably determine, for Ricardian economics, the size and rate of growth of aggregate output, and the pattern of distribution of this output among the major classes of productive factors which produce that output. It is true that no Ricardian could *entirely* exorcise the human element from the economic explanations. Wealth must, after all, be defined in terms of human needs and desires. The economic explanations must rely upon the behaviour of 'economic men'. But the central point is that in the Ricardian view, the nature of wealth and the behaviour of economic men can be treated as physical, or at least biological, constants. The explanations need place no reliance upon human resourcefulness, human valuations, human expectations, human discoveries. The inexorable course of economic history is one which proceeds almost regardless of what mere mortals may wish, desire, believe, or decide. (The circumstance that it is this view of economic history which was to characterize Marxist economics was to have much to do with the dramatic tensions which were later to develop between the Marxists and the Austrians – the heirs to the Mengerian anti-Ricardian legacy.)

As opposed to this Ricardian view of the economy, Menger saw a way to understand economic history in diametrically opposite terms. Economic outcomes, while certainly vitally affected by physical and biological realities, are directly caused only by the actions of human beings. From this Mengerian perspective the physical and biological realities recede into the background; they become the passive material of the world upon which acting man impinges. Admittedly, what acting man can achieve is sharply constrained by the natural scarcities which circumscribe the world and which, indeed, impose the need to economize; but what is achieved, and the entire array of prices, patterns of outputs, and structure of production methods, are achieved through human actions and are vitally affected by man's beliefs, desires, expectations and knowledge.

Understanding Menger's revolutionary perspective upon the economic process in this way rather than as an approach focused narrowly upon the foundations of the theory of economic value permits us, perhaps, to solve a certain puzzle which has been introduced into Mengerian scholarship by the work of Erich Streissler (1990). What we have seen is that Menger's revolutionary perspective consists not in the theory of subjective value which it generated, but in its understanding of the prime causal role of human action in the determination of economic phenomena. It is only in terms of this appreciation of Menger's vision that we can account for the fact that, of the marginal utility pioneers, only Menger perceived the outlines, at least, of a marginal productivity theory of resource prices. For Menger the subjective theory of value was merely an implication of the subjective appreciation of the economic process. Streissler has, in a paper of surpassing scholarship, drawn attention to earlier German economists such as Hermann, Rau, Hufeland, Schäffle, Mischler and Schuz, whose value theories incorporated subjectivist insights long before Menger. He has therefore labelled as 'myth' the doctrine that Carl Menger developed his 'novel insights quite independently and in actual constrast to German economics' of the time (op. cit., p. 31).

Yet it is difficult to ignore Menger's own apparent conviction of the revolutionary character of his work. Hayek has reported that Menger 'is said to have once remarked that he wrote the *Grundsätze* in a state of morbid excitement' (Hayek, 1934). While subsequent historians of economics may perhaps have created something of a myth concerning Menger's supposed independence of predecessors, it seems safe to assert that Menger's revolutionary *overall* perspective owes little to the precursors Streissler has identified. It is one thing to show that subjective theories of value preceded Menger and may well have influenced Menger's own theory of value, either directly or indirectly. It would be quite another thing to claim that Menger's vision of an economy created and shaped by human action was not a totally original one. Streissler's thesis, of course, implies no such claim. And indeed the integration of earlier ideas concerning subjectively determined values into Menger's own subjectivist perspective on how economic phenomena in general are generated, *would* certainly constitute a most revolutionary advance in economic understanding.

Having characterized Menger's innovation as consisting in its vision of economic phenomena as being caused by human action, it is necessary immediately to point out the incompleteness of that vision (see Kirzner, 1992, chapter 4). A critic of the above suggested interpretation of Menger's essential contribution might well draw attention to crucial passages in Menger's writings which appear to contradict that interpretation. In the preface to his *Grundsätze*, for example, Menger was concerned to counter the views of those 'who question the existence of laws of economic behaviour by referring to human free will.' Menger responded to these views by asserting, *inter alia*, that 'whether and under what conditions an *economic exchange* of goods will take place between two economizing individuals, and the limits within which a *price* can be established if an exchange does occur – these and many other matters are fully as independent of my will as any law of chemistry is of the will of the practising chemist.' Reference to the freedom of the human will can never justify the 'denial of the conformity to definite laws of phenomena that condition the outcome of the economic activity of men and are entirely independent of the human will. It is precisely phenomena of this description, however, which are the objects of study in our science' (Menger, 1981, pp. 48ff.).

Although these passages might admit of interpretation not inconsistent with what we have claimed to be Menger's subjectivist perspective, we certainly cannot and do not claim that Menger believed himself to have seen how it is *precisely* the freely-exerted wills of human beings which generate powerful tendencies towards definite outcomes. We do not claim that Menger at all clearly understood the entrepreneurial role exercised by alert market participants in achieving a tendency towards market coordination. Our claim is simply that he saw the causal source of market phenomena in the actions of the human participants in the market process; and that it was this vision of Menger's which, consciously or unconsciously, inspired subsequent generations of Austrians towards a more completely subjective theory of the market process.

On the Distinctiveness of the Austrian School: Paradox confronted

Our statement of Menger's revolutionary perspective on the entire economic process can perhaps help us resolve some of the paradoxes noted earlier regarding perceptions of the distinctiveness of the Austrian School. We noted how the emergence of the Austrian School during the 1880s attracted professional attention in England and the U.S.A. The methodological and doctrinal characteristics of the school were considered sufficiently novel to confer a certain distinctiveness upon it. And yet, within a few short decades, it came to be thought that there was little that set the economics of Vienna apart from that of other neoclassical schools. No doubt some fraction of this change in perceptions can be attributed to developments that had occurred, during these decades, in the economics of other neoclassical schools. (It was during these decades that equilibrium theorizing came to be refined and widely introduced explicitly into mainstream discussions.) But attention to changes within Austrian Economics itself can, in the light of our statement of Menger's overall vision of the economy, offer still further insights.

What seems to have occurred is that Menger's subjective view of the determination of economic phenomena came rather rapidly to be reduced, in Austrian Economics, to the subjective theory of value. In the work of both Böhm-Bawerk and Wieser, it was the subjective theory of value which was emphasized; certainly there is little in their work which recognizes, let alone expands upon, Menger's groping glimpse of a fully subjective theory of the market process. Böhm-Bawerk's theory of capital and interest reflected his emphasis upon subjective intertemporal rankings of value (time-preferences); as such it represented an extension of marginal utility theory. But the macroeconomics of Böhm-Bawerk's vision of a capital-using market economy owes very little to subjectivism. Indeed the late Ludwig Lachmann has pronounced Böhm-Bawerk's vision to be a fundamentally Ricardian one [Lachmann, 1977, p. 253].

After World War I, with both Menger and Böhm-Bawerk no longer alive (Menger died in 1921), with Menger's book seen as something of a dated classic work rather than as the basis for current advanced research, the development of economics in Vienna seems to have been in a direction definitely at variance with that adumbrated, at least, in Menger's original anti-Ricardian vision. The theory of consumer choice that was being refined during the 1920s, based on marginal utility theory, was hardly different, on fundamentals, from that which was being developed in Marshallian and in Walrasian economics. (See in this edition, Volume II, paper 17.) Human choice was still viewed in rather mechanical terms, with the outcome seen as more or less already implicit in the relevant operative constraints and assumed marginal utility schedules (see Ebeling). There was little in the economics of Vienna in the 1920s that could draw attention to the problems of uncertainty, information and ignorance. Even expectations were hardly in the forefront of Austrian economists' minds at that time. While Austrian Economics could hardly be confused with the Ricardian perspective, the same was after all true also of Marshallian and Walrasian economics. It is true that Marshallian economics did explicitly seek to retain an explanatory role for the physical realities which condition production possibilities, while Austrian economics did not. But this difference (if indeed it was noticed at all) must have appeared as not much more than a matter of detail in the theory of value, rather than as reflecting any deep-seated philosophical differences regarding the nature of economic explanations.

On the surface at least, a certain unanimity among the major theoretical schools of the 1920s must have seemed to prevail. As noted earlier, Robbins's *Nature and Significance* did not seek to improve British economics by introducing Austrian theoretical innovations. Rather he sought to teach British economists how their own Marshallian doctrines could be expressed more tightly and understood more satisfyingly when placed consistently within a continental framework which emphasizes individual allocative decisions and the manner in which they interact in markets. While there *was* a sense that new frontiers were beckoning to be conquered (perhaps by extensions of Austrian capital theory, or monetary theory, for example), the settled territory already well behind the front lines was seen as shared in common by economists of all schools.

For the Austrians themselves, especially those old enough to remember the pre-war dominance of the Historical School in German-language economics, this unanimity was perceived to be reinforced by the shared theoretical and anti-historicist methodological approach. No doubt it was this that led Mises to declare in 1932 that, although it is 'customary to distinguish several schools', in modern economics, the fact is 'that these three schools of thought differ only in their mode of expressing the same fundamental idea and that they are divided more by their terminology and by peculiarities of presentation than by the substance of their teachings' (Mises [1933], 1960, p. 214).

As we shall see, however, this unanimity was superficial. Although in 1932 it might have *seemed* to Mises that 'the substance' of the teachings of the major schools was a commonly shared one, nonetheless it would become apparent in the years ahead that in fact Austrian economic thought pointed in a direction very different from that towards which the confluence of Marshallian and Walrasian thought was to proceed. In fact it would be Mises himself, more than anyone else, who very soon came to emphasize the sharp differences which separated his own economics from that of the neoclassical mainstream. And it seems plausible to claim that it was the Mengerian subjectivist legacy, with all its incompleteness, which was to inspire those subsequent developments in Austrian Economics which would reestablish unmistakably the unfashionable distinctiveness of Austrian Economics. A number of these subsequent developments seemed to have occurred in the course of, and as a result of the celebrated interwar debate on the possibility of rational economic calculation under central planning. (See Kirzner, 1992, chapter 6.) But before we turn to examine the impact of this debate upon the future history of the Austrian School, it may be useful to consider what an eminent Austrian-trained economist, thoroughly steeped in the economics of Vienna circa 1930, was to see years later as the basic tenets of Austrian Economics. This list will be revealing in its confirmation of the fundamental *lack* of distinctiveness in Austrian Economics at that date, ascribed to it by its staunchest adherents.

Fritz Machlup and the Essentials of Austrian Economics

Fritz Machlup was one of the remarkable young economists, educated at the University of Vienna in the 1920s, who were participants in Mises's famous *Privat-seminar* at that time, and who were, in later phases of their careers, to become world famous in their profession. Machlup, whose work on Austrian Economics during the interwar period is represented in the present collection by paper 20 in Volume II was to migrate to the U.S. in the 1930s and establish a brilliant and prolific teaching and research record. On a number of occasions Machlup sought to identify the essential components of Austrian Economics (see Machlup, 1981, 1982).

For Machlup these components were (i) *methodological individualism*: in 'the explanation of economic phenomena we have to go back to the actions (or inaction) of individuals'; (ii) *methodological subjectivism*: in 'the explanation of economic phenomena we have to go back to the judgments and choices made by individuals on the basis of whatever knowledge they have or believe to have and whatever expectations they entertain ...'; (iii) *tastes and preferences*: demand is determined by subjective valuations of goods and services; (iv) *opportunity costs*: the true character of economic costs is that they reflect the alternative opportunities that must be foregone; (v) *marginalism*; (vi) *time structure of production*.

A brief glance at this list must confirm the judgment that the Austrian Economics of which Machlup was writing was hardly different from that of the mainstream Anglo-American approach. In the latter, too, (at least insofar as it is expressed in mainstream microeconomics), methodological individualism and subjectivism play a role. Of course the mainstream theory of consumer demand has a place for tastes and preferences. And marginalism and the jargon of opportunity costs are, of course, among the most fundamental elements in the professional vocabulary of all the modern economists.

Two items are strikingly absent from Machlup's list which, from the perspective of late twentieth-century Austrian Economics, would seem utterly essential. These are (vii) the emphasis upon market *process* (rather than upon market equilibrium conditions); and (viii) the recognition that economic choices are made in an open-ended context of Knightian uncertainty, in which the determination of the relevant parameters of the choice context (constraints and preferences) is itself an integral part of the act of choice. That Machlup omitted these elements of the modern Austrian position expresses, certainly, the extent to which the Austrian Economics of 1930 was to develop in the subsequent half-century – the age of Mises and Hayek. At the same time these omissions explain, in part, why an economics which would seem so unfashionable in the 1970s, a half century earlier could be thought to be so close to the mainstream. What we wish to show now is how, partly as a result of the economic calculation debate, the legacy of Mengerian subjectivism was to generate, within the Austrian Economics of the 1920s, a ferment of intellectual development that would eventually produce a variety of Austrian Economics which someone trained in the earlier decades (such as a Fritz Machlup) might find it difficult to comprehend fully.

It will be this ferment of intellectual development which will account for the difference in 'flavour' between many of the papers in Volume II of the present collection (covering the interwar period), and many of those in Volume III (covering the decades after World War II, the age of Mises and Hayek).

The Socialist Economic Calculation Debate

It was Mises's famous 1920 article (paper 22 in Volume III of this collection) which set off the debate. Although, as was later established (see Hayek, 1935; Mises [1922], 1936, p. 135 fn.), several turn-of-the-century economists had raised the question of how socialist planners might grapple with the allocative problems of a complex society, it was Mises who placed the calculation problem squarely before the economics profession. He pointed out that rational planning in a complex economy demands that planners distinguish between the values of different resource quantities. Only by reference to such values (reflecting the alternative uses that might be served by these resources elsewhere in the economy) might planners be able efficiently to steer resources away from less important uses towards more valuable purposes. Such indexes of value emerge in capitalist economies, of course, as a result of competitive markets in resource services. But because such resource markets must, by the very definition of socialism, be absent in the centrally planned economy, the central planners necessarily find themselves without the basic tools necessary for economic calculation. It was this Misesian thesis which came to be perceived as the 'Austrian' side of the calculation debate.

A flurry of German-language responses in the 1920s sought to defend the possibility of socialist economic calculation. But it was not until the 1930s that a series of more sophisticated responses emerged, and these happened to be in the English language. For the purpose of our brief survey here it is sufficient to focus attention upon the contributions asserting the viability of socialist calculation which were made by Oskar Lange and Abba P. Lerner (see Lange [1936] 1964; Lerner, 1944). It was these contributions which persuaded the mainstream writers (but not the Austrians themselves!) that Mises's critique of socialist planning was, while important and insightful, not necessarily fatal for the possibility of rational central planning.

The Lange-Lerner thesis (it is generally treated as a single thesis, although it was developed in separate contributions by these two economists) acknowledges the force of Mises's basic argument. Mises is certainly correct in drawing attention to the critical need for resource prices, in order for efficient production decisions to be made that should not mis-allocate scarce social resources. However where Mises erred, in the opin-ion of Lange and Lerner, is in his assertion that without capitalist markets for the services of productive resources no prices can be imagined for these services. Prices, Lange and Lerner maintain, are simply magnitudes attached to economic goods which govern the decisions being made con-cerning the utilization of these goods. (The statement by Wicksteed ([1910] 1933, p. 28) is cited, in which a wider sense of the meaning of price is held to be 'the terms on which alternatives are offered to us'.) There is no reason, in principle, why these magnitudes must be those emerging from the exchanges made in markets. A central planning author-ity could announce these non-market prices and instruct the managers of socialist enterprises on the manner in which these prices should govern production decisions. By periodically monitoring the aggregate outcomes of these managerial decisions, the central planners can adjust these non-market prices periodically (in a manner not fundamentally different from that in which market prices fluctuate in response to the surpluses and shortages occurring in resource markets). In brief, Lange and Lerner are suggesting an artificial resource 'market' in which socialist managers 'com-pete' for scarce resources on the basis of 'prices' announced by the central planners. This is not the place to examine critically the substantive con-tent of this Lange-Lerner response to the Austrian challenge to the possi-bility of socialist efficiency. We are concerned only to trace those develop-ments in Austrian Economics that occurred during the age of Mises and Hayek which, we argue, can be attributed to the impact of the socialist calculation debate.

As has been extensively demonstrated by Professor Don Lavoie (see Lavoie, 1985), the position articulated by Lange and Lerner reflects the mainstream understanding of the nature of price and the centrality of market equilibrium. The position taken by Mises and by Hayek, on the other hand, reflects a different Austrian appreciation of the nature of market prices, and also the Austrian perspective on the centrality of dynamic, entrepreneur-driven market processes (rather than of equilib-rium states of affairs). In subsequent literature it was considered that the Lange-Lerner solution had effectively disposed of Mises's challenge to the possibility of socialist efficiency. This must be attributed to the dominance of the mainstream equilibrium paradigm and to the unfamiliarity of that literature with the Austrian market process paradigm. The responses by Mises and by Hayek to the Lange-Lerner literature must, *ex post*, be pronounced to have proven unconvincing. This must be partly attributed, in turn, to the circumstance that both Mises and Hayek were at least in the earlier stages of the calculation debate, not yet completely aware of the paradigmatic contrast between the mainstream and the Austrian perspectives. Indeed, it was only their exposure to the Lange-Lerner arguments which gradually compelled Mises and Hayek to recognize clearly the process character of their own understanding of markets. Understandably their early responses to the Lange-Lerner arguments failed to come to grips with the roots of the disagreement. While both Mises and Hayek certainly sensed the inadequacy of a non-market price system for overcoming the problems of mutual ignorance which beset the disequilibrium economy, at that stage of the development of Austrian Economics, they were not able to spell out the nature of that inadequacy convincingly.

It should be emphasized that our contention is not that the calculation debate taught the Austrians to advance from an equilibrium view to a *different* view – a process view – of markets. We maintain, rather, that for the Austrians, the debate induced a more complete and clear understanding of what was already implicit in their theory of the market. In arguing that the calculation debate was an important catalyst in the development of Austrian Economics we are asserting that the debate led to the crystallization, in the work of Mises and Hayek, of insights which had indeed not been specifically articulated until then, but which were nonetheless deeply embedded in the Mengerian perspective. These insights had, during the interwar period, not been explicitly articulated, which permitted the general view at that time that Austrian Economics differed only in language and style from the Marshallian and Walrasian mainstream. It was the emerging clarity with which these insights came to be perceived and articulated by Mises and Hayek, as the calculation debate faded during the years of World War II, which ushered in an era in which Austrian Economics became unfashionably distinctive and, in fact, professionally marginalized. That era is the period beginning about 1940, covered in Volume III of the present collection.

A superficial reading of Mises's 1920 paper might, we acknowledge, see it as a not particularly sophisticated statement of neoclassical equilibrium theory. It could be said that Mises pointed out the allocative-efficiency properties of an equilibrium set of competitive prices, and claimed that capitalism achieves its efficiency by presenting market participants with a set of prices reasonably approximating the structure of the relevant equilibrium set. The reader might be excused for missing insights concerning the capacity of prices to inspire those processes of entrepreneurial discovery and learning, *in disequilibrium markets*, which were to be so characteristic of later Misesian and Hayekian economics. The explanation for this is, however, not that the 1920 Mises was an equilibrium theorist, but that the importance of the distinction between the equilibrium and the process perspectives had at that time not yet come to be recognized. (Indeed many contemporary statements of neoclassical economics were based similarly on perspectives which relied upon *both* an appreciation of the dynamic character of competitive market processes *and* upon a conviction that market prices are reasonable approximations of equilibrium prices.)

In considering attempts to defend the possibility of socialist efficiency by reference to non-market prices, Mises and Hayek reached a more careful appreciation of the nature and function of market prices in the course of dynamic processes of equilibration, as distinct from the allocative properties of prices in the attained state of equilibrium.

From Menger to Mises: the Search for Subjectivism

In his autobiographical sketch (Mises, 1978, p. 33) Mises recounts how he first read Menger's *Grundsätze* as a student in 1903. 'It was the reading of this book,' he remarks, 'that made an "economist" of me.' Certainly the central message which Menger sought to convey was the *subjective* character of the fundamental elements in economic theorizing, such as 'goods', 'resources', 'structure of production'. For Menger these ideas are not to be understood as inhering in economic objects themselves, but as emerging from the attitudes towards these economic objects, of valuing and acting human beings. (See particularly in this volume, papers 2 and 3.) If we claim that the age of Mises and Hayek, the age of lowest general professional esteem for the school, represented the most consistent development and deepening of the Mengerian legacy, we do so on the basis of the more fully developed subjectivism which has characterized Misesian and Hayekian economics. It was Hayek who put his finger on the centrality of subjectivism for Mises's life's work. In a footnote (to an oft-quoted remark hailing subjectivism as the fountain of advances in economic theory; see Hayek, 1955, p. 31) Hayek observes that this development of economic theory on the basis of the consistent application of subjectivism 'has probably been carried out most consistently by L. V. Mises.' He adds his belief 'that most peculiarities of [Mises's] views which at first strike many readers as strange and unacceptable are due to the fact that in the consistent development of the subjectivist approach he has for a long time moved ahead of his contemporaries' (Hayek, op. cit. pp. 209–10). Here Hayek has delicately drawn attention to the decided unfashionability, at the middle of the twentieth-century, of the Austrian Economics expounded by Mises. If in 1930 the subjectivism of the Viennese School had permitted its adherents to enjoy the comfort and prestige of being close to the gravitational centre of the profession, by 1950 the consistent extension of this subjectivism had expelled the heirs of Mengerian subjectivism to the outer reaches of professional exile. If in 1930 the Austrian School was at the peak of professional recognition, by 1950 the school was considered to have become utterly extinct leaving as vestigial remains only the persons and writings of Mises and Hayek.

Yet (as we shall argue in the Introduction to Volume III) it was precisely during this time of professional eclipse that Mises and Hayek made original contributions that would eventually inspire a modest but significant Austrian revival. This revival would occur after 1970 (the closing date for coverage in these volumes) but it was during the age of Mises and Hayek that the groundwork was being laid. In the course of the rebuilding of Austrian Economics that was to occur in the latter portion of the twentieth century, Mengerian subjectivism was again and again to be the lodestar. What has encouraged younger members of the profession to rediscover the Austrian tradition has been a sense of dissatisfaction with the mechanical quality of a mainstream economics in which human aspirations, human errors, and human discoveries are downplayed, ignored, or simply assumed away. In searching for a mode of economic understanding sensitive to these elements in the human condition, it is the work of Menger which has proven most fertile; and it is the development of the Mengerian tradition spurred by the work of Mises that latter-day Austrians have found most helpful. From the perspective of the closing years of the twentieth century, therefore, it is in the gradual deepening and maturing of Mengerian subjectivism that the history of the Austrian School finds its unity and its *raison d'etre*.

Austrian Economics and Economic Ideology

No survey of the Austrian School, no matter how cursory, can ignore widespread impressions which link it to libertarian ideology in general, and to vigorous (if not virulent) opposition to socialism in particular. Although our story, in the preceding pages, has made little mention of ideological considerations (even in our account of the socialist economic calculation debate), we must certainly confront this issue forthrightly. Briefly, our position can be summarized in the following two propositions.

First, the intellectual content of Austrian Economics, throughout its history, *can* be disengaged from any ideological accompaniments that may have been present. To dismiss any portion of this intellectual history as merely the propagandistic pseudo-academic facade for ideological pre-judgments is not only to be grossly unfair to the economists concerned, but also to manufacture shoddy excuses for avoiding to grapple with important theoretical argumentation. Intellectual honesty requires, on these grounds alone, that any ideological disagreements with Austrians be laid aside if Austrian Economics is to be treated with the seriousness it deserves.

Second, the ideological dimension of the Austrian School cannot be denied. Many of its members have in fact been prominently identified with a political position close to classical liberalism (or even, for some, to libertarianism). This appears to have been true of Menger (see on this Boehm, 1985; Kirzner, 1992, chapter 5; Streissler, 1990), of Böhm-Bawerk, and, certainly, of both Mises and Hayek. Although socialism in the twentieth century has usually been viewed as the ideological opposi-tion against which Austrians were doing battle, we should not forget that the original ideological enemy was not socialism *per se*, but rather author-itarian government domination over private activity, as under the Prussian monarchy. (On this see Mises, 1969.) Yet it was the Austrian Böhm-Bawerk who sharply criticized the Marxist labour theory of value and its ideological entailments; it was the Marxist Bukharin, later to be liquidated by Stalin, who pronounced the Austrians the 'most powerful opponent' of Marxism (Bukharin, [1914] 1972, p. 9). A recent example of (fearful?) interest on the part of Marxists in Austrian Economics and its current revival is the impressive work of Stavros Ioannides (1992). And, as we have seen, it was Mises and Hayek who denied the viability of socialist planning.

It is not our objective here to explore the precise interrelationship between the pure intellectual content of Austrian Economics and the broadly classical liberal ideological stance of many (or most) of its most prominent exponents. Although we insist on the epistemological inde-pendence of the former from the latter, we certainly recognize that the intellectual content of Austrian Economics, and its development during the century covered in these volumes, did not occur in an ideological vacuum. Austrian support for free market policies was, in the view of the Austrians themselves, at least, solidly based on Austrian understanding of the way free markets work. The stimulus to explore the subtle webs of causation which prevail in markets was, for Austrians (as for most econ-omists in the history of the science) strongly related to the overall policy objective of improving the well-being of society in general. We draw attention to these rather obvious aspects of Austrian Economics simply to alert the reader who may have an interest in pursuing the ideological dimension of those changes and developments in Austrian Economics between 1870 and 1970 as reflected, perhaps, in the papers collected in these volumes.

* * *

The Papers in Volume I of the Present Collection

Volume I covers that period in the development of the Austrian School which is the best known in the conventional history of economic thought. (Indeed, in much of that history the term 'Austrian School' refers strictly and exclusively to this period.) From the perspective of this conventional history, what occurred in Vienna, Innsbruck, and Prague between 1871 and 1914 was the emergence of a separate tributary of ideas that would, however, flow into, merge with and reinforce the mainstream of modern neoclassical economics with its very success in this latter function ensuring its eventual loss of identity. In the preceding sections of this Introduction we have offered a sharply differing view of the historical significance of this early period of Austrian economic thought. For us the work of Menger, Böhm-Bawerk and Wieser was historically significant primarily in that it pointed beyond itself to a more fully subjectivist tradition which that work was to generate. Although the Austrian work sampled in this volume is better known to the profession than that presented in Volumes II and III, we urge that the papers in this first volume, several of them made available in English for the first time, be freshly examined from the perspective of the thesis advanced in this Introduction.

These papers offer methodological statements by each of the three founders of the school (papers 1, 5, 11). They offer expositions of the subjective theory of value (Menger, papers 2, 3; Wieser, papers 8, 9). They include Menger's classic statement of his theory of spontaneous evolution of economic institutions (paper 4); Böhm-Bawerk's elucidations of the Austrian perspectives on the foundations of capital and interest theory (papers 6, 7); and Wieser's application of Austrian theory to the applied area of urban ground rent (paper 10). Finally, these papers include a classic debate between Böhm-Bawerk and his outstanding Czech student Franz Čuhel, on the cardinality or ordinality of the concept of utility (papers 12, 13). We wish to suggest briefly here that much of the work offered in this volume illustrates the extent and force of the subjectivist insights which, we have argued, provided the initial spark which set the Austrian tradition into motion.

The Austrian defences of the deductive method express an epistemological assertion concerning the causal role of human decisions. For economists of the Historical School, human decisions played no such decisive role in the generation of economic regularities; any such regularities were seen as emerging from the welter of observable economic events. The Austrian position, often denigrated as pointless quibbling over trivial matters in scholastic dispute, actually reveals a unique perspective on the nature of economic causation and on what can be known concerning that causation (see Bostaph, 1978). That perspective stemmed from a Mengerian subjectivist understanding of the manner in which economic phenomena express human preferences and decisions.

Menger's theory of spontaneous institutional evolution, central to his view of the nature and scope of social science, relies heavily on subjectivist insights. The dynamics of the emergence of money as an institution is driven by human perceptions of differential marketability among exchangeable goods, generating decisions concerning exchanges which themselves cause further snow-balling effects on marketability. Although the process is not a planned one, it is driven, step by step, by the planned actions of choosing, evaluating human beings.

Čuhel's critique of Böhm-Bawerk's cardinalism illustrates at once both the radical subjectivism implicit in the Mengerian legacy, and the limitations of that subjectivism as it was expressed in the work of Menger's immediate, and most eminent, followers. The Čuhel–Böhm-Bawerk debate represents a fascinating anticipation of the cardinalist-ordinalist debates in British economics three or four decades later. But whereas Hicksian ordinalism stemmed primarily from an application of Occam's Razor (i.e. from the consideration that demand theory can be developed without recourse to a cardinal utility), Čuhel's ordinalism arises from his subjectivist (introspective) appreciation of the nature of human preferences and choices. Admittedly, Čuhel's ordinalism was significantly rooted in psychological (rather than in purely economic) insights. But his rebellion against Böhm-Bawerk's cardinalism, had it been completely successful, would have helped weaken the view that choices (and hence all market phenomena) are somehow 'determined' by a law which ensures the achievement of maximum possible total cardinal utility for each market participant. Such a (mainstream) view of microeconomics changes the nature of the choices made by choosing, imagining, dreaming and purposeful human beings. Such a microeconomics makes it appear as if market phenomena emerge without human action, emerging, instead, automatically as it were from the 'data' (including individual utility functions in the data), being merely the outcomes of maximization exercises which are inevitably and mechanically fulfilled. Čuhel's ordinalism might have steered economics towards a more consistently Mengerian-subjectivist understanding of how market phenomena emerge through individual acts of conscious valuations and comparisons. The influence which Čuhel's work exercised on the thinking of Ludwig von Mises is a matter of record (see Mises, [1912] 1953, p. 41; 1978, p. 57). It is reasonable to attribute Mises's own radical subjectivism, at least in part, to this influence.

That Austrians were aware of the danger that their 'subjective' theory of value might permit itself to become embedded within a mechanical, positivist analytic framework, is clear from Wieser's highly critical review essay on Schumpeter's first (1908) book. (See paper 11 in this volume.) Schumpeter, writing his book under the influence of the emerging positivist perspective associated with the Viennese physicist Ernst Mach, had seen economic phenomena as governed deterministically by the mechanics of utility maximization. Just as physical bodies are held to be located in the cosmos by the rigid operation of gravitational laws, so also the location of 'economic quantities' is governed rigidly by the principle of utility maximization. Wieser, apparently sensing the danger of this kind of positivist thinking for subjectivist economics, carefully but effectively criticizes Schumpeter's position.

The papers in this volume thus illustrate the variety of aspects of economics explored by the Austrian founders. They illustrate in particular, we wish to emphasize, both the centrality of Mengerian subjectivism to their work, and the ambiguities in the degree of consistency with which they pursued that subjectivism. As argued earlier, it was the fate of Mengerian Subjectivism which would dictate the course of subsequent intellectual history for the Austrian School.

LIST OF REFERENCES

Alter, Max, *Carl Menger and the Origins of Austrian Economics* (Boulder: Westview Press, 1990).

Boehm, Stephan, 'The Political Economy of the Austrian School', P. Roggi, (ed.), *Gli Economisti e la Political Economica* (Naples: Edizioni Scientifiche Italiene, 1985).

Bostaph, Samuel, 'The Methodological Debate Between Carl Menger and the German Historicists', *Atlantic Economic Journal* 6 (3) September 1978, pp. 3–16.

Bukharin, Nikolai, *The Economic Theory of the Leisure Class* (New York: Monthly Review Press, 1927; translated from the Russian original of 1914 by M. Lawrence).

Caldwell, Bruce, (ed.), *Carl Menger and his Legacy in Economics* (Durham, NC: Duke University Press, 1990).

Ebeling, Richard M., 'Action Analysis and Economic Science, the Economic Contributions of Ludwig von Mises', unpublished manuscript.

Hayek, Friedrich A., 'Introduction', C. Menger, *Principles of Economics* (New York: New York University Press, 1981), originally published as 'Introduction', *Collected Works of Carl Menger* (London: London School of Economics, 1934).

——, *Collectivist Economic Planning* (London: Routledge and Kegan Paul, 1935).

——, *The Counter-Revolution of Science. Studies on the Abuse of Reason* (Glencoe, IL.: Free Press, 1955).

——, contribution to Hicks, J. R. and Weber, W., *Carl Menger and the Austrian School of Economics* (Oxford: Clarendon Press, 1973).

Ioannides, Stavros, *The Market, Competition and Democracy, A Critique of Neo-Austrian Economics* (Aldershot, Hants, England: Edward Elgar, 1992).

Kirzner, Israel M., 'The Economic Calculation Debate: Lessons for Austrians', *The Review of Austrian Economics* (1988).

——, 'Carl Menger and The Subjectivist Tradition in Economics', *The Meaning of Market Process, Essays in the Development of Modern Austrian Economics* (London: Routledge, 1992).

——, 'Menger, Classical Liberalism and the Austrian School of Economics', *The Meaning of Market Process* (1992).

Lachmann, Ludwig M., *Capital, Expectations, and the Market Process, Essays on the Theory of the Market Economy* (Kansas City: Sheed Andrews and McMeel, 1977).

Lange, O., 'On the Economic Theory of Socialism', B. E. Lippincott (ed.), *On the Economic Theory of Socialism* (New York: McGraw-Hill, 1964).

Lavoie, Don, *Rivalry and Central Planning: The Socialist Calculation Debate Reconsidered* (Cambridge: Cambridge University Press, 1985).

Lerner, Abba P., *The Economics of Control* (New York: Macmillan, 1944).

Leser, N. (ed.), *Die Wiener Schule der Nationalökonomie* (Vienna: Hermann Bohlau, 1986).

Machlup, Fritz, 'Ludwig von Mises: the Academic Scholar who would not Compromise', *Wirtschaftspolitischen Blätter*, 4, (1981).

——, 'Austrian Economics', D. Greenwald (ed.), *Encyclopedia of Economics* (New York: McGraw-Hill, 1982).

Menger, Carl, *Principles of Economics* (New York: New York University Press, 1981), originally published in 1871 as *Grundsätze der Volkwirthschaftslehre*.

——, *Investigations into the Method of the Social Sciences with Special*

Reference to Economics, trans. F. J. Nock (New York: New York University Press, 1985) originally published in 1883 as *Untersuchungen über der Methode der Socialwissenschaften und der Politischen Oekonomie insbesondere*.

Mises, Ludwig von, *The Theory of Money and Credit* (New Haven: Yale University Press, 1953); the original German-language version was published in 1912.

——, *Socialism: An Economic and Sociological Analysis* (London: Jonathan Cape, 1936), translated from the German-language *Die Gemeinwirtschaft*, 1st edn 1922, 2nd edn 1932.

——, *Epistemological Problems of Economics* (Princeton, NJ: Van Nostrand, 1960) translated from the German original, *Grundprobleme der Nationalökonomie*, 1933.

——, *Notes and Recollections* (South Holland, IL: Libertarian Press, 1978).

——, *The Historical Setting of the Austrian School of Economics* (New Rochelle, NY: Arlington House, 1969).

Robbins, Lionel, *The Nature and Significance of Economic Science* (London: Macmillan, 1932; 2nd edn 1935).

Smith, Barry and Grassl, Wolfgang, *Austrian Economics, Historical and Philosophical Background* (New York: New York University Press, 1986).

Streissler, Erich, 'The Intellectual and Political Impact of the Austrian School of Economics', *History of European Ideas*, 92 (1988).

——, [in Caldwell, op. cit.] 'The Influence of German Economics on the Work of Menger and Marshall', pp. 31–68 (1990).

——, 'Menger, Böhm-Bawerk, and Wieser: The Origins of the Austrian School', K. Hennings and W. J. Samuels, eds, *Neoclassical Economic Theory, 1870 to 1930* (Boston, MA: Kluwer, 1990).

Wicksteed, Philip, *The Common Sense of Political Economy* [1910] (London: Routledge and Kegan Paul, 1933).

EDITORIAL NOTE

Some of the papers contain references to page numbers in the original texts. These have been retained so that readers can refer to the originals if they so wish.

ACKNOWLEDGEMENTS

Gustav Fischer Verlag, Stuttgart-Hohenheim, for their kind permission to reproduce:
  Hans Mayer, 'Imputation'
  ——, 'Market'
  Ludwig von Mises, 'Monetary Stabilization and Cyclical Policy'
Kluwer Academic Publishers, Norwell, Mass., for their kind permission to reproduce:
  Ludwig von Mises, 'The Treatment of "Irrationality" in the Social Sciences'
  ——, 'Epistemological Relativism'
Van Nostrand Reinhold, New York, for their kind permission to reproduce:
  Carl Menger, 'Toward a Systematic Classification of the Economic Sciences'
  Friedrich von Wieser, 'The Theory of Urban Ground Rent'
Springer-Verlag KG, Vienna, for their kind permission to reproduce:
  Gottfried Haberler, 'Economics as an Exact Science'
The Macmillan Press Ltd, Basingstoke, for their kind permission to reproduce:
  Paul Rosenstein-Rodan, 'Marginal Utility'
University of Chicago Press, Chicago, and Routledge & Kegan Paul, Andover, for their kind permission to reproduce:
  F. A. Hayek, 'Competition as a Discovery Procedure'

For full bibliographical details see the editorial note preceding each paper.

Despite our best efforts to trace the owners of copyright in the following papers, we have been unable to do so, and would welcome notification from the authors or their heirs that they agree to our inclusion of the material in this edition.

  Carl Menger, 'The General Theory of the Good' and 'Economy and Economic Goods', trans. *Principles of Economics* (Glencoe, IL: Free Press, 1950).

Eugen von Böhm-Bawerk, 'On the Relationship between the Third Reason for Higher Valuation of Present Goods and the Two Other Reasons', trans. *Capital and Interest* (South Holland, IL: Libertarian Press, 1959).

Oskar Morgenstern, 'The Time Moment in Value Theory', *Selected Writings of Oskar Morgenstern*, ed. A. Schotter (New York: New York University Press, 1976).

The Founding Era

Carl Menger, 'Toward a Systematic Classification of the Economic Sciences', 1889, Louise Sommer (ed.), *Essays in European Economic Thought* (Princeton, NJ: Van Nostrand, 1960), pp. 1–38.

This paper by the founder of the Austrian School, Carl Menger (1840–1921) was first published in the original German as 'Grund-züge einer Klassifikation der Wirtschaftswissenschaften' in *Jahr-bücher für Nationalökonomie und Statistik*, New Series (1889), xix, pp. 465–96. It was republished in *Collected Works of Carl Menger* (edited by F. A. Hayek) London School of Economics and Political Science, 1934–6: vol. iii, pp. 187–218. It made an important contribution to the 'Methodenstreit' – the debate over method – which raged between the Austrian School and the German Historical School at the time of its first publication.

1

Toward a Systematic Classification of the Economic Sciences

CARL MENGER

Ever since the appearance of my 'Inquiry into the Methods of the Social Sciences' discussion concerning the epistemology and methodology of economics has been incessant. In the literature that has since proliferated on this subject, including even some recently published university lectures, the position I have taken has become the object of sometimes contradictory judgments. In particular, the views I have set forth regarding the types of problems to be solved by inquiry in the field of economics, as well as my treatment of the important related question of a systematic classification of the economic sciences, have met with no less vehement opposition than friendly acceptance. All this, and even the many misunderstandings which usually accompany discussions of questions of such a general nature, would yet not have persuaded me to re-enter the controversy. However, in view of the present state of economic studies in Germany, I am convinced that only full clarity concerning the whole complex of problems requiring investigation in the field of economics can save us from adopting one-sided attitudes, with all their pernicious consequences both practical and theoretical.

The Historical School describes the origin and development of social phenomena, and – with the exception of a few especially biased authors – it makes a serious effort to discover their laws, in the sense of external regularities in their coexistence and succession. However, this school refrains from analyzing complex economic phenomena: it does not trace them back to their psychological causes or to ultimate component elements that would still be accessible to perceptual verfication. Such a procedure cannot provide us with a *theoretical understanding* of economic events.

To be sure, many abuses have brought theoretical analysis into disrepute.

3

This is especially true of efforts to arrive at knowledge and understanding of economic facts by way of an aprioristic construction. But no less harmful has been the failure to realize that economic phenomena are temporal events and therefore show developments that ought to attract the attention of theoretical inquiry. To the great detriment of our science, the adherents of this school regard the mere *description* of concrete economic events and of external regularities in their relations as the only legitimate goal of economic study. They thereby overlook the fact that historical investigation is no substitute for theoretical analysis, nor is the latter either excluded or rendered superfluous by the fact – equally neglected by the Historical School – that economic phenomena exhibit a development in the course of time. Historicism has simply turned its back on theoretical analysis. But is it not the task of our science to find the particular form that is adequate to the specific character of economic events? In trying to avoid the mistakes of aprioristic social philosophy, and to a certain extent also those of the social physicists and social biologists, the Historical School has fallen into the still greater error of renouncing theoretical analysis, and with it theoretical understanding, of social phenomena. Thus the scientific character of economics has become altogether questionable. The solution of the methodological problems involved is an urgent necessity of our science.

Although the attacks directed against me in this controversy challenge me to a reply, I do not intend to deal here with economic theory or with the diverse tasks which it has to fulfill. In view of the present state of our understanding of methodological issues, questions concerning the nature of economic theory – including its different branches and its distinctive problems, as conditioned by the specific character of its object – must doubtless be considered as providing the most controversial, and therefore the most attractive, theme for investigations into the methodology of that science. However, any study of the above-mentioned problem seems to me to be quite futile as long as *the preliminary question of the position of economic theory within the entire domain of the economic sciences in general* remains unresolved. The Historical School has failed to pay enough attention to the distinctive character of the problems confronting the sciences of history and statistics on the one hand, and economic theory and applied economics on the other; nor has it taken into sufficient consideration the essential differences among these main branches of inquiry within the field of political economy itself. The exponents of historicism have not maintained a sharp enough distinction between the 'method of historical inquiry' and the so-called 'historical method in economic theory and applied economics.' They have especially mis-interpreted the specific place of questions of applied economics within the complex of

4

problems to be solved by theoretical analysis. In their eyes the only worthwhile goal of scientific research is a compilation – arranged on the basis of external principles of classification – of historical, statistical, theoretical, morphological, and practical studies referring to economics. Under such circumstances how is it possible to deal specifically with the whole set of problems to be solved by economic *theory* without having previously clarified either its position within the domain of the other economic sciences or the outlines of a system of classifying the economic sciences in general?

1. On the Classification of the Economic Sciences

The results of the investigation of reality by the different sciences have in practice been divided into separate domains in accordance with two essentially distinct principles of classification: on the one hand, according to the nature of the objects of inquiry, i.e., the different *fields* of reality which constitute the subject matter of scientific cognition; and on the other hand, according to the different lines of scientific inquiry, i.e., the different *methods of approaching* reality.

The distinction between the sciences of nature and the sciences of man, the division of the former into sciences of organic nature and of inorganic nature, the further subdivisions within the different fields of the organic and of the inorganic world (petrography, botany, zoology, and so forth), and the constitution of separate sciences of law, political theory, sociology, economics, etc., all rest upon the first principle of classification.

However, the progress of the sciences and a deepening interest in specialized problems of research has led to further classifications based upon the second principle. Within each specific field of reality different lines of approach have gradually developed into distinct disciplines and sciences corresponding to the need for an independent presentation of their results.

The search for an understanding of reality may be pursued, within each field, in two basic directions. It may be oriented towards knowledge of *concrete* phenomena and their concrete relations in space and time, or towards knowledge of their *general* nature and their general interrelations (i.e., relations of coexistence and succession among generally determined phenomena).

The first approach leads either to the *statistical*[1] or to the historical sciences: to the former if the concrete phenomena of particular fields of reality are viewed from the static standpoint, and to the latter if we take the point of view of evolution. The second direction ramifies into the

5

morphological and the *theoretical* sciences, respectively: the former if what we are aiming at is knowledge of the generic form of the phenomena in a given field (their common structure), and the latter if the object of our knowledge is their relations and internal connections (i.e., their laws).

Our scientific interest, however, is not confined only to the exploration and the understanding of reality. Besides the above-mentioned lines of inquiry, there is within each field a tendency toward the establishment of principles and procedures aiming at a purposeful *shaping* of phenomena, i.e., effective interference with the course of events. The systematically organized results of these efforts are characterized as the *practical* or applied sciences.

The different lines of approach which we have mentioned – the statistical, the historical, the morphological, the theoretical, and the practical – have to be distinguished, by virtue of their formal differences from one another, not only within each distinct field of reality, but also within each subdivision in its turn; and the same holds true with regard to the further ramifications within these major types of science.[2]

The classification of the natural sciences according to the different kinds of natural substance, on the one hand, and the different lines of approach to them, on the other, has in part been long since completed and is in part still going on. Nobody in the field of the natural sciences would confuse the descripion of *concrete* natural substances in their static state, or of the course of *concrete* natural events of historical significance, with a *morphology* of natural phenomena. Even in treating of phenomena belonging to the same field, one does not fail to make a distinction between, for instance, the history of the animal world and systematic zoology, or between the history of man and a morphology of the races of mankind. In the same way a line of division is drawn between the morphological and the theoretical natural sciences. For instance, systematic petrography, botany, zoology, and anatomy are separated from physics, chemistry, and physiology. Finally, the same holds true of the theoretical and the applied sciences. The natural scientist does not confuse pure chemistry with applied chemistry, or mechanics and physics with so-called mechanical technology, or anatomy and physiology with surgery and thereapeutics.

To be sure, in particular cases practical considerations, such as regard for the appropriate arrangement of the scientific data or the rather rudimentary state of development of a particular branch of inquiry, might nevertheless induce one to combine the results of different approaches in the natural sciences purely for purposes of presentation. But no investigator of nature would conceive of 'progressing' to the development of a single, comprehensive natural science embracing all statistical-historical, morphological, theoretical, and practical knowledge concerning nature, or even concerning one of its specific fields, assembled in a loosely organized conglomeration – a veritable mass of ἄμορφος ὕλη!* The distinction between the historical-statistical, the morphological, the theoretical, and the applied sciences – and within these major types between still further articulated subdivisions – is accepted without question by every clear-thinking natural scientist. In the field of the political sciences too, no doubt exists as to the difference between, for example, statistics, the history of political institutions, political theory, and applied political science. The same holds true in the field of jurisprudence with regard to the distinction between the history of law, legal doctrine, and legislative policies.

In the domain of the economic sciences, however, the above-mentioned development is in many respects still in an imperfect, and even embryonic, state. The classification of the economic sciences into the historical-statistical, the morphological, the theoretical, and the applied is far from being generally recognized. The confounding of historical-statistical descriptions, morphological studies, 'laws of economic phenomena,' and principles and procedures for effective action in the economic sphere is still the rule in the literature on political economy, while a separation of the economic sciences according to their formal differences would still appear to be the exception. Moreover, it should be emphasized that this practice of indiscriminately lumping together the results of different types of scientific approach is not dictated exclusively by considerations of a didactic nature,[3] nor is it confined only to writings devoted to popular instruction; it is widely prevalent also in works with pretensions to a strictly scientific character.

The explanation of this fact is to be found primarily in the hitherto rudimentary development of the economic sciences. Many other disciplines likewise present the appearance, in the early phases of their development, of a conglomerate mass, assembled on external principles, of historical-statistical, morphological, theoretical, and practical information about a definite field of phenomena. In other realms of inquiry also, disciplines corresponding to different lines of inquiry have branched off only gradually and tentatively and have thus developed into independent sciences. As soon as economists have a clear understanding of the importance that a systematic approach has for the *demonstration*, and especially for the *understanding*, of the internal interrelations of the results of scientific inquiry, and as soon as they become aware of the impossibility of coherently presenting the results of different lines of approach within one and the same system, the natural course of development of scientific knowledge in the domain of economics will necessarily lead to a systematic ramification of the economic sciences similar to that which has already taken place in all other fields.

2. On the Necessity of Separating Economic History, Economic Theory, Morphology, and Applied Economics[4]

It is in many respects the methodological insufficiency of the Historical School that hampers the above development in German political economy, and that has even reversed the progress made thus far. The economists of this school envision a *universal science of economics* that should embrace any and every kind of knowledge about things economic in a neatly uniform order. They vehemently reject the idea of marking off one discipline from another, although such a division would in no way destroy the intrinsic coherence of each. They even stigmatize this separation as a regressive step, as 'an artificial dismemberment of an intrinsically coherent subject matter'; or if there is agreement in principle regarding the classification of the economic sciences, it is interpreted in such a way as in reality to annul it altogether.

Now such a universal science of economics reveals itself not only as an absurdity from the point of view of scientific systematics, but as an impossibility if the above postulate of scientific procedure is taken at all seriously. I have no intention of discussing the altogether fantastic notion of dealing even with economic history and statistics within a 'system' of political economy which also includes morphological, theoretical, and practical information about economics. I simply cannot conceive of a system of political economy, or even of a treatment of it to some extent and in some sense organized, which would simultaneously embrace the whole of the economic history and all of the economic statistics of all ages and all nations. The *independent* treatment of economic history and economic policy is an absolute necessity. This, and only this, is what we are concerned with; neither the citation of historical-statistical facts for the purpose of exemplifying the theoretical and practical truths of political economy nor the use of history and statistics as ancillary sciences in laying its foundations is at issue here.

Nor is what has been said above in any way opposed to those summaries of economic history and economic ideas which usually precede the exposition of our science. They are but introductions to the study of political economy – synopses of the respective sciences serving the above-mentioned didactic purpose – which in no way obviate the need for, or replace an independent treatment of, economic history, economic statistics, and economic literature. The assertion that economic history and statistics as such can be dealt with in a system of 'political economy' embracing at once morphological, theoretical, and practical questions rests on a misunderstanding.[5]

3. On the Idea of Combining Economic Theory and Applied Economics Within a Unified System

However, serious doubts must be voiced regarding the idea of organizing economic theory and the principles of economic policy into a systematically unified science. Each of these has its own particular system corresponding to the specific formal principles upon which it is constituted. To unite them would involve one or the other of two alternatives: either one would have to fit the principles of economic policy into the system of economic theory and demonstrate the laws of certain economic phenomena in an incidental way by establishing an external connection between the principles and procedures of the economic policies relating to them, on the one hand, and theoretical knowledge on the other; or one would have to accompany the systematic exposition of the principles of economic policy with incidental theoretical demonstrations. Both of these alternatives not only are logically possible, but, as experience has abundantly taught us, are actually feasible. Whoever recalls the historical development of scientific knowledge and appreciates the importance, for both methodology and systematics, of a division of the sciences based on formal principles, will recognize in such procedures nothing but a symptom of the still undeveloped state of the economic sciences.[6]

It is the failure to appreciate this fact for which I reproach my opponents. Their error consists in regarding the union of economic theory and applied economics, rather than their separation, as progress and even as a methodological postulate. Actually our efforts should be directed towards furthering the separate treatment of the theoretical and the practical, since this is of the greatest importance for the development of our science. But wherever, because of the backwardness of the latter, such a separation is not yet advisable, scientists should endeavor to prepare the way for it. There are, however, economists of the Historical School who tend to regard the above-mentioned development as a kind of regress, and who conversely consider any retrogression in this respect as scientific progress.

The argument of F. J. Neumann in favour of the opposed view[7] is quite untenable. It is not true that the division of political economy into economic theory and applied economics must necessarily lead to 'awkward repetitions.' This opinion rests upon two prepossessions, both widespread among German economists: that each individual science must present *all*

9

the results of inquiry referring to a definite field of phenomena, and that there are no sciences which *presuppose* the knowledge of other sciences. Physiology is based on a knowledge of anatomy, while surgery and therapy presuppose a knowledge of both these sciences; chemical technology rests on a knowledge of chemistry; mechanics, on a knowledge of mathematics; etc. The opinion that the classification of the sciences according to formal principles leads to repetitions is so far from being correct that it is in fact diametrically opposed to the truth. The function of economics is not to provide us with an incomplete and arbitrary collection of theoretical and useful information organized on external principles. On the contrary, it has the task of organizing all the results of scientific inquiry relating to economics into an intrinsically coherent and well-articulated system. Once our economists realize this, the most expeditious means of attaining such a goal will be seen to consist in separating the theoretical and the applied sciences.

Still less convincing as an argument *against* such a separation is Neumann's contention that it would often necessitate defining different concepts specifically for each of the two divisions, theoretical and applied, of the economic sciences. Even if this were the case, the separate definition of the 'concepts' in question would be a problem of economics the evasion of which could hardly be considered as a scientific solution. Neumann does not seem to be aware that he has here touched upon a sore point of the economic sciences. It is true that some of the most important terms are understood in a totally different sense by economic theory and by applied economics. One need only think, for example, of the way in which such concepts as capital, ground rent, interest, and so on, are used in economic theory, on the one hand, and, on the other, in public finance, particularly in treating of the taxation of profits. But can this conceptual confusion be used as an argument *against* the separation of economic theory from applied economics?

Finally, Neumann's proposal to replace the separation between economic theory and economic policy by a division of 'political economy' into a *general* branch and a *specialized* branch rests upon a methodological misunderstanding, as I have already demonstrated elsewhere.[8] Economic theory no less than applied economics has its general and its specialized branches. But applied economics can no more be regarded as a specialized branch of economic theory, or the latter as the general branch of applied economics, than chemical technology can be considered as a specialized branch of chemistry, or surgery as a specialized branch of anatomy.[9] It is true that even if no distinction is made in the treatment of economic theory and applied economics, however imperfect such a system might be, a general and a specialized branch would still have to be distinguished, just as they are in every methodically organized scientific work. This fact, however, has nothing to do with the question that concerns us here. The bifurcation of each branch of economics into a general and a specialized section, and the separation of the economic sciences into the theoretical and the applied, are two distinct methodological problems that should not be confused with each other. The former refers to the intrinsic systematics of particular economic sciences; the latter, to the classification of the economic sciences in general.

4. Can There Be Independently Valid Morphological Sciences of Economic Phenomena?

It is doubtful whether the development of economics will lead to an independent systematic morphology of economic phenomena, nor can we be at all certain what place the results of morphological inquiry will have within the system of the economic sciences in general.

Not every theoretical discipline has an independent morphology as its counterpart. Even within the realm of the natural sciences, those which are purely theoretical, i.e., essentially the result of analytic-synthetic methods, such as chemistry and physics, do not have any particular morphologies corresponding to them. Wundt has rightly pointed out, with respect to the problem of a real separation between the individual branches of the different natural sciences, that, for example, the classification of chemical compounds is usually not separated from the theory of chemical phenomena.[10] However, he explains this 'strange circumstance' on the one hand by 'the relatively undeveloped state of chemistry, in which the function of description and explanation are not yet sharply distinguished,' and, on the other, by 'the deep-rooted traditions of natural history, according to which only things found in nature, and not those artificially produced, are treated as objects of the separate systematic sciences.' Here Wundt, excellent epistemologist though he is, seems to me to have misunderstood the real reason for a practice that is of great importance to economic inquiry as well.

Morphological knowledge, as far as it is the result of a real analytical reduction of complex phenomena to their elementary factors and of an isolating synthesis of the latter, has no independent significance. It subserves the needs of theoretical work, and its treatment comes to be bound up, for purposes of convenience, with that of the laws of synthesis of the respective phenomena, i.e., with the corresponding theoretical sciences. Indeed, in the absence of such morphological knowledge, these laws cannot even be formulated. The systematic presentation of the combined

11

results of both approaches is thus seen to be dictated not by considerations of convenience alone, but also by their intrinsic congruity. The situation is quite different, however, where our immediate concern is not with *understanding* complex natural phenomena by means of analysis and isolating synthesis, but with *describing* them, as in minerology, botany, zoology, etc. Here, of course, the description of forms, the morphology of the respective fields of phenomena, assumes an independent significance, and the synthesis of the results of inquiry in separate systematic sciences corresponds only to the independent interest that we take in such knowledge.

Science is presented with a similar problem in the field of economics. Here too the question may arise – not whether the morphological approach is justified in general, for no doubt exists on that score – but whether, side by side with economic theory, a morphology of economic phenomena is of independent interest and whether the latter should accordingly be assigned an independent position, alongside economic theory, within the system of the economic sciences.

To this question the methodological principles that we have here set forth provide an answer that proves to be in full accord with the actual development of economics up to the present day. The elementary factors that theoretical analysis discloses in complex economic phenomena have no independent significance within the system of economic science; their morphology does not correspond to any independent scientific need.

It is therefore altogether appropriate that they should be treated as an integral part of economic theory as far as the latter deals with the laws of synthesis of elementary economic phenomena. What usually introduces systematic treatises on economic theory under the rubric of 'Principles of Economics,' but is incorporated into the body of the presentation by the more rigorously systematic economists, is chiefly nothing but a morphological description of the essential elementary factors of complex economic phenomena. There is as little scientific need for an independent morphology of these elementary economic factors as there is in the case of elementary natural phenomena and the combinations of them that are obtained by means of an isolating synthesis.

On the other hand, it seems to me that at least where our primary and immediate concern is not with *understanding* complex economic phenomena by way of analytic-synthetic inquiry, but with *describing* them in all their complexity and multi-formity (in which noneconomic factors also play a role), their systematic morphology does take on an independent scientific interest. In addition to the effort to achieve a theoretical understanding of economic phenomena – and even long before the need for it appears in inquiry – there is an endeavor to study them in their complexity, as they are presented by experience, and in their multiformity, which is the product of the simultaneous operation of a diversity of spatial and temporal influences. It is here that morphology enters the system of economic science. Serving as a supplement to the historical sciences, where they offer but a collective image of concrete economic events within definite spatial limits, it has the task of presenting a systematic survey of the complex phenomena of economics in general.

To be sure, the first steps taken in this direction have so far been pitifully inadequate. No doubt, too, the results of such lines of investigation not only could be, but, in the present state of economics, are in fact already, an integral part of that science, particularly in its more highly specialized branches. Yet it does not seem to me to be altogether out of the question that methodological studies in the field of economics might some day emerge from their present subordinate position as a part of economic theory or as themes for monographical dissertations and finally develop into a fully independent systematic science.

5. A Survey of the System of Economic Sciences

A complete system of the actual economic sciences will therefore comprise the following:

1. The historical sciences of economics: *economic statistics* and *economic history*. The former has to investigate concrete economic phenomena from the point of view of statics and within definite spatial limits, while the latter has to study them from an evolutionary standpoint and to combine them into a unitary, organic structure.

2. *The morphology of economic phenomena*, whose function consists in the classification of economic facts in accordance with their genera, species, and subspecies, as well as the demonstration of their generic form, i.e., the description of the common structures of different groups of homogeneous phenomena.

3. *Economic theory*, which has the task of investigating and establishing the laws of economic phenomena, i.e., the regularities in their coexistence and successsion, as well as their intrinsic causation. I have already called attention to the appropriateness of combining the morphography of basic economic phenomena with economic theory (see above p. 12).

4. *Practical or applied economics*, which teaches us the principles and procedures by which generally determined economic aims may be most effectively realized in different circumstances and in the light of existing scientific knowledge.

6. The Classification of the Economic Sciences as Conceived by the Historical School

The economists of the Historical School view the classification of the economic sciences from an essentially different methodological standpoint.

Here the confusion between historiography and sociology, i.e., between economic history and political economy (regarded as a branch of sociology), first makes itself apparent. I have already commented upon the difference between the tasks of these sciences and have pointed out the impossibility of dealing with history and statistics – the history of all ages and all nations – in a single system of sociology, and with economic history and economic statistics in a single system of political economy. If a certain number of social philosophers still cling to this error, the reason is that they consider it as the function of historical inquiry not to investigate and describe the evolution of *concrete* nations and their cultures, but rather to discover the *laws* of their development. However, distinguished historians have long since rejected this view as an error and as a misunderstanding of the essential task of historiography. Roscher's definition of political economy as 'the philosophy of economic history' is a belated echo of this antiquated conception of history.

Even greater is the conceptual confusion concerning the relationship between economic theory and applied economics.[11]

Every variety of positivism, even a type less extreme than that embraced by the economists of the Historical School, finds it difficult to form a correct conception of the applied sciences.[12]

One will search in vain in Comte's classification of the sciences for a clear and consistent treatment of this problem, nor does the methodology of the Historical School offer any really serious solution of it. Within the system of the social sciences, what relation does the science of administration have to sociology? And what position do the principles of economic policy hold, especially in relation to economic theory, within the system of the economic sciences? To such questions, which can hardly be avoided by the methodology of our science, no satisfactory answer has been given either by Comte's positivism or by the historicism of German political economy. The latter has even denied the independent significance of applied economics.

It is true that the sciences which treat of the principles and procedures for the realization of generally determined human goals have no *absolute* significance, in the sense in which the word is understood in the attacks that the Historical School has launched against this idea. However, this is not a serious objection to the validity of such disciplines. It is patently erroneous to assume that identical procedures in different circumstances, especially in different ages and in different nations, lead to identical results and have in this sense an absolute meaning. However, this mistaken conception of the nature and the tasks of the applied sciences has no bearing on their validity. The function of these disciplines is to demonstrate how given, generally determined goals of human action can be attained under different typical conditions *by methods specifically appropriate to different kinds of circumstances.*

I do not propose to deal here with the question whether the physiocratic or the classical school of economics has really laboured under the aforementioned error as completely as our historicists would have us believe. I leave to others the task of elucidating this point and of rectifying, in respect to the doctrines of *applied* economics, the distortions in the treatment of our science for which the Historical School is responsible, in the same way that this correction has already been made in respect to the history of the development of all the principal doctrines of economic theory. In any case, the above conception of applied economics is an error, but one which is in no way crucial to the question of the independent validity of that discipline in the sense in which we have defined it.

However, it is said, 'the applied sciences, whatever they may do in the way of investigating and demonstrating the *different* procedures suited for the attainment of different typical objectives in different typical circumstances, are nevertheless deficient in that they fail to take into consideration the distinctive peculiarity of each of the *concrete* cases actually encountered in practice; and consequently, at least in this respect, there is a mistaken absolutism in the solutions that they offer.'

This objection too rests upon a prepossession, viz., the mistaken idea that applied economics is to be conceived, if at all, only in the sense of a 'set of prescriptions' for the concrete cases encountered in actual practice.

The applied sciences do not offer us 'recipes' for taking action in every single *concrete* case. There are no sciences of this kind – sciences which would exhaust the whole of life's fullness and multiformity and which would prescribe for us from the very outset the procedure to be followed in each individual *concrete* situation. No applied science, no matter how complete, could possibly do this. Applied sciences in this sense exist only in the fantasy of our historicists. What the applied sciences can and do provide are not recipes for concrete cases. Therapy, technology, and the principles of economic policy are not mere sets of prescriptions. They show us how *generally* determined human goals of a specific kind can be most effectively realized in the light of diverse circumstances. Evidently what is referred to here is the attainment, by means of a *variety* of

15

procedures, of different kinds of objectives under similar conditions and of the same kinds of objectives in different types of circumstances. This is far from providing us with prescriptions for every occasion. The ends aimed at by men are unique in each concrete case, and so are the circumstances in which they have to be attained. No applied science, no matter how highly specialized, could possibly exhaust the individual particularity of every single situation encountered in actual experience.

Here, *in this respect*, the practical man is required to have recourse to his essential insight into phenomena and their interrelationships and to rely upon his own inventiveness. Just as the applied sciences in general are based upon the theoretical, so the scientifically trained technician tries, on the basis of his theoretical insight, to modify, to refine, and to adapt to the unique requirements of each concrete case the procedures indicated by the applied sciences as suited for goals and conditions that are determined only in a general way. It is *only in combination with his theoretical insight* that his knowledge of the applied sciences enables him to specify, in each concrete case, the procedure appropriate to it – or, if one will, the 'prescription' for it. Indeed, there are many situations in practical life, with its ever-changing conditions and exigencies, in which the applied sciences, at their current level, are completely useless, leaving the practical man at the mercy of his own theoretical insight and his native faculty for synthesis and invention. There are instances when even the surgeon, the therapist, and the technologist have only their theoretical insight into the essential nature of things and their interrelations to fall back upon. Although the applied sciences, no matter how fully elaborated, can never, as we have said, be merely a set of prescriptions, yet, in combination with the theoretical sciences, they serve, in innumerable cases that constitute the rule of practical life, as the guiding star of the scientifically trained technician.[13]

What, then, it may be asked, is the use of the applied sciences after all? Can they not be dispensed with entirely, as too round-about? Is it not more appropriate for practical purposes to familiarize oneself exclusively with theory, or at least with history, and thus determine directly, on the basis of these sciences, the procedure corresponding to each concrete case?

Whoever argues in this way – and our economists of the Historical School actually seem to have fixed upon a position very much like this – misunderstands the exigencies of practical life. Historical knowledge, however comprehensive, and theoretical insight, however profound, into the essential nature of things and their interrelations, are far from sufficient in themselves to enable one to decide in a concrete case with the required certainty, rapidity, and completeness upon the most appropriate procedure for getting things done. Theoretical insight has to be associated with the faculty of synthesis and inventiveness, and these are endowments

16

that are to be found only among a limited number of exceptional and especially talented minds. The applied sciences provide us with the sum total of the results achieved in man's effort to find appropriate procedures for the attainment of his practical goals. This knowledge represents the accomplishment not only of scientific research, but also of the greatest inventive geniuses – the really 'practical' men in the strict sense of the word – and includes as well a stock of particular experiences accumulated in practice. Whether because of the imperfect state of development of this kind of knowledge, the ever-changing patterns and requirements of life's practical situations, or special peculiarities of circumstance, the applied sciences may fail to offer an immediate and well-founded prescription for action in a concrete case; yet even then they provide a systematic survey of all the procedures that have been found to be effective in attaining similar goals, and they thereby, to some extent at least, lighten the task of selecting, on the basis of theoretical insight, the means appropriate to the end in view in a given case.

Thus, besides the theoretical sciences, the applied sciences have an eminently independent significance. To call into question, for instance, the utility of surgery, of therapy, of technology, or of the principles of economic policy would argue a complete disregard for the requirements of practical life. These disciplines challenge the sagacity, the experience, the ingenuity, and the diligence of their practitioners to the utmost degree. To place them on a par with 'cookbooks for handy reference,' as Kleinwächter does,[14] is an aberration comparable to that of certain 'practical' men who consider theorizing as idle toying with ideas.[15]

However, it is said, the applied sciences are not sciences in the strict sense of the word, but only scientific studies.

This objection, I believe, does indeed amount to playing with the word 'science.' It is true that some epistemologists refuse to call these disciplines sciences on the ground that the name 'science' in its strictest sense is to be applied only to those disciplines which provide us with an *understanding* of things and which are susceptible of *systematic* demonstration. On this basis, as we know, even *history* has been denied the character of a science. This is a serious error. As far as the applied sciences are concerned, such a judgment is mistaken because disciplines that lend themselves to systematic treatment not only *describe* the procedures for the attainment of generally determined human ends, but also provide us with an *understanding* of them. The applied sciences not only enable us to act in a mechanical way, but at the same time make us aware of the reasons for our action. They are fully entitled to be regarded as sciences in the strict sense of the term in so far as they provide a systematic account of human goals in any one field of endeavor and demonstrate the appropriate methods of

17

attaining them. Terminological controversies over whether these disciplines are properly to be called sciences in some particular sense of the word or whether they are to be labeled 'mere scientific studies' will not affect in any way their independent significance and value in the sphere of scientific knowledge, which is all that concerns us here.

7. Further Observations on the Classification of the Economic Sciences as Conceived by the Historical School

It is incorrect to assert that the applied sciences in general and applied economics in particular establish general principles 'without taking circumstances into account.' It is also incorrect to say that they are 'just sets of prescriptions' and that they can be replaced by theoretical disciplines or even by mere historical studies. On the contrary, these sciences are of the greatest independent significance for both theoretical research and practical life. Their development in both breadth and depth requires no less talent and zeal than does that of the historical, morphological, and theoretical disciplines. Why, then, in the light of all this, are these practical sciences rejected by our economists of the Historical School? The reply is: It is the task of science to be concerned solely with fact and not with value. Science has to teach us what *has been, what is*, and how what is *has come to be*; but not, what *ought to be*.

Accordingly, it is asserted, disciplines like surgery, therapy, technology, or the principles of economic policy are not sciences, and the effort to elaborate and perfect them is misdirected, for they do not teach us what *was*, what *is*, or how what is *has come to be*, but rather, on the basis of this knowledge, they concern themselves, in a certain sense, with what *ought to be*.[16]

Let us, by all means, give to positivism its due share of credit for having liberated us from aprioristic speculation in the sciences that have the real world for their object. However, its helpless incapacity to deal with the applied sciences, and especially with the applied social sciences, seems to me not so much a proof of the invalidity of the latter as a symptom of the *insufficiency* of the positivistic conception of the social sciences. If we understand by the term 'applied sciences' disciplines having the task of teaching us the most effective way in which certain human goals *could* be realized under given conditions and in the light of our judgment at the time, then I am inclined to believe that the applied sciences will continue in full vigor and enjoy a flourishing development long after the insufficiency of positivism, even in the field of *theoretical* inquiry, will have become generally recognized.

18

The objections cited here against the independent validity of applied economics are thus seen to be complete misconceptions. They are certainly far from justifying the opinion that in the field of social inquiry in general, and of economics in particular, the applied sciences should be replaced by a mere description of what was and what is, i.e., by 'economic history and especially a record of the outcome of the attempts that have hitherto been made to improve economic conditions.'

History and statistics, together with the common experience of life, are important foundations of the theoretical sciences. The latter, however, for their part constitute the foundation of the applied disciplines. These too rely upon experience and, what is more, upon an experience that is comprehensive, well-founded, and systematically organized. They are far from rejecting experience or from minimizing its significance. Economic history, economic theory, and the morphology of economic phenomena are important, and even indispensable, auxiliary sciences for applied economics. However, the latter has an independent function, which is essentially different from that of the above-mentioned sciences. As long as the practising surgeon and the therapist do not confine themselves to the study of human history, anatomy, and physiology, or the practising technologist to that of chemistry, mechanics, and physics, there will continue to exist, side by side with history and sociology, applied social sciences of the greatest significance for both theory and practice, even though positivism cannot fit them into its system.

The present confusion concerning the *methods of the applied sciences* in this field will come to an end as soon as it is realized that the cognitive goals of the latter are essentially *different* from those of the other economic sciences. In basing themselves upon historical and theoretical disciplines, the applied sciences draw upon experience to the greatest extent. But in their endeavor to establish the principles and procedures for attaining the goals of human action, they do not confine themselves to the mere description of what the inventive spirit of man has already accomplished. They are not concerned exclusively with past experience. They are equally the product of inventive genius and the faculty of intellectual synthesis. Progress in the applied sciences is the result not only of the scientist's zeal in collecting data, but also of his ingenuity and resourcefulness. The assumption that social scientists should, as a matter of principle, restrict themselves solely to the historical description of the results of man's activity involves the renunciation on the part of science of any concern for meeting new needs and even for influencing in any way the conduct of affairs in all those cases for which no precedent so far exists. Not scientific knowledge, but administrative authority would then determine every innovation in the field of applied economics.

It should be clear from what has been said so far that the applied, as well as the historical and the theoretical, social sciences have an independent significance and validity – that their cognitive goals and their methodologies are different – and also, as I have shown above, that their separate treatment is essential for the intrinsic systematics of each of these sciences.[17] Hence no doubt should exist any longer concerning the relationship between the *morphologies* of social phenomena and the applied social sciences. I have elsewhere pointed out that the morphological approach is valid also in the domain of political economy. And beyond that, I must say that it is indeed gratifying to note, in the methodological discussions of the economists of the Historical School, the increasing emphasis that has recently been placed upon morphological considerations. I welcome this as a sign of the growing conviction among them that our science has the task not only of investigating and describing *concrete* economic phenomena and their development – of being, in other words, something more than mere historiography – but also of dealing with their *generic* aspects. In any case, those who hold to the opinion that a morphology of economic phenomena could be substituted for applied economics in general, or for the sciences of business management in particular, simply fall into a new error. Indeed, a morphology of economic phenomena could by no means take the place even of economic theory, although the connection between theoretical knowledge and certain branches of morphological investigation, particularly those that are concerned with evolutionary changes, is quite as close here as it is in the natural sciences. Those who regard a morphology of economic phenomena and of their historical development as the only legitimate branch of inquiry in the field of economics (besides, perhaps, economic history and economic statistics) fail to understand the independent function and significance not only of applied economics, but of economic theory as well. The one-sidedness manifested by such a confusion of the morphological and the theoretical in the field of economic inquiry surpasses even that involved in the lumping together of economic theory and applied economics.

8. Rebuttal of Some Recent Attacks on My Methodological Position

While I was preparing this paper, my attention was called to Brentano's *Über die Ursachen der heutigen sozialen Not,*[18] and Kleinwächter's *Wesen, Aufgabe, und System der Nationalökonomie.*[19] Both these authors take the opportunity to present their methodological views, which in part are in direct opposition to my own. Since their conception of the classification of the economic sciences reflects the prevailing view on this subject, it seems appropriate to give it some attention here.

Brentano takes the position of the 'vicar of Wakefield,' that the honest man who marries and raises a large family does more good than the man who stays single and babbles about the population. But instead of drawing from this the obvious conclusion that the honest man who organizes cartels or shares in their profits is more useful than the one who only lectures on them, Brentano derives the practical application that 'endless chatter about *what* should be done and *how* it should be done without ever getting anything done' – in other words, concern with the goals and the methods of inquiry – amounts to the 'contraction of intellectual debts.'[20]

Now I too am of the opinion that a methodology, no matter how fully elaborated, is not sufficient in itself for the development of the sciences.

There is, to be sure, between the elaboration of a systematic method and the satisfactory completion and perfection of a science an immeasurable distance that can be bridged only by the genius of the scientist. An active talent for inquiry has often, even in the absence of a fully developed method, created a science or transformed it in an epoch-making way – something that no methodology by itself has ever succeeded in doing. Techniques of procedure, although of incomparable importance for the performance of the subsidiary tasks of science, are of minor significance for those great problems that only the genius can solve.[21]

However, as long as such a genius has not yet appeared in the field of economics, erroneous methodological doctrines still hamper the development of important branches of our science. Under these conditions I think the value of methodological inquiry can hardly be overemphasized by any of us. 'It is,' says Kant, 'already a great and necessary proof of good sense or judgment to know what questions one should ask from a rational point of view.' Economic inquiry has the aim of teaching us not only this, but also what to do in order to get reasonable replies to reasonable questions. Why, then, just in this field, should such investigations imply the 'contraction of intellectual debts'?

In this respect the natural sciences are in an enviable position, because they have long since had an essential awareness of their cognitive goals and procedures. Nevertheless, they do not by any means reject methodological questions, least of all where serious doubts arise concerning the aims and methods of inquiry. Suppose there were to appear a group of natural scientists who refused to recognize as valid any but a descriptive approach to nature, limiting themselves, for example, to the morphology of natural phenomena or even only to the theory of evolution, and who would accordingly reject not only the mathematical sciences as an idle game played with abstract concepts, but even the applied natural sciences as a mere aberration from the true path of inquiry. In that case, provided that their more sober-minded colleagues did not simply prefer to pass over

21

such prejudices in silence, methodological questions would immediately come to the fore also in the field of the natural sciences.

In the domain of the social sciences, however, we are not in the same fortunate position. It is not at all clear what social phenomena are specifically or in what way their distinctive nature must determine the goals and methods of inquiry. There is more than enough room here for misunderstanding and prejudice. Even attitudes as one-sided as those we have described above are within the realm of possibility. Indeed, it is by no means inconceivable that such prejudices might gain currency within certain scholarly circles and that men obsessed by them might have the power to decide on the most momentous issues affecting our economic life. Under such circumstances it can hardly be gainsaid that methodological questions, far from being entirely without significance, are of paramount and urgent importance and demand of all of us our best efforts toward their clarification.

The need for a thoroughgoing reorganization of the social sciences is an undeniable fact. However, I shall not enter here into the discussion of whether such an undertaking is still to be regarded in our time as naive and unconsidered, or whether criticisim of other investigators' work is even possible in the absence of clarity concerning methodological issues. But there is no doubt that the finest flower of the German mind sprang from the ground of inquiries concerning *'what* should be done and *how* it should be done.' Indeed, it is precisely this that constitutes, to a considerable extent, the distinctive feature manifested by the development of German thought. Scholarly zeal, very respectable, to be sure, but rather confused as to the aims and methods of scientific inquiry, is what I think is responsible for the biased tendency of the German Historical School of economists. It is not as unlikely as Brentano seems to believe that a deeper study of methodological questions may make German economists once again aware of the types of problems to be solved by our science and may thus put an end to the one-sidedness that has had such a pernicious effect upon the development of the economic sciences in Germany. However, I am of the opinion that we can attain to a broad view of the types of problems to be solved by economics only by way of comprehensive methodological investigations subserving no extraneous ends of any kind. Incidental methodological dissertations, on the other hand, subjoined to specialized studies of other questions, often serve the sole purpose of placing the particular merits of these works in the right light. Being little more than adornments added to special investigations of quite a different kind, they necessarily bear within themselves the seeds of partiality.

The foundation of a methodology of the social sciences is the most important epistemological task of our time. Our most distinguished epistemologists have directed their scholarly endeavors for the most part towards the great goal of contracting that 'intellectual debt.' Indeed, I myself would like to be such a contractor of intellectual debts. Would that I could solve the methodological problems in the field of the social sciences! Even the more modest service of having advanced their solution by an essential step deserves – considering the present level of methodological understanding – to be esteemed at least as highly as any purely descriptive monograph, even one as meritorious as Brentano's own study of the trade unions of England.

Brentano speaks in similarly derogatory way of the endeavors of the 'new abstract school' to bring about the reform that economic theory so urgently needs if it is to become a truly scientific foundation for applied economics, and thereby also for economic policy. Although attacking these 'new abstract thinkers,' he does not find them guilty of errors in the field of economic theory. He is even fair-minded and candid enough to recognize the progress that it owes this particular group of scientists.[22] And yet this progress, strangely enough, has come not from the Historical School, which has been in existence now for about half a century, but precisely from the 'abstract school,' which is charged with being remote from life. In spite of this, Brentano does not miss any opportunity to demonstrate his disdain for 'abstract theory,' which he seems to regard as an idle game played with ideas. Why? Because abstract theory has not succeeded in abolishing poverty![23] The investigations of the 'abstract scholars' seem to him of no value whatsoever, and the adherents of the 'abstract school' appear even 'incomprehensible' as long as their theoretical inquiries have not succeeded in 'conjuring away either poverty or the dangers to the social order resulting from it.'[24]

I shall deal with this idea in greater detail in another place, where I propose to discuss the different lines of theoretical inquiry with particular reference to mathematical economics. There I shall further examine the circumstances connected with the reproach that 'abstract' economics is only a conceptual game or, as some would have us believe, a system of abstract theorems contradicting experience and derived by way of deduction from certain a priori axioms. These and other similar prejudices that have recently been championed with much zeal, especially in German economics, I shall make the object of an exhaustive inquiry. But here I must observe, in opposition to Brentano's thesis, that the judgment he passes on the theoretical work of the 'abstract scholars' seems untenable to me no matter what branch of economic theory is involved. Brentano seems to forget that economic theory, even when it is interpreted, as it may be, as a science having the real world for its object, has to investigate the nature of economic phenomena and their interrelations and thereby to provide us with an *understanding* of them. On the other hand, it is the task of the applied (or so-called 'practical') sciences, and specifically of applied economics, to teach us the principles and procedures for effective intervention in the economic system in the light of different circumstances. Brentano overlooks the fact that theoretical economics or some specialized branch of it can not very well be reproached for solving the problems peculiar to it and not those that are properly within the sphere of the *applied* sciences.[25]

How biased Brentano's point of view is may be seen from the fact that he declares 'abstract' economic theory to be of no value, but not on the ground that it is *utterly* incapable of solving problems of economic welfare. He scorns all the 'controversies about concepts in which the abstract school is absorbed' only because 'abstract' economic theory is unable to solve a special problem of public welfare, viz., the abolition of 'social danger.' He reminds one of those well-known medical specialists who hold that the natural sciences are all very well, yet scorn them because theories cannot cure a diseased eye or heal a sore leg, and who therefore cannot understand how anyone can devote time and effort and even his entire life to such theoretical inquiries.

Moreover, Brentano does not realize that by demanding this kind of achievement from *science* he puts his own morphological studies in a bad light. After all, Brentano did not originate the idea of trade unionism, of arbitration offices, etc., nor has he, as far as I know, directly called them into being. He is not the Schulze-Delitzch of these institutions, but only a distinguished expositor and historian of them. Even if they were to abolish poverty, as Brentano predicted and still in part assumes, even if his forecast of their operation and development had proved to be perfectly correct, he still could claim for himself only the merit of being their monographer, i.e., a theorist in economics. Not he, but the institutions he describes, would have abolished poverty, and they would have done so even without his descriptions. Yet it would hardly be reasonable to reproach him for this, since he has accomplished, to the best of his ability, what the scientific description of different kinds of economic phenomena has the task of accomplishing. For this reason, it seems to me, it would only be fair if he too demanded of theorists that they do no more than the theoretical sciences or particular branches of them can do by their very nature, namely, what their specific tasks require them to do.

Brentano's attack upon 'abstract' economic theory is mistaken. But I myself am inclined to think that the latter is open to justifiable criticism on quite another score, namely, its failure, in its present state of development, to solve the very problems with which an 'abstract' theory of economists has to be specifically concerned.

Economic theory, in my opinion, will do justice to its task only when it provides us not alone with knowledge of the external regularities in the coexistence and succession of economic phenomena, i.e., with empirical laws, but also with an *understanding* of them in their intrinsic relations. Only in this way can the theoretical foundation be laid for the solution of *all* the problems of economic policy. The inability to abolish poverty is not the only respect in which the science of economic welfare has proved its practical insufficiency in consequence of the present defective theoretical understanding of the nature of economic phenomena and their essential interrelations. The helplessness of administrative authorities in the face of economic crises and the uncertain and fumbling attempts made by even the most distinguished statesmen in dealing with problems of monetary, commercial, industrial, and agricultural policy are only too evident symptoms of the unsatisfactory state of applied economics, which, in its turn, reflects the backwardness of economic theory. The inadequacies of economic policy are but the corollary of an economic theory that leaves to the arbitrary judgment of politicians the answer to such questions as whether duties on grains raise their price in predominantly grain-importing countries, whether higher grain prices raise the price of bread, or whether duties on coffee, petroleum, and tobacco or other indirect taxes raise the price of the corresponding articles of consumption.

No one is more deeply conscious than we theorists, whose heads, according to Brentano, are filled with 'abstractions,' of the imperfection, even the fundamental weaknesses, of the prevailing economic theory and of its insufficiency as a basis for applied economics. Where we differ from Brentano, however, is in the conviction that science as well as economic policy can be perfected only by a deeper understanding of the nature of economic phenomena and their essential interrelations. It is our belief that in economics, as in all other fields of practical activity, only the progressive improvement of all branches of theory can bring about progress in the applied sciences and thereby also the perfection of practice itself. It is therefore one of the most important tasks of those of us who work in this field to cultivate the study of economic theory in all its branches.

However, this task will in no way be advanced by erroneous and biased conceptions concerning the cognitive goals of economic theory or by depreciatory remarks in regard to the endeavors to reform it or particular branches of it. In his criticism of our theoretical investigations Brentano adopts an unfair attitude from the very outset by demanding of them that they forthwith abolish poverty – in other words, that they do the impossible. Nor is he, it seems to me, quite just in his judgment of what these investigations have already accomplished within the sphere of their competence or what, assuming that they are correct, they are called upon to accomplish.

I should like to add here only one remark regarding Brentano's attitude toward the applied sciences.

I believe that in struggling against the idea that life 'may be controlled' by *theory*,[26] Brentano has fallen prey to an altogether baseless apprehension resulting solely from his defective conception of the system of the economic sciences. To be sure, false theories can lead, and often enough have led, the applied sciences based upon them into errors on their part. Erroneous theories in the field of anatomy and physiology, for instance, have had a pernicious influence on surgery and therapy, and thereby indirectly also upon medical practice. In the same way, false economic theories have been responsible for errors in the principles of economic policy. Erroneous ideas concerning the nature of the wealth of nations and the function of money in the national economy have, for example, contributed essentially to aggravate the errors of mercantile economic policy; and the erroneous theory of value developed by the classical school has unquestionably had an essential influence on practical affairs in the demand of the socialists that the entire product, or its equivalent value in money, should belong to the workers. False theoretical doctrines can doubtless give rise to false principles for the conduct of practical affairs and to ineffective procedures or inappropriate policies based upon them, but a *theory* that could 'control' life is a contradiction in terms. Economic theory too can offer us only a true or a false statement of the laws of economic phenomena; it can represent life falsely, but it can no more control life than chemistry or physics can.[27] Hence the question whether the economic sciences have the task of 'controlling' life, if it arises at all, can in any case refer only to applied economics.

But if by 'the control of life' one means to refer to the fact that applied economics has the task of teaching us the principles and procedures for an effective policy of intervention on the part of the state, or of associations analogous and subordinated to it, then the above question must be answered unconditionally in the affirmative, for this is precisely the function that applied economics is, by its very nature and, indeed, by definition, called upon to perform. It 'controls' the economic system in just about the same way as nature is 'controlled' by technology, or the human body by surgery and therapy. In any case, this reproach is one that the specialists in the field of applied economics will find it easy to treat rather lightly.

If the reproach contained in the passage quoted above has any justification at all, it surely cannot mean that applied economics is to be blamed for performing its specific function of aiming at the improvement of life in general, but for going about this task *in the wrong way*.

Here, indeed, the question arises whether applied economics should in principle confine itself to recording the results of past experience and whether – at least from the standpoint of a strict scientific method – it should be absolutely prevented from *also* proposing such ways and means of attaining human goals as are not borrowed from past experience, but are the result of intellectual synthesis and inventive thought.

In this regard, I believe that a science that would confine itself to the description of existing institutions and administrative measures and to waiting for their results with the intention of also 'describing' them at a later date must, in principle, abandon any claim to a leading position in questions of economic policy and dwindle to that of a mere history of the activity of administrative authorities and institutions of collective self-help. No one can possibly deny the importance of experience to the applied sciences, nor would anyone even wish to call it into question in the slightest degree. In requiring that disciplines for the conduct of practical affairs be founded upon the theoretical sciences, we are demanding for the former the most comprehensive empirical foundation, one which can be subjected to the most penetrating criticism and which includes everything that enables us to acquire 'an insight into life.' To restrict these disciplines exclusively to the task of describing past institutions and tendencies and their effects would argue a complete disregard of the innumerable innovations in the economic system that are to be attributed to the work of specialists in applied economics.

Brentano apparently fails to recognize the great practical importance of the creative and inventive spirit or its influence upon the applied sciences. If those working in the field of the applied sciences, as well as men engaged in practical affairs, had always shared Brentano's opinion that science should confine itself to 'observing nature' and to noting the principles of its development, and if they had made this the exclusive rule of their conduct, then we should have run the risk of still having to live in caves and of clothing ourselves in hides 'discovered in nature,' and – in the absence of any higher ethical principles – of preserving the institutions of slavery and serfdom to this very day. Brentano seems to have taken too literally Roscher's dictum that the sole task of our science should be 'the simple description, first, of the economic nature and needs of the different peoples of the world; then, of the laws and institutions designed for their satisfaction; and finally, of the greater or lesser effects they have had,' and that whatever exceeds this 'simple description' is to be regarded quite literally as a 'collection of prescriptions.'[28]

What may well be the strongest point in favour of the conception of applied economics and its task that we have set forth here is that it opens the way for the presentation of new proposals for the organization of

27

economic life. As long as these are sound and are realized in practice, people can always be found to 'describe' the different ways of organizing the management of practical affairs and to 'observe nature' once again in order to learn their underlying principles. In any case, however, nothing seems to me more certain than that in the field of economics 'a real service can be rendered to science, fatherland, and humanity' not only by 'descriptions,' but also by intellectual synthesis and the inventive spirit, especially when these are combined with an ever-growing fund of experience.

NOTES

1. For my conception of the *statistical* sciences, see my *Untersuchungen über die Methode de Sozialwissenschaften* (1883) pp. 253ff.
2. See my *Untersuchungen über die Methode der Sozialwissenschaften* (1883), pp. 3 ff. and pp. 249 ff. For other discussions of this point, see L. Cossa, *Guida allo studio dell' econ. pol.* (1878), pp. 14 ff.; M. Block, *Journal des ècon* (1883), pp. 67 ff.; E. Sax, *Das Wesen und die Aufgaben der Nationalökonomie* (Vienna, 1884), pp. 21 ff.; E. v. Philippovich, *Über die Angabe und Methode der polit. Ökonomie* (Freiburg, 1886), pp. 3 ff.; L. Walras, *Elèments d'èc. pol.* (1889), pp. 34 ff.
3. A presentation combining theoretical with practical knowledge is justified wherever certain parts of a theory are of specific importance for a particular applied science. In demonstrating a particular practical application of the natural sciences, one may draw upon all the theoretical knowledge relevant to one's purpose, setting it forth either by way of introduction or by means of incidental references in the body of the presentation itself. The economist who deals with a particular practical application of economic theory, or of any branch of it, may do likewise. The author of a work on monetary, commercial, and agricultural policy or on indirect taxation may use whatever theoretical knowledge is specifically required to support his thesis, either in his introduction or in incidental references in the body of his work. He may do the same with the results of the sciences of history, statistics, technology, husbandry, forestry, mining, etc. But it is clearly understood that this in no way obviates the need for an *independent* presentation of the above-mentioned sciences.
4. See my essay 'Zur Kritik der pol. Ök.' in Grünhut's *Zeitchr. für das privat– und offentl. Recht* (1887), pp. 754 ff.

28

5. See my *Untersuchungen über die Methode der Sozialwissenschaften* (1883), pp. 352 ff. and *Die Irrtümer des Historismus in der deutschen Nationalökonomie* (1884), pp. 12 ff. The experts in the field of historical research are in substantial agreement on this point. Bernheim, in his *Lehrbuch der historischen Methode* (1889), pp. 68 ff., vehemently criticizes the conceptual confusion of those social philosophers who regard the science of history, not as an independent discipline, but as a branch of sociology, with allegedly the same aims, tasks, and methods as the latter. Bernheim says, 'This is almost as erroneous as it would be to regard history as a branch of politics, merely because both are concerned with the state. Sociology, it is true, is concerned with the same object as history, i.e., with human society, but in a totally different way. . . .The whole outlook and approach of society is fundamentally different from that of history, since the latter endeavors to learn what man, as a member of society, has everywhere become, how this development has taken place, what has been accomplished by every social group, every people, every prominent personality, in all their individuality. . . . Sociology is an auxiliary science of history. But it is no way the aim of the latter to establish general types and factors, or even laws, of development. . . . The sociologists belonging to the biased group that fails to recognize this fact declare the only theme of historical science to be what they themselves seek to abstract from history for their own purposes.'

6. The separation of economic theory from the applied sciences as far as *presentation* is concerned is no more an 'unnatural dissection of a homogeneous subject matter' than is the separate treatment of chemistry and chemical technology or of mechanics and mechanical technology. The assumption that such a separation of the sciences necessarily involves a disintegration of *knowledge* must in any event be considered as one of the most naive of existing prejudices. A scientifically trained physician is familiar not only with therapy, but also with anatomy and physiology, although these sciences have long since been treated as independent.

7. G. Schönberg, *Handbuch d. pol. Ök.*, (1885), i, pp. 134 ff.

8. See my *Untersuchungen über die Methode der Sozialwissenschaften,* pp. 246 ff.

9. This error is especially obvious in Kleinwächter's characterization of the relationship between economic theory and the principles of applied economics as that of 'different *parts* or *chapters*' of one and the same science. (See *Jahrbücher,* New Series, xviii (1889), p. 603.) Brentano also makes a distinction between general *or* theoretical

29

economics and specialized *or* applied economics. (*Die klassische Nationalökonomie*, pp. 28 ff.)

10. *Logik* (1883), ii, p. 230.

11. On the confusion of *economic theory* with the *general* branch and of *applied economics* with the *specialized* branch of political economy, see above pp. 10–11.

12. 'Every practice presupposes an ideal; the thing to be done is never a fact: empiricism leaves every practice to the hazard of the passions.' (C. Secrétan, *Études sociales* (1889), p. 205).

13. We must distinguish in the domain of economics, just as we do in other fields of human activity, between the so-called *practical sciences* and *practice* itself. The former have the task of teaching us the procedures by which certain economic aims, determined only in a general way, can be most effectively realized in different circumstances. In actual practice, on the other hand, on the basis of the above-mentioned sciences and of one's own (theoretical) insight into the essential nature of things and their interrelations, one has to determine and to follow the procedure uniquely appropriate to the concrete case with which one has to deal. The confusion in the field of economics between the practical sciences and practical activity is one of the chief reasons why there are so many methodological misunderstandings. What chiefly contributes to this error is the fact that the practical sciences are often designated as the *applied* sciences, since they are based upon the theoretical sciences and presuppose a knowledge of them. It is clear, however, that the applied sciences in the above sense should not be confused with practice. Surgery, a practical science, is, in its relation to anatomy and physiology, an applied science. Yet no one would confuse the activity of a practising surgeon with the *science* of surgery.

14. Ibid., p. 603. Kleinwächter seems to be ignorant of the reasons why the words '*or* the so-called practical arts' are an appropriate addition to the expression 'the applied sciences.' The reason lies in the double meaning of this term, which designates on the one hand, especially in the older philosophy, ἡ περὶ γἀνθρὠπινα φιλοσωφία, i.e., *all* the sciences of man, and, on the other hand, the *applied* sciences in the modern sense (as opposed to the *theoretical* sciences). The added words are intended to eliminate a possible doubt as to the *meaning* in which the expression 'applied science' is employed. In any case, it takes a rather extravagant fancy to draw from them the conclusion that Kleinwächter does that the applied sciences are something like 'cookbooks for handy reference that the Minister of the Interior or of Commerce consults each time he proceeds to draft a bill

or an ordinance, in the same way as a cook refers to her cookbook when she has to prepare a roast in an unusual way.' In my opinion, an official usually knows that there are no prescriptions in the art of public administration, but only general principles and procedures to be *reasonably* applied in the specific cases in which he is called upon to act. Besides, he does not wait until the moment when he begins to draw up a law before familiarizing himself with the principles of legislation. A minister who behaved in that way would be like a military commander who would 'look up' the general principles of strategy only immediately before or during the battle. Such a bizarre conception of the manner in which public affairs are conducted can hardly avail to disprove the independent validity of the applied sciences.

15. Those who are opposed to treating applied economics as an independent science might find it worthwhile to consider how the founder of the strictly scientific treatment of mechanical technology characterizes the very essence of that science: 'Technology,' say Karl Karmarsch, 'is often denied a separate status as a science – although only by those who do not understand its nature and aims. One would think that its entire content consists of a combination of fragments of chemistry and mechanics. ... Technology is based on natural history, physics, chemistry, and mechanics. ... But the mere combination of all these *auxiliary sciences* in one person does not necessarily constitute a technologist.' And he rightly emphasizes that from an accumulation of purely descriptive literature technology developed only after its material had been interpreted, investigated, and treated in a scientific way. (*Geschichte der Technologie* (1872), pp. 1 ff.)

16. In view of what has been said above, it is hardly necessary to observe that the applied sciences do not force upon us any *absolute 'ought,'* but that they only teach us the way in which certain generally determined ends can be attained in the light of our judgment at a particular time and *provided that we want to attain them at all*. The applied sciences do not contain, as Kleinwächter thinks (*Jahrbücher für Nationalökonomie und Statistik*, New Series (1889), xviii, pp. 603 ff.), a command to pursue any aims in particular. They merely show us how we have to act (or, if one will, how we *ought to act*), on the basis of our judgment at a particular time, if we *want* to attain a given end; whereas it is the historical, the morphological, and the theoretical sciences that provide us with knowledge of the past and the present and of the nature of phenomena and their interrelations. This distinction between the tasks of the applied sciences, on the one hand, and those of history, statistics, morphology, and the theoretical sciences,

on the other, is expressed, in a way that can hardly be misunderstood by any unprejudiced person, in the statement that the former do not deal with what *is*, but with what *ought to be*.

17. See above pp. 7–8.
18. *Über die Ursachen der heutigen sozialen Not. Ein Beitrag zur Morphologie der Volkswirtschaft.* Lecture delivered on the occasion of assuming the professorship at the University of Lepzig, April 27, 1889 (Leipzig, 1889).
19. In *Jahrbücher für Nationalökonomie und Statistik,* New Series (Jena, 1889), xviii, pp. 601 ff.
20. Loc. cit., p. 1.
21. See my *Untersuchungen über die Methode der Sozialwissenschaften* (1883), pp. xi ff.
22. *Die klassische Nationalökonomie* (1888), p.7; *Die Ursachen der sozialen Not* (1889), p.3.
23. From an essentially different standpoint F.J. Neumann, in the recently published first part of his *Grundlagen der Volkswirtschaftslehre* (Tübingen, 1889), opposes the tendencies of the Austrian school of economists. Neumann has been concerned with economic theory not only in his 'younger years' or in a merely cursory way. Unlike many of his German colleagues, who became aware of the untenability of 'classical theory' and perhaps also of their own incapacity for reforming it, Neumann has not thrown theory overboard completely or confined himself exclusively to the investigation of 'parallelism in economic history' and a rootless eclecticism. Neither has he ever failed to recognize the importance of economic theory to applied economics and to economic policy. We can unqualifiedly agree with Neumann's statement that it was precisely practical problems that impelled him to embark upon theoretical investigations and showed him how to set in order the theoretical foundations to which one has to revert in the discussion of the above questions (ibid., p. v.).

In economic theory itself an essential progress in Neumann's thought is also to be noted. He arrives at the conclusion (pp. 251 ff.) that the standpoint represented by the opponents of the theory of value that he had himself hitherto favoured – a theory of particular importance for our science because of its bearing upon the theory of prices and the doctrines connected with it – is to be given 'preference over the interpretations of Hufeland, Lotz, Hermann, etc.,' the very men whose essential views he had formerly espoused. By openly acknowledging this revolution in his fundamental doctrines, he has rendered an inestimable service to economic theory.

However, the reader of Neumann's work will find this concession scarcely conceivable. His book is introduced by a criticism, extending over some two hundred and fifty pages, partly petty, partly even mis-interpreting the very authors to whom he owes his present better insight. Many of his objections against particular details of some of the theories that he now recognizes as essentially valid are to be attributed simply to the fact that in the introductory section of his work, devoted to general doctrines, he takes only a partial view of the necessary consequences that the standpoint he now accepts has for the special-ized doctrines of economic theory. This lack of clarity is what is mainly responsible for the chief deficiency of his work: his trivial prolixity and a tendency toward the consistent evasion of the crucial points in the problems he discusses.

24. *Die Ursachen der sozialen Not*, p. 5. Brentano directs this criticism in particular against those authors who have attacked the basic error in the theory of modern socialism. As if those who seek to refute the socialists' erroneous idea that labour is the sole source of value or other similar errors in fact 'believed,' as Brentano maintains, that by doing so they could immediately conjure away all the dangers to the social order! Such dangers can be created by erroneous theories only in an *indirect* way; hence, it stands to reason that their refutation can likewise contribute only in an *indirect* way toward removing those dangers. However, this is not a valid objection to the refutation of erroneous theories. Brentano, after all, seems to have forgotten that he has himself only recently devoted a lecture, which he also had printed and published (*Die klassische Nationalökonomie* (Leipzig, 1888)), to the criticism of economic theories that he regarded as erroneous, without, as far as I know, succeeding in abolishing poverty, not even – and this is what seems to me, under the circumstances, to be a far more serious failing on his part – the poverty still existing here and there in the field of economic theory.

25. Brentano so far fails to recognize the limits of the different economic sciences and the nature of economic theory that he even suspects the efforts to reform the latter to be a method of justifying and sanctioning the existing economic order, in evident disregard of the fact that inquiry into the nature of economic phenomena and their interrela-tions does not contain any value judgment implying their 'perfection.' (*Die Ursachen der sozialen Not*, p. 28.)

26. Loc. cit., pp. 29 ff.

27. An essentially different question has been raised by Wundt, *Logik* (1883), ii, pp. 591 ff. His problem is whether 'abstract' economic theories (which, in his sense, are true only under specific assump-tions) may be *directly* transformed into prescriptions for practical

33

action. I believe that – quite apart from erroneous doctrines – even correct 'abstract' theories cannot properly constitute the sole and immediate basis of the principles of practical action. One must take into consideration differences of circumstance as well as empirical probabilities. Even principles of practical action are not universally applicable prescriptions, but rather rules for the conduct of affairs that have to be applied with due regard for the distinctive peculiarity of each concrete case. Abstract theory can serve as the foundation of an applied science, just as the latter can form the basis of actual practice, only by virtue of a determinative procedure – if one may be permitted to use such an expression.

However, this is not, I think, a peculiar feature of the economic sciences, but a general characteristic of the relationship of 'abstract' theories to the applied sciences based upon them. Technologists, surgeons, and therapists, for example, apply the laws of physics, chemistry, mechanics, and even physiology, not directly, but only by means of the above-mentioned determinative procedure. The difference here is only one of degree, not of kind. In any case, the fact referred to by Wundt, that in abstract theorizing about economic questions our conception of 'what *ought to be*' helps to determine our view of 'what *is*,' as far as this does not involve a complete confusion between theoretical and applied science, is not, I believe, a feature peculiar to 'abstract' economic theory alone. No doubt science has often enough been led astray by certain practical motives that have operated to give it a tendentious direction. However, it is not only 'abstract' economic theories that are open to this reproach, but also, as recent experience has demonstrated, the 'concrete' ones as well – including even economic history and statistics. To impute to those who work in the field of 'abstract' economic theory a special propensity toward biased distortions of this kind or even merely toward error would be, it seems to me, more than unfair.

28. *Grundlagen der Nationalökonomie* (1854), §26 and §29.

Carl Menger, 'The General Theory of the Good' and 'Economy and Economic Goods' in Menger's *Grundsätze* (1871), chapters 1 and 2, trans. *Principles of Economics* (Glencoe IL: Free Press, 1950), pp. 51–113.

This is the English translation of the first two chapters in Menger's famous *Grundsätze der Volkswirthschaftslehre* (Wien: Wilhelm Braunmüller, 1871). Although that volume was described on its title page as 'Erster, Allgemeiner Theil' (i.e. the First, General, Part), Menger did not in fact publish any further parts to this book. A second edition, with substantial changes in the arrangement of chapters as well as in the text, was published posthumously in 1923, edited by Menger's son, Karl Menger, Jr. The present translation, by James Dingwall and Bert F. Hoselitz, was first published in 1950. Many of Menger's best-known ideas and insights are contained in this chapter, and also in the second chapter which follows.

2

The General Theory of the Good

CARL MENGER

All things are subject to the law of cause and effect. This great principle knows no exception, and we would search in vain in the realm of experience for an example to the contrary. Human progress has no tendency to cast it in doubt, but rather the effect of confirming it and of always further widening knowledge of the scope of its validity. Its continued and growing recognition is therefore closely linked to human progress.

One's own person, moreover, and any of its states are links in this great universal structure of relationships. It is impossible to conceive of a change of one's person from one state to another in any way other than one subject to the law of causality. If, therefore, one passes from a state of need to a state in which the need is satisfied, sufficient causes for this change must exist. There must be forces in operation within one's organism that remedy the disturbed state, or there must be external things acting upon it that by their nature are capable of producing the state we call satisfaction of our needs.

Things that can be placed in a causal connection with the satisfaction of human needs we term *useful things*.[1] If, however, we both recognize this causal connection, and have the power actually to direct the useful things to the satisfaction of our needs, we call them *goods*.[2]

If a thing is to become a good, or in other words, if it is to acquire goods-character, all four of the following prerequisites must be simultaneously present:

1. A human need.
2. Such properties as render the thing capable of being brought into a causal connection with the satisfaction of this need.
3. Human knowledge of this causal connection.
4. Command of the thing sufficient to direct it to the satisfaction of the need.

Only when all four of these prerequisites are present simultaneously can a thing become a good. When even one of them is absent, a thing cannot acquire goods-character,[3] and a thing already possessing goods-character would lose it at once if but one of the four prerequisites ceased to be present.[4]

Hence a thing loses its goods-character: (1) if, owing to a change in human needs, the particular needs disappear that the thing is capable of satisfying, (2) whenever the capacity of the thing to be placed in a causal connection with the satisfaction of human needs is lost as the result of a change in its own properties, (3) if knowledge of the causal connection between the thing and the satisfaction of human needs disappears, or (4) if men lose command of it so completely that they can no longer apply it directly to the satisfaction of their needs and have no means of re-establishing their power to do so.

A special situation can be observed whenever things that are incapable of being placed in any kind of causal connection with the satisfaction of human needs are nevertheless treated by men as goods. This occurs (1) when attributes, and therefore capacities, are erroneously ascribed to things that do not really possess them, or (2) when non-existent human needs are mistakenly assumed to exist. In both cases we have to deal with things that do not, in reality, stand in the relationship already described as determining the goods-character of things, but do so only in the opinions of people. Among things of the first class are most cosmetics, all charms, the majority of medicines administered to the sick by peoples of early civilizations and by primitives even today, divining rods, love potions, etc. For all these things are incapable of actually satisfying the needs they are supposed to serve. Among things of the second class are medicines for diseases that do not actually exist, the implements, statues, buildings, etc., used by pagan people for the worship of idols, instruments of torture, and the like. Such things, therefore, as derive their goods-character merely from properties they are imagined to possess or from needs merely imagined by men may appropriately be called *imaginary* goods.[5]

As a people attains higher levels of civilization, and as men penetrate more deeply into the true constitution of things and of their own nature, the number of true goods becomes constantly larger, and as can easily be understood, the number of imaginary goods becomes progressively smaller. It is not unimportant evidence of the connection between accurate knowledge and human welfare that the number of so-called imaginary goods is shown by experience to be usually greatest among peoples who are poorest in true goods.

Of special scientific interest are the goods that have been treated by some writers in our discipline as a special class of goods called 'relationships.'[6] In this category are firms, goodwill, monopolies, copyrights, patents, trade licenses, authors' rights, and also, according to some writers, family connections, friendship, love, religious and scientific fellowships, etc. It may readily be conceded that a number of these relationships do not allow a rigorous test of their goods-character. But that many of them, such as firms, monopolies, copyrights, customer good-will, and the like, are actually goods is shown, even without appeal to further proof, by the fact that we often encounter them as objects of commerce. Nevertheless, if the theorist who has devoted himself most closely to this topic[7,8] admits that the classification of these relationships as goods has something strange about it, and appears to the unprejudiced eye as an anomaly, there must, in my opinion, be a somewhat deeper reason for such doubts than the unconscious working of the materialistic bias of our time which regards only materials and forces (tangible objects and labour services) as things and, therefore, also as goods.

It has been pointed out several times by students of law that our language has no term for 'useful actions' in general, but only one for 'labour services.' Yet there is a whole series of actions, and even of mere inactions, which cannot be called labour services but which are nevertheless decidedly useful to certain persons, for whom they may even have considerable economic value. That someone buys commodities from me, or uses my legal services, is certainly no labour service on his part, but it is nevertheless an action beneficial to me. That a well-to-do doctor ceases the practice of medicine in a small country town in which there is only one other doctor in addition to himself can with still less justice be called a labour service. But it is certainly an inaction of considerable benefit to the remaining doctor who thereby becomes a monopolist.

Whether a larger or smaller number of persons regularly performs actions that are beneficial to someone (a number of customers with respect to a merchant, for instance) does not alter the nature of these actions. And whether certain inactions on the part of some or all of the inhabitants of a city or state which are useful to someone come about voluntarily or through legal compulsion (natural or legal monopolies, copyrights, trade marks, etc.), does not alter in any way the nature of these useful inactions. From an economic standpoint, therefore, what are called clienteles, goodwill, monopolies, etc., are the useful actions or inactions of other people, or (as in the case of *firms*, for example) aggregates of material goods, labour services, and other useful actions and inactions. Even relationships of friendship and love, religious fellowships, and the like, consist obviously of actions or inactions of other persons that are beneficial to us.

If, as is true of customer good-will, firms, monopoly rights, etc., these useful actions or inactions are of such a kind that we can dispose of them, there is no reason why we should not classify them as goods, without finding it necessary to resort to the obscure concept of 'relationships,' and without bringing these 'relationships' into contrast with all other goods as a special category. On the contrary, all goods can, I think, be divided into the two classes of *material goods* (including all forces of nature insofar as they are goods) and of *useful human actions* (and inactions), the most important of which are labour services.

2. The Causal Connections between Goods

Before proceeding to other topics, it appears to me to be of pre-eminent importance to our science that we should become clear about the causal connections between goods. In our own, as in all other sciences, true and lasting progress will be made only when we no longer regard the objects of our scientific observations merely as unrelated occurrences, but attempt to discover their *causal connections* and the laws to which they are subject. The bread we eat, the flour from which we bake the bread, the grain that we mill into flour, and the field on which the grain is grown – all these things are goods. But knowledge of this fact is not sufficient for our purposes. On the contrary, it is necessary in the manner of all other empirical sciences, to attempt to classify the various goods according to their inherent characteristics, to learn the place that each good occupies in the causal nexus of goods, and finally, to discover the economic laws to which they are subject.

Our well-being at any given time, to the extent that it depends upon the satisfaction of our needs, is assured if we have at our disposal the goods required for their direct satisfaction. If, for example, we have the necessary amount of bread, we are in a position to satisfy our need for food directly. The causal connection between bread and the satisfaction of one of our needs is thus a direct one, and a testing of the goods-character of bread according to the principles laid down in the preceding section presents no difficulty. The same applies to all other goods that may be used directly for the satisfaction of our needs, such as beverages, clothes, jewelry, etc.

But we have not yet exhausted the list of things whose goods-character we recognize. For in addition to goods that serve our needs directly (and which will, for the sake of brevity, henceforth be called 'goods of first order') we find a large number of other things in our economy that cannot be put in any direct causal connection with the satisfaction of our needs, but which possess goods-character no less certainly than goods of first order. In our markets, next to bread and other goods capable of satisfying human needs directly, we also see quantities of flour, fuel, and salt. We find that implements and tools for the production of bread, and the skilled labour services necessary for their use, are regularly traded. All these things, or at any rate by far the greater number of them, are incapable of satisfying human needs in any direct way – for what human need could be satisfied by a specific labour service of a journeyman baker, by a baking utensil, or even by a quantity of ordinary flour? That these things are nevertheless treated as goods in human economy, just like goods of first order, is due to the fact that they serve to produce bread and other goods of first order, and hence are indirectly, even if not directly, capable of satisfying human needs. The same is true of thousands of other things that do not have the capacity to satisfy human needs directly, but which are nevertheless used for the production of goods of first order, and can thus be put in an indirect causal connection with the satisfaction of human needs. These considerations prove that the relationship responsible for the goods-character of these things, which we will call goods of *second* order, is fundamentally the same as that of goods of first order. The fact that goods of first order have a direct and goods of second order an indirect causal relation with the satisfaction of our needs gives rise to no difference in the essence of that relationship, since the requirement for the acquisition of goods-character is the existence of some causal connection, but not necessarily one that is direct, between things and the satisfaction of human needs.

At this point, it could easily be shown that even with these goods we have not exhausted the list of things whose goods-character we recognize, and that, to continue our earlier example, the grain mills, wheat, rye, and labour services applied to the production of flour, etc., appear as goods of *third* order, while the fields, the instruments and appliances necessary for their cultivation, and the specific labour services of farmers, appear as goods of *fourth* order. I think, however, that the idea I have been presenting is already sufficiently clear.

In the previous section, we saw that a causal relationship between a thing and the satisfaction of human needs is one of the prerequisites of its goods-character. The thought developed in this section may be summarized in the proposition that it is not a requirement of the goods-character of a thing that it be capable of being placed in *direct* causal connection with the satisfaction of human needs. It has been shown that goods having an indirect causal relationship with the satisfaction of human needs differ in the closeness of this relationship. But it has also been shown that this difference does not affect the essence of goods-character in any way. In this connection, a distinction was made between goods of first, second, third, fourth, and higher orders.

41

Again it is necessary that we guard ourselves, from the beginning, from a faulty interpretation of what has been said. In the general discussion of goods-character, I have already pointed out that goods-character is not a property inherent in the goods themselves. The same warning must also be given here, where we are dealing with the order or place that a good occupies in the causal nexus of goods. To designate the order of a particular good is to indicate only that this good, in some particular employment, has a closer or more distant causal relationship with the satisfaction of a human need. Hence the order of a good is nothing inherent in the good itself and still less a property of it.

Thus I do not attach any special weight to the orders assigned to goods, either here or in the following exposition of the laws governing goods, although the assignment of these orders will, if they are correctly understood, become an important aid in the exposition of a difficult and important subject. But I do wish especially to stress the importance of understanding the causal relation between goods and the satisfaction of human needs and, depending upon the nature of this relation in particular cases, the more or less direct causal connection of the goods with these needs.

3. The Laws Governing Goods-character

A. *The goods-character of goods of higher order is dependent on command of corresponding complementary goods.*

When we have goods of first order at our disposal, it is in our power to use them directly for the satisfaction of our needs. If we have the corresponding goods of second order at our disposal, it is in our power to transform them into goods of first order, and thus to make use of them in an indirect manner for the satisfaction of our needs. Similarly, should we have only goods of third order at our disposal, we would have the power to transform them into the corresponding goods of second order, and these in turn into corresponding goods of first order. Hence we would have the power to utilize goods of third order for the satisfaction of our needs, even though this power must be exercised by transforming them into goods of successively lower orders. The same proposition holds true with all goods of higher order, and we cannot doubt that they possess goods-character if it is in our power actually to utilize them for the satisfaction of our needs.

This last requirement, however, contains a limitation of no slight importance with respect to goods of higher order. For it is never in our power to make use of any particular good of higher order for the satisfaction of our needs unless we also have command of the other (complementary) goods of higher order.

Let us assume, for instance, that an economizing individual possesses no bread directly, but has at his command all the goods of second order necessary to produce it. There can be no doubt that he will nevertheless have the power to satisfy his need for bread. Suppose, however, that the same person has command of the flour, salt, yeast, labour services, and even all the tools and appliances necessary for the production of bread, but lacks both fuel and water. In this second case, it is clear that he no longer has the power to utilize the goods of second order in his possession for the satisfaction of his need, since bread cannot be made without fuel and water, even if all the other necessary goods are at hand. Hence the goods of second order will, in this case, immediately lose their goods-character with respect to the need for bread, since one of the four prerequisites for the existence of their goods-character (in this case the fourth prerequisite) is lacking.

It is possible for the things whose goods-character has been lost with respect to the need for bread to retain their goods-character with respect to other needs if their owner has the power to utilize them for the satisfaction of other needs than his need for bread, or if they are capable, by themselves, of directly or indirectly satisfying a human need in spite of the lack of one or more complementary goods. But if the lack of one or more complementary goods makes it impossible for the available goods of second order to be utilized, either by themselves alone or in combination with other available goods, for the satisfaction of any human need whatsoever, they will lose their goods-character completely. For economizing men will no longer have the power to direct the goods in question to the satisfaction of their needs, and one of the essential prerequisites of their goods-character is therefore missing.

Our investigation thus far yields, as a first result, the proposition that the goods-character of goods of *second* order is dependent upon complementary goods of the same order being available to men with respect to the production of at least one good of first order.

The question of the dependence of the goods-character of goods of higher order than the second upon the availability of complementary goods is more complex. But the additional complexity by no means lies in the relationship of the goods of higher order to the corresponding goods of the next lower order (the relationship of goods of third order to the corresponding goods of second order, or of goods of fifth order to those of fourth order, for example). For the briefest consideration of the causal relationship between these goods provides a complete analogy to the relationship just demonstrated between goods of second order and goods

43

of the next lower (first) order. The principle of the previous paragraph may be extended quite naturally to the proposition that the goods-character of goods of higher order is directly dependent upon complementary goods of the same order being available with respect to the production of at least one good of the next lower order.

The additional complexity arising with goods of higher than second order lies rather in the fact that even command of all the goods required for the production of a good of the next lower order does not necessarily establish their goods-character unless men also have command of all their complementary goods of this next and of all still lower orders. Assume that someone has command of all the goods of third order that are required to produce a good of second order, but does not have the other complementary goods of second order at his command. In this case, even command of all the goods of third order required for the production of a single good of second order will not give him the power actually to direct these goods of third order to the satisfaction of human needs. Although he has the power to transform the goods of third order (whose goods-character is here in question) into goods of second order, he does not have the power to transform the goods of second order into the corresponding goods of first order. He will therefore not have the power to direct the goods of third order to the satisfaction of his needs, and because he has lost this power, goods of third order lose their goods-character immediately.

It is evident, therefore, that the principle stated above – the goods-character of goods of higher order is directly dependent upon complementary goods of the same order being available with respect to the production of at least one good of the next lower order – does not include all the prerequisites for the establishment of the goods-character of things, since command of all complementary goods of the same order does not by itself give us the power to direct these things to the satisfaction of our needs. If we have goods of third order at our disposal, their goods-character is indeed directly dependent on our being able to transform them into goods of second order. But a further requirement for their goods-character is our ability to transform the goods of second order in turn into goods of first order, which involves the still further requirement that we must have command of certain complementary goods of second order.

The relationships of goods of fourth order, fifth, and still higher orders are quite analogous. Here again the goods-character of things so remote from the satisfaction of human needs is directly dependent on the availability of complementary goods of the same order. But it is dependent also upon our having command of the complementary goods of the next lower order, in turn of the complementary goods of the order below this, and so on, in such a way that it is in our power actually to direct the goods of higher order to the production of a good of first order, and thereby finally to the satisfaction of a human need. If we designate the whole sum of goods that are required to utilize a good of higher order for the production of a good of first order as its complementary goods in the wider sense of the term, we obtain the general principle that *the goods-character of goods of higher order depends on our being able to command their complementary goods in this wider sense of the term.*

Nothing can place the great causal interconnection between goods more vividly before our eyes than this principle of the mutual interdependence of goods.

When, in 1862, the American Civil War dried up Europe's most important source of cotton, thousands of other goods that were complementary to cotton lost their goods-character. I refer in particular to the labour services of English and continental cotton mill workers who then, for the greater part, became unemployed and were forced to ask public charity. The labour services (of which these capable workers had command) remained the same, but large quantities of them lost their goods-character since their complementary good, cotton, was unavailable, and the specific labour services could not by themselves, for the most part, be directed to the satisfaction of any human need. But these labour services immediately became goods again when their complementary good again became available as the result of increased cotton imports, partly from other sources of supply, and partly, after the end of the American Civil War, from the old source.

Conversely, goods often lose their goods-character because men do not have command of the necessary labour services, complementary to them. In sparsely populated countries, particularly in countries raising one predominant crop such as wheat, a very serious shortage of labour services frequently occurs after especially good harvests, both because agricultural workers, few in numbers and living separately, find few incentives for hard work in times of abundance, and because the harvesting work, as a result of the exclusive cultivation of wheat, is concentrated into a very brief period of time. Under such conditions (on the fertile plains of Hungary, for instance), where the requirements for labour services, within a short interval of time, are very great but where the available labour services are not sufficient, large quantities of grain often spoil on the fields. The reason for this is that the goods complementary to the crops standing on the fields (the labour services necessary for harvesting them) are missing, with the result that the crops themselves lose their goods-character.

When the economy of a people is highly developed, the various complementary goods are generally in the hands of different persons. The producers of each individual article usually carry on their business in a mechanical way, while the producers of the complementary goods realize just as little that the goods-character of the things they produce or manufacture depends on the existence of other goods that are not in their possession. The error that goods of higher order possess goods-character by themselves, and without regard to the availability of complementary goods, arises most easily in countries where, owing to active commerce and a highly developed economy, almost every product comes into existence under the tacit, and as a rule quite unconscious, supposition of the producer that other persons, linked to him by trade, will provide the complementary goods at the right time. Only when this tacit assumption is disappointed by such a change of conditions that the laws governing goods make their operation manifestly apparent, are the usual mechanical business transactions interrupted, and only then does public attention turn to these manifestations and to their underlying causes.

B. *The goods-character of goods of higher order is derived from that of the corresponding goods of lower order.*

Examination of the nature and causal connections of goods as I have presented them in the first two sections leads to the recognition of a further law that goods obey as such – that is, without regard to their economic character.

It has been shown that the existence of human needs is one of the essential prerequisites of goods-character, and that if the human needs with whose satisfaction a thing may be brought into causal connection completely disappear, the goods-character of the thing is immediately lost unless new needs for it arise.

From what has been said about the nature of goods, it is directly evident that goods of first order lose their goods-character immediately if the needs they previously served to satisfy all disappear without new needs arising for them. The problem becomes more complex when we turn to the entire range of goods causally connected with the satisfaction of a human need, and inquire into the effect of the disappearance of this need on the goods-character of the goods of higher order causally connected with its satisfaction.

Suppose that the need for direct human consumption of tobacco should disappear as the result of a change in tastes, and that at the same time all other needs that the tobacco already prepared for human consumption might serve to satisfy should also disappear. In this event, it is certain that all tobacco products already on hand, in the final form suited to human consumption, would immediately lose their goods-character. But what would happen to the corresponding goods of higher order? What would be the situation with respect to raw tobacco leaves, the tools and appliances used for the production of the various kinds of tobacco, the specialized labour services employed in the industry, and in short, with respect to all the goods of second order used for the production of tobacco destined for human consumption: What, furthermore, would be the situation with respect to tobacco seeds, tobacco farms, the labour services and the tools and appliances employed in the production of raw tobacco, and all the other goods that may be regarded as goods of third order in relation to the need for tobacco? What, finally, would be the situation with respect to the corresponding goods of fourth, fifth, and higher orders?

The goods-character of a thing is, as we have seen, dependent on its being capable of being placed in a causal connection with the satisfaction of human needs. But we have also seen that a *direct* causal connection between a thing and the satisfaction of a need is by no means a necessary prerequisite of its goods-character. On the contrary, a large number of things derive their goods-character from the fact that they stand only in a more or less *indirect* causal relationship to the satisfaction of human needs.

If it is established that the existence of human needs capable of satisfaction is a prerequisite of goods-character in all cases, the principle that the goods-character of things is immediately lost upon the disappearance of the needs they previously served to satisfy is, at the same time, also proven. This principle is valid whether the goods can be placed in *direct* causal connection with the satisfaction of human needs, or derive their goods-character from a more or less *indirect* causal connection with the satisfaction of human needs. It is clear that with the disappearance of the corresponding needs the entire foundation of the relationship we have seen to be responsible for the goods-character of things ceases to exist.

Thus quinine would cease to be a good if the diseases it serves to cure should disappear, since the only need with the satisfaction of which it is causally connected would no longer exist. But the disappearance of the usefulness of quinine would have the further consequence that a large part of the corresponding goods of higher order would also be deprived of their goods-character. The inhabitants of quinine-producing countries, who currently earn their livings by cutting and peeling cinchona trees, would suddenly find that not only their stocks of cinchona bark, but also, in consequence, their cinchona trees, and tools and appliances applicable only to the production of quinine, and above all the specialized labour services, by means of which they previously earned their livings, would at once lose their goods-character, since all these things would, under the changed circumstances, no longer have any causal relationship with the satisfaction of human needs.

47

If, as the result of a change in tastes, the need for tobacco should disappear completely, the first consequence would be that all stocks of finished tobacco products on hand would be deprived of their goods-character. A further consequence would be that the raw tobacco leaves, the machines, tools, and implements applicable exclusively to the processing of tobacco, the specialized labour services employed in the production of tobacco products, the available stocks of tobacco seeds, etc., would lose their goods-character. The services, presently so well paid, of the agents who have so much skill in the grading and merchandising of tobaccos in such places as Cuba, Manila, Puerto Rico, and Havana, as well as the specialized labour services of the many people, both in Europe and in those distant countries, who are employed in the manufacture of cigars, would cease to be goods. Even tobacco boxes, humidors, all kinds of tobacco pipes, pipe stems, etc., would lose their goods-character. This apparently very complex phenomenon is explained by the fact that all the goods enumerated above derive their goods-character from their causal connection with the satisfaction of the human need for tobacco. With the disappearance of this need, one of the foundations underlying their goods-character is destroyed.

But goods of first order frequently, and goods of higher order as a rule, derive their goods-character not merely from a single but from more or less numerous causal connections with the satisfaction of human needs. Goods of higher order thus do not lose their goods-character if but one, or if, in general, but a part of these needs ceases to be present. On the contrary, it is evident that this effect will take place only if *all* the needs with the satisfaction of which goods of higher order are causally related disappear, since otherwise their goods-character would, *in strict accordance with economic law*, continue to exist with respect to needs with the satisfaction of which they have continued to be causally related even under the changed conditions. But even in this case, their goods-character continues to exist only to the extent to which they continue to maintain a causal relationship with the satisfaction of human needs, and would disappear immediately if the remaining needs should also cease to exist.

To continue the previous example, should the need of people for the consumption of tobacco cease completely to exist, the tobacco already manufactured into products suited to human consumption, and probably also the stocks of raw tobacco leaves, tobacco seeds, and many other goods of higher order having a causal connection with the satisfaction of the need for tobacco, would be completely deprived of their goods-character. But not all the goods of higher order used by the tobacco industry would necessarily meet this fate. The land and agricultural implements used in the cultivation of tobacco, for instance, and perhaps also many tools and machines used in the manufacture of tobacco products, would retain their goods-character with respect to other human needs since they can be placed in causal connection with these other needs even after the disappearance of the need for tobacco.

The law that the goods-character of goods of higher order is derived from the goods-character of the corresponding goods of lower order in whose production they serve must not be regarded as a modification affecting the substance of the primary principle, but merely as a restatement of that principle in a more concrete form.

In what has preceded we have considered in general terms all the goods that are causally connected both with one another and with the satisfaction of human needs. The object of our investigation was the whole causal chain up to the last link, the satisfaction of human needs. Having stated the principle of the present section, we may now, in the section following, turn our attention to a few links of the chain at a time – by disregarding the causal connection between goods of third order for instance, and the satisfaction of human needs for the time being, and by observing only the causal connection of goods of that order with the corresponding goods of any higher order of our choice.

4. Time and Error

The process by which goods of higher order are progressively transformed into goods of lower order and by which these are directed finally to the satisfaction of human needs is, as we have seen in the preceding sections, not irregular but subject, like all other processes of change, to the law of causality. The idea of causality, however, is inseparable from the idea of time. A process of change involves a beginning and a becoming, and these are only conceivable as processes in time. Hence it is certain that we can never fully understand the causal interconnections of the various occurrences in a process, or the process itself, unless we view it in time and apply the measure of time to it. Thus, in the process of change by which goods of higher order are gradually transformed into goods of first order, until the latter finally bring about the state called the satisfaction of human needs, time is an essential feature of our observations.

When we have the complementary goods of some particular higher order at our command, we must transform them first into goods of the next lower order, and then by stages into goods of successively still lower orders until they have been fashioned into goods of first order, which alone can be utilized directly for the satisfaction of our needs. However short the time periods lying between the various phases of this process may often appear (and progress in technology and in the means of transport tend continually to shorten them), their complete disappearance is nevertheless inconceivable. It is impossible to transform goods of any given order into the corresponding goods of lower order by a mere wave of the hand. On the contrary, nothing is more certain than that a person having goods of higher order at his disposal will be in the actual position of having command of goods of the next lower order only after an appreciable period of time, which may, according to the particular circumstances involved, sometimes be shorter and sometimes longer. But what has been said here of a single link of the causal chain is even more valid with respect to the whole process.

The period of time this process requires in particular instances differs considerably according to the nature of the case. An individual, having at his disposal all the land, labour services, tools, and seed required for the production of an oak forest, will be compelled to wait almost a hundred years before the timber is ready for the axe, and in most cases actual possession of timber in this condition will come only to his heirs or other assigns. On the other hand, in some cases a person who has at his disposal the ingredients and the necessary tools, labour service, etc., required for the production of foods or beverages, will be in a position to use the foods or beverages themselves in only a few moments. Yet however great the difference between the various cases, one thing is certain: the time period lying between command of goods of higher order and possession of the corresponding goods of lower order can never be completely eliminated. Goods of higher order acquire and maintain their goods-character, therefore, not with respect to needs of the immediate present, but as a result of human foresight, only with respect to needs that will be experienced when the process of production has been completed.

After what has been said, it is evident that command of goods of higher order and command of the corresponding goods of first order differ, with respect to a particular kind of consumption, in that the latter can be consumed *immediately* whereas the former represent an earlier stage in the formation of consumption goods and hence can be utilized for direct consumption only after the passage of an appreciable period of time, which is longer or shorter according to the nature of the case. But another exceedingly important difference between immediate command of a consumption good and indirect command of it (through possession of goods of higher order) demands our consideration.

A person with consumption goods directly at his disposal is certain of their quantity and quality. But a person who has only indirect command of them, through possession of the corresponding goods of higher order, cannot determine with the same certainty the quantity and quality of the goods of first order that will be at his disposal at the end of the production process.

A person who has a hundred bushels[9] of grain can plan his disposition of this good with that certainty, as to quantity and quality, which the immediate possession of any good is generally able to offer. But a person who has command of such quantities of land, seed, fertilizer, labour services, agricultural implements, etc., as are normally required for the production of a hundred bushels of grain, faces the chance of harvesting more than that quantity of grain, but also the chance of harvesting less. Nor can the possibility of a complete harvest failure be excluded. He is exposed, moreover, to an appreciable uncertainty with respect to the quality of the product.

This uncertainty with respect to the quantity and quality of product one has at one's disposal through possession of the corresponding goods of higher order is greater in some branches of production than it is in others. An individual who has at his disposal the materials, tools, and labour services necessary for the production of shoes, will be able, from the quantity and quality of goods of higher order on hand, to draw conclusions with a considerable degree of precision about the quantity and quality of shoes he will have at the end of the production process. But a person with command of a field suitable for growing flax, the corresponding agricultural implements, as well as the necessary labour services, flaxseed, fertilizer, etc., will be unable to form a perfectly certain judgment about the quantity and quality of oilseed he will harvest at the end of the production process. Yet he will be exposed to less uncertainty with respect to the quantity and quality of his product than a grower of hops, a hunter, or even a pearl-fisher. However great these differences between the various branches of production may be, and even though the progress of civilization tends to diminish the uncertainty involved, it is certain that an appreciable degree of uncertainty regarding the quantity and quality of a product finally to be obtained will always be present, although sometimes to a greater and sometimes to a less extent, according to the nature of the case.

The final reason for this phenomenon is found in the peculiar position of man in relation to the causal process called production of goods. Goods of higher order are transformed, in accordance with the laws of causality, into goods of the next lower order; these are further transformed until they become goods of first order, and finally bring about the state we call satisfaction of human needs. Goods of higher order are the most important elements of this causal process, but they are by no means the only ones. There are other elements, apart from those belonging to the world of goods, that affect the quantity and quality of the outcome of the causal

51

process called production of goods. These other elements are either of such a kind that we have not recognized their causal connection with our well-being, or they are elements whose influence on the product we well know but which are, for some reason, beyond our control.

Thus, until a short time age, men did not know the influence of the different types of soils, chemicals, and fertilizers, on the growth of various plants, and hence did not know that these factors sometimes have a more and sometimes a less favourable (or even an unfavourable) effect on the outcome of the production process, with respect to both its quantity and its quality. As a result of discoveries in the field of agricultural chemistry, a certain portion of the uncertainties of agriculture has already been eliminated, and man is in a position, to the extent permitted by the discoveries themselves, to induce the favourable effects of the known factors in each case and to avoid those that are detrimental.

Changes in weather offer an example from the second category. Farmers are usually quite clear about the kind of weather most favourable for the growth of plants. But since they do not have the power to create favourable weather or to prevent weather injurious to seedlings, they are dependent to no small extent on its influence upon the quantity and quality of their harvested product. Although weather, like all other natural forces, makes itself felt in accordance with inexorable causal laws, it appears to economizing men as a series of accidents, since it is outside their sphere of control.

The greater or less degree of certainty in predicting the quality and quantity of a product that men will have at their disposal due to their possession of the goods of higher order required for its production, depends upon the greater or less degree of completeness of their knowledge of the elements of the causal process of production, and upon the greater or less degree of control they can exercise over these elements. The degree of uncertainty in predicting both the quantity and quality of a product is determined by opposite relationships. Human uncertainty about the quantity and quality of the product (corresponding goods of first order) of the whole causal process is greater the larger the number of elements involved in any way in the production of consumption goods which we either do not understand or over which, even understanding them, we have no control – that is, the larger the number of elements that do not have goods-character.

This uncertainty is one of the most important factors in the economic uncertainty of men, and, as we shall see in what follows, is of the greatest practical significance in human economy.

5. The Causes of Progress in Human Welfare

'The greatest improvement in the productive powers of labour,' says Adam Smith, 'and the greater part of the skill, dexterity, and judgment with which it is anywhere directed, or applied, seem to have been the effects of the division of labour.'[10] And: 'It is the great multiplication of the productions of all the different arts, in consequence of the division of labour, which occasions, in a well-governed society, that universal opulence which extends itself to the lowest ranks of the people.'[11]

In such a manner Adam Smith has made the progressive division of labour the central factor in the economic progress of mankind – in harmony with the overwhelming importance he attributes to labour as an element in human economy. I believe, however, that the distinguished author I have just quoted has cast light, in his chapter on the division of labour, on but a single cause of progress in human welfare while other, no less efficient, causes have escaped his attention.

We may assume that the tasks in the collecting economy of an Australian tribe are, for the most part, divided in the most efficient way among the various members of the tribe. Some are hunters; others are fishermen; and still others are occupied exclusively with collecting wild vegetable foods. Some of the women are wholly engaged in the preparation of food, and others in the fabrication of clothes. We may imagine the division of labour of the tribe to be carried still further, so that each distinct task comes to be performed by a particular specialized member of the tribe. Let us now ask whether a division of labour carried so far, would have such an effect on the increase of the quantity of consumable goods available to the members of the tribe as that regarded by Adam Smith as being the consequence of the progressive division of labour. Evidently, as the result of such a change, this tribe (or any other people) will achieve either the same result from their labour with less effort or, with the same effort, a greater result than before. It will thus improve its condition, insofar as this is at all possible, by means of a more appropriate and efficient allocation of occupational tasks. But this improvement is very different from that which we can observe in actual cases of economically progressive peoples.

Let us compare this last case with another. Assume a people which extends its attention to goods of third, fourth, and higher orders, instead of confining its activity merely to the tasks of a primitive collecting economy – that is, to the acquisition of naturally available goods of lowest order (ordinarily goods of first, and possibly second, order). If such a people progressively directs goods of ever higher orders to the satisfaction of its needs, and especially if each step in this direction is accompanied by an appropriate division of labour, we shall doubtless observe that progress in welfare which Adam Smith was disposed to attribute exclusively to the latter factor. We shall see the hunter, who initially pursues game with a club, turning to hunting with bow and hunting net, to stock farming of the simplest kind, and in sequence, to ever more intensive forms of stock farming. We shall see men, living initially on wild plants, turning to ever more intensive forms of agriculture. We shall see the rise of manufacturers, and their improvement by means of tools and machines. And in the closest connection with these developments, we shall see the welfare of this people increase.

The further mankind progresses in this direction, the more varied become the kinds of goods, the more varied consequently the occupations, and the more necessary and economic also the progressive division of labour. But it is evident that the increase in the consumption goods at human disposal is not the exclusive effect of the division of labour. Indeed, the division of labour cannot even be designated as the most important cause of the economic progress of mankind. Correctly, it should be regarded only as one factor among the great influences that lead mankind from barbarism and misery to civilization and wealth.

The explanation of the effect of the increasing employment of goods of higher order upon the growing quantity of goods available for human consumption (goods of first order) is a matter of little difficulty.

In its most primitive form, a collecting economy is confined to gathering those goods of lowest order that happen to be offered by nature. Since economizing individuals exert no influence on the production of these goods, their origin is independent of the wishes and needs of men, and hence, so far as they are concerned, accidental. But if men abandon this most primitive form of economy, investigate the ways in which things may be combined in a causal process for the production of consumption goods, take possession of things capable of being so combined, and treat them as goods of higher order, they will obtain consumption goods that are as truly the results of natural processes as the consumption goods of a primitive collecting economy, but the available quantities of these goods will no longer be independent of the wishes and needs of men. Instead, the quantities of consumption goods will be determined by a process that is in the power of men and is regulated by human purposes within the limits set by natural laws. Consumption goods, which before were the product of an accidental concurrence of the circumstances of their origin, become products of human will, within the limits set by natural laws, as soon as men have recognized these circumstances and have achieved control of them. The quantities of consumption goods at human disposal are limited only by the extent of human knowledge of the causal connections between things, and by the extent of human control over these things. Increasing understanding of the causal connections between things and human welfare, and increasing control of the less proximate conditions responsible for human welfare, have led mankind, therefore, from a state of barbarism and the deepest misery to its present stage of civilization and well-being, and have changed vast regions inhabited by a few miserable, excessively poor, men into densely populated civilized countries. Nothing is more certain than that the degree of economic progress of mankind will still, in future epochs, be commensurate with the degree of progress of human knowledge.

6. Property

The needs of men are manifold, and their lives and welfare are not assured if they have at their disposal only the means, however ample, for the satisfaction of but one of these needs. Although the manner, and the degree of completeness, of satisfaction of the needs of men can display an almost unlimited variety, a certain harmony in the satisfaction of their needs is nevertheless, up to a certain point, indispensable for the preservation of their lives and welfare. One man may live in a palace, consume the choicest foods, and dress in the most costly garments. Another may find his resting place in the dark corner of a miserable hut, feed on leftovers, and cover himself with rags. But each of them must try to satisfy his needs for shelter and clothing as well as his need for food. It is clear that even the most complete satisfaction of a single need cannot maintain life and welfare.

In this sense, it is not improper to say that all the goods an economizing individual has at his command are mutually interdependent with respect to their goods-character, since each particular good can achieve the end they all serve, the preservation of life and well-being, not by itself, but only in combination with the other goods.

In an isolated household economy, and even when but little trade exists between men, this joint purpose of the goods necessary for the preservation of human life and welfare is apparent, since all of them are at the disposal of a single economizing individual. The harmony of the needs that the individual households attempt to satisfy is reflected in their property.[12] At a higher stage of civilization, and particularly in our highly developed exchange economy, where possession of a substantial quantity of any one economic good gives command of corresponding quantities of all other goods, the interdependence of goods is seen less clearly in the economy of the individual members of society, but appears much more distinctly if the economic system as a whole is considered.

We see everywhere that not single goods but combinations of goods of different kinds serve the purposes of economizing men. These combinations of goods are at the command of individuals either directly, as is the case in the isolated household economy, or in part directly and in part indirectly, as is the case in our developed exchange economy. Only in their entirety do these goods bring about the effect that we call the satisfaction of our requirements, and in consequence, the assurance of our lives and welfare.

The entire sum of goods at an economizing individuals's command for the satisfaction of his needs, we call his *property*. His property is not, however, an arbitrarily combined quantity of goods, but a direct reflection of his needs, an integrated whole, no essential part of which can be diminished or increased without affecting realization of the end it serves.

NOTES

1. *'Nützlichkeiten.'* [*Trans. note*].
2. See the first three paragraphs of Appendix A (p. 286) for the material originally appearing here as a footnote. [This reference is to the Appendix printed in the original translation (1950) of Menger's *Grundsätze* – Ed.].
3. *Güterqualität.* Later Menger uses such terms as *'Waarencharakter'* (commodity-character), 'ökonomischer Charakter' (economic character), *'nichtökonomischer Charakter'* (noneconomic character), *'Geldcharakter'* (money-character), etc. It is only in the present instance that he uses *'Qualität'* instead of 'Charakter.' Since the meanings are the same, we have chosen the translation 'goods-character' to make the constructions parallel. [*Trans. note*].
4. From this it is evident that goods-character is nothing inherent in goods and not a property of goods, but merely a relationship between certain things and men, the things obviously ceasing to be goods with the disappearance of this relationship.
5. Aristotle (*De Anima* iii.10. 433ᵃ 25–38) already distinguished between true and imaginary goods according to whether the needs arise from rational deliberation or are irrational.
6. *'Verhältnisse.'* There is no English word or phrase that is capable of expressing the same meaning as *'Verhältnisse'* in this context. The English terms 'intangibles' and 'claims' are closest, but less broad in meaning. We have chosen the English word 'relationships' as corresponding most closely to the primary meaning of *'Verhältnisse.'* The

reader can obtain the full meaning of the term, however, only from the text itself. [*Trans. note*].

7. A. E. F. Schäffle, *Die national-ökonomische Theorie der ausschlies-senden Absazverhältnisse* (Tübingen, 1867), p. 2.

8. See the last paragraph of Appendix A (p. 288) for the material originally appearing here as a footnote. [This reference is to the Appendix printed in the original translation (1950) of Menger's *Grundsätze* – Ed.].

9. *'Metzen.'* One *Metze* is equal to 3.44 liters, or approximately 3 quarts. But here as elsewhere in the translation we have chosen approximate modern equivalents since the old Austrian units of weight and measure are unfamiliar not only to English and American but even to present-day German-speaking readers. In any case, the units are used only for illustrative purposes. [*Trans. note*].

10. Adam Smith, *An Inquiry into the Nature and Causes of the Wealth of Nations*, Modern Library Edition (New York, 1937), p. 3.

11. Ibid., p. 11.

12. Lorenz v. Stein, *Lehrbuch der Volkswirthschaft* (Wien, 1858), pp. 36 ff.

3

Economy and Economic Goods

CARL MENGER

Needs arise from our drives and the drives are imbedded in our nature. An imperfect satisfaction of needs leads to the stunting of our nature. Failure to satisfy them brings about our destruction. But to satisfy our needs is to live and prosper. Thus the attempt to provide for the satisfaction of our needs is synonymous with the attempt to provide for our lives and well-being. It is the most important of all human endeavors, since it is the prerequisite and foundation of all others.

In practice, the concern of men for the satisfaction of their needs is expressed as an attempt to attain command of all the things on which the satisfaction of their needs depends. If a person has command of all the consumption goods necessary to satisfy his needs, their actual satisfaction depends only on his will. We may thus consider his objective as having been attained when he is in possession of these goods, since his life and well-being are then in his own hands. The quantities of consumption goods a person must have to satisfy his needs may be termed his *requirements*[1] The concern of men for the maintenance of their lives and well-being becomes, therefore, an attempt to provide themselves with their requirements.

But if men were concerned about providing themselves with their requirements for goods only when they experienced an immediate need of them, the satisfaction of their needs, and hence their lives and well-being, would be very inadequately assured.

If we suppose the inhabitants of a country to be entirely without stocks of foodstuffs and clothing at the beginning of winter, there can be no doubt that the majority of them would be unable to save themselves from destruction, even by the most desperate efforts directed to the satisfaction of their needs. But the further civilization advances, and the more men come to depend upon procuring the goods necessary for the satisfaction of their needs by a long process of production (pp. 49 ff.), the more compelling becomes the necessity of arranging in advance for the satisfaction of their needs – that is, of providing their requirements for future time periods.

Even an Australian savage does not postpone hunting until he actually experiences hunger. Nor does he postpone building his shelter until inclement weather has begun and he is already exposed to its harmful effects.[2] But men in civilized societies alone among economizing individuals plan for the satisfaction of their needs, not for a short period only, but for much longer periods of time. Civilized men strive to ensure the satisfaction of their needs for many years to come. Indeed, they not only plan for their entire lives, but as a rule, extend their plans still further in their concern that even their descendants shall not lack means for the satisfaction of their needs.

Wherever we turn among civilized peoples we find a system of large-scale advance provision for the satisfaction of human needs. When we are still wearing our heavy clothes for protection against the cold of winter, not only are ready-made spring clothes already on the way to retail stores, but in factories light cloths are being woven which we will wear next summer, while yarns are being spun for the heavy clothing we will use the following winter. When we fall ill we need the services of a physician. In legal dispute we require the advice of a lawyer. But it would be much too late, for a person in either contingency to meet his need, if he should only then attempt to acquire the medical or legal knowledge and skills himself, or attempt to arrange the special training of other persons for his service, even though he might possess the necessary means. In civilized countries, the needs of society for these and similar services are provided for in good time, since experienced and proven men, having prepared themselves for their professions many years ago, and having since collected rich experiences from their practices, place their services at the disposal of society. And while we enjoy the fruits of the foresight of past times in this way, many men are being trained in our universities to meet the needs of society for similar services in the future.

The concern of men for the satisfaction of their needs thus becomes an attempt to *provide in advance* for meeting their requirements in the future, and we shall therefore call a person's requirements those quantities of goods that are necessary to satisfy his needs within the time period covered by his plans.[3]

There are two kinds of knowledge that men must possess as a prerequisite for any successful attempt to provide in advance for the satisfaction of their needs. They must become clear: (a) about their requirements – that is, about the quantities of goods they will need to satisfy his needs during the time period over which their plans extend, and (b) about the quantities of goods at their disposal for the purpose of meeting these requirements.

All provident activity directed to the satisfaction of human needs is based on knowledge of these two classes of quantities. Lacking knowledge of the first, the activity of men would be conducted blindly, for they would be ignorant of their objective. Lacking knowledge of the second, their activity would be planless, for they would have no conception of the available means.

In what follows, it will first be shown how men arrive at a knowledge of their requirements for future time periods; it will then be shown how they estimate the quantities of goods that will be at their disposal during these time periods; and finally a description will be given of the activity by which men endeavor to direct the quantities of goods (consumption goods and means of production) at their disposal to the most effective satisfaction of their needs.

1. Human Requirements

A. Requirements for goods of first order consumption goods)

Human beings experience directly and immediately only needs for goods of first order – that is, for goods that can be used deemed for the satisfaction of their needs (p. 40). If no requirements for these goods existed, none for goods of higher order could arise. Requirements for goods of higher order are thus dependent upon requirement for goods of first order, and an investigation of the latter constitutes the necessary foundation for the investigation of human requirements in general. We shall first, accordingly, be occupied with human requirements for goods of first order, and then with an exposition of the principles according to which human requirements for goods of higher order are regulated.

The quantity of a good of first order necessary to satisfy a concrete human need[4] (and hence also the quantity necessary to satisfy all the needs for a good of first order arising in a certain period of time) is determined directly by the need itself (by the needs themselves) and bears a direct quantitative relationship to it (them). If, therefore, men were always correctly and completely informed, as a result of previous experience, about the concrete needs they will have, and about the intensity with which these needs will be experienced during the time period for which they plan, they could never be in doubt about the quantities of goods necessary for the satisfaction of their needs – that is, about the magnitude of their requirements for goods of first order.

But experience tells us that we are often more or less in doubt whether certain needs will be felt in the future at all. We are aware, of course, that we will need food, drink, clothing, shelter, etc., during a given time period. But the same certainty does not exist with respect to many other goods, such as medical services, medicines, etc., since whether we shall experience a need for these goods or not often depends upon influences that we cannot foresee with certainty.

Even with needs that we know in advance will be experienced in the time period for which we plan, we may be uncertain about the quantities involved. We are well aware that these needs will make themselves felt, but we do not know beforehand in exactly what degree – that is, we do not know the exact quantities of goods that will be necessary for their satisfaction. But these are the very quantities here in question.

In the case of needs about which there is uncertainty as to whether they will arise at all in the time periods for which men make their plans, experience teaches us that, in spite of their deficient foresight, men by no means fail to provide for their eventual satisfaction. Even healthy persons living in the country are, to the extent permitted by their means, in possession of a medicine chest, or at least a few drugs for unforeseen emergencies. Careful householders have fire extinguishers to preserve their property in case of fire, weapons to protect it if necessary, probably also fire- and burglar-proof safes, and many similar goods. Indeed, even among the goods of the poorest people I believe that some goods will be found that are expected to be utilized only in unforeseen contingencies.

The circumstance that it is uncertain whether a need for a good will be felt during the period of our plans does not, therefore, exclude the possibility that we will provide for its eventual satisfaction, and hence does not cause the reality of our requirements for goods necessary to satisfy such needs to be in question. On the contrary, men provide in advance, and as far as their means permit, for the eventual satisfaction of these needs also, and include the goods necessary for their satisfaction in their calculations whenever they determine their requirements as a whole.[5]

But what has been said here of needs whose appearance is altogether uncertain is fully as true where there is no doubt that a need for a good will arise but only uncertainty as to the intensity with which it will be felt, since in this case also men correctly consider their requirements to be fully met when they are able to have at their disposal quantities of goods sufficient for all anticipated eventualities.

A further point that must be taken into consideration here is the *capacity* of human needs *to grow*. If human needs are capable of growth and, as is sometimes maintained, capable of infinite growth, it could appear as if this growth would extend the limits of the quantities of goods necessary for the satisfaction of human needs continually, indeed even to complete infinitely, and that therefore any advance provision by men with respect to their requirements would be made utterly impossible.

On this subject of the capacity of human needs for infinite growth, it appears to me, first of all, that the concept of infinity is applicable only to unlimited progress in the development of human needs, but not to the quantities of goods necessary for the satisfaction of these needs during a given period of time. Although it is granted that the series is infinite, each individual element of the series is nevertheless finite. Even if human needs can be considered unlimited in their development into the most distant periods of the future, they are nevertheless capable of quantitative determination for all given, and especially for all economically significant, time periods. Thus, even under the assumption of uninterrupted progress in the development of human needs, we have to deal with finite and never with infinite, and thus completely indeterminate, magnitudes if we concern ourselves only with definite time periods.

If we observe people in provident activity directed to the satisfaction of their future needs, we can easily see that they are far from letting the capacity of their needs to grow escape their attention. On the contrary, they are most diligently concerned to take account of it. A person expecting an increase in his family or a higher social position will pay due attention to his increased future needs in the construction and furnishing of dwellings and in the purchase of carriages and similar durable goods. As a rule, and as far as his means will permit, he will attempt to take account of the higher claims of the future, not in a single connection only, but with respect to his holdings of goods as a whole. We can observe an analogous phenomenon in the activities of municipal governments. We see municipalities constructing waterworks, public buildings (schools, hospitals, etc.), parks, streets, and so on, with attention not only to the needs of the present, but with due consideration to the increased needs of the future. Naturally this tendency to give attention to future needs is even more distinctly evident in the activities of national governments.

To summarize what has been said, it appears that human requirements for consumption goods are magnitudes whose quantitative determination with respect to future time periods poses no fundamental difficulties. They are magnitudes about which, in activities directed to the satisfaction of their needs, men actually endeavor to attain clarity within feasible limits and insofar as a practical necessity compels them – that is, their attempts to determine these magnitudes are limited, on the one hand, to those time periods for which, at any time, they plan to make provision and, on the other hand, to a degree of exactness that is sufficient for the practical success of their activity.

B. *Requirements for goods of higher order (means of production)*

If our requirements for goods of first order for a coming time period are already directly met by existing quantities of these goods, there can be no question of a further provision for these same requirements by means of goods of higher order. But if these requirements are not met, or are not completely met, by existing goods of first order (that is, if they are not met directly), requirements for goods of higher order for the time period in question do arise. These requirements are the quantities of goods of higher order that are necessary, in the existing state of technology of the relevant branches of production, for supplying our full requirements for goods of first order.

The simple relationship just presented with respect to our requirements for the means of production is to be observed, however, as we shall see in what follows, only in rare cases. An important modification of this principle arises from the causal interrelationships between goods.

It was demonstrated earlier (pp. 42 ff.) that it is impossible for men to employ any one good of higher order for the production of corresponding goods of lower order unless they are able, at the same time, to have the complementary goods at their disposal. Now what was said earlier of goods in general becomes more sharply precise here when we take into account the available quantities of goods. It was shown earlier that we can change goods of higher order into goods of lower order, and thus use them for the satisfaction of human needs, only if we have the complementary goods simultaneously at our disposal. This principle can now be restated in the following terms: *We can bring quantities of goods of higher order to the production of given quantities of goods of lower order, and thus finally to the meeting of our requirements, only if we are in the position of having the complementary quantities of the other goods of higher order simultaneously at our disposal.* Thus, for instance, even the largest quantity of land cannot be employed for the production of a quantity of grain, however small, unless we have at our disposal the (complementary) quantities of seed, labour services, etc., that are necessary for the production of this small quantity of grain.

Hence requirements for a single good of higher order are never encountered. On the contrary, we often observe that, whenever the requirements for a good of lower order are not at all or are only incompletely met, requirements for each of the corresponding goods of higher order are experienced only jointly with quantitatively corresponding requirements for the other complementary goods of higher order.

Suppose, for example, that with still unfilled requirements for 10,000 pairs of shoes for a given time period, we can command the quantities of tools, labour services, etc., necessary for the production of this quantity of shoes but only enough leather for the production of 5,000 pairs. Or else suppose that we are in a position to command all the other goods of higher order necessary for the production of 10,000 pairs of shoes but only enough labour services for the production of 5,000 pairs. In both instances, there can be no doubt that our *full requirements*, with respect to the given time period, would extend to such quantities of the various goods of higher order necessary for the production of shoes as would suffice for the production of 10,000 pairs. Our *effective requirements*, however, with respect to the other complementary goods, would, in each case, extend to such quantities only as are needed for the production of 5,000 pairs. The remaining requirements would be *latent*, and would only become *effective* if the other, lacking, complementary quantities should also become available.

From what has been said, we derive the principle, *with respect to given future time periods, our effective requirements for particular goods of higher order are dependent upon the availability of complementary quantities of the corresponding goods of higher order.*

When cotton imports to Europe declined considerably because of the American Civil War, requirements for cotton piece goods remained evidently quite unaffected since that war could not change the needs for these goods significantly. To the extent to which there were future requirements for cotton piece goods that were not already met by finished manufactured products, there were also, as a result, requirements for the corresponding quantities of goods of *higher* order necessary for the production of cotton cloth. Hence these requirements also could not, on the whole be altered significantly in any way by the civil war. But since the available quantity of one of the necessary goods of higher order, namely raw cotton, declined considerably, the natural consequence was that a part of the previous requirements for goods complementary to raw cotton with respect to the production of cotton cloth (labour services, machines, etc.) became *latent*, and the *effective* requirements for them diminished to such quantities as were necessary for processing the available quantities of raw cotton. As soon, however, as imports of raw cotton revived again, the effective requirements for these goods also experienced an increase – to the exact extent, of course, that the *latent* requirements diminished.

Immigrants, bringing with them viewpoints acquired in highly developed mother countries, often fall into the error of striving from the outset for an extended landed property to the neglect of more important considerations, and even without regard to whether the corresponding quantities of the other goods, complementary to the land, are available in their settlements. Yet nothing is more certain than that they can progress in using the land for the satisfaction of their needs only to the extent that they are able to acquire the corresponding complementary quantities of seed grain, cattle, agricultural instruments, etc. Their course of action betrays an ignorance of the above principle, which makes itself so inexorably felt that men must either submit to its validity or bear the injurious consequences of its neglect.

The further civilization progresses with a highly developed division of labour, the more accustomed do people in various lines become to producing quantities of goods of higher order under the implicit and as a rule correct assumption that other persons will produce the corresponding quantities of the complementary goods. Manufacturers of opera glasses very seldom produce the glass lenses, the ivory or tortoise-shell cases, and the bronze parts, used in assembling the opera glasses. On the contrary, it is known that the producers of these glasses generally obtain the separate parts from specialized manufacturers or artisans and only assemble these parts, adding perhaps a few finishing touches. The glass-cutter who makes the lenses, the fancy-goods worker who makes their ivory or tortoise-shell cases, and the bronze-worker who makes the bronze castings, all operate under the implicit assumption that requirements for their products do exist. And yet nothing is more certain than that the effective requirements for the products of each one of them are dependent upon the production of the complementary quantities in such a fashion that, if the production of glass lenses were to suffer an interruption, the effective requirements for the other goods of higher order necessary for the production of telescopes, opera-glasses, and similar goods, would become latent. At this point, economic disturbances would appear that laymen usually consider completely abnormal, but which are, in reality, entirely in accordance with economic laws.

C. *The time limits within which human needs are felt*

In our present investigation, the only topic still remaining to be taken into consideration is the problem of time, and we must demonstrate for what time periods men actually plan their requirements.

On this question, it is clear, in the first place, that our requirements for goods of first order appear to be met, with reference to a given future time period, if, within this time period, we will be in the position of having *directly* at our disposal the quantities of goods of first order that we require. It is different if we must meet our requirements for goods of first or, in general, of lower order indirectly (that is, by means of quantities of

66

the corresponding goods of higher order), because of the lapse of time that is inevitable in any production process. Let us designate as Period I the time period that begins now and extends to the point in time when a good of first order can be produced from the corresponding goods of second order now at our disposal. Let us call Period II the time period following Period I and extending to the point in time when a good of first order can be produced from the goods of third order now available to us. And similarly, let us designate the following time periods III, IV, and so on. A sequence of time periods is thus defined for each particular kind of good. For each of these time periods we have immediate and direct requirements for the good of the first order, and these requirements are actually met since, during these time periods, we come to have direct command of the necessary quantities of the good of first order.

Suppose, however, that we should try to meet our requirements for a good of first order during Period II by means of goods of fourth order. It is clear that this would be physically impossible, and that an actual provision of our requirements for the good of first order within the posited time period could result only from the use of goods of first or second order.

The same observation can be made not only with respect to our requirements for goods of first order, but with respect to our requirements for all goods of lower order in relation to the available goods of higher order. We cannot, for example, provide our requirements for goods of third order during Period V by obtaining command, during that time period, of the corresponding quantities of goods of sixth order. On the contrary, it is clear that for this purpose we would already have had to obtain command of the latter goods during Period II.[6]

If the requirements of a people for grain for the current year were not directly covered in late autumn by the then existing stocks of grain, it would be much too late to attempt to employ the available land, agricultural implements, labour services, etc., for that purpose. But autumn would be the proper time to provide for the grain requirements of the following year by utilizing the above-mentioned goods of higher order. Similarly, to meet our requirements for the labour services of competent teachers a decade from now, we must already, at the present time, educate capable persons for this purpose.

Human requirements for goods of higher order, like those for goods of lower order, are not only magnitudes that are quantitatively determined in strict accordance with definite laws, and that can be estimated beforehand by men where a practical necessity exists, but they are magnitudes also which, within certain time limits, men do calculate with an exactness sufficient for their practical affairs. Moreover, the record of the past demonstrates that, on the basis of previous experience as to their needs and as to the processes of production, men continually improve their ability to estimate more exactly the quantities of the various goods that will be needed to satisfy their needs, as well as the particular time periods within which these requirements for the various goods will arise.

2. The Available Quantities

If it is generally correct that clarity about the objective of their endeavors is an essential factor in the success of every activity of men, it is also certain that knowledge of requirements for goods in future time periods is the first prerequisite for the planning of all human activity directed to the satisfaction of needs. Whatever may be the external conditions, therefore, under which this activity of men develops, its success will be dependent principally upon correct foresight of the quantities of goods they will find necessary in future time periods – that is, upon correct advance formulation of their requirements. It is clear also that a complete lack of foresight would make any planning of activity directed to the satisfaction of human needs completely impossible.

The second factor that determines the success of human activity is the knowledge gained by men of the means available to them for the attainment of the desired ends. Wherever, therefore, men may be observed in activities directed to the satisfaction of their needs, they are seen to be seriously concerned to obtain as exact a knowledge as possible of the quantities of goods available to them for this purpose. How they proceed to do so is the subject that will occupy us in this section.

The quantities of goods available, at any time, to the various members of a society are set by existing circumstances, and in determining these quantities the only problems they have are to measure and take inventory of the goods at their disposal. The ideal result of these two varieties of provident human activity is the complete enumeration of the goods available to them at a given point in time, their classification into perfectly homogeneous categories, and the exact determination of the number of items in each category. In practical life, however, far from pursuing this ideal, men customarily do not even attempt to obtain results as fully exact as is possible in the existing state of the arts of measuring and taking inventory, but are satisfied with just the degree of exactness that is necessary for practical purposes. Yet it is significant evidence of the great practical importance that exact knowledge of the existing quantities of goods available to them has for many people that we find a quite exceptional degree of exactness of this knowledge among merchants, industrialists, and such persons generally as have developed a high degree of provident activity. But even at the lowest levels of civilization we encounter a certain amount of knowledge of the available quantities of goods, since it is evident that a complete lack of this knowledge would make impossible any provident activity of men directed to the satisfaction of their needs.

To the degree to which men engage in planning activity directed to the satisfaction of their needs, they endeavor to attain clarity as to the quantities of goods available to them at any time. Wherever a considerable trade in goods already exists, therefore, we will find men attempting to form a judgment about the quantities of goods currently available to the other members of the society with whom they maintain trading connections.

As long as men have no considerable trade with one another, each man obviously has but a small interest in knowing what quantities of goods are in the hands of other persons. As soon, however, as an extensive trade develops, chiefly as a result of division of labour, and men find themselves dependent in large part upon exchange in meeting their requirements, they naturally acquire a very obvious interest in being informed not only about all the goods in their own possession but also about the goods of all the other persons with whom they maintain trading relations, since part of the possessions of these other persons is then accessible to them, if not directly, yet indirectly (by way of trade).

As soon as a society reaches a certain level of civilization, the growing division of labour causes the development of a special professional class which operates as an intermediary in exchanges and performs for the other members of society not only the mechanical part of trading operations (shipping, distribution, the storing of goods, etc.), but also the task of keeping records of the available quantities. Thus we observe that a specific class of people has a special professional interest in compiling data about the quantities of goods, so-called *stocks* in the widest sense of the word, currently at the disposal of the various peoples and nations whose trade they mediate. The data they compile cover trading regions that are smaller or larger (single counties, provinces, or even entire countries or continents) according to the position the intermediaries in question occupy in commercial life. They have, moreover, an interest in many other general kinds of information, but we will have occasion to discuss this at a later point.

The keeping of such statistical records, insofar as they relate to the quantities of goods currently at the disposal of sizeable groups of individuals, or even at the disposal of whole nations or groups of nations, meets, however, with not inconsiderable difficulties, since the exact determination of these stocks can be made only by means of a census. The procedure of a census presupposes a complicated apparatus of public officials, covering an entire trading area and equipped with the necessary powers. Such an apparatus can be supplied only by national governments, and by these only within their own territories. Moreover, a census fails to be efficient even within these limits, as is known to every expert, when it deals with goods whose available quantities are not easily accessible to official enumeration.

Censuses, too, can be undertaken conveniently only from time to time. Indeed, it is ordinarily possible to undertake them only at considerable intervals of time. Hence the data obtained at a certain point in time for all goods whose available quantities are subject to severe fluctuations will not infrequently already have lost practical value, even though the figures may lay claim to reliability.

Government activity directed to the determination of the quantities of goods available at any time to a given people or nation is, therefore, naturally confined: (1) to goods whose quantities are subject only to slight changes, as is the case with land, buildings, domestic animals, transportation facilities, etc., since a census of such items, taken at a particular point in time, maintains its validity for later points in time as well, and (2) to goods whose available quantities are subject to such a degree of public control that the correctness of the figures obtained is thereby guaranteed, at least in some degree.

With the signal interest that the business world, under the circumstances just described, has in as exact a knowledge as possible of the quantities of goods available in certain trading areas, it is understandable that it is not satisfied with the incomplete results of this activity of governments, performed, as it is for the most part, with little commercial understanding and always covering only particular countries or parts of countries rather than entire trading areas. On the contrary, the business world itself attempts to provide independently, and not infrequently at considerable financial sacrifice, as inclusive and as exact information as is possible of the quantities in question. This need has produced many organs serving the special interests of the business world, whose task consists, in considerable part, of informing the members of each branch of production about the current state of stocks in the various trading areas.[7]

Among these organs are the correspondents who are maintained by large business houses at the major markets for each of their commodities. One of the chief duties of these correspondents is to keep their employers continuously informed about the condition of commodity stocks. For every important commodity there is also a considerable number of periodically published business reports that serve the same purpose. Anyone who carefully follows the grain reports of Bell in London or Meyer in Berlin, the sugar reports of Licht in Magdeburg, the cotton reports of Ellison and

70

Haywood in Liverpool, etc., will find reliable information in them about the current state of commodity stocks (and many other data of importance to the business world, which I will discuss later) based on investigations of various kinds and on ingenious calculation where investigation is not feasible. These estimates of commodity stocks have a very definite influence, as we shall see, on economic phenomena, notably price formation. The cotton reports of Ellison and Haywood, for example, contain periodical information about current stocks of the different grades of cotton in Liverpool, in England in general, on the continent, and in America, India, Egypt and the other producing regions; they inform us regularly about the quantities of cotton in process of shipment on the high seas (floating cargo), about the ports to which they are consigned, and whether the quantities in England are still in the hands of the wholesalers, already in the warehouses of spinners or other buyers, or assigned for export, etc.

These reports are based on public censuses of all kinds, which the business world immediately strives to make serviceable if they prove at all trustworthy, on information gathered by expert correspondents in various places, and in part also on the estimates of experienced businessmen of proven reliability. They cover not only the stocks available at any given time but also the quantities of goods expected to be at the disposal of men in future time periods.[8] In the above-mentioned reports of Licht, for example, one finds not only news of the fluctuations of sugar stocks in all the trading areas in contact with Germany, but also a comprehensive collection of facts concerning raw material and manufacturing production. In particular, one finds current reports on the area of land planted in sugar cane and sugar beets, on the present condition of the cane and beet crops, on the expected influence of the weather on the time and quantitative and qualitative results of the harvest, on the harvest itself, on the capacities of sugar factories and refineries, on the number of these plants that are active and the number that are idle, on the amount of foreign and domestic output that is expected to reach the German market and the times of expected arrival, on technical progress in methods of sugar production, on disturbances in the distributive apparatus, etc. Similar data on other commodities are contained in the other business reports mentioned in the previous paragraph.

Such reports are usually sufficient to inform the business world about the available quantities of certain commodities in the more or less extensive trading areas relevant to each commodity, and to provide it with a basis for judging prospective changes in stocks. Where actual uncertainties exist, the reports serve to draw attention to this circumstance, so that, in all cases, where the outcome of a particular transaction depends upon the larger or smaller available quantity of a good, its risky character is brought to the attention of the business world.

71

3. The Origin of Human Economy and Economic Goods

A. *Economic goods*

In the two preceding sections we have seen how separate individuals, as well as the inhabitants of whole countries and groups of countries united by trade, attempt to form a judgment on the one hand about their requirements for future time periods and, on the other, about the quantities of goods available to them for meeting these requirements, in order to gain in this way the indispensable foundation for activity directed to the satisfaction of their needs. The task to which we now turn is to show how men, on the basis of this knowledge, direct the available quantities of goods (consumption goods and means of production) to the greatest possible satisfaction of their needs.

An investigation of the requirements for, and available quantities of, a good may establish the existence of any one of the three following relationships:

(a) that requirements are larger than the available quantity.
(b) that requirements are smaller than the available quantity.
(c) that requirements and the available quantity are equal.

We can regularly observe the first of these relationships – where a part of the needs for a good must necessarily remain unsatisfied – with by far the greater number of goods. I do not refer here to articles of luxury since, with them, this relationship seems self-evident. But even the coarsest pieces of clothing, the most ordinary living accommodations and furnishings, the most common foods, etc., are goods of this kind. Even earth, stones, and the most insignificant kinds of scrap are, as a rule, not available to us in such great quantities that we could not employ still greater quantities of them.

Wherever this relationship appears with respect to a given time period – that is, wherever men recognize that the requirements for a good are greater than its available quantity – they achieve the further insight that no part of the available quantity, in any way practically significant, may lose its useful properties or be removed from human control without causing some concrete human needs, previously provided for, to remain unsatisfied, or without causing these needs now to be satisfied less completely than before.

The first effects of this insight upon the activity of men intent to satisfy their needs as completely as possible are that they strive: (1) to maintain at their disposal every unit of a good standing in this quantitative relationship, and (2) to conserve its useful properties.

A further effect of knowledge of this relationship between requirements and available quantities is that men become aware, on the one hand, that under all circumstances a part of their needs for the good in question will remain unsatisfied and, on the other hand, that any inappropriate employment of partial quantities of this good must necessarily result in part of the needs that would be provided for by appropriate employment of the available quantity remaining unsatisfied.

Accordingly, with respect to a good subject to the relationship under discussion, men endeavor, in provident activity directed to the satisfaction of their needs: (3) to make a choice between their more important needs, which they will satisfy with the available quantity of the good in question, and needs that they must leave unsatisfied, and (4) to obtain the greatest possible result with a given quantity of the good or a given result with the smallest possible quantity – or in other words, to direct the quantities of consumer's goods available to them, and particularly the available quantities of the means of production, to the satisfaction of their needs in the most appropriate manner.

The complex of human activities directed to these four objectives is called economizing, and goods standing in the quantitative relationship involved in the preceding discussion are the exclusive objects of it. These goods are *economic* goods in contrast to such goods as men find no practical necessity of economizing – for reasons which, as we shall see later, can be traced to quantitative relationships accessible to exact measurement, just as this has been shown to be possible in the case of economic goods.[9]

But before we proceed to demonstrate these relationships and the phenomena of life ultimately determined by them, we will consider a phenomenon of social life which has assumed immeasurable significance for human welfare and which, in its ultimate causes, springs from the same quantitative relationship that we became acquainted with earlier in this section.

So far we have presented the phenomena of life that result from the fact that the requirements of men for many goods are greater than the quantities available to them in a very general way, and without special regard to the social organization of men. What has been said to this point therefore applies equally to an isolated individual and to a whole society, however it may be organized. But the social life of men, pursuing their individual interests even as members of society, brings to view a special phenomenon in the case of all goods whose available quantities are less than the requirements for them. An account of this phenomenon may find its place here.

If the quantitative relationship under discussion occurs in a society (that is, if the requirements of a society for a good are larger than its available

73

quantity), it is impossible, in accordance with what was said earlier, for the respective needs of all individuals composing the society to be completely satisfied. On the contrary, nothing is more certain than that the needs of some members of this society will be satisfied either not at all or, at any rate, only in an incomplete fashion. Here human self-interest finds an incentive to make itself felt, and where the available quantity does not suffice for all, every individual will attempt to secure his own requirements as completely as possible to the exclusion of others.

In this struggle, the various individuals will attain very different degrees of success. But whatever the manner in which goods subject to this quantitative relationship are divided, the requirements of some members of the society will not be met at all, or will be met only incompletely. These persons will therefore have interests opposed to those of the present possessors with respect to each portion of the available quantity of goods. But with this opposition of interest, it becomes necessary for society to protect the various individuals in the possession of goods subject to this relationship against all possible acts of force. In this way, then, we arrive at the economic origin of our present legal order, and especially of the so-called *protection of ownership*, the basis of property.

Thus human economy and property have a joint economic origin since both have, as the ultimate reason for their existence, the fact that goods exist whose available quantities are smaller than the requirements of men. Property, therefore, like human economy, is not an arbitrary invention but rather the only practically possible solution of the problem that is, in the nature of things, imposed upon us by the disparity between requirements for, and available quantities of, all economic goods.

As a result, it is impossible to abolish the institution of property without removing the causes that of necessity bring it about – that is, without simultaneously increasing the available quantities of all economic goods to such an extent that the requirements of all members of society can be met completely, or without reducing the needs of men far enough to make the available goods suffice for the complete satisfaction of their needs. Without establishing such an equilibrium between requirements and available amounts, a new social order could indeed ensure that the available quantities of economic goods would be used for the satisfaction of the needs of different persons than at present. But by such a redistribution it could never surmount the fact that there would be persons whose requirements for economic goods would either not be met at all, or met only incompletely, and against whose potential acts of force, the possessors of economic goods would have to be protected. Property, in this sense, is therefore inseparable from human economy in its social form, and all plans of social reform can reasonably be directed only toward an appropriate distribution of economic goods but never to the abolition of the institution of property itself.

B. *Non-economic goods*

In the preceding section I have described the every-day phenomena that result from the fact that requirements for certain goods are larger than their available quantities. I shall now demonstrate the phenomena arising from the opposite relationship – that is, as a consequence of a relationship in which the requirements of men for a good are smaller than the quantity of it available to them.

The first result of this relationship is that men not only know that the satisfaction of all their needs for such goods is completely assured, but know also that they will be incapable of exhausting the whole available quantity of such goods for the satisfaction of these needs.

Suppose that a village is dependent for water on a mountain stream with a normal flow of 200,000 pails of water a day. When there are rainstorms, however, and in the spring, when the snow melts on the mountains, the flow rises to 300,000 pails. In times of greatest drought it falls to but 100,000 pails of water daily. Suppose further that the inhabitants of the village, for drinking and other uses, usually need 200, and at the most 300, pails daily for the complete satisfaction of their needs. Their highest requirement of 300 pails is in contrast with an available minimum of at least 100,000 pails per day. In this and in every other case where a quantitative relationship of this kind is found, it is clear not only that the satisfaction of all needs for the good in question is assured, but also that the economizing individuals will be able to utilize the available quantity only *partially* for the satisfaction of their needs. It is evident also that partial quantities of these goods may be removed from their disposal, or may lose their useful properties, without any resultant diminution of the satisfaction of their needs, provided only that the aforementioned quantitative relationship is not thereby reversed. As a result, economizing men are under no practical necessity of either preserving every unit of such goods at their command or conserving its useful properties.

Nor can the third and fourth of the above-described phenomena of human economic activity be observed in the case of goods whose available quantities exceed requirements for them. If such a relationship should exist, what sense would there be in any attempt to make a choice between needs that men should satisfy with the available quantity and needs that they will resign themselves to leaving unsatisfied, when they are unable to exhaust the whole quantity available to them even with the most complete satisfaction of all their needs? And what could move men to achieve the greatest possible result with each quantity of such goods, and any given result with the least possible quantity?

It is clear, accordingly, that all the various forms in which human economic activity expresses itself are absent in the case of goods whose available quantities are larger than the requirements for them, just as naturally as they will necessarily be present in the case of goods subject to the opposite quantitative relationship. Hence they are not objects of human economy, and for this reason we call them *non-economic* goods.

To this point we have considered the relationship underlying the non-economic character of goods in a general way – that is, without regard to the present social organization of men. There remains only the task of indicating the special social phenomena that result from this quantitative relationship.

As we have seen, the effort of individual members of a society to attain command of quantities of goods adequate for their needs to the exclusion of all other members has its origin in the fact that the quantity of certain goods available to society is smaller than the requirements for them. Since it is therefore impossible, when such a relationship exists, to meet the requirements of all individuals completely, each individual feels prompted to meet his own requirements to the exclusion of all other economizing individuals. Thus, when all the members of a society compete for a given quantity of goods that is insufficient, under any circumstances, to satisfy completely all the needs of the various individuals, a practical solution to this conflict of interests is, as we have seen, only conceivable if the various portions of the whole amount at the disposal of society pass into the possession of some of the economizing individuals, and if these individuals are protected by society in their possession to the exclusion of all other individuals in the economy.

The situation with respect to goods that do not have economic character is profoundly different. Here the quantities of goods at the disposal of society are larger than its requirements, with the result that all individuals are able to satisfy their respective needs completely, and portions of the available amount of goods remain unused because they are useless for the satisfaction of human needs. Under such circumstances, there is no practical necessity for any individual to secure a part of the whole sufficient to meet his requirements, since the mere recognition of the quantitative relationship responsible for the non-economic character of the goods in question gives him sufficient assurance that, even if all other members of society completely meet their requirements for these goods, more than sufficient quantities will still remain for him to satisfy his needs.

As experience teaches, the efforts of single individuals in society are therefore not directed to securing possession of quantities of non-economic goods for the satisfaction of their own individual needs to the exclusion of other individuals. These goods are therefore neither objects of economy nor objects of the human desire for property. On the contrary, we can actually observe a picture of communism with respect to all goods standing in the relationship causing non-economic character; for men are communists whenever possible under existing natural conditions. In towns situated on rivers with more water than is wanted by the inhabitants for the satisfaction of their needs, everyone goes to the river to draw any desired quantity of water. In virgin forests, everyone fetches unhindered the quantity of timber he needs. And everyone admits as much light and air into his house as he thinks proper. This communism is as naturally founded upon a non-economic relationship as property is founded upon one that is economic.

C. *The relationship between economic and non-economic goods*

In the two preceding sections we examined the nature and origin of human economy, and demonstrated that the difference between economic and non-economic goods is ultimately founded on a difference, capable of exact determination, in the relationship between requirements for and available quantities of these goods.

But if this has been established, it is also evident that the economic or non-economic character of goods is nothing inherent in them nor any property of them, and that therefore every good, without regard to its internal properties or its external attributes, attains economic character when it enters into the quantitative relationship explained above, and loses it when this relationship is reversed.[10]

Economic character is by no means restricted to goods that are the objects of human economy in a social context. If an isolated individual's requirements for a good are greater than the quantity of the good available to him, we will observe him retaining possession of every unit at his command, conserving it for employment in the manner best suited to the satisfaction of his needs, and making a choice between needs that he will satisfy with the quantity available to him and needs that he will leave unsatisfied. We will also find that the same individual has no reason to engage in this activity with respect to goods that are available to him in quantities exceeding his requirements. Hence economic and non-economic goods also exist for an isolated individual. The cause of the economic character of a good cannot therefore be the fact that it is either

77

an 'object of exchange' or an 'object of property.' Nor can the fact that some goods are products of labour while others are given us by nature without labour be represented with any greater justice as the criterion for distinguishing economic from non-economic character, in spite of the fact that a great deal of clever reasoning has been devoted to attempting to interpret actual phenomena that contradict this view in a sense that does not. For experience tells us that many goods on which no labour was expended (alluvial land, water power, etc.) display economic character whenever they are available in quantities that do not meet our requirements. Nor does the fact that a thing is a product of labour by itself necessarily result in its having goods-character, let alone economic character. Hence the labour expended in the production of a good cannot be the criterion of economic character. On the contrary, it is evident that this criterion must be sought exclusively in the relationship between requirements for and available quantities of goods.

Experience, moreover, teaches us that goods of the same kind do not show economic character in some places but are economic goods in other places, and that goods of the same kind and in the same place attain and lose their economic character with changing circumstances.

While quantities of fresh drinking water in regions abounding in springs, raw timber in virgin forests, and in some countries even land, do not have economic character, these same goods exhibit economic character in other places at the same time. Examples are no less numerous of goods that do not have economic character at a particular time and place but which, at this same place, attain economic character at another time. These differences between goods and their changeability cannot, therefore, be based on the properties of the goods. On the contrary, one can, if in doubt, convince oneself in all cases, by an exact and careful examination of these relationships, that when goods of the same kind have a different character in two different places at the same time, the relationship between requirements and available quantities is different in these two places, and that wherever, in one place, goods that originally had non-economic character become economic goods, or where the opposite takes place, a change has occurred in this quantitative relationship.

According to our analysis, there can be only two kinds of reasons why a non-economic good becomes an economic good: an increase in human requirements or a diminution of the available quantity.

The chief causes of an increase in requirements are: (1) growth of population, especially if it occurs in a limited area, (2) growth of human needs, as the result of which the requirements of any given population increase, and (3) advances in the knowledge men have of the causal connection between things and their welfare, as the result of which new useful purposes for goods arise.

I need hardly point out that all these phenomena accompany the transition of mankind from lower to higher levels of civilization. From this it follows, as a natural consequence, that with advancing civilization non-economic goods show a tendency to take on economic character, chiefly because one of the factors involved is the magnitude of human requirements, which increase with the progressive development of civilization. If to this is added a diminution of the available quantities of goods that previously did not exhibit economic character (timber, for instance, through the clearance or devastation of forests associated with certain phases of cultural development), nothing is more natural than that goods, whose available quantities on an earlier level of civilization by far outstripped requirements, and which therefore did not show economic character, should become economic goods with the passage of time. In many places, especially in the new world, this transition from non-economic to economic character can be proven historically for many goods, especially timber and land. Indeed the transition can be observed even at the present time. Despite the fact that information in this field is only fragmentary, I believe that in Germany, once so densely forested, but few places are to be found where the inhabitants have not, at some time, experienced this transition – in the case of firewood, for example.

From what has been said, it is clear that all changes by which economic goods become non-economic goods, and conversely, by which the latter become economic goods can be reduced simply to a change in the relationship between requirements and available quantities.

Goods that occupy an intermediate position between economic and non-economic goods with respect to the characteristics they exhibit may lay claim to a special scientific interest.

In this class must be counted, above all, such goods in highly civilized countries as are produced by the government and offered for public use in such large quantities that any desired amount of them is at the disposal of even the poorest member of society, with the result that they do not attain economic character for the consumers.

Public school education, for instance, in a highly developed society is usually such a good. Pure healthy drinking water also is considered a good of such importance by the inhabitants of many cities that, wherever nature does not make it abundantly available, it is brought by aquaducts to the public fountains in such large quantities that not only are the requirements of the inhabitants for drinking water completely met but also, as a rule, considerable quantities above these requirements are available. While instruction by a teacher is an economic good for those in need of such

CLASSICS IN AUSTRIAN ECONOMICS: VOLUME I

instruction in societies at a low level of civilization, this same good becomes a non-economic good in more highly developed societies, since it is
provided by the state. Similarly, in many large cities pure and healthy
drinking water, which previously had economic character for consumers,
becomes a non-economic good.

Conversely, goods that are naturally available in quantities exceeding
requirements may attain economic character for their consumers if a
powerful individual excludes the other members of the economy from
freely acquiring and using them. In densely wooded countries, there are
many villages surrounded by natural forests abounding in timber. In such
places, the available quantity of timber by far exceeds the requirements of
the inhabitants, and uncut wood would not have economic character in the
natural course of events. But when a powerful person seizes the whole
forest, or the greater part of it, he can regulate the quantities of timber
actually available to the inhabitants of his village in such a way that timber
nevertheless acquires economic character for them. In the heavily wooded
Carpathians, for instance, there are numerous places where peasants (the
former villeins) must buy the timber they need from large landholders,
even while the latter let many thousands of logs rot every year in the forest
because the quantities available to them far exceed their present requirements. This, however, is a case in which goods that would not possess
economic character in the natural course of events artificially become
economic goods for the consumers. In such circumstances, these goods
actually manifest all the phenomena of economic life that are characteristic
of economic goods.[11]

Finally, goods belong in this category that do not exhibit economic
character at the present time but which, in view of future developments,
are already considered by economizing men as economic goods in many
respects. More precisely, if the available quantity of a non-economic good
is continually diminishing, or if the requirements for it are continually
increasing, and the relationship between requirements and available quantity is such that the final transition of the good in question from non-
economic to economic status can be foreseen, economizing individuals will
usually make portions of the available quantity objects of their economic
activity. They will do this even when the quantitative relationship responsible for the non-economic character of the good still actually prevails, and
will, when living as members of a society, usually guarantee themselves
their individual requirements by taking possession of quantities corresponding to these requirements. The same reasoning applies to non-
economic goods whose available quantities are subject to such violent
fluctuations that only command of a certain surplus in normal times
assures command of requirements in time of scarcity. It applies also to all

non-economic goods with respect to which the boundary between requirements and available quantities is already so close (the third case mentioned on p. 72, above all, belongs in this category) that any misuse or ignorance on the part of some members of the economy may easily become injurious to the others, or when special considerations (considerations of comfort or cleanliness for example) apparently make expedient the seizure of partial quantities of the non-economic goods. For these and similar reasons the phenomenon of property can also be observed in the case of goods that appear to us still, with respect to other aspects of economic life, as non-economic goods.

Finally, I would like to direct the attention of my readers to a circumstance that is of great importance in judging the economic character of goods. I refer to differences in the quality of goods. If the total available quantity of a good is not sufficient to meet the requirements for it, every appreciable part of the total quantity becomes an object of human economy and thus an economic good whatever its quality. And if the available quantities of a good are greater than the requirements for it, and there are therefore portions of the total stock that are utilized for the satisfaction of no need whatever, all units of the good must, in accordance with what has already been said about the nature of non-economic goods, have non-economic character if they are all of exactly the same quality. But if some portions of the available stock of a good have certain advantages over the other portions, and these advantages are of such a kind that various human needs can be better satisfied or, in general, more completely satisfied by using these rather than the other, less useful, portions, it may happen that the goods of better quality will attain economic character while the other (inferior) goods still exhibit non-economic character. Thus, in a country with a superabundance of land, for instance, land that is preferable because of the composition of the soil or by reason of its location may already have attained economic character while poorer lands still exhibit non-economic character. And in a city situated on a river with drinking water of inferior quality, quantities of spring water may already be objects of individual economy when the river water does not, as yet, show economic character.

Thus, if we sometimes find that different portions of the whole supply of a good differ in character at the same time, the reason, in this case too, always lies solely in the fact that the available quantities of the goods of better grade are smaller than requirements while the poorer goods are available in quantities exceeding requirements (requirements not covered by the goods of better grade). Such instances do not, therefore, constitute exceptions, but are, on the contrary, a confirmation of the principles stated in this chapter.

D. *The laws governing the economic character of goods*

In our investigation of the laws governing human requirements, we have reached the result that the existence of requirements for goods of higher order is dependent: (1) on our having requirements for the corresponding goods of lower order, and also (2) on these requirements for goods of lower order being not already provided for, or at least not completely provided for. We have defined an economic good as a good whose available quantity does not meet requirements completely, and thus we have the principle that *the existence of requirements for goods of higher order is dependent upon the corresponding goods of lower order having economic character.*

In places where pure and healthy drinking water is present in quantities exceeding the requirements of the population, and where this good therefore does not exhibit economic character, requirements for the various implements or means of transportation serving exclusively for carrying or piping and filtering drinking water cannot arise. And in regions in which there is a natural superabundance of firewood (trees, to be exact), and in which, as a result, this good has non-economic character, obviously all requirements for goods of higher order suitable exclusively for the production of firewood are absent from the very beginning. In regions, on the other hand, where firewood or drinking water have economic character, requirements for the corresponding goods of higher order will certainly exist.

But if it has now been established that human requirements for goods of higher order are determined by the economic character of the corresponding goods of lower order, and that requirements for goods of higher order cannot arise at all if they are not applicable to the production of economic goods, it follows that requirements for goods of higher order can never, in this event, become larger than their available quantities, however small, and hence that it is impossible from the very beginning for them to attain economic character.

From this we derive the general principle that the *economic character of goods of higher order depends upon the economic character of the goods of lower order for whose production they serve.* In other words, no good of higher order can attain economic character or maintain it unless it is suitable for the production of some economic good of lower order.

If, therefore, goods of lower order displaying economic character are under consideration, and if the question arises as to the ultimate causes of their economic character, it would be a complete reversal of the true relationship, if one were to assume that they are economic goods because the goods employed in producing them displayed economic character before the production process was undertaken. Such a supposition would contradict, in the first place, all experience, which teaches us that, from goods of higher order whose economic character is beyond all doubt, completely useless things may be produced, and in consequence of economic ignorance, actually are produced – things that do not even have goods-character let alone economic character. Moreover, cases can be conceived where, from economic goods of higher order, things can be produced that have goods-character but not economic character. By way of illustration, one need only imagine persons using costly economic goods to produce timber in virgin forests, to store up drinking water in regions abounding in freshwater springs, or to make air, etc.!

The economic character of a good thus cannot be a consequence of the circumstance that it has been produced from economic goods of higher order, and this explanation would have to be rejected in any case, even if it were not involved in a further internal contradiction. The explanation of the economic character of goods of lower order by that of goods of higher order is only a pseudo-explanation, and apart from being incorrect and in contradiction with all experience, it does not even fulfill the formal conditions for the explanation of a phenomenon. If we explain the economic character of goods of first order by that of goods of second order, the latter by the economic character of goods of third order, this again by the economic character of goods of fourth order, and so on, the solution of the problem is not advanced fundamentally by a single step, since the question as to the last and true cause of the economic character of goods always still remains unanswered.

Our previous explanation, however, demonstrates that man, with his needs and his command of the means to satisfy them, is himself the point at which human economic life both begins and ends. Initially, man experiences needs for goods of first order, and makes those whose available quantities are smaller than his requirements the objects of his economic activity (that is, he treats them as economic goods) while he finds no practical inducement to bring the other goods into the sphere of his economic activity.

Later, thought and experience lead men to ever deeper insights into the causal connections between things, and especially into the relations between things and their welfare. They learn to use goods of second, third, and higher orders. But with these goods, as with goods of first order, they find that some are available in quantities exceeding their requirements while the opposite relationship prevails with others. Hence they divide goods of higher order also into one group that they include in the sphere of their economic activity, and another group that they do not feel any practical necessity to treat in this way. This is the origin of the economic character of goods of higher order.

4. Wealth

Earlier (p. 56) we called 'the entire sum of goods at a person's command' his *property*. The entire sum of *economic* goods at an economizing individuals's command[12] we will, on the other hand, call his *wealth*.[13, 14] The non-economic goods at an economizing individual's command are not objects of his economy, and hence must not be regarded as parts of his wealth. We saw that economic goods are goods whose available quantities are smaller than the requirements for them. Wealth can therefore also be defined as *the entire sum of goods at an economizing individual's command, the quantities of which are smaller than the requirements for them*. Hence, if there were a society where all goods were available in amounts exceeding the requirements for them, there would be no economic goods nor any 'wealth.' Although wealth is thus a measure of the degree of completeness with which one person can satisfy his needs in comparison with other persons who engage in economic activity under the same conditions, it is never an absolute measure of his welfare,[15] for the highest welfare of all individuals and of society would be attained if the quantities of goods at the disposal of society were so large that no one would be in need of wealth.

These remarks are intended to introduce the solution of a problem which, because of the apparent contradictions to which it leads, is capable of creating distrust as to the accuracy of the principles of our science. The problem arises from the fact that a continuous increase in the amounts of economic goods available to economizing individuals would necessarily cause these goods eventually to lose their economic character, and in this way cause the components of wealth to suffer a diminution. Hence we have the queer contradiction that a continuous increase of the objects of wealth would have, as a necessary final consequence, a diminution of wealth.[16]

Suppose that the quantity of a certain mineral water available to a people is smaller than requirements for it. The various portions of this good at the command of the several economizing persons, as well as the mineral springs themselves, are therefore economic goods, and hence constituent parts of wealth. Suppose now that this medicinal water should suddenly begin to flow in several brooks in such abundant measure as to lose its previous economic character. Nothing is more certain, than that the quantities of mineral water that were at the command of economizing individuals before this event, as well as the mineral springs themselves, would now cease to be components of wealth. Thus it would indeed be the case that a progressive increase in the component parts of wealth would finally have caused a diminution of wealth.

This paradox is exceedingly impressive at first sight, but upon more exact consideration, it proves to be only an apparent one. As we saw earlier, economic goods are goods whose available quantities are smaller than the requirements for them. They are goods of which there is a partial deficiency, and the wealth of economizing individuals is nothing but the sum of these goods. If their available quantities are progressively increased until they finally lose their economic character, a deficiency no longer exists, and they move out of the category of goods constituting the wealth of economizing individuals – that is, they leave the class of goods of which there is a partial deficiency. There is certainly no contradiction in the fact that the progressive increase of a good of which there was previously a deficiency finally brings about the result that the good ceases to be in short supply.

On the contrary, that the progressive increase of economic goods must finally lead to a reduction in the number of goods of which there was previously a deficiency is a proposition that is as immediately evident to everyone as the contrary proposition that a long continued diminution of abundantly available (non-economic) goods must finally make them scarce in some degree – and thus components of wealth, which is thereby increased.

The above paradox, which was raised not only with regard to the extent of objects of wealth but in an analogous manner also with regard to the value and price of economic goods,[17] is therefore only an apparent one, and is founded upon a misinterpretation of the nature of wealth and its components.

We have defined wealth as the entire sum of economic goods at the command of an economizing individual. The existence of any item of wealth presupposes, therefore, an economizing individual, or at any rate one in whose behalf acts of economizing are performed. Quantities of economic goods destined for a specific purpose are therefore not wealth in the economic sense of the word. The fiction of a legal person may be valid for purposes of legal practice or even for purposes of juridical constructions but not for our science which decidedly rejects all fictions. So-called 'trust funds'[18] are therefore quantities of economic goods devoted to specific purposes, but they are not wealth in the economic sense of the word.

This leads to the question of the nature of *public wealth*. States, provinces, communities, and associations generally have quantities of economic goods at their disposal in order to satisfy *their* needs, and to realize *their* ends. Here the fiction of a legal person is not necessary for the political economist. Without calling upon any fiction, he can observe an economizing unit, a social organization, whose personnel administer certain economic goods that are available to it for the purpose of satisfying its needs, and direct them to this objective. Hence no-one will hesitate to admit the existence of governmental, provincial, municipal and corporate wealth.

The situation is different with what is designated by the term *'national wealth'*. Here we have to deal not with the entire sum of economic goods available to a nation for the satisfaction of *its* needs, administered by government employees, and devoted by them to its purposes, but with the totality of goods at the disposal of the separate economizing individuals and associations of a society for their individual purposes. Thus we have to deal with a concept that deviates in several important respects from what we term wealth.

If we employ the fiction of conceiving of the totality of economizing persons in a society, each striving for the satisfaction of his special needs, and driven not infrequently by interests opposed to the interests of others, as *one* great economizing unit, and if we further assume that the quantities of economic goods at the disposal of the separate economizing individuals are not applied to the satisfaction of their special needs but to the satisfaction of the needs of the totality of individuals composing the economy, then we do, of course, arrive at the concept of a sum of economic goods at the disposal of an economizing unit (here, at the disposal of society) that are available for the purpose of satisfying its collective needs. Such a concept could correctly be designated by the term national wealth. But under our present social arrangements, the sum of economic goods at the disposal of the individual economizing members of society for the purpose of satisfying their special individual needs obviously does not constitute wealth in the economic sense of the term but rather a complex of wealths linked together by human intercourse and trade.[19]

The need for a scientific designation for the sum of goods just mentioned is, however, so just, and the term 'national wealth' for that concept is so generally accepted and sanctioned by usage, that we would serve this need badly if we were to drop the existing term as we become clearer about the correct nature of the so-called national wealth.

It is, then, only necessary that we guard against the error that must arise if we pay no attention to the distinction discussed here. In all questions where the issue is merely the quantitative determination of the so-called national wealth, the sum of the wealths of the individuals of the nation may be designated as national wealth. But when inferences running from the magnitude of the national wealth to the welfare of a people, or when phenomena resulting from contacts between the various economizing individuals, are involved, the concept of national wealth in the literal sense of the term must necessarily lead to frequent errors. In all these cases, the national wealth must be regarded rather as a complex composite of the wealths of the members of society, and we must direct our attention to the different size of these individual wealths.

NOTES

1. *'Bedarf.'*. The reader is first referred to Menger's own note on this term (note 3 of this chapter). Since Menger uses the term *Bedarf* in both of the senses mentioned in his note, and since he uses the term *'Nachfrage'* (demand) at several points, even if infrequently, we feel it best to translate *'Bedarf'* as 'requirements' throughout to preserve as exactly as possible Menger's own terminology. [*Trans. note*].

2. Even some animals lay by stores and thus ensure in advance that they will not lack food and a warm abode in winter.

3. The word 'requirements' (*Bedarf*) has a double meaning in our language. It is used on the one hand to designate the quantities of goods that are necessary to satisfy a person's needs completely, and on the other to designate the quantities that a person intends to consume. In the latter meaning, a man receiving a rent of 20,000 Thalers and accustomed to using it all for consumption has very great requirements, whereas a rural labourer whose income amounts to 100 Thalers has very small requirements, and a beggar in the depths of extreme poverty no requirements whatsoever. In the former meaning, the requirements of men also differ greatly due to differences in their education and habits. But even a person devoid of all means has requirements equal to the quantities of goods that would be necessary to meet his needs. Merchants and industrialists generally employ the term 'requirements' in the narrower sense of the word, and often mean by it the 'expected demand' for a good. In this sense also, one says that there are requirements for a commodity 'at a given price' but not at another price, etc.

4. The term 'concrete human need' recurs from time to time in the text. Menger uses the term to refer to a need (or rather a portion of a need) that is satisfied by consumption of a single unit of a good. When an individual consumes successive units of a good, Menger pictures him as satisfying successive 'concrete needs' of diminishing psychological

importance. At some points he adopts a different terminology, and speaks of the consumption of successive units of commodity as successive 'acts of satisfaction.' See also note 3 of chapter iii and Appendix D for some suggestions regarding the meaning of 'concrete.' [This reference is to the Appendix printed in the original translation (1950) of Menger's *Grundsätze* – Ed.].

5. See E. B. de Condillac, *Le commerce et le gouvernement,* in E. Daire (ed.), *Mélanges d'économie politique* (Paris, 1847), p. 248.

6. In this paragraph Menger implicitly assumes his time periods to be of equal duration. Reference to the definitions of the second paragraph preceding will confirm that this need not be the case. [*Trans. note*].

7. The next paragraph appears here as a footnote in the original. [*Trans. note*].

8. The remainder of this paragraph appears here as a footnote in the original. [*Trans. note*].

9. See the first five paragraphs of Appendix B (p. 288) for the material originally appearing here as a footnote. [This reference is to the Appendix printed in the original translation (1950) of Menger's *Grundsätze* – Ed.].

10. The next paragraph originally appears here as a footnote. [*Trans. note*].

11. Using a mode of expression already current in our science, we could, by analogy, call the latter *quasi-economic* goods (as opposed to true economic goods), and the former *quasi-non-economic* goods.

12. A good is at a person's 'command' in the economic sense of the term if he is in a position to employ it for the satisfaction of his needs. Either physical or legal obstacles can prevent a good from being at one's command. A minor's wealth, for example, is not at his guardian's command in this sense of the word.

13. F. B. W. von Hermann, *Staatswirthschaftliche Untersuchungen* (München, 1874), p. 21.

14. See the last two paragraphs of Appendix B (p. 291) for the material originally appearing here as a footnote. [This reference is to the Appendix printed in the original translation (1950) of Menger's *Grundsätze* – Ed.].

15. Since wealth provides only a relative measure of the degree of completeness with which an individual can satisfy his needs, some writers have defined wealth as a sum of *economic* goods, when applying the term to the economy of a single individual, and as the sum of *all* goods when applying it to the social economy. The main reason for doing this was that they had in mind the relative welfare of the different individuals in the first definition and the absolute welfare of society in

the second. See especially, James Maitland, Earl of Lauderdale, *An Inquiry into the Nature and Origin of Public Wealth* (Edinburgh, 1804), pp. 39 ff., esp. pp. 56 ff. The question recently raised by Wilhelm Roscher (*System der Volkswirthschaft*, 20th edn (Stuttgart, 1892), i, pp. 16 ff.), about whether or not social wealth is to be estimated by its use value and private wealth by its exchange value can be traced to the same distinction.

16. See already Lauderdale, op. cit., p. 43.
17. Pierre-Joseph Proudhon, *Système des contradictions économiques*, 3rd edn (Paris, 1867), i, pp. 59 ff.
18. '*Zweckvermögen.*' [*Trans. note*].
19. See Carl Dietzel, *Die Volkswirthschaft und ihr Verhältniss zu Gesellschaft und Staat* (Frankfurt am Main, 1864), pp. 106 ff.

Carl Menger, 'On the Origin of Money', *Economic Journal*, June 1892, pp. 239–55.

This paper by Carl Menger was published originally in English (translated, apparently from an original German manuscript, by Caroline A. Foley) in the second volume of the Royal Economic Society's new *Economic Journal*, in June 1892. In the same year Menger's longer German article on the same topic appeared in Volume iii of the continental encyclopedia of the social sciences, *Handwörterbuch der Staatswissenschaften*. This paper contains Menger's complete statement of his well-known theory of the spontaneous institution of money, already outlined in Menger's *Grundsätze* of 1871 and his *Untersuchungen über die Methode der Socialwissenschaften und der Politischen Oekonomie insbesondere* of 1883.

4

On the Origin of Money

CARL MENGER

I. Introduction

There is a phenomenon which has from of old and in a peculiar degree attracted the attention of social philosophers and practical economists, the fact of certain commodities (these being in advanced civilizations coined pieces of gold and silver, together subsequently with documents representing those coins) becoming universally acceptable media of exchange. It is obvious even to the most ordinary intelligence, that a commodity should be given up by its owner in exchange for another more useful to him. But that every economic unit in a nation should be ready to exchange his goods for little metal disks apparently useless as such, or for documents representing the latter, is a procedure so opposed to the ordinary course of things, that we cannot well wonder if even a distinguished thinker like Savigny finds it downright 'mysterious.'

It must not be supposed that the *form* of coin, or document, employed as current-money, constitutes the enigma in this phenomenon. We may look away from these forms and go back to earlier stages of economic development, or indeed to what still obtains in countries here and there, where we find the precious metals in an uncoined state serving as the medium of exchange, and even certain other commodities, cattle, skins, cubes of tea, slabs of salt, cowrie-shells; etc.; still we are confronted by this phenomenon, still we have to explain why it is that the economic man is ready to accept a certain kind of commodity, *even if he does not need it, or if his need of it is already supplied*, in exchange for all the goods he has brought to market, while it is none the less what he needs that he consults in the first instance, with respect to the goods he intends to acquire in the course of his transactions.

And hence there runs, from the first essays of reflective contemplation

91

in social phenomena down to our own times, an uninterrupted chain of disquisitions upon the nature and specific qualities of money in its relation to all that constitutes traffic. Philosophers, jurists, and historians, as well as economists, and even naturalists and mathematicians, have dealt with this notable problem, and there is no civilized people that has not furnished its quota to the abundant literature thereon. What is the nature of those little disks or documents, which in themselves seem to serve no useful purpose, and which nevertheless, in contradiction to the rest of experience, pass from one hand to another in exchange for the most useful commodities, nay, for which every one is so eagerly bent on surrendering his wares? Is money an organic member in the world of commodities, or is it an economic anomaly? Are we to refer its commercial currency and its value in trade to the same causes conditioning those of other goods, or are they the distinct product of convention and authority?

II. Attempts at Solution hitherto

Thus far it can hardly be claimed for the results of investigation into the problem above stated, that they are commensurate either with the great development in historic research generally, or with the outlay of time and intellect expended in efforts at solution. The enigmatic phenomenon of money is even at this day without an explanation that satisfies; nor is there yet agreement on the most fundamental questions of its nature and functions. Even at this day we have no satisfactory theory of money.

The idea which lay first to hand for an explanation of the specific function of money as a universal current medium of exchange, was to refer it to a general convention, or a legal dispensation. The problem, which science has here to solve, consists of giving an explanation of a general, homogeneous course of action pursued by human beings when engaged in traffic, which taken concretely, makes unquestionably for the common interest, and yet which seems to conflict with the nearest and immediate interests of contracting individuals. Under such circumstances what could lie more contiguous than the notion of referring the foregoing procedure to causes lying outside the sphere of individual considerations? To assume that certain commodities, the precious metals in particular, had been exalted into the medium of exchange by general convention or law, in the interest of the commonweal, solved the difficulty, and solved it apparently the more easily and naturally inasmuch as the shape of the coins seemed to be a token of state regulation. Such in fact is the opinion of Plato, Aristotle, and the Roman jurists, closely followed by the mediæval writers. Even the more modern developments in the theory of money have not in substance got beyond this standpoint.[1]

Tested more closely, the assumption underlying this theory gave room to grave doubts. An event of such high and universal significance and of notoriety so inevitable, as the establishment by law or convention of a universal medium of exchange, would certainly have been retained in the memory of man, the more certainly inasmuch as it would have had to be performed in a great number of places. Yet no historical monument gives us trustworthy tidings of any transactions either conferring distinct recognition on media of exchange already in use, or referring to their adoption by peoples of comparatively recent culture, much less testifying to an initiation of the earliest ages of economic civilization in the use of money.

And in fact the majority of theorists on this subject do not stop at the explanation of money as stated above. The peculiar adaptability of the precious metals for purposes of currency and coining was noticed by Aristotle, Xenophon, and Pliny, and to a far greater extent by John Law, Adam Smith and his disciples, who all seek a further explanation of the choice made of them as media of exchange, in their special qualifications. Nevertheless it is clear that the choice of the precious metals by law and convention, even if made in consequence of their peculiar adaptability for monetary purposes, presupposes the pragmatic origin of money, and selection of those metals, and that presupposition is unhistorical. Nor do even the theorists above mentioned honestly face the problem that is to be solved, to wit, the explaining how it has come to pass that certain commodities (the precious metals at certain stages of culture) should be promoted amongst the mass of all other commodities and accepted as the generally acknowledged media of exchange. It is a question concerning not only the origin but also the nature of money and its position in relation to all other commodities.

III. The Problem of the Genesis of a Medium of Exchange

In primitive traffic the economic man is awaking but very gradually to an understanding of the economic advantages to be gained by exploitation of existing opportunities of exchange. His aims are directed first and foremost, in accordance with the simplicity of all primitive culture, only at what lies first to hand. And only in that proportion does the value in use of the commodities he seeks to acquire, come into account in his bargaining. Under such conditions each man is intent to get by way of exchange just such goods as he directly needs, and to reject those of which he had no need at all, or with which he is already sufficiently provided. It is clear then, that in these circumstances the number of bargains actually concluded must lie within very narrow limits. Consider how seldom it is the case, that a commodity owned by somebody is of less value in use than another commodity owned by somebody else! And for the latter just the opposite relation is the case. but how much more seldom does it happen that these two bodies meet! Think, indeed, of the peculiar difficulties obstructing the immediate barter of goods in those cases, where supply and demand do not quantitatively coincide; where, *e.g.*, an indivisible commodity is to be exchanged for a variety of goods in the possession of different persons, or indeed for such commodities as are only in demand at different times and can be supplied only by different persons! Even in the relatively simple and so often recurring case, where an economic unit, A, requires a commodity possessed by B, and B requires one possessed by C, while C wants one that is owned by A – even here, under a rule of mere barter, the exchange of the goods in question would as a rule be of necessity left undone.

These difficulties would have proved absolutely insurmountable obstacles to the progress of traffic, and at the same time to the production of goods not commanding a regular sale, had there not lain a remedy in the very nature of things, to wit, *the different degrees of saleableness (Absatzfähigkeit) of commodities*. The difference existing in this respect between articles of commerce is of the highest degree of significance for the theory of money, and of the market in general. And the failure to turn it adequately to account in explaining the phenomena of trade, constitutes not only as such a lamentable breach in our science, but also one of the essential causes of the backward state of monetary theory. *The theory of money necessarily presupposes a theory of the saleableness of goods*. If we grasp this, we shall be able to understand how the almost unlimited saleableness of money is only a special case, – presenting only a difference of degree – of a generic phenomenon of economic life – namely, the difference in the saleableness of commodities in general.

IV. *Commodities as more or less Saleable*

It is an error in economics, as prevalent as it is patent, that all commodities, at a definite point of time and in a given market, may be assumed to stand to each other in a definite relation of exchange, in other words, may be mutually exchanged in definite quantities at will. It is not true that in any given market 10 cwt. of one article = 2 cwt. of another = 3 lbs. of a third article, and so on. The most cursory observation of market-phenomena teaches us that it does not lie within our power, when we have bought an article for a certain price, to sell it again forthwith at that same price. If we but try to dispose of an article of clothing, a book, or a work of art, which we have just purchased, in the very same market, even though it be at once, before the same juncture of conditions has altered, we shall easily convince ourselves of the fallaciousness of such an assumption. The price at which any one can at pleasure buy a commodity at a given market and a given point of time, and the price at which he can dispose of the same at pleasure, are two essentially different magnitudes.

This holds good of wholesale as well as retail prices. Even such marketable goods as corn, cotton, pig-iron, cannot be voluntarily disposed of for the price at which we have purchased them. Commerce and speculation would be the simplest things in the world, if the theory of the 'objective equivalent in goods' were correct, if it were actually true, that in a given market and at a given moment commodities could be mutually converted at will in definite quantitative relations – could, in short, at a certain price be as easily disposed of as acquired. At any rate there is no such thing as a general saleableness of wares in this sense. The truth is, that even in the best organized markets, while we may be able to purchase when and what we like at a definite price, viz.: the *purchasing price*, we can only dispose of it again when and as we like at a loss, viz.: at the *selling price*.[2]

The loss experienced by any one who is compelled to dispose of an article at a definite moment, as compared with the current purchasing prices, is a highly variable quantity, as a glance at trade and at markets of specific commodities will show. If corn or cotton is to be disposed of at an organised market, the seller will be in a position to do so in practically any quantity, at any time he pleases, at the current price, or at most with a loss of only a few pence on the total sum. If it be a question of disposing, in larger quantities, of cloth or silk-stuffs at will, the seller will regularly have to content himself with a considerable percentage of diminution in the price. Far worse is the case of one who at a certain point of time has to get rid of astronomical instruments, anatomical preparations, Sanskrit writings, and such hardly marketable articles!

If we call any goods or wares *more or less saleable*, according to the greater or less facility with which they can be disposed of at a market at any convenient time at current purchasing prices, or with less or more diminution of the same, we can see by what has been said, that an obvious difference exists in this connection between commodities. Nevertheless, and in spite of its great practical significance, it cannot be said that this phenomenon has been much taken into account in economic science. The reason of this is in part the circumstance, that investigation into the phenomena of price has been directed almost exclusively to the *quantities* of the commodities exchanged, and not as well to the greater or less *facility* with which wares may be disposed of at normal prices. In part also the reason is the thorough-going abstract method by which the saleableness of goods has been treated, without due regard to all the circumstances of the case.

The man who goes to market with his wares intends as a rule to dispose of them, by no means at any price whatever, but at such as corresponds to the general economic situation. If we are going to inquire into the different degrees of saleableness in goods so as to show its bearing upon practical life, we can only do so by consulting the greater or less facility with which they may be disposed of at prices corresponding to the general economic situation, that is, at *economic* prices.[3] A commodity is more or less saleable according as we are able, with more or less prospect of success, to dispose of it at prices corresponding to the general economic situation, at *economic* prices.

The *interval of time*, moreover, within which the disposal of a commodity at the economic price may be reckoned on, is of great significance in an inquiry into its degree of saleableness. It matters not whether the demand for a commodity be slight, or whether on other grounds its saleableness be small; if its owner can only bide his time, he will finally and in the long run be able to dispose of it at economic prices. Since, however, this condition is often absent in the actual course of business, there arises for practical purposes an important difference between those commodities, on the one hand, which we expect to dispose of at any given time at economic, or at least approximately economic, prices, and such goods, on the other hand, respecting which we have no such prospect, or at least not in the same degree, and to dispose of which at economic prices the owner foresees it will be necessary to wait for a longer or shorter period, or else to put up with a more or less sensible abatement in the price.

Again, account must be taken of the *quantitative* factor in the saleableness of commodities. Some commodities, in consequence of the development of markets and speculation, are able at any time to find a sale in practically any quantity at economic, or approximately economic, prices. Other commodities can only find a sale at economic prices in smaller quantities, commensurate with the gradual growth of an effective demand, fetching a relatively reduced price in the case of a greater supply.

V. Concerning the Causes of the different Degrees of Saleableness in Commodities

The degree to which a commodity is found by experience to command a sale, at a given market, at any time, at prices corresponding to the economic situation (economic prices), depends upon the following circumstances.

1. Upon the number of persons who are still in want of the commodity in question, and upon the extent and intensity of that want, which is unsupplied, or is constantly recurring.

2. Upon the purchasing power of those persons.

3. Upon the available quantity of the commodity in relation to the yet unsupplied (total) want of it.

4. Upon the divisibility of the commodity, and any other ways in which it may be adjusted to the needs of individual customers.

5. Upon the development of the market, and of speculation in particular. And finally,

6. Upon the number and nature of the limitations imposed politically and socially upon exchange and consumption with respect to the commodity in question.

We may proceed, in the same way in which we considered the degree of the saleableness in commodities at definite markets and definite points of time, to set out the *spatial and temporal limits* of their saleableness. In these respects also we observe in our markets some commodities, the saleableness of which is almost unlimited by place or time, and others the sale of which is more or less limited.

The *spatial* limits of the saleableness of commodities are mainly conditioned –

1. By the degree to which the want of the commodities is distributed in space.

2. By the degree to which the goods lend themselves to transport, and the cost of transport incurred in proportion to their value.

3. By the extent to which the means of transport and of commerce generally are developed with respect to different classes of commodities.

4. By the local extension of organised markets and their intercommunication by 'arbitrage.'

5. By the differences in the restrictions imposed upon commercial intercommunication with respect to different goods, in interlocal and, in particular, in international trade.

The time-limits to the saleableness of commodities are mainly conditions –

1. By the permanence in the need of them (their independence of fluctuation in the same).

2. Their durability, *i.e.* their suitableness for preservation.

3. The cost of preserving and storing them.

4. The rate of interest.

5. The periodicity of a market for the same.

6. The development of speculation and in particular of time-bargains in connection with the same.

7. The restrictions imposed politically and socially on their being transferred from one period of time to another.

All these circumstances, on which depend the different degrees of, and the different local and temporal limits to, the saleableness of commodities, explain why it is that certain commodities can be disposed of with ease and certainty in definite markets, *i.e.* within local and temporal limits, at any time and in practically any quantities, at prices corresponding to the general economic situation, while the saleableness of other commodities is confined within narrow spatial, and again, temporal, limits; and even within these the disposal of the commodities in question is difficult, and, in so far as the demand cannot be waited for, is not to be brought about without a more or less sensible diminution in price.

VI. *On the Genesis of Media of Exchange*[4]

It has long been the subject of universal remark in centres of exchange, that for certain commodities there existed a greater, more constant, and more effective demand than for other commodities less desirable in certain respects, the former being such as correspond to a want on the part of those able and willing to traffic, which is at once universal and, by reason of the relative scarcity of the goods in question, always imperfectly satisfied. And further, that the person who wishes to acquire certain definite goods in exchange for his own is in a more favourable position, if he brings commodities of this kind to market, than if he visits the markets with goods which cannot display such advantages, or at least not in the same degree. Thus equipped he has the prospect of acquiring such goods as he finally wishes to obtain, not only with greater ease and security, but also, by reason of the steadier and more prevailing demand for his own commodities, at prices corresponding to the general economic situation – at economic prices. Under these circumstances, when any one has brought goods not highly saleable to market, the idea uppermost in his mind is to exchange them, not only for such as he happens to be in need of, but, if this cannot be effected directly, for other goods also, which, while he did not want them himself, were nevertheless more saleable than his own. By so doing he certainly does not attain at once the final object of his trafficking, to wit, the acquisition of goods needful to *himself*. Yet he draws nearer to that object. By the devious way of a mediate exchange, he gains the prospect of accomplishing his purpose more surely and economically than if he had confined himself to direct exchange. Now in point of fact this seems everywhere to have been the case. Men have been led, with increasing knowledge of their individual interests, each by his own economic interests, without convention, without legal compulsion, nay, even without any regard to the common interest, to exchange goods destined for exchange (their 'wares') for other goods equally destined for exchange, but more saleable.

With the extension of traffic in space and with the expansion over ever longer intervals of time of prevision for satisfying material needs, each individual would learn, from his own economic interests, to take good heed that he bartered his less saleable goods for those special commodities which displayed, beside the attraction of being highly saleable in the particular locality, a wide range of saleableness both in time and place. These wares would be qualified by their costliness, easy transportability, and fitness for preservation (in connection with the circumstance of their corresponding to a steady and widely distributed demand), to ensure to the possessor a power, not only 'here' and 'now,' but as nearly as possible unlimited in space and time generally, over all other market-goods at economic prices.

And so it has come to pass, that as man became increasingly conversant with these economic advantages, mainly by an insight become traditional, and by the habit of economic action, those commodities, which relatively to both space and time are most saleable, have in every market become the wares, which it is not only in the interest of every one to accept in exchange for his own less saleable goods, but which also are those he actually does readily accept. And their superior saleableness depends only upon the relatively inferior saleableness of every other kind of commodity, by which alone they have been able to become *generally* acceptable media of exchange.

It is obvious how highly significant a factor is habit in the genesis of such generally serviceable means of exchange. It lies in the economic interests of each trafficking individual to exchange less saleable for more saleable commodities. But the willing acceptance of the medium of exchange presupposes already a knowledge of these interests on the part of those economic subjects who are expected to accept in exchange for their wares a commodity which in and by itself is perhaps entirely useless to them. It is certain that this knowledge never arises in every part of a nation at the same time. It is only in the first instance a limited number of economic subjects who will recognise the advantage in such procedure, an advantage which, in and by itself, is independent of the general recognition of a commodity as a medium of exchange, inasmuch as such an exchange, always and under all circumstances, brings the economic unit a good deal nearer to his goal, to the acquisition of useful things of which he really stands in need. But it is admitted, that there is no better method of enlightening any one about his economic interests than that he perceive

99

the economic success of those who use the right means to secure their own. Hence it is also clear that nothing may have been so favourable to the genesis of a medium of exchange as the acceptance, on the part of the most discerning and capable economic subjects, for their own economic gain, and over a considerable period of time, of eminently saleable goods in preference to all others. In this way practice and habit have certainly contributed not a little to cause goods, which were most saleable at any time, to be accepted not only by many, but finally by all, economic subjects in exchange for their less saleable goods: and not only so, but to be accepted from the first with the intention of exchanging them away again. Goods which had thus become generally acceptable media of exchange were called by the Germans, *Geld*, from *gelten*, *i.e.* to pay, to perform, while other nations derived their designation for money mainly from the substance used,[5] the shape of the coin,[6] or even from certain kinds of coin.[7]

It is not impossible for media of exchange, serving as they do the commonweal in the most emphatic sense of the word, to be instituted also by way of legislation, like other social institutions. But this is neither the only, nor the primary mode in which money has taken its origin. This is much more to be traced in the process depicted above, notwithstanding the nature of that process would be but very incompletely explained if we were to call it 'organic,' or denote money as something 'primordial,' of 'primæval growth,' and so forth. Putting aside assumptions which are historically unsound, we can only come fully to understand the origin of money by learning to view the establishment of the social procedure, with which we are dealing, as the spontaneous outcome, the unpremeditated resultant, of particular, individual efforts of the members of a society, who have little by little worked their way to a discrimination of the different degrees of saleableness in commodities.[8]

VII. *The Process of Differentiation between Commodities which have become Media of Exchange and the Rest*

When the relatively most saleable commodities have become 'money,' the event has in the first place the effect of substantially increasing their originally high saleableness. Every economic subject bringing less saleable wares to market, to acquire goods of another sort, has thenceforth a stronger interest in converting what he has in the first instance into the wares which have become money. For such persons, by the exchange of their less saleable wares for those which as money are most saleable, attain not merely, as heretofore, a higher probability, but the certainty of being able to acquire forthwith equivalent quantities of every other kind of commodity to be had in the market. And their control over these depends simply upon their pleasure and their choice. *Pecuniam habens, habet omnem rem quem vult habere.*

On the other hand, he who brings other wares than money to market, finds himself at a disadvantage more or less. To gain the same command over what the market affords, he must first convert his exchangeable goods into money. The nature of his economic disability is shown by the fact of his being compelled to overcome a difficulty before he can attain his purpose, which difficulty does not exist for, *i.e.* has already been overcome by, the man who owns a stock of money.

This has all the greater significance for practical life, inasmuch as to overcome this difficulty does not lie unconditionally within reach of him who brings less saleable goods to market, but depends in part upon circumstances over which the individual bargainer has no control. The less saleable are his wares, the more certainly will he have either to suffer the penalty in the economic price, or to content himself with awaiting the moment, when it will be possible for him to effect a conversion at economic prices. He who is desirous, in an era of monetary economy, to exchange goods of any kind whatever, which are not money, for other goods supplied in the market, cannot be certain of attaining this result at once, or within any predetermined interval of time, at economic prices. And the less saleable are the goods brought by an economic subject to market, the more unfavourably, for his own purposes, will his economic position compare with the position of those who bring money to market. Consider, *e.g.*, the owner of a stock of surgical instruments, who is obliged through sudden distress, or through pressure from creditors, to convert it into money. The prices which it will fetch will be highly accidental, nay, the goods being of such limited saleableness, they will be fairly incalculable. And this holds good of all kinds of conversions which in respect of time are compulsory sales.[9] Other is his case who wants at a market to convert the commodity, which has become *money*, forthwith into other goods supplied at that market. He will accomplish his purpose, not only with certainty, but usually also at a price corresponding to the general economic situation. Nay, the habit of economic action has made us so sure of being able to procure in return for money any goods on the market, whenever we wish, at prices corresponding to the economic situation, that we are for the most part unconscious of how many purchases we daily propose to make, which, with respect to our wants and the time of concluding them, are compulsory purchases. Compulsory sales, on the other hand, in consequence of the economic disadvantage which they commonly involve, force themselves upon the attention of the parties implicated in unmistakable fashion. What therefore constitutes the peculiarity of a commodity which has become money is, that the possession of it procures for us at any time, *i.e.* at any moment we think fit, assured control over every commodity to be had on the market, and this usually at prices adjusted to the economic situation of the moment: the control, on the other hand, conferred by other kinds of commodities over market goods is, in respect of time, and in part of price as well, uncertain, relatively if not absolutely.

Thus the effect produced by such goods as are relatively most saleable becoming money is an increasing differentiation between their degree of saleableness and that of all other goods. And this difference in saleableness ceases to be altogether gradual, and must be regarded in a certain aspect as something absolute. The practice of every-day life, as well as jurisprudence, which closely adheres for the most part to the notions prevalent in every-day life, distinguish two categories in the wherewithal of traffic – goods which have become money and goods which have not. And the ground of this distinction, we find, lies essentially in that difference in the saleableness of commodities set forth above – a difference so significant for practical life and which comes to be further emphasized by intervention of the state. This distinction, moreover, finds expression in language in the difference of meaning attaching to 'money' and 'wares,' to 'purchase' and 'exchange.' But it also affords the chief explanation of that superiority of the buyer over the seller, which has found manifold consideration, yet has hitherto been left inadequately explained.

VIII. How the Precious Metals became Money

The commodities, which under given local and time relations are most saleable, have become money among the same nations at different times, and among different nations at the same time, and they are diverse in kind. The reason why the *precious metals* have become the generally current medium of exchange among here and there a nation prior to its appearance in history, and in the sequel among all peoples of advanced economic civilisation, is because their saleableness is far and away superior to that of all other commodities, and at the same time because they are found to be specially qualified for the concomitant and subsidiary functions of money.

There is no centre of population, which has not in the very beginnings of civilization come keenly to desire and eagerly to covet the precious metals, in primitive times for their utility and peculiar beauty as in themselves ornamental, subsequently as the choicest materials for plastic and architectural decoration, and especially for ornaments and vessels of every kind. In spite of their natural scarcity, they are well distributed geographically, and, in proportion to most other metals, are easy to extract and elaborate. Further, the ratio of the available quantity of the precious metals to the total requirement is so small, that the number of those whose need of them is unsupplied, or at least insufficiently supplied, together with the extent of this unsupplied need, is always relatively large – larger more or less than in the case of other more important, though more abundantly available, commodities. Again, the class of persons who wish to acquire the precious metals, is, by reason of the kind of wants which by these are satisfied, such as quite specially to include those members of the community who can most efficaciously barter; and thus the desire for the precious metals is as a rule more effective. Nevertheless the limits of the effective desire for the precious metals extend also to those strata of population who can less effectively barter, by reason of the great divisibility of the precious metals, and the enjoyment procured by the expenditure of even very small quantities of them in individual economy. Besides this there are the wide limits in time and space of the saleableness of the precious metals; a consequence, on the one hand, of the almost unlimited distribution in space of the need of them, together with their low cost of transport as compared with their value, and, on the other hand, of their unlimited durability and relatively slight cost of hoarding them. In no national economy which has advanced beyond the first stages of development are there any commodities, the saleableness of which is so little restricted in such a number of respects – personally, quantitatively, spatially, and temporally – as the precious metals. It cannot be doubted that, long before they had become the generally acknowledged media of exchange, they were, amongst very many peoples, meeting a positive and effective demand at all times and places, and practically in any quantity that found its way to market.

Hence arose a circumstance, which necessarily became of special import for their becoming money. For any one under those conditions, having any of the precious metals at his disposal, there was not only the reasonable prospect of his being able to convert them in all markets at any time and practically in all quantities, but also – and this is after all the criterion of saleableness – the prospect of converting them at prices corresponding at any time to the general economic situation, *at economic prices*. The proportionately strong, persistent, and omnipresent desire on the part of the most effective bargainers has gone farther to exclude prices of the moment, of emergency, of accident, in the case of the precious metals, than in the case of any other goods whatever, especially since these, by reason of their costliness, durability, and easy preservation, had become the most popular vehicle for hoarding as well as the goods most highly favoured in commerce.

Under such circumstances it became the leading idea in the minds of the more intelligent bargainers, and then, as the situation came to be more generally understood, in the mind of every one, that the stock of goods destined to be exchanged for other goods must in the first instance be laid out in precious metals, or must be converted into them, even if the agent in question did not directly need them, or had already supplied his wants in that direction. But in and by this function, the precious metals are already constituted generally current media of exchange. In other words, they hereby function as commodities for which every one seeks to exchange his market-goods, not, as a rule, in order to consume them but entirely because of their special saleableness, in the intention of exchanging them subsequently for other goods directly profitable to him. No accident, nor the consequence of state compulsion, nor voluntary convention of traders effected this. It was the just apprehending of their individual self-interest which brought it to pass, that all the more economically advanced nations accepted the precious metals as money as soon as a sufficient supply of them had been collected and introduced into commerce. The advance from less to more costly money-stuffs depends upon analogous causes.

This development was materially helped forward by the ratio of exchange between the precious metals and other commodities undergoing smaller fluctuations, more or less, than that existing between most other goods, – a stability which is due to the peculiar circumstances attending the production, consumption, and exchange of the precious metals, and is thus connected with the so-called intrinsic grounds determining their exchange value. It constitutes yet another reason why each man, in the first instance (*i.e.* till he invests in goods directly useful to him), should lay in his available exchange-stock in precious metals, or convert it into the latter. Moreover the *homogeneity* of the precious metals, and the consequent facility with which they can serve as *res fungibiles* in relations of obligation, have led to forms of contract by which traffic has been rendered more easy; this too has materially promoted the saleableness of the precious metals, and thereby their adoption as money. Finally the precious metals, in consequence of the peculiarity of their *colour*, their *ring*, and partly also of their *specific gravity*, are with some practice not difficult to recognise, and through their taking a durable stamp can be easily controlled as to quality and weight; this too has materially contributed to raise their saleableness and to forward the adoption and diffusion of them as money.

IX. Influence of the Sovereign Power

Money has not been generated by law. In its origin it is a social, and not a state-institution. Sanction by the authority of the state is a notion alien to it. On the other hand, however, by state recognition and state regulation, this social institution of money has been perfected and adjusted to the manifold and varying needs of an evolving commerce, just as customary rights have been perfected and adjusted by statute law. Treated originally by weight, like other commodities, the precious metals have by degrees attained as coins a shape by which their intrinsically high saleableness has experienced a material increase. The fixing of a coinage so as to include all grades of value (*Wertstufen*), and the establishment and maintenance of coined pieces so as to win public confidence and, as far as is possible, to forestall risk concerning their genuineness, weight, and fineness, and above all the ensuring their circulation in general, have been everywhere recognised as important functions of state administration.

The difficulties experienced in the commerce and modes of payment of any country from the competing action of the several commodities serving as currency, and further the circumstance, that concurrent standards induce a manifold insecurity in trade, and render necessary various conversions of the circulating media, have led to the legal recognition of certain commodities as money (to legal standards). And where more than one commodity has been acquiesced in, or admitted, as the legal form of payment, law or some system of appraisement has fixed a definite ratio of value amongst them.

All these measures nevertheless have not first made money of the precious metals, but have only perfected them in their function as money.

KARL MENGER

Translated by CAROLINE A. FOLEY, M.A.

NOTES

1. Cf. Roscher, *System der Volkswirthschaft*, i. § 116; my *Grundsätze der Volkswirtschaftslehre* (1871), p. 255, et seq.; M. Block, *Les Progrés de la Science èconomique depuis A. Smith* (1890), ii, p. 59, et seq.
2. We must make a distinction between the higher purchasing prices for which the buyer is rendered liable through the wish to purchase at a definite point of time, and the (lower) selling prices, which he, who is obliged to get rid of goods within a definite period, must content

himself withal. The smaller the difference between the buying and selling prices of an article, the more saleable it usually proves to be.

3. The height of saleableness in a commodity is not revealed by the fact that it may be disposed of at any price whatever, including such as result from distress or accident. In this sense all commodities are pretty well equally saleable. A high rate of saleableness in a commodity consists in the fact that it may at every moment be easily and surely disposed of at a price corresponding to, or at least not discrepant from, the general economic situation − at the economic, or approximately economic, price.

The price of a commodity may be denoted as *uneconomic* on two grounds: (1) in consequence of error, ignorance, caprice, and so forth; (2) in consequence of the circumstance that only a part of the supply is available to the demand, the rest for some reason or other being withheld, and the price in consequence not commensurate with the actually existing economic situation.

4. Cf. My article on 'Money' in the *Handwörterbuch der Staatswissenschaften*, Dictionary of Social Science (Jena, 1891), iii., p. 730 et seq.

5. The Hebrew *Keseph*, the Greek ἀργύριον, the Latin *argentum*, the French *argent*, &c.

6. The English *money*, the Spanish *moneda*, the Portuguese *moeda*, the French *monnaie*, the Hebrew *maoth*, the Arabic *fulus*, the Greek νόμισμα, &c.

7. The Italian *danaro*, the Russian *dengi*, the Polish *pienondze*, the Bohemian and Slavonian *penize*, the Danish *penge*, the Swedish *penningar*, the Magyar *penz*, &c. (i.e. *denare = Pfennige = penny*).

8. Cf. on this point my *Grundsätze der Volkswirtschaftslehre* (1871), pp. 250 et seq.

9. Herein lies the explanation of the circumstance why compulsory sales, and cases of distraint in particular, involve as a rule the economic ruin of the person upon whose estate they are carried out, and that in a greater degree the less the goods in question are saleable. Correct discernment of the uneconomic character of these processes will necessarily lead to a reform in the available legal mechanism.

Eugen von Böhm-Bawerk, 'The Historical vs the Deductive Method in
Political Economy', *Annals of the American Academy of Political and
Social Science*, vol. 1 (1891), pp. 244–71.

Eugen von Böhm-Bawerk (1851–1914) was one of the most illus-
trious founding members of the Austrian School. This is a translation (by Henrietta Leonard) of an article in Conrad's *Jahrbücher
für Nationalökonomie*, volume liv, reviewing a book by Gustav
Schmoller, leader of the German Historical School, dedicated to
Professor Wilhelm Roscher in honour of the fiftieth anniversary of
his doctorate. (Although Roscher was a leader of the 'older' German Historical School of Economics, Menger had dedicated his
Grundsätze to him in 1871.) Schmoller's book included a republi-
cation of his blistering review of Menger's *Untersuchungen* (1883)
on methodology. Böhm-Bawerk used his review to restate the Austrian position.

5

The Historical *vs* the Deductive Method in Political Economy

EUGEN von BÖHM-BAWERK

The offering which the most prominent leader of the younger generation of the historical school has made to the founder and head of that school, Wilhelm Roscher, at the fiftieth anniversary of his doctorate, is a most fitting tribute.[1] It is as if Schmoller had presented a laurel-wreathed portrait of the veteran's intellectual self. A vigorous sketch, which forms the centre of the book (pp. 147–171), shows Roscher's place and significance in political economy, and around this Schmoller has set a frame of older sketches, consisting chiefly of the literary portraits which he has made of other economists, as occasion served, during the twenty-five years between 1863 and 1888, and made, too, in the light of the historical school. It is this latter element which gives unity to the book. Embodied in these portraits a whole literary epoch stands before us – an epoch which includes the beginning and growth of the political economy founded by Roscher upon historical method, its battles and victories and renewed battles. The life-stage upon which Roscher's scientific mission was fulfilled is thus faithfully exhibited to us.

It is but suitable to the occasion that the reviewer, too, should devote his first words to that portion of the work which immediately concerns the person of the celebrated master. As Schmoller expressly says in a preface addressed to Roscher, he has no wish to honour the *jubilar* 'with a panegyric such as is customary at celebrations of this sort,' and he has not attempted it. On the contrary, he has sought to analyze psychologically, and with the strictest objectivity, the character and the work of his master. He has therefore, as is reasonable, placed duly in the light all the merits and superiorities of the man, but he has also not hesitated at least to indicate his weaker points. We have thus a character sketch which is,

109

above all else, true, and which, in spite of a few wrinkles that the brush of the painter has not softened, is extraordinarily honourable to its subject and creditable to its author.

As is natural, Schmoller honours Roscher above all, as the road breaker of historical investigation in political economy. He shows how Roscher began as a philologist and historian, later to find his life-work in transplanting abstract political economy to historical ground. He rightly values Roscher's rare historical gifts, his happy tact in interpreting and estimating an often incomplete set of facts, and his enormous, many-sided learning. He does not fail to point out, in this connection, that certain peculiarities 'for which historical minds are not usually distinguished' are also lacking in Roscher. He reviews the master's most important works – his researches in historico-political science, his history of the literature of economics, and his system of political economy, which last is his most widely-known, but not his most important work. He shows that important inequalities exist between the different volumes of the 'System;' that in the two special volumes which treat of the economics of agriculture, of trade and manufacture, the peculiarities of Roscher's historical tendencies are seen at their best, while the first volume on general theoretical economy and the volume on finance are of less value. He enlivens the description by means of comparisons, in which he contrasts Roscher as a systematic writer with Rau, and as a literary historian with Dühring, and finally he sums up his study with the following concise and significant words: 'Roscher has the poly-historical feature in common with the older Göttingen writers of the history of civilization; he has caught from Rau and the whole elder generation the deepest respect for Adam Smith, Ricardo and Malthus. His temper is that of a sensitive, markedly conservative, scholar, who strives to destroy nothing suddenly, but slowly to rebuild. He wishes quite as much to remain a dogmatic economist as to enlarge the tenets of the old school by historical work. He stands between two scientific epochs, closing the old and opening the new.'

It is not my task to review separately each of the essays collected into the present book. They are all more or less famililar to the public. I will merely indicate which of them are best known. They are the essays on Schiller (1863), on Fichte (1864–65), List (1884), Carey (1886), Lorenz von Stein (1866), Knies (1883), Schäffle (1879–88), Funck-Brentano (1876), Henry George (1882), Hertzka (1886), besides an essay on the more recent view of statistics of population and of morals (1869), and a critical review of the writings of K. Menger and W. Dilthey on the methodology of political and social science (1883).

I am led, however, to notice one theme which forms the essential centre, a theme which we meet in each of the essays, but which is treated most clearly and decisively in the last – perhaps not without the intention of giving it the impressive position of a 'last word.' This theme is the method of investigation in political science.

I am encouraged to do this by the following considerations: In the first place, the question has lost nothing of urgency since the first appearance of the essay referred to; the question how political science should be pursued, whether by 'exact' or historical methods, is just as pressing to-day, just as important and as far from being settled, as it was years ago. It seems to me that the occasion of the reprinting of the essay is for more than one reason more favourable to a fruitful discussion of its contents than was that of its appearance. It is well known that the year 1883 was a hot one for the discussion of methods, and passion is seldom a good counsellor in scientific debate. The excitement has long since cooled, and I, for one, will make an honest endeavor to treat the subject *sine ira et studio*, and with the most unimpassioned objectivity. Moreover, Schmoller himself has set me a noteworthy example, in that, although he still upholds his fundamental thesis, he has yet by a trifling change of style removed the personal bitterness against his former opponent. And finally, during the last six years much has come to light which essentially facilitates a fruitful discussion of the question. There is no task more thankless than an abstract discussion of methods. It is extremely difficult to form a true conception of a method and still more difficult to pass just judgment upon it when it is presented only *in abstracto*, without an exhibition of its operations. From this fact the so-called empirical method suffered greatly six years ago. None, or at least few, had seen its workings, and we were at liberty, therefore, to form of it any conception which might please our fancy. To-day the case is different. To-day we have before us a whole series of works based on that method. He who will, can by concrete examples see how the empirical method works, to what it is applicable, and to what it is not. In short, if it be true that experiment outweighs theory – and in questions of method this precept seems to me undubitable – we are to-day far better equipped than we were six years ago to make an impartial estimate of the rival methods of investigation.

As a believer in frank statement of opinion, I am willing straightway to admit that I am a defender of the method called by Menger 'exact,'[2] and attacked by Schmoller; and in order that there may be no misunderstanding as to the extent of this admission – a misunderstanding which after certain singular events of recent date I have cause enough to fear – I wish by express explanation to place beyond the possibility of doubt, what is in question and what I advocate. I expressly affirm, therefore, that so far as I am concerned, I have absolutely no thought of casting doubt upon the complete right of the historico-statistical method to a wide and important province in economic inquiry; I have still less intention of denying and belittling the enormous services that historical and statistical work has rendered and still renders to economic science; and least of all is it my intention – an intention which, through a singular misunderstanding, has often, and again quite lately, been imputed to the advocates of the abstract method – to assume an attitude either hostile or even indifferent to social and political reforms. Quite recently we have heard Brentano accuse the 'abstract' school of thinking that with the refutation of certain socialistic errors, 'the perfection of the present economic organization is demonstrated;' the conduct of the school gives rise, he says, to the idea that 'all is in order in the economic world, and there is no misery except what people bring upon themselves;' 'incomprehensible' to him are the followers of that school 'which thinks that by newly formulating old truths, by a new definition of interest, or by the argument that differences in productiveness of land, and hence rents will be found even in a socialistic state, it can get rid of these difficulties.'[3] There is, indeed, something incomprehensible in the matter, but it is the fact that Brentano could impute to me and my scientific associates views which we not only have never anywhere expressed, but which are diametrically opposed to our scientific convictions. It should be entirely superfluous to stop to defend one's self against the imputation of such antediluvian ideas; but, when an economist of Brentano's standing has not disdained to speak such slanders, I, too, may not disdain once emphatically to contradict them. I state here then, once and for all, that so far as I am concerned, and I am confident that in this instance my colleagues of the abstract school will not gainsay me, such opinions are utterly foreign and repulsive to us. It really does not seem to me possible to overlook the existence of much that is lamentable and in need of reform in the present condition of society. I consider an indifferent, *laissez-faire, laissez-passer* attitude toward them wholly wrong; I sympathize most warmly with active efforts at reform in favour of the economically weak and oppressed classes, and endeavor as far as is in my power to further them. To be sure, I have as yet written no book on the subject; but can that fairly be made the ground for charging me with the very opposite of what I believe, and as a teacher always profess?

If now, we put all misunderstanding aside, the *status controversiæ* may be reduced to the following simple terms: The question is not whether the historical method or the 'exact' method is the correct one, but solely whether, alongside of the unquestionably warranted historical method of economics, we shall not recognize the 'isolating' method. Many, I among them, maintain that it should be so recognized. Many others, most of them adherents of the historical school, reply in the negative. It is a practical negative when Schmoller, for example, relegates to a despicable 'little corner of the great structure of our science' all that can be accomplished by that method (p. 293), or when he emphatically declares that a new era of political science is opening, 'but only through the conversion of the whole historical and descriptive material now in our possession, *not* through the further distillation of the abstract theses of the old dogmatism, already a hundred times distilled,' (p. 279.)[4]

In favour of the equality of the two methods, which is denied by the historical school, I will now attempt to set forth certain experiences and impressions which have, in the course of years, been forced upon me, and which do not seem to have been sufficiently emphasized thus far in the progress of the strife. If my plain speaking shall seem to take a polemic character, it will be entirely against my will. My desire is rather to heal the strife than to embitter it. Certain truths must be spoken unless all hope of coming to an understanding be explicitly renounced. In any case, I beg those who differ with me to believe that I am able to separate the personal side of the discussion from the material, and that, in spite of the unavoidable opposition which I am forced to offer to certain statements of the leaders of the historical school, I continue most gladly to pay tribute to their real and important services to our science.

It is admitted on all hands that the deductive method which, generally speaking, is one of the two processes upon which the mind is dependent for the extention of its knowledge, is applied with rich results in almost all sciences, even in those which are pronouncedly empirical, like physics and astronomy. If this mode of reasoning were to be entirely, or almost entirely, banished from political economy, it would be necessary to point to very positive reasons for distrusting so well tried a method.

If now we review the grounds upon which stand the objections of the historical school to the 'abstract-deductive' method – and I use this name because it is convenient as a name, not because I am entirely satisfied with it – we meet two principal arguments. On the one hand it is sought from the peculiarly complex nature of social phenomena to *deduce* that the method of investigation in question is not adequate; into this territory I shall not to-day venture, since far too much has already been deduced both for and against the option. Only in passing, I would point out the curious fact that though the historical school looks so contemptuously on deduction, yet to establish the proposition that abstract-deductive reasoning is not applicable to political economy, they make a brave use of abstract deductions. On the other hand, and chiefly, they combat the method with an argument drawn from experience: the classical political economy worked by this method; it erred; therefore, they conclude, the method is proved to be unfit for the inquiries of political economy.

In this favourite argument of to-day the unprejudiced thinker finds something quite remarkable, and that is the extraordinary assurance with which claim is here laid to strictness of experimental proof. In most cases one scarcely ventures to regard a general statement as proved by experience until its correctness has been established by a whole series of separate concurrent instances of as many various sorts as possible, while here the pretended experimental proof that abstract deduction accomplishes nothing in political economy rests upon one single instance – that of the classical school! And what sort of an instance is that? The case of a young science in its beginnings! When did ever a science win the whole truth at the first throw? Has not every one, even the most rigorously empirical – have not astronomy, physics, history, floundered for centuries from one error to another, fished up out of each phase of error scattered grains of truth, one here, another there, and slowly, very slowly, gathered them into the upward tending structure? And what no other method has been able to do the abstract-deductive method is expected to accomplish for political economy. Rich treasures it has, indeed, brought to light, as its opponents well know, and of these, too, not a few. But that at the first onset it should bring forth the whole truth, and nothing but the truth, that is too great a miracle to ask. Because it has not wrought the miracle shall it be now and always denied all confidence?

The rashness of this judgment is not the only peculiar feature which the historical economy's conception of the classical exhibits; therewith is associated a singular contradiction in its estimate of the classical economy, a strangely inconsistent coupling of depreciation with exaggeration of the ability of the latter. That is to say, on the one hand the body of classical doctrine is somewhat shortly and dryly designated a mass of fatal error, and therefore repudiated; on the other hand, a superhuman ability is imputed to the same men whose achievements are so bitterly censured. It is implied that all knowledge which could be derived by their methods they had derived to perfection from the material within their reach, so that a 'further distillation of the abstract theses of the old dogmatism already a hundred times distilled' offers absolutely no prospect of further gain. The men are thus in the same breath represented as both fallible and infallible – fallible in the choice of methods, infallible in the use of them.

It seems to me that under such conceptions the scientific situation cannot fail to be misunderstood. The classical economists have probably accomplished more in some directions than the historical economists are willing to allow. With that point I am not now concerned. It is quite certain that in other directions they have accomplished very much less. They are far from having distilled from familiar facts and hypotheses all that could have been derived by their method – quite the contrary. They have but very imperfectly distilled, and in countless cases they have been unable to derive the best conclusion from their premises. Their theory swarms with vital questions, not of method alone, which they have wrongly handled. Instead of many examples take one, the very popular and important doctrine of value. The experience from which the general theory of value is to be derived was about as complete for the classical economists as it is for us. What did they make of it? Some declared that the creative principle and measure of value was the amount of human labour involved; others, more numerous, that it was the cost of production. Both definitions are false, as every one to-day knows. But – and this is the point to be emphasized – they were branded false, not by the discovery of some new and startling fact which advanced empirical investigation has brought to light, but by the everyday experiences of the world, experiences which were necessarily as familiar to the classical economists as they are to us. It was not that in this case their empirical knowledge was insufficient, but that they here, as in countless other cases, 'distilled' badly.

If the question under consideration were only to correct a somewhat platonic, adscititious judgment as to what rank in personal esteem is to be accorded to the heroes of the classical economy, it would be scarcely worth while to bring it up here. I think, however, its significance goes much deeper. I think, in fact, that herein lies the key not only to an understanding of the position of the historical economists in regard to methods, but also to an understanding of their great mistake. Had the classical school indeed fully accomplished all that could be accomplished by their methods, the historical school would then be quite right in maintaining that further progress could be made only by a change of method. They conceive the present condition of our science to be that of a mine out of which each man in his turn has dug a certain amount of ore, that ore being now completely exhausted. If one hopes to find more metal here, he will not be likely to smelt again the barren slag, but rather dig for new ore; or, as Schmoller would have it, he will not be likely for the one-hundred-and-first time to distil what has been distilled one hundred times already, but would collect new material out of the store of historical and statistical experience.

The case of our science is, however, not this. It is more correctly conceived as follows: From the universal experience of mankind, from history and statistics, an enormous treasure of empirical raw material was even before our day brought to the furnace. The classical economy, which, in spite of its prematurely given name was only an incipient, embryonic science, with its well-meaning but primitive and untaught art extracted much gold, but that which required a finer process it could not reach. What then shall we do who come after? The answer, both metaphorical and literal, is a simple one. We have evidently a double task:

we must by means of an improved, more careful, process, a stricter 'distillation,' extract the countless grains of truth still in the old one, and we must at the same time mine new empirical material for future refining, the richer the better. But what would the historical school have instead? They would first of all open an era devoted to the collection of materials. They would have, first of all, in addition to the enormous mountain of raw material which lies still unworked, a second mass, if possible still larger than the first, before we begin again to 'distill.'[5]

Under some circumstances this might be all very well, but under the given conditions it seems to me a highly unsuitable plan, and for more than one reason. In the first place we should not in science, any more than in everyday life, put off till to-morrow what can be done to-day. In the second place each ray of light, even the dimmest which theory has yet drawn from the old facts, helps to lighten the search for the new. Empirical investigation, even in its lowest form – the collection and tabulation of facts – is far from being merely mechanical work which one could do just as well with his eyes shut. For he who would merely gather facts with success must be a seer who knows what he wishes to find, and when and how he can find it. Consciously to give up the present preparation for a 'distilling theory' is consciously to prefer carrying on the work of collection in the dark rather than in the twilight, or in the twilight rather than in full day. And finally, I cannot repress a grave doubt whether the historical school will be either able or willing, when the future to which they point us shall have become the present, to redeem the promises with which they put us off. They promise to build us a theoretical structure sometime in the future if only they first be allowed to provide for it the broader empirical foundation which they deem necessary. That would be all very fine if we could be sure that the historical school is to-day hindered in construction by nothing else than a lack of material. There are those who suspect that the present theoretical sterility of the historical economy is due to quite another trouble – not to the lack of material from which to construct, but to their manner of treating it. To speak plainly, there are those who suspect that in order to extract an adequate general theory from the given empirical material, just that due measure of abstraction and use of deduction is necessary which the historical school definitely reject. In favour of this view there is much that could be said, upon which, for fear of becoming prolix, I will not enter; I shall later on have occasion in another connection to make some remarks that will serve to support it. But assumed that this view is the correct one – a supposition which is not at all precluded by previous experience – what of it? It follows that the historical school, if they continue in their present course, will after twenty or fifty years of collecting material be as far as ever from a constructive theory.

They will have to put off the fulfillment of their promise from decade to decade, until, tired of fruitless expectation, men seek its fulfillment elsewhere; and hereby precious years and scores of years will have been irrevocably lost to German political economy.

It is far from my intention by these remarks to depreciate the value of empirical investigation. To prevent the possibility of any misunderstanding, I will be still more explicit. In my opinion there is not the slightest doubt that the extension of the empirical material of the science is advantageous to its development. A difference of opinion can exist only in regard to the respective degrees in which, in the present actual circumstances, the purveyance of new empirical material on the one hand, and on the other hand the 'abstract-deductive' consumption of the old material will further that development. In regard to this question, which is less a question of principle than one of fact, it seems to me that they of the historical persuasion err, misled by their previously mentioned misconception of the actual condition of the science. They too highly magnify the office of empiricism. Starting with the optimistic assumption that the former 'distillation' accomplished all that was then possible, and that the advance of political economy is hindered only by the lack of 'descriptive empirical material,' they can naturally expect nothing from repeated distillation of the old material, and are forced to stake everything upon the enrichment of it; this enrichment from empiricism they regard not only as advantageous, but as the only means in the present condition of affairs to the accomplishment of our end.

This conception seems to me not to correspond with the facts. The case appears to me to be rather as follows: The problems of political economy, from a technical point of view, fall into two classes. Upon those of one class the mark of the historical school is indelibly stamped. Nor would I proceed otherwise than by the historical-statistical method if I had to study, for example, the influence of retail trade upon price or the economic influence of the division of property in land. Even here we cannot do wholly without deductive reasoning, as is shown by the masterly combination of sharp-sighted deduction with solid empiricism in the works of many of the strongest advocates of the historical method – Nasse, Conrad, Miaskowski, Schanz, Schönberg, and others. But at any rate, for this class of problems the rule holds good that if one wishes to further the solution of them he must begin by enlarging his knowledge of facts. Every addition to our experience is in such a case valuable and fruitful. Without claiming to define with precision the limits of this class, it may be said to include most practical or social-political problems as well as questions of detail attaching to theoretical problems.

With the second class of problems, however, the case is different. For

117

them experience has already done all, or nearly all, that it can do. It has thousands and millions of times over brought to our notice certain obvious outward relations, and a further pursuit of empirical investigation would have no other result than to bring out, perhaps ten thousand or ten million times, the same familiar outward relations. The difficulty, and at the same time the scientific problem, is not in acquiring facts, but in mastering and correctly interpreting the facts long since acquired. A few examples will make this clear more quickly than will any abstract analysis. Man's estimate of the value of property has been millions of times observed. Science has to answer the question, What is the final principle and measure of our estimate of value – the labour involved, or the cost of production, or the degree of service rendered, or the estimated final utility, etc.? I do not suppose anyone thinks we shall be nearer the answer to the question when we shall have collected a second or third or tenth million of estimates of values, when we shall have emptied all the arsenals of history and statistics in the determination to find out what meat and grain were worth to the citizens of Elberfeld in the Fifteenth Century, or what cotton is worth to-day in England, Sweden, Turkey and India, although I would not deny that for certain details of the theory of value this information will always be useful. All the elements for the solution of the problem are contained in the first million of instances – perhaps in the first thousand – as surely as in the last. The art is merely to set them free, and to that end it is not greater extension, but greater profundity, that is needed. Again, the existence of a certain empirical relation between cost and market price has long been beyond a doubt. Science has to answer the question on which side is the cause and on which the effect – whether the high cost of production is the cause or the effect of a high price of the product. Here, again, the increase of empirical material is of no benefit. Numerous observed instances tend to support the former notion, as when, after rise in the price of hops, a rise in the price of beer follows. Other instances support the latter view; for example, the rise in the price of brick-kilns after a rise in the price of bricks. And in every thousand and every million of instances cases of both sorts will be found side by side in almost equal proportion, so that after the tenth thousand you are no wiser than you might have been after the first. Here, then, it is not a greater accumulation of observed cases that will help, but a deeper insight into them. And thus it is with the whole category of theoretical problems – as the question of the true character of the influence of supply and demand upon price, of the true function of capital in production, of the origin of interest, of the relation between saving and the accumulation of capital, etc. The most general and fundamental questions of theory belong, as it seems to me, to this class of problems.

118

Hence springs a double consequence: first it is not for all questions of political economy equally that we are to look for advantage from the further accumulation of empirical material, for in important spheres of investigation such accumulation is useless and purposeless, and advance is to be expected only through more effectual 'distillation' of facts already known; secondly, in the same spheres mere quiescence and hope from the future are out of place. What can be done at all can be done as well, and better, to-day than after twenty years more of industrious observation. These years would bring us nothing but disillusionment and a mass of superfluous material, and we must even then begin what I and my colleagues are doing to-day, and what the historical economists would prevent us from doing – the intellectual exploitation of the treasures of experience by all the methods which our mental constitution allows, and among them by the method of abstract-deductive 'distillation!'

If it is instructive to hear what a man says in regard to a question of practical conduct, it is still more instructive to observe how, under the given conditions, he himself acts. For such observation the conduct of the adherents of the historical school in this connection furnishes an excellent opportunity. It is noticeable that in questions which, like those above mentioned, from their nature require abstract-deductive treatment, the historical economists invariably have used, and still use, the very same abstract deduction which they, in words, repudiate. In the elder generation this is extremely easy to prove – is even notorious. They still treat chiefly theoretical problems, or, at least, discuss them, and that being the case, they felt themselves forced into the method which the nature of the problems demanded. Everybody knows that Roscher filled the greater part of his 'Grundlagen der Nationalökonomie' with the scouted doctrines of the classical economists. In Knies' highly-esteemed works on 'Wert' and 'Geld und Kredit' abstract-deductive reasoning predominates,[6] and Hildebrand takes the same road when he is led to an opportune digression upon some similar subject – value, for instance, and the explanation of the phenomenon that useful things often possess little value, while comparatively useless things possess great value.

The same trait in the younger generation of the historical school is, at first sight, less striking. Theoretical-problems of a general nature are to-day almost entirely avoided, and – I say it with no depreciatory double meaning – if the history of the development of this or that municipal guild or the price of grain in a certain place, or the population of some mediæval town, or any similar subject, is to be investigated, little occasion is offered for delving into theoretical problems. But yet it is not possible entirely to avoid contact with the latter. It is absolutely impossible to make a report upon a question of economics, much less to discuss it, without touching

119

upon general theoretical conceptions and propositions. For example, whoever has occasion to explain a rise in the price of meat by a rise in the cost of raising cattle indirectly recognizes the law, although it may be with many limiting clauses, that between the price of goods and the cost of production a causal relation exists; or whoever, in speaking of a fall in rates of interest, says that the 'price of capital' is lower unconsciously acknowledges himself an adherent of the view that there is such a thing as real, independent 'use' of perishable and representative commodities, and that the existence of interest on capital must be explained by the real existence of that 'use' as an independent element. In this wise the younger generation let slip, unconscious, veiled acknowledgments, perhaps the more significant because unintentional.

The instructive point is that the substance of these acknowledgments is almost always borrowed from the older abstract-deducting teaching. 'Naturam expellas furca, tamen usque redibit.' The historical school have discarded abstract deduction, but they cannot write three pages on economic questions, even in the historical style, without general theory, and one can construct no general theory without the use of abstract deduction. For facts are not so accommodating as to present themselves to the eye of the investigator ranked in a scale ascending from the most special facts to ultimate, general facts. Even if such an orderly structure really exists, it is seldom or never immediately visible in its completeness; single links, single terms of the scale, are almost always hidden at first, and their existence must be assumed by a deductive operation, the results of which are afterward to be verified by experimental test. To take again one example instead of many: If we let only the facts, which are obviously perceptible, speak for themselves, we shall never discover whether the value of materials is the cause or the effect of the value of the product. It is easy to see that there is a relation between the two, but the whole structure is to our eyes so distorted by complications that by simple observation we cannot tell which of the two facts occupies the lower and which the higher place in the scale of causation. What the outward eye cannot here unaided see, the mind must construct by means of a series of abstract speculations. The theory of final utility, as is well known, was thus worked out, and in such a manner that the internal series, as well as the experimental proof, was actually complete.

What position, now, does the historical school[7] take upon this and similar questions? As already shown, they must have one view or another, and it is impossible to arrive at one without an abstract-deductive operation; the historical-school on principle deny even the intention of performing such an operation; hence there is no other course left for them either consciously or unconsciously, to appropriate what others before them have deduced – in other words, to appropriate the doctrines of the old classical economists. The historical economists have thrown them out at the front door of science only to have them slip in again through a back door into their own works. Anyone who will take the trouble to observe may gather an imposing array of utterances which can be construed in no other way than as acceptance, probably involuntary, of the officially repudiated classical doctrines.

This state of affairs naturally has dubious consequences. The least of them, since it is only personal, is that the historical school lay themselves open to the charge of inconsequence. Far more serious is the objective injury done by the historical school, in that, while scouting for all present and future time the use of abstract deduction as a 'further distillation of the old dogmas already a hundred times distilled,' they yet remain fast in the same sorry slough of dogma in which the first imperfect attempts of the old economists involved them. To deny a fault is to hinder its correction. If they decline the more recent advances in the theory of value or of capital because they are acquired by abstract-deductive methods, but yet cannot themselves avoid referring to value, the influence of cost upon price, the productiveness of capital and the like, they remain grounded on the same contradictory, half-apprehended, or misapprehended conceptions which the classical economists brought to light. That adherents of the historical school themselves occasionally find fault with the doctrines does not help the matter at all. A bad doctrine is never made better by fault-finding alone, and whoever depends upon a creed which he himself finds worthless has a worthless creed indeed upon which to depend.

It seems to me that from one point of view the attitude of the historical school toward abstract-deductive theory is the same as that of loose, theory-disdaining routine to all theory. The man of routine who arrogantly rejects theory usually rejects only the new and advanced theory, while he remains unconsciously fettered by the superannuated notions which have filtered into practice, into the judgments and prejudices of 'common sense.' And the historian who purposes to reject abstract deduction in general, in reality rejects only its newer, improved results, and thereby remains, the more unsuspectingly, the more surely, under the dominion of the old false deductions.[8]

If a tendency of method is more faithfully mirrored in the works than in the words of its followers, we can in no way better obtain a fair presentation of the attitude of the party of the defendant than by holding up the glass to them. How do those economists really proceed whom it is the fashion to name the 'abstract-deductive school?'

Supported by certain ambiguous words of Menger,[9] which were assuredly not intended by him to convey the meaning which our opponents

121

have found it easy to foist upon them, the opinion has become widespread that the so-called abstract-deductive method is unempirical, starting with hypotheses which have no correspondence with the fact, and therefore spinning abstract conclusions without concern as to their empirical reality.[10] No representation could be further from the truth than this. The abstract-deductive method as presented in the German literature by C. Menger, Wieser, Sax, myself and others, is in its very essence a genuinely empirical method. It is by no means exclusively and finally abstract-deductive, for which reason I can accept the name only with qualifications; it has no fancy for *à priori* axioms as a basis for its inferences, nor does it confine itself to inferences and deductions. On the contrary, it starts exactly as the historical school would have it start, with observation of actual conditions and endeavors from this empirical material to derive general laws. But it recognizes the utility – for technical reasons above referred to – of tracing causal connections, not only from special to general, but also, for the sake of experiment, from general to special. It thereby often discovers links in the chain of causes which were, of course, present in the complex, empirical facts, but which were there so deeply inwrapt that they would hardly, if ever, have been discovered by a purely inductive method. To the eye taught by preliminary deduction where and how to look, the same facts are easier to find and to verify, as the astronomer Leverrier, in an often-quoted but none the less forcible example, from given empirical premises, the disturbances of the orbit of Uranus, deduced the existence, the motion and orbit of the planet Neptune, and then actually found the planet in the orbit he had calculated.

However, we will not make words, but proceed to look at facts. Take a practical example. The best known among the doctrines of the abstract-deductive school is the theory of value based on final utility. How did they arrive at it? By some soaring *à priori* speculation? Not at all. In the first place they simply observed how men practically regard property, and they found that men value it not, as the theory of abstract value teaches, according to the utility of the whole species; neither, as the labour theory teaches, according to the amount of labour embodied in it, nor according to the cost of production, but they value it simply according to the effective increase of well-being which they expect to secure by the possession of it. A further empirical investigation, rightly conducted, and supported by deduction, gave this result; that invariably we must regard as the dependent effective increment of utility that one which, in a given case, one can most easily determine, if necessary, to do without, *i.e.*, that consumption of utility which, among all the consumptions made possible by the possessions of the given individual, is of least importance, or the so-called 'final utility.' With such a key in hand one can tirelessly investigate all the changes and complications of practical life, the commonest as well as the most fantastic, and need not rest until the test has been everywhere successful. Not long since one of the leaders of the historical method by no means friendly heretofore to the abstract-deductive method, was impelled to recognize that the theory of the measure of value was derived from 'an immediate observation of life!' I can claim a similar genuinely empirical basis for my researches in the theory of capital; for example, my inquiries into the productive function of capital, into the relation of saving to the accumulation of capital, into the existence and the rationale of the lower estimate placed upon future than upon present possessions of property under certain conditions, into the exceptions to this rule, into the origin of interest and the like. And if Schmoller rightly demands that political economy should provide itself with a sound psychological foundation (p. 282), he will find his demand nowhere so nearly met as in the works of the so-called abstract-deductive school, in the works of a Jevons or Sidgewick, a Menger or Wieser; indeed, it would not at all surprise me if in the future this school should come to be called the 'psychological school of political economy.'

Again, it is a mistake to say, as has been said, that we would deduce everything from a single premise, the postulate of an enlightened self-interest, without troubling ourselves about other highly important factors of social economy – habit, custom, humanity, nationality and the like. Whoever will fairly review our works will find, indeed, that we now and then expressly concern ourselves with the working of an enlightened self-interest only, and analyze it in detail; but he will also find that we never forget the influence of the other factors, and still less deny it. At times we also devote care and attention to this influence; but life is short and art is long, and since we are not able to exhaust all things, we must often content ourselves with merely noticing the existence of such incidental influences, the necessity of taking them into account and filling in the gaps which for the present have been left open. For a typical example I venture to refer to my analysis of the theory of price already familiar to the reader, the first, general part of which I worked out in detail and then added the second part as a necessary complement.[11]

A careful inquiry would probably lead to the conclusion that the doctrines of the classical school, decried as highly abstract-deductive, were by no means abstract-deductive in their origin, but were, in the last analysis, empirical. It seems to me highly probable that the doctrines of demand and supply, the theories of value based upon labour, cost of production, etc., were not originally the results of speculation, but were the products of crude empirical observation. However that may be, we who are living have a right to be judged, not by what an old prejudice fables about us, but rather by what we actually do, and in view of our actual attitude the charge of denying or ignoring living realities must in the end be withdrawn from our account.

'By their fruits ye shall know them' are the words Schmoller has put at the end of his reprinted essay on Menger. I accept the principle gladly. As to the adequacy of a method there is no juster index, and for us none more expedient than the sum of what the method has accomplished. But as a matter of course we demand that the principle, as a test of our method, should be applied to what we ourselves have done. This protest is directed against a treatment as remarkable as it is common, which Brentano not long since brought heavily to bear upon us in a dissertation upon the classical economists. It is a favourite practice to criticise the abstract-deductive economists of the past, and there nothing is easier than to point out errors and misconceptions under which our grandfathers laboured 80 or 100 years ago, in the childhood of our science, and then to extend the same judgment, without qualification, to the abstract-deductive economists of the present day. That is unjust. If we are to be judged, make out the case against us and not against our grandfathers. For our own faults we will willingly be answerable, but to be made answerable for faults committed by others which we have ourselves no less strongly reprehended than have the historical school, we must decline.

If we strike a balance between what the historical school have done in the province of theory and what we have done, it seems to me we have no cause to blush at the result. I say advisedly in the province of *theory*. For it is only here that the question of method is in dispute. In the province of practical social politics, for technical reasons, the historical-statistical method is so unquestionably superior that I do not hesitate to declare that a purely abstract-deductive legislative policy in economic and social matters would be as much of an abomination to me as to others, but when Schmoller lays claim to the same superiority of the historical method in the province of theory proper[12] he seems to me to be out of touch with the facts. A glance at what has been done in Germany in the last thirty or forty years in the department of theory seems to me, rather, to show the following results: The historical school has unquestionably merited much in the province of criticism of theory, although the lion's part in the critical revolution which shattered the sovereignty of the classical economy was taken not so much by the historians as by the Socialists and the Socialists of the chair – by Rodbertus, Lassalle, Wagner and Schäffle. In the province of positive theory, however, the efforts of the historical school have been confined almost exclusively to questions of detail. They have made, for instance, quite remarkable investigations into the influence of retail trade upon price; into the fluctuations between the prices of different classes of goods in long periods of time, as well as into countless details of the subject of money, exchange, banks, etc. On the other hand, the great questions of general theory have either not been touched at all by the historical school, or else, as in the case of Knies, have been treated by another than the historical method. All the positive advances which general theory has made in recent times are notoriously due to other methods. In proof of this I would call to mind the investigations of Knies and Wagner in money and credit; the rich German literature on value which has lately culminated in the theory of final utility; the corrections made with the help of this theory in the much scouted old law of supply and demand; the accompanying illumination of the theory of cost, till then either not understood or misunderstood; and perhaps I might name certain very recent investigations into the subject of capital, of wages and the theory of economic contribution,[13] as among those which have brought general theory a step forward.

Let us trust to the future for proof. I make, but one modest request – not at all for a blind acceptance of abstract deduction, but merely for a truce to the blind repudiation of it which has become fashionable; that the historical school should once and for all cease to pursue a course of treatment entirely contrary to the empirical principle in the name of which it is carried on; – namely, an *à priori* repudiation of the results of our method of investigation, upon the ground of the preconceived opinion that nothing good can come of the method. I particularly do not desire, what an incomprehensible obstinacy still fondly accuses us of desiring, that the abstract-deductive method be put forward into a place of unseemly and exclusive sovereignty. I wish merely to protect it against its unseemly exclusion, against the continuance of an intolerance in methods which has lasted already far too long to the injury of German science. I desire no battle between the methods; I desire rather their reconciliation and fruitful coöperation; I would awaken the feeling not only that there is room for us all in the vast field of political economy, but that there is need of us all, with all our variety of talents and methods; that, instead of turning our intellectual weapons against one another and wilfully refusing to use a better way than our own when it is offered us, we should unite our forces and turn them against the common enemy, the untold army of problems of one of the most difficult of sciences.

I venture to hope that this call to reconciliation will not pass unheard. I notice with pleasure that Schmoller himself has lately expressed some opinions which betoken an approach to the standpoint I have been defending. 'I admit,' he writes, in a discussion of Roscher's science of finance,[14] 'that a great part of the financial questions of to-day do not bear historical treatment. The problems of the incidence of taxation have been, up to this time, so little approachable by empirical investigation that the collective theories on the subject are limited to the deductive consideration and presentation of the views of various authors.' And in his characterization of Roscher he says: 'Greatly as the empirical history and statistics of price have cleared away the old errors the fundamental phenomena of fluctuations in price yet recur with tolerable regularity, and hence historical investigation is not so very necessary. The same is true of many elementary natural and psychological phenomena which constitute and influence economic life. Concerning so many things, historical tradition is so faint that, for this reason, other forms of investigation must predominate.'[15] It is necessary only to extend to a somewhat greater tale of problems what Schmoller has here observed of one problem, in order to arrive at that standpoint which I have reached in my foregoing analysis.

My hope is strengthened by the perception that the same call for harmonious coöperation in methods is raised in highly-reputed quarters, and, what seems to me especially important, raised by men who belong to or stand near to the historical school. Let me here refer the reader to Wagner's very remarkable paper on this subject,[16] to the calm and clear exposition of it by Philippovich,[17] to Conrad's thoughtful expression of opinion, in which, with praiseworthy objectivity, he warns his colleagues not to run to an extreme in the opposite direction, as the old classical school once did in theirs. If this school held too strictly to general rules, and gave too little attention to exceptions, the present scientific tendency is the reverse – to 'the exaggeration of exceptions and disregard of the great average.' And since Conrad considers the present stage, 'in which we are inclined to underestimate, in the study of detail, the significance of larger features, and to let ourselves be deceived by obvious exceptions,' an imperfect and transitory stage, this master of empirical research gives his followers a hint of the claims and the significance of general theory, which could not have been milder in expression nor plainer in meaning.[18] And on the other side of the ocean, where the strife between abstract-deductive and historical method is raging, we see one of the most gifted of the younger investigators, Prof. Simon N. Patten, who has drunk the empiricism of Germany at its source, and carried it over to America, nevertheless break a lance in behalf of the indispensability of the abstract-deductive method and its equal rights.[19]

My strongest hope, however, is based upon the undeniable and encouraging upward swing upon which theoretical investigation proper has just entered in so many nations. Where it has been established by unquestionable practical success that truth can be acquired by the abstract-deductive method, then her most stiff-necked opponents can no longer deny her the place she deserves, and there will be an end of a conflict the very possibility of which will be inconceivable to the coming generation. And then we shall finally realize what I to-day most profoundly desire; then will be little or nothing *written* about method, and so much the more will be *done* by all methods.

E. v. BÖHM-BAWERK.

Ministry of Finance, Vienna.

Translated by HENRIETTA LEONARD.

NOTES

1. This article is a translation of an article in Conrad's *Jahrbücher für Nationalökonomie* (vol. liv, p. 75) by Professor Dr v. Böhm-Bawerk, in which he reviews a late work of Professor Schmoller's on the Literature of the Political and Social Sciences ('Zur Literaturgeschichte der Staats- und Sozialwissenschaften'). The book is dedicated to Professor Roscher, in honour of the fiftieth anniversary of his doctorate.

2. While there is still so much to be cleared up in the subject itself, it is scarcely worth while to quarrel over the name. I will, therefore, briefly remark that the method in question is spoken of by many, especially by its opponents, as the '*a priori*' method, by others as the 'abstract-deductive' method, neither of which is quite correct, as we shall see. Menger, not without calling forth sharp opposition, calls it the 'exact' method. I would rather call it the 'isolating' method; for, as I not long since pointed out (*Göttingische gel. Anzeigen*, 1 June, 1889, review of Brentano's '*Klassische Nationalökonomie*'), its essence consists in, first of all, observing the different aspects of complex phenomena separately, but let it be understood, what is often forgotten, that it should not content itself with a partial view, or mistake the part isolated in thought for the whole, but, as far as possible, should construct out of the clearly grasped parts a complete whole.

3. 'Ueber die Ursachen der heutigen sozialen Not,' (Leipzig, 1889), pp. 4–5, 28.

4. Cf. also Brentano's 'Die Klassische Nationalökonomie,' *passim*, especially pp. 4 et seq., 28 et seq.

5. Cf. Schmoller 'Zur Litteratur-Geschichte, etc.,' p. 278 et seq. Brentano's Die Klassiche Nationalökonomie, p. 28 et seq.

6. Schmoller himself says of Knies, that 'in one of his youthful works he had, indeed, demanded the historical method, but that in his riper works on 'Money and Credit,' which will always belong to the best

that German theoretical political economy has produced, he has, in all essentials, abandoned this method for the more or less abstract method by which Menger himself works.' 'Litt. Gesch.', p. 293.

7. Under this head I include, as the connection shows, only the historians of the strictest orthodoxy, the methodically *exclusive* writers; not those numerous economists who, although they have been active chiefly in historical or statistical investigation, have yet kept in sympathy with the 'dogmatic' economists.

8. To what a compromising extent this contentment with the old incorrect platitudes and this unfamiliarity with the statements of theory – boldly criticised, however – and their substance can, in certain cases, be carried, out of sheer rabidity in method, is well shown in W. Sombart's latest criticisms of Wieser's 'Naturlichen Wert' (Schmoller's Jahrbuch, vol. xiii (1889), part 4, p. 238). I wish this critique the greatest publicity, for the critical reading of it will make the spirit in which it was written more repulsive to the unprejudiced mind than I could make it by the most cogent arguments. Moreover, I am far from wishing to measure the whole school by such extravagance.

9. 'Nothing is so sure as that the results of the "exact" method of theoretical investigation, measured by the standard of reality ... appear inadequate and *unempirical.' Methode der Sozialwissenschaften*, pp. 54 and 59.

10. 'Menger ... supposes that political economy is an exact science, *i.e.*, that it desires, in a one-sided way, to derive from what it considers first elements a quantity of safe, deductive conclusions, *in opposition to which empirical realities* may be contemptuously put to one side as something immaterial.' Schmoller, Litt. und Gesch., p. 283.

11. *Jahrbuch für Nationalökonomie und Statistik*, N. F. Bd. xiii, pp. 477, et seq., especially 486–8.

12. Wherever healthy tendencies to new theoretical formulation show themselves to-day, the truth of this observation (that all help is to be expected from the empirical method) is strikingly evident. P. 280.

13. [The theory of the respective contributions made by a number of cöoperating factors or elements, as land, labour, and capital to the total value of their joint product. Such a theory is the counterpart, and in the thought of the Austrian economists the basis of a theory of distribution. – Ed.].

14. *Jahrbuch für Gesetzgebung, Verwaltung, und Volkwirthschaft*, Vol. xii (1888), p. 256.

15. *Zur Litteraturgeschichte*, p. 156.

16. 'Systematische Nationalökonomie,' *Jahrbuch für Nationalökonomie und Statistik*, N. F., vol. xii, pp. 197 et seq., especially p. 241.

17. *Ueber Aufgabe und Methode der politischen Oekonomie* (Freiburg, 1886).
18. 'Referat über den Einfluss des Detailhandels auf die Preise, erstattet in den Verhandlungen des Vereins für Sozialpolitik von 1888'; siehe die *Schriften dieses Vereines*, vol. xxxviii, p. 152.
19. 'The ultimate laws of a science cannot be investigated in any other way.' *The Consumption of Wealth* (Philadelphia, 1888), Introduction, p. vii. Compare, also, the same author's essay on Malthus and Ricardo, read at the third annual meeting of the American Economic Association, at Philadelphia, December 29th, 1888, p. 12, ff; beside these, the spirited review of Schmoller's book in the *Göttingen Gelehrten Anzeigen*, September 1st 1889, by H. Dietzel, which I did not see until after the completion of this article.

Eugen von Böhm-Bawerk, 'Professor Clark's Views on the Genesis of Capital', *Quarterly Journal of Economics* IX (1895), pp. 113–31.

This paper was first published in the January 1895 issue of the U.S. journal, *Quarterly Journal of Economics*. It is the first of two papers in which Böhm-Bawerk addressed his critics. This title, *The Positive Theory of Capital and its Critics*, is the generic title of both papers.

It is an important statement of Böhm-Bawerk's position in his famous debate with the U.S. economist John Bates Clark on the foundations of capital theory. This was echoed in a later debate which erupted in the 1930s between Austrian economist F. A. Hayek and the American Frank H. Knight (see this volume, items 20 and 28).

6

The Positive Theory of Capital and its Critics

Professor Clark's Views on the Genesis of Capital

EUGEN von BÖHM-BAWERK

The American public has kindly given to my theory of capital, which appeared a few years ago, more than ordinary attention. I look upon the numerous critical attacks which have been made in American periodicals, either upon my theory as a whole or upon details of it, as by no means unwelcome evidence of this attention. In spite of repeated requests I have until now refrained from replying to these criticisms. My own time and strength have been taken up with other matters; and I wished further to let some time elapse, so that the public as well as the author might return to the subject with less bias and more calmness than usually characterize the first heated utterances. Since, too, the critical reviews of my theory have appeared with almost undiminished frequency even down to the present moment, I may hope to find still some interest manifested in the subject. Turning now, as time and opportunity offer, to answer some objections most worthy attention, I will remark that I do not pretend either to answer all the objections raised or to observe any systematic or chronological sequence. In this article I wish to take issue with an opponent whose views I am wont much oftener to share – as, I may add, it is my greater pleasure to do – than to oppose. Unfortunately, however, his attack, as chivalrous in spirit as it is subtle in thought, makes it plain to me that as regards the theory of capital we are diametrically opposed to each other, – to be sure, in one point only, but this is a point of fundamental consequence in the whole conception of the matter.

In his ingenious article on 'The Genesis of Capital'[1] Professor Clark makes the serious charge that I have, through my conception of capital, 'side-tracked' the whole theory of capital. The trouble is held to lie in this: that I have failed to make a certain distinction which he thinks one is bound to make. One is bound to distinguish, namely, between 'concrete capital goods' and 'true capital' itself. Capital goods are the concrete instruments of production; that is, raw materials, machinery, tools, and the like. True capital, however, is a 'permanent fund' distinct from these, a 'sum or amount of productive wealth.' The concrete capital goods are replaced, are consumed, or worn out, whereas the true capital abides. Indeed, they must be replaced and used up, that the true capital may abide. Let us quote from Professor Clark, in order to make his somewhat subtle distinction clear:

The raw materials in a workshop are, in time, finished, sold and used up by customers. Tools and machines are worn out and replaced. True capital abides, because the things that at any one instant constitute it do not abide. Stop the selling of goods and the wearing out of tools, and you waste true capital. Lock up the mill and the full warehouse, and you ruin the owner. It is clear that, in scientific study, we cannot confine our attention to capital goods, and we certainly cannot treat them as equivalent to true capital for purposes of analysis. [Again,] a waterfall consists in particles of water. Can one say the same things of the fall that he does of the water? The water moves; the fall stays where it is. The water appears in globules condensed in the atmosphere, and it ultimately merges itself in the sea. The fall does not appear nor disappear. Capital goods are, like particles of water, vanishing elements. True capital is like the fall; it is an abiding element, owing its continuance to the constant wasting and replenishing of its substance.

My mistake is that, in explaining interest, my expositions always relate to concrete capital goods and treat them as identical with true capital. The cardinal principle upon which I base my explanation of interest – namely, that present goods have a higher value than future goods of like kind and quantity – appears to Professor Clark to be 'the wedgelike end of the switching-rail that takes the wheel of the scientific car from the rail on which it belongs.' According to this principle, he declares that concrete capital, goods, – for example, a driving-horse or pleasure carriage of 1893 – must be compared with concrete goods of the same kind, – that is, with a driving-horse or pleasure-carriage of 1894. Professor Clark thinks, however, that the things compared with each other in actual practical life are not identical concrete goods, but 'sums of wealth.' 'We do indeed compare a *sum of wealth* existing to-day with a like sum to be used later,' but the two sums 'at the two dates represent quite different goods.'

To prove his statement and to refute mine, he cites the case of a 'typical capitalist' who has saved two hundred dollars in the course of the year, and is considering whether to 'capitalize' the sum or not. Professor Clark holds that, according to my theory, the capitalist must proceed as follows:

From the income of a period now closed he defrays the more necessary expenses of that period, and finds, say, two hundred dollars remaining in his hands. He may use this as he likes, and concludes that, if he spends it now, he will buy the driving-horse of the illustration. He further decides that he will actually spend it at a future time, – say at the end of a year, – and *for that identical thing*. The prospective horse is to-day worth a hundred and ninety dollars; and the rate of interest is five per cent.

Really, thinks Professor Clark, the capitalist will proceed altogether differently. For the sums saved are never, as a matter of fact, spent for the identical goods for which they would have been spent, had the saving not taken place. For either the capitalization is a genuine, permanent one – and in this case the capitalized sums never are spent at all – or it is only a *quasi* temporary one, a saving 'for a rainy day,' and in this case there will be purchased in the moment of need articles totally different from those which the man saving denies himself at the present moment. He denies himself luxuries. He will purchase necessities. In all cases there is a comparison, not between present and future goods *of like kind*, but between present and future 'sums of wealth.'

So writes Professor Clark. If I would, I might make my reply simple. I might limit myself to showing that Professor Clark's attempt to refute my theory by reference to a concrete case is based entirely upon a misunderstanding of my theory, – a misunderstanding for which I think I am not responsible. For I interpret the concrete case of the 'typical capitalist' with two hundred dollars savings exactly as does Professor Clark. The latter is perfectly correct. Surely, the man who saves will not deny himself a driving-horse in 1893, in order to buy himself just such a horse in 1894. Either he will in the future consume only the interest or, if on a 'rainy day' he must spend the saving, he will spend it for more necessary or useful articles. My theory also teaches exactly this. According to it the man who saves will weigh whether the two hundred dollars will have a greater value for him if consumed now as 'present dollars,' or if reserved for later use as 'future dollars.'[2] It is evident that in the first half of this valuation the man who saves will consider the marginal employment which he would have for the two hundred dollars at the *present moment*; in our case, the use which the possession of a driving-horse would be of to him. But this, too, upon which I have dwelt repeatedly,[3] is self-evident: that in the second half of this valuation, in the weighing of the 'future goods,' the man who saves will consider, not the state of his needs at the present moment, but the relation between demand and supply in that *future period* in which the sum of wealth in question will be used. Therefore, the man saving for a rainy day will take as the basis of his valuation those necessary wants for the satisfaction of which he will use the two hundred dollars in the future moment of need; and the 'true capitalist' in an analogous way will estimate the value of the future interest returns by the various necessary or useful articles which, according to the state of his total income at the future periods in question, will lie for him on the margin of the attainable.

How, on the other hand, Professor Clark came to the odd conclusion that, according to my theory, the man who saves can take into consideration for the future nothing else but the worth of a driving-horse, and that the amount saved must be henceforth forevermore devoted to the purchase of such a horse, is a mystery to me. This conclusion seems to me really to have no foundation either in his example or in my theory. Not in the example; for in that the 'concrete present goods' which are to be saved are not a driving-horse, but two hundred dollars. And, in my theory, such an understanding of the matter could find justification only if I were to teach that in the comparison of present and future goods there must always be taken into consideration an identical use for both. But, as already stated, I teach the very opposite of this. According to my theory, the superiority of present over future goods is based upon the very fact that one can, as a rule, make a *different* and, indeed, more advantageous use of goods now present than one can make of an equal quantity of goods which are not to be at one's disposal until some future moment.

Clearly, my conception of capital, at least in this example which Professor Clark selects for its refutation, has not the dangerous quality ascribed to it of shunting science off on a wrong line. My conception leads quite directly to the conclusion which Professor Clark pronounces correct. But I will not stop with this example. I think I can give assurance that my conception is not more misguiding in any other case. By means of a few words of explanation I hope not only to prove this, but at the same time to bring into strong light the error to which Professor Clark seems to me to have fallen victim in his polemic.

Professor Clark declares expressly[4] that his objection is not to the recognition of time as an element in the problem of interest. In the proposition, which he attacks so sharply, – namely, that present goods are worth more than future goods of *like kind and quantity*, – it is more especially the last Italicized words which arouse Professor Clark's opposition. But what is the significance and force of these words? Why do I add at all to my proposition that present goods on the great average are worth more than future goods – a proposition with which, most probably, Professor Clark, too, is ready to agree – the further qualification that excites his dislike and misgivings? namely, that they are worth more than future goods of '*like kind and quantity*.'

Simply because, without the second half of the proposition, the first half would be neither intelligible nor complete. What, indeed, is the thought to be expressed? It is the superiority which the difference of time gives to present over future goods. Now, every one will admit that the circumstance of present *diamonds*, for example, being worth more than future *pebbles*, has as little to do with this superiority as has the circumstance that *two thousand* present dollars are worth more than *one thousand* future dollars. On the other hand, this superiority is most nicely tested and expressed in the statement that one thousand present dollars are worth more than one thousand future dollars, or that ten present tons of iron are worth more than ten future tons of iron. In other words, to express clearly and correctly the superiority which difference of time gives present goods over future goods, one must compare things of *like kind*, – for example, dollars with dollars, and not diamonds with pebbles, – and of *like quantity*, one thousand with one thousand, and not one thousand with two thousand. It is this supplement, as harmless as it is logically essential, that I intended to make in the addition to which Professor Clark objects, 'goods of like kind and quantity.'

I add that I do not believe that this supplement can be expressed equally correctly in any other form. Especially would it be inadmissible – and Professor Clark perhaps had this in mind – to place over against each other like sums of *value* instead of like sums of *wealth*. For, in order to express the superiority of the present sums of value, one would have to make the logically inconsistent assertion that a certain present value is *greater* than an *equally great* future value, a proposition which, as to logical correctness, differs in no wise from the familiar, facetious thesis that a pound of iron is heavier than a pound of feathers.

It is time now to pass from the defence of my own position to the attack upon that of my honoured opponent. I have just said that *perhaps* Professor Clark had in mind the inadmissible form of comparison cited. I can assert nothing definite here, since Professor Clark on this question avoids precise statement, and by preference employs vague terms which admit of double interpretation. He speaks of a 'sum of wealth' or an 'amount of wealth.' This may mean as well an amount of goods as an amount of value. But I think I can under these circumstances maintain with certainty that, if Professor Clark would force himself to a precise definition of his meaning, he would have to assert either exactly what I assert or something positively false. For either he means by his amount of wealth an amount of goods – and in this case, if he is to demonstrate the superiority of present goods, he must necessarily have reference in both halves of the comparison to goods 'of like kind and quantity' – or he means an amount of value, and then the assertion that a definite present value is greater than an equally great future amount of value contains the self-contradiction just criticised.

I would say the same of the whole conception of capital which Professor

Clark opposes to my conception as a supposed improvement. It is related that Caliph Omar, after the conquest of Alexandria, had the celebrated Alexandrian Library burned, saying, 'Either the books contain only what the Koran contains, and so are superfluous, or they contain something else, and are therefore harmful.' I believe the saying of Caliph Omar may be turned aptly against Professor Clark's new theory. Over against the concrete capital goods Professor Clark wishes to put a 'true capital' which shall differ from those goods as does the waterfall from the falling water. Now, I know no capital other than the concrete goods which constitute it; and I believe the world of facts knows no other. Everything accomplished by the so-called capital in the world of mechanics and commerce is accomplished solely by the concrete, useful capital goods – or it is not accomplished at all. Therefore, science, whose business it is to hold up the mirror to the world of reality, must have reference to concrete capital goods in all explanations in which it attributes any influence at all to capital, if it would not offer fancies in place of geniune explanations. Calling anything other than the concrete capital goods by the name of capital is either to use a mere figure of speech or to assert something positively false. For the purposes of science this figure can at least be dispensed with. The figure also becomes dangerous the moment one ceases to be aware that one is using a mere figure of speech.

To repeat, the figure at least may be dispensed with. Professor Clark is mistaken in thinking that his conception of true capital is necessary to express any scientific truth which could not be expressed as well, and even better – because more naturally – by the aid of the conception of concrete capital goods. For example, he lays great stress upon the fact that the goods which constitute capital are being constantly replaced, whereas the sum total of capital abides. This is perfectly correct. My theory, too, recognizes and states this fact, just as does that of Professor Clark. But I do not understand why one needs a new conception of capital to express it. It is expressed perfectly correctly and exactly by saying that the total value of all capital goods is maintained unchanged through the constant replacement of pieces used up or destroyed by means of new pieces of equal value.

Not only is this form of expression as correct as Professor Clark's proposition that 'capital has remained unaltered'; it is a more correct mode of expression. As appears, for example, where the renewal of the capital goods used up takes a false or one-sided turn, and so prepares the way for a partial overproduction and a crisis, which, however, is not as yet felt in the market. Here the sum of values of the capital goods may remain for the time being unaltered; and Professor Clark, who calls this sum of values capital, must consequently, to be consistent, say 'Capital has remained

136

unaltered.' As a matter of fact, however, a very real change has taken place in the capital, – a change of which the pernicious consequences are soon enough manifest in the approach of a crisis. Of course, Professor Clark himself will not deny this, but will probably explain that his proposition, 'Capital has remained unaltered,' should not here be taken quite literally. Thus, however, is made plain just what I wished to show; namely, that this proposition is nothing more than a misleading figure of speech which cannot be taken literally.

In the example just discussed the danger that one may go astray is not great, because the truth reveals itself too clearly. In some of its applications, however, Professor Clark's figure of speech is less innocent, as when Professor Clark asserts repeatedly, with great emphasis, that true capital is never encroached upon. The bare fact upon which this assertion rests is simply that all concrete capital goods are at some time expended or consumed, but that the capitalist always creates a new sum of wealth equal to the amount of capital goods used up, so that the final effect in one sense is as if he had not expended any of his capital. For example, a cloth manufacturer consumes 100,000 dollars' worth of wool, coal, and machinery in the production of 100,000 dollars' worth of cloth (with a profit of several thousand dollars additional), sells the cloth for that sum, and with the proceeds procures a new stock of wool, machinery, and fuel, equivalent in value to the stock consumed. When one goes with Professor Clark into such an account of the matter, the assertion that capital is not consumed is seen to be another inexact, shining figure of speech, which must not be taken at all literally. Any one taking it literally falls into a fatal error, into which, forsooth, science has already fallen once. I refer to the familiar and at one time widely disseminated doctrine that saving is a social evil and the class of spendthrifts a useful factor in social economy, because what is saved is not spent and so producers cannot find a market.

In justice to Professor Clark be it said that, though he has in his theory, as it were, invited others to make this error, he has not himself fallen into it. But there are, nevertheless, positive errors into which Professor Clark allows himself also to be beguiled by his own figure of speech. Jevons and I have maintained that the peculiar character of capitalistic production lies in this: that a certain space of time, a certain production-period, elapses between the application of labour and the attainment of the finished product. Professor Clark thinks that this is true only of concrete capital goods, and not at all of true capital. Of course, a man must wait a certain time if he wishes to work up a raw hide into a concrete piece of leather, and that on a concrete machine into a concrete pair of shoes ready to be drawn on his feet. Since, however, in that permanent fund which true capital represents there are always on hand shoes in every stage of completion, the labourer can, without any waiting at all, procure forthwith a pair of shoes ready-made which are the virtual product of his own industry. Upon these observations Professor Clark thinks he can rest the proposition which he declares with great emphasis, over and over again; namely, that true capital – in contrast with concrete capital goods – has no production-periods, but on the contrary 'annihilates' production-periods. It has the power to 'synchronize all industry and its fruition.' 'Industry and its fruition are simultaneous.' 'To-day we work, and to-day we eat; and the eating is the effect of working.' And, to give his idea the greatest possible sharpness of expression, Professor Clark with strong emphasis designates the ready-made goods obtained on the spot and without any waiting by the labourer as the '*true* and *immediate* fruit' of his labour.[5]

Upon this sentence I pronounce once more my former judgment. It employs a figure of speech wholly wanting in scientific accuracy and misleading. The bit of truth involved in it, as Professor Clark will, surely, willingly grant me, is clearly enough set forth in my theory, and, plainly put, it is as follows: a labourer who in the year 1894 dresses a hide, out of which in the year 1895 a pair of shoes will be made, can in the year 1894 in immediate exchange for his raw product, leather, obtain a pair of shoes ready-made, *if* and *because* there was on hand in society in the year 1894 a separate stock of concrete capital goods in more advanced stages of production, out of which to create in the year 1894 a pair of finished shoes. I lay stress particularly upon this, that to make possible the above exchange there must be on hand *concrete capital goods of a definite sort*. Professor Clark's 'permanent fund' may be ever so large; but were it to contain no concrete capital goods that could be worked up into shoes, obviously the currier could not obtain a pair of ready-made shoes at once, but must wait until the shoes made out of *his* leather are forthcoming. Professor Clark's figure of speech therefore leads away from the truth in two particulars: production-periods are not at all 'annihilated,' but make themselves on occasions very keenly felt; the fact that one is at once provided with commodities whose own production-periods, because begun earlier, are sooner brought to an end than the production-periods of the unfinished products given in exchange, is the happy consequence of the existence, not of any mystical permanent fund, but of those very concrete capital goods whose periods expire earlier.

Again, a third time Professor Clark's figure of speech leads astray when it is laid down with special stress that the finished commodities, which the labourer obtains in exchange for his own raw, mediate goods, are the '*true* and *immediate* fruit' of his labour. The true and immediate fruit of his labour is the leather he has tanned, and nothing else. The finished shoes, made by another labourer out of leather prepared by others still, are the fruit of strange labour and are acquired immediately by the producer of raw materials only in exchange for his own true product. As is well enough seen and felt when either production or distribution is so blocked that the true immediate product becomes unsalable! By the way, I should make no objection whatever, were Professor Clark content with remarking that the products which the labourer obtains through exchange may be looked upon as, in a certain but less literal sense, *also* the fruit of his labour. Such an observation, for example, would be quite in order, as a refutation of the economically unsound notion that 'the labourer eats his master's bread.' When, however, Professor Clark sets up his thesis avowedly in confutation of the opinion that the product of the labourer is completed only after the lapse of a certain period; when in this connection he holds the commodities obtained through exchange to be the *true* and *immediate* fruit of the labourer's exertions; and when, further, for this way of thinking he claims the monopoly of 'scientific' thinking, – he places himself, as I believe, in direct opposition to the facts in the matter and to scientific truth.

It is very significant that Professor Clark finds himself forced to make one concession whereby he really gainsays his whole theory. Accustomed to take a wide survey of facts, he could not overlook a group of facts which very palpably did not come under his rule. In the following note he has in mind this group: 'In a dynamic condition of society industries are often started that are wholly new. In these cases some time is required before any goods are ready for consumption, and during this interval owners must wait for their expected products. After the series of goods in various stages of advancement has once been established, the normal action of capital is revealed. Thenceforward there is no waiting.'[6] Here, then, Professor Clark instances an exception to his rule. Let us look at this exception somewhat more closely. Above all, note that the exception has a much broader application than Professor Clark declares it to have. For it applies not only to industries newly set up, but to old industries as well, whenever the quantity of a certain product is to be increased, – for instance, to meet a growing demand. When, for example, the normal production of an article has in the past amounted to 30,000 pieces a year, and that amount is to be raised to 40,000 pieces a year, clearly there are ready at our immediate disposal only 30,000 pieces; and for the additional 10,000 pieces obviously we must wait until the whole production-period of the 10,000 pieces has expired, be that period long or short, as mechanical conditions determine.

How, I ask then, according to his theory, will Professor Clark explain away this exception to his rule? If true capital really is, as Professor Clark avers, a thing different from concrete capital goods, and possesses in contradistinction to these the power to 'annihilate' production-periods, why does it manifest this its peculiar power only in a normal, unprogressive state of affairs, and not also in a dynamic economy? I do not know what Professor Clark will say in explanation. To me the matter appears quite clear and simple. Professor Clark's true capital is a mystical conception, manifesting the virtue ascribed to it neither under dynamic nor static conditions. In a static economy the inaccuracy of the Clarkian theory is not palpably exposed for this reason, – that here it is not put to the test. For in a static economy everything runs smoothly because of the harmonious interlocking of the production-periods of the concrete capital goods existing in various stages of completion and *by virtue of these very goods*, just as everything would go on were Professor Clark's theory really true. In any interval of time the concrete production-periods closed are just as many as the new ones begun. So it comes about that at any one time just so many finished products are turned out as enable each producer to exchange his own raw product immediately for the finished product of another's labour. One may therefore, if he will, with theoretical inaccuracy but practically with impunity, imagine that, through some mystical quality of true capital, production-periods have been quite done away with in the world, so that one harvests as the 'true and immediate fruit' of one's *own* labour a something brought to maturity with magic despatch; exactly as I may with theoretical inaccuracy but practically with impunity, ascribe to a talisman worn about my neck the power to save me from drowning so long as I take care not to go in the water. As the power of the talisman is really put to the test first in the water, so is the power of true capital first in a dynamic economy. Here, where concrete capital goods are, as it were, changing their stratification, and production-periods no longer interlock in a perfect circle, it might be demonstrated whether or not true capital has the power ascribed to it, the power to do away with production-periods. Now, Professor Clark, in the example cited above, concedes that his true capital cannot stand this test. Is it, then, an injustice to place this true capital in the same category with the talisman which preserves from drowning only upon dry land?

A theory not borne out by the facts cannot be saved by a metaphor, not even by a metaphor so ingenious and alluring as Professor Clark's waterfall and the single drops of falling water. I believe, too, that on stricter analysis this metaphor itself turns against him, as well as the facts of economic activity. I believe that science has as little need in scientific exposition of a conception of a waterfall different from the conception of falling water as it has for a conception of true capital different from the conception of concrete capital goods. Any physicist would smile, were one to tell him that any of the physical or mechanical effects produced by the waterfall – for example, the driving of the mill, the generation of electrical power, the wearing out of the rocky bed – were not produced by the concrete falling drops of water, but through an apprehensible entity different from these, the 'waterfall.' Whatever the concrete falling of water does not effect is not effected by the 'waterfall.' If by a sudden heavy gust of wind or a displaced stone a single wave of the waterfall is forced somewhat out of its course, so that no 'concrete water' strikes the floats of the mill-wheel placed therein, the mill stops, although the waterfall as a whole has been neither moved from the place nor dried up, nor even lessened in volume.

I have in these lines inveighed at such length and so fiercely against Professor Clark that a false impression might easily be given of the general bearing of our respective opinions, did I not add some further remarks. For I believe we very nearly agree on most concrete questions connected with the theory of capital. I believe that Professor Clark is inclined to concur with me in many concrete deductions from my theory of capital, especially after some misunderstandings are explained; and on my side I can say that I am in full agreement with many of Professor Clark's positive asseverations. Thus I can subscribe almost word for word, especially to the three theses – laid down by Professor Clark at the end of his article – concerning the real character of the 'abstinence' undergone by the one who saves, and concerning the weighing of present assured satisfactions given up against less certain future enjoyments spread through a longer interval of time. And I may add that it is ever a genuine satisfaction to me to find myself in agreement with an author whom I esteem so highly.

But whence comes this strange unison in the midst of dissent? I believe it is owing to an excellence in my esteemed opponent to which I have already once adverted; namely, to his extraordinarily shrewd observation of facts. He has, I think, set up an unfortunate general concept; but his own fine scientific tact happily always keeps him at least from drawing those deductions from his generalization which would bring him into conflict with facts. Arrived at the danger point, either he breaks off his deductions or he evades the issue, as we have seen, by instancing an exception. With himself the error involved always remains a purely Platonic, academic error.

Unhappily, however, it does not remain so for science as a whole; and this it is that has led me to join issue, first and so positively, with the writer among all my critics whose doctrine differs perhaps least from mine in its consequences. In him I combat above all else the dangerous example through the imitation of which his less adroit and wary followers will, or would, do far more harm than he himself. Professor Clark is not the first to seek a conception of capital distinct from the real concrete goods of which capital, in fact, consists; and I fear he will not be the last. He has had forerunners in every decade of this century and among most diverse peoples, – in J.B. Say, in Hermann, in MacLeod, in the Germans Kühnast and Schellwien, and probably in many others too. There seems to dwell in the human heart an enervating proneness for playing the poet in matters of science, and for placing by the side of the common natural things and forces with which we have to do in the world of prose visionary doubles in the form of all sorts of mystical beings and powers, to which a semblance of reality is imparted by means of an 'elegant' abstraction. I hold this practice to be fraught with greatest danger to science. If one departs from the bare truths of nature by only a hair's breadth, scientific accuracy of thought is irretrievably lost; the sway of truth gives place to that of words and sounding phrases. I have expressed my opinion on this subject repeatedly, and without reserve, in my work on Capital and Interest,[7] and I feel bound at this time to repeat it with the greater stress, because I esteem more highly in other matters the authority of the eminent scholar who believes it necessary on this question to take a stand diametrically opposed to mine. It is, indeed, a difference of opinion almost grotesquely intensified, as to which science must judge between us two. Professor Clark has shown such kindly appreciation of all that I have written concerning capital except in this one point only. At this very point, however, he believes that I have turned the whole doctrine of capital into a wrong course. On the other hand, I would believe that, if any modest excellence attaches to my work on the theory of capital, it is this, that I have endeavored to place the conception of capital upon a sound, natural basis, – to write, as it were, a solid natural history of capital in place of a mythology of capital.

Vienna   E. Böhm-Bawerk

NOTES

1. *Yale Review*, November, 1893, pp. 302–15.
2. Strictly speaking, the example chosen by Professor Clark is not a case of comparing present and future *goods*, but only one of comparing present and future *uses* of one and the same sum of wealth. But, since the decisive ideas are the same in both cases, I am perfectly willing to test my theory by this example. I have therefore given the example the form best suited to this purpose.
3. *Positive Theory*, pp. 245 and 247.
4. Ibid.
5. *Yale Review*, November, 1893, p. 303.

6. Ibid., p. 312.
7. See, for example, the *Positive Theory*, p. 58 et seq.; still more emphatically in a passage of my *Geschichte und Kritik der Kapitalzinstheorien* (p. 484 et seq. of the German edition) not contained in the English edition of this work. The notion was involved also in the criticism of a theory of interest recently brought out by the German Schellwien. As I did not imagine that this theory was familiar to the English reading public, or of special interest to it, the whole paragraph referring to the matter was, in accordance with my wish, left out of the English edition. I am almost inclined now to regret this; for Schellwien's theory gives an illustration as instructive as, to my mind, it is deterrent of a case where Professor Clark's fundamental idea, that capital itself must be differentiated from the capital 'goods' of which capital is made up, is used as the basis of reasoning by a somewhat less careful and circumspect writer than Professor Clark.

Eugen von Böhm-Bawerk, 'On The Relationship between the "Third Reason" for Higher Valuation of Present Goods and the Two Other Reasons', [1912], published in E. von Böhm-Bawerk, *Capital and Interest* (South Holland IL: Libertarian Press, 1959), Vol. 3, Essay xii, pp. 150–93, footnotes pp. 235–40.

The German original of this paper was Exkurs XII in the volume entitled *Exkurse zur 'Positiven Theorie des Kapitales'*, containing Eugen von Böhm-Bawerk's detailed, polemical responses to criticisms levelled at his earlier book on capital and interest. The present version is from the English translation by Hans Sennholz of that volume.

Reference in the notes at the end of this paper to other Essays refer to other essays in the volume of Exkurse. When Böhm-Bawerk in his notes refers to 'this edition' of *Positiven Theorie*, he is referring to the third edition together with which this Exkurs was published.

7

On the Relationship between
the 'Third Reason' for Higher Valuation
of Present Goods and
the Two Other Reasons[1]

EUGEN von BÖHM-BAWERK

My 'third reason' pertains to the higher productivity of more time-consuming roundabout methods of production. It attempts to demonstrate this as the most important of several cooperating reasons leading to higher valuation of present goods over future goods and thus to the emergence of interest. As I have repeatedly stated, the facts to which I refer in the deduction of my third reason basically coincide with the very facts on which the once commonly accepted productivity theory exclusively based its explanation of interest, with a few changes in interpretation. And their acceptance is an express or tacit assumption also for the competing use and abstinence theories.[2] I am particularly referring to the fact that utilization or employment of capital leads to higher productivity. Even in the socialist interest theory the higher productivity of production assisted by 'intermediary products' plays a certain role which, of course, is projected in a different light. According to Rodbertus, the first 'economic' condition of interest is the productivity of labour exceeding the absolutely necessary minimum for the sustenance of workers. This excess productivity of labour is to be ascribed, among others, to employment of better production methods and improved tools, which means the technical advantages of 'capitalist' production.[3] In such a situation and in view of the notorious relationship so manifest in real life between the degree of capital productivity and the rate of interest obtainable for the use of capital, it is certainly not surprising if I concede to these facts a prominent

145

place of their own in my explanation of the interest phenomenon. As a matter of fact it would seem inconceivable to most economists if an interest theory were to completely delete from its list of interest causes the higher productivity of capitalist production methods.[4]

The capital theory is full of surprises. And it is one of the strangest and thereby most interesting surprises that several distinguished scholars, noted for their theoretical sagacity, recently have directed their criticisim against just this part of my explanation of interest. Irving Fisher and Bortkiewicz both deny the validity of my 'third reason.' Without denying the facts to which I refer[5] Bortkiewicz believes he must doubt 'that this fact can contribute to the explanation of interest.'[6] Fisher, on the other hand, arrives at the statement that I demonstrated correctly the value superiority of present goods over future goods, but 'the result ... has nothing whatever to do with that assumption (that longer methods of production lead generally to a greater output).'[7] Thus both writers omit the higher productivity of capitalist production methods from the list of causative factors of interest. And both endeavor to prove that only due to an error of logic could I concede a place on this list to technology. In reality, what I ascribe to my 'third reason' as its specific effect on the value supremecy of present goods is said to constitute merely an effect of the first or second reason.

The circumstance that these objections do not pertain to accuracy or inaccuracy of facts, but rather to trains of thought, has lent a peculiar character to the polemics. It has become unusually abstract and difficult. I consider its development to be one of the most irksome on a generally irksome road, partially due, no doubt, to the material. Discussions on formal cogency of thought dealing with a subject of greatest material difficulty require, from the outset, every kind of polemic sagacity and subtlety. But the participants in the dispute have added another factor. I doubt that all the polemics could have developed without a certain pleasure in artificial dialectics and sophistical paradoxes. At any rate, so much of this has entered the dispute that one of my opponents has gained the impression he was accused of arguing with 'scholastic reasons.'[8] To be sure he then announces he is opposing 'scholasticism with scholasticism.'

The reader may judge this for himself later. I would like to make one remark in advance. I do not believe that any reader or opponent of mine doubts in the least that the phenomenon of interest would vanish, or at least be seriously affected in scope and extent, if the fact of higher productivity of capitalist production methods would suddenly cease to exist. If this is correct, we can hardly assume that the one who searches for a natural relationship between this fact and the phenomenon of interest must resort to 'scholastic reasons.' Rather, we may judge it as an indication that the neglect of this relationship must lead to artificial reasoning. I shall demonstrate this at the proper place.

Fisher and Bortkiewicz concur in a certain point of conclusion. They both agree that my 'third reason' must be eliminated from the list of reasons for the value supremacy of present goods. But they differ essentially in detail and especially in the manner of presentation. No matter how we may judge Fisher's conclusions he attempts a broad and productive critique. He is not content with raising objections, but seeks to find his way out and gain clarity on the doubtful points. The result is that he does not want to abandon much of the content of the disputed theory, but merely would like to alter the systematic arrangement of the thoughts appealed to for the solution of the interest problem. He embarks upon an exceedingly interesting attempt at finding a simplifying and 'successful generalization' which in my preface[9] I myself had declared to be the goal of the future development. Bortkiewicz, on the other hand, apparently made only the negative part of critique his task. He does this so exclusively that he reminds us of the trial lawyer who is more interested in an accumulation of numerous objections than in their clarification. At any rate, he took less pains on what I just called 'finding his way out' than on raising objections, leaving much to be desired on the fruitfulness of his critique. Because of their different presentations I shall present them separately in my reply. I shall begin with the chronologically earlier expositions by Bortkiewicz.

A. Bortkiewicz

This writer[10] first describes my demonstration of the higher valuation of present means of production as presented on page 274 ff. of the second edition of *Positive Theory of Capital*,[11] in the following abstract: 'He (Böhm-Bawerk) compares *several producers*[12] of whom the *first* possesses a certain quantity of means of production in the present, the *second* the same quantity one year hence, the *third* two years hence. The greater productivity of the more time-consuming production methods finds expression in the fact that the *various producers* can supply unequal product quantities at the same point of time, whereby the *first* will always enjoy an advantage over the second, the second over the third, etc. In his *Positive Theory of Capital* he illustrates this situation by Table 1. [*Corresponding to table on p. 272 in this edition.*]

TABLE I
PRODUCT UNITS YIELDED DURING ECONOMIC YEAR
BY ONE LABOR MONTH OF THE YEAR

Economic Year	1888	1889	1890	1891
1888	100	—	—	—
1889	200	100	—	—
1890	280	200	100	—
1891	350	280	200	100
1892	400	350	280	200
1893	440	400	350	280
1894	470	440	400	350
1895	500	470	440	400"

Bortkiewicz unfortunately confuses the issue right from the beginning by making an imputation contrary to the text – an act derogatory of his critical conscientiousness. Its origin is an entire mystery to me. In the passage quoted above he makes me compare 'several' 'different' producers. I submit, on the other hand, that my text contains nothing upon which to base this conjecture. On the contrary, I repeated frequently and explicitly that the comparison pertains to means of production invested in various years and in the possession of 'one and the same person.'[13] Indeed, the crucial point in my argumentation[14] is the identity of the person for whom the valuation comparison of various obtainable products is made. This error is all the more inexplicable as Bortkiewicz literally quotes[15] the passage in which I applied the comparison to 'one and the same person' with great logical emphasis and clarity of expression. With a little control over his own objections he should have noticed the conflict of his assumption with the text.

During the course of his polemics Bortkiewicz repeatedly resumes this erroneous imputation.[16] Therefore I believe I need not answer arguments materially based on this imputation since they are devoid of all application. I rather shall deal only with that part of his argumentation that can be treated independently of this error although it may still be affected by it. His by far most interesting objection, noticed also by other theorists, fortunately belongs to this part.

Bortkiewicz presents it as follows. At first in a long quotation he cites my explanatory expositions following the foregoing table on pages 276 to 278 of the second edition of my *Positive Theory of Capital*.[17] He then proceeds:

'So much by Böhm-Bawerk. Above all his table which is his basis for the foregoing explanation requires a correction which on first glance may appear unimportant, but in reality in very essential. Böhm–Bawerk fails to state whether the numerical series in each column must be thought of as continuous or terminating. Naturally we must assume the latter since the prolongation of the production period is limited already for physical reasons. Indeed it is irrelevant for the main question discussed here whether the series comes to an end after 7, 8 or 20 years. Therefore, let us assume that production can require no additional number of years than provided for in Böhm-Bawerk's schedule. This is 7 years.'

'Now we cannot assume that the plans of various producers do not cover more than 7 years from the present (1888). The one, for instance, who will be able to dispose of one labour month only in 1889 will anticipate already today, in 1888, that he can obtain 500 product units in 1896. The one who will have one labour month in 1890 will assume that in 1896 he can produce 470 and in 1897 500 units. If we add these considerations to the table, it will be modified as shown in Table II.

'If we now compare the production returns of one labour month from 1888 with one from 1889, etc., we can no longer maintain that the older means of production in every conceivable employment yield more consumers' goods than the newer means, thus giving rise to a surplus of value. For 100 is indeed more than 0, 200 more than 100, 500 more than 470. But if we compare, for instance, one labour month from 1888 with one from 1889, we must add 0 on the one side, and 500 on the other. The conclusion would then not be cogent if we do not know the value relationship between the annual outputs of consumers' goods.'

'But we may also conduct the comparison in a diagonal way. Then we

TABLE II

PRODUCT UNITS YIELDED DURING ECONOMIC YEAR
BY ONE LABOR MONTH OF THE YEAR

Economic Year	1888	1889	1890	1891
1888	100	—	—	—
1889	200	100	—	—
1890	280	200	100	—
1891	350	280	200	100
1892	400	350	280	200
1893	440	400	350	280
1894	470	440	400	350
1895	500	470	440	400
1896	—	500	470	440
1897	—	—	500	470
1898	—	—	—	500

149

actually arrive at equal product quantities produced in different periods of time. The question is whether these temporal differences affect our valuations. The answer obviously depends on whether we recognize the causes which, according to Böhm-Bawerk, determine the value difference between present and future consumers' goods. Thus, in my belief, we must go back to the first two causes of interest.'

'This fact should not surprise us. For according to the marginal utility theory, the means of production receive value from their consumption goods for whose production they are used. Thus if means of production from different periods are concerned we must assume that value differences between them can arise only insofar as their consumers' goods are produced in different periods of time. If, for the sake of argument, we eliminate time as a value factor for consumers' goods, it loses its significance also for producers' goods. This can be readily seen as soon as we conduct the comparison between the respective outputs as described above, that is, in a descending sequence of diagonals.'

'We will also be soon convinced if we compare figures on the same horizontal line. The *plus* and *minus* deviations will then balance each other out. Böhm-Bawerk conducts his comparison in this very fashion, but he arrives at a different result because he arbitrarily and, unsuitably for the problem, interrupts the series to be compared. He makes the farthest point of the respective production periods coincide with the farthest point of the period covered by the economic plan of the producer. He does this without mention of any reasons.'

The crucial point of our dispute is designated correctly in the introductory and concluding words of this long polemic. It pertains to the justification and the meaning of 'interruption' of the numerical series included in the table of comparison. It is evident that the comparison cannot be continued into infinity, that it must be interrupted somewhere. It is also self-explanatory that the *absolute* length of the compared series is entirely unimportant and that it is 'irrelevant' whether we terminate the series with 7, 8, or 20 years. But it is most decisive – which Bortkiewicz has perceived correctly – whether the last compared year, no matter what its absolute figure may be, is assumed to lie within or beyond a certain limit *in its relationship to other suppositions.*

According to Bortkiewicz, the seventh year, with which I conclude my schematic comparison, designates the outer limit to which the *prolongation of the roundabout way of production* can be continued.[18] And he maintains that the schematic comparison must extend beyond this outer limit. In other words, he wants to include valuation figures deduced from productive utilizations in which the higher productivity of longer production processes can no longer play a role. And this in turn means he wants production plans and productive utilizations no longer enjoying the advantage of higher productivity of longer production methods to enter into the role of the plans and utilizations that determine the valuation of our means of production. This, however, is a supposition which I can maintain is 'unsuitable for the problem' and conflicts with the suppositions under which we must analyze it.

The view that Bortkiewicz's supposition does not suit the investigation of our controversial problem cannot be better introduced than by an affirmative presentation of the object of inquiry for which it would actually be suitable. This is the illustration of a state of affars in which an economy is so saturated with present goods that no lengthening of roundabout methods leading to higher productivity is obstructed by an insufficient supply of present goods. Only under this condition could we responsibly design production plans and dispose of our means of production by applying them to the provision for wants that lie beyond the temporal zone within which roundabout methods lead to higher productivity. Then also our valuation of producers' goods could be deduced from such reasonable employments (for we never value our producers' goods on grounds of employments that are unreasonable and economically out of the question; but according to the law of marginal utility we value them on grounds of the economically *last* permissible, that is, economically *permissible* employment). Then indeed it would be conceivable, which Bortkiewicz demonstrates correctly, that we value two non-synchronal quantities of producers' goods (e.g. one month of labour from the year 1888 and one month from 1889) as means for the attainment of the *same maximum quantity of products* that can be produced with the longest technically still advantageous method. Then an eventual difference in the valuation of both can no longer result from a difference in the *product quantity* they yield, but merely from the difference in the *period of time* in which they yield identical quantities. Then indeed a value supremacy of the older (present) means of production is feasible only if either my 'first' or 'second reason' independently establishes this priority, that is, if we would prefer to obtain the same product already one year earlier because of an unfavourable state of demand and supply that arose for other independent reasons, or because of the intervention of psychological causes for a lower valuation of the future.

It will hardly have escaped attentive readers that I did not maintain my thesis – that the higher productivity of longer roundabout methods of production lends value supremacy to present means of production over future means – for such a situation. I rather base my thesis on the opposite assumption which from the outset has been the centerpoint of my train of thought and which I later repeated with the greatest possible emphasis on every occasion. This is the assumption that the supply of present goods does *not* suffice for a complete realization of all lengthenings leading to higher productivity. Already in my first edition I explained the emergence of the agio on present goods with the express intermediary condition that it must arise from the quantitative superiority of the demand for present goods over their supply. And I already offered reasons for this fact, observable in every economy, in my first edition in the following words: 'Even in the wealthiest nation, supply is limited by the momentary state of wealth. Demand, however, is practically boundless; at any rate it extends as far as productivity can be enhanced by a lengthening of the production process. Even in the richest nation this limit lies far beyond its present wealth.'[19]

Bortkiewicz wants me to conduct the comparison under the supposition that the employments from which we deduce our decisive valuations of means of production extend beyond the zone of higher productivity of longer roundabout methods. Now what does this expectation mean? It means that I am to verify my thesis under assumptions for which I did not advance it. It means that first I am to exclude the efficacy of my reason through the assumption of special circumstances, but then prove it positively. Or, it means that I am to investigate and prove the influence of unused opportunities of technically more productive method lengthenings on the value supremacy of present goods under the supposition that no such unused opportunities still exist![20]

My analysis was to prove whether and how the availability of unused opportunities for technically more productive process lengthenings can and must exert an influence on the emergence of interest. Therefore it certainly was neither 'arbitrary' nor 'unsuitable for the problem,' but rather required by its very nature, that I mentioned the case in question in my suppositions and that in the unavoidable 'interruption' of my series I assumed the border of the higher productivity zone to lie beyond and not before my point of interruption. For in reality the period of time for whose wants we plan to provide through the use of our means of production and which can exert an influence on our valuations of producers' goods, never and nowhere extends beyond the zone of higher productivity of longer roundabout methods. We will observe that in economic calculations we never make investments for the sake of[21] wants that lie beyond this zone. We will nowhere experience consciously employing our means of production in such a way that their yield will benefit remoter wants if postponement of the yield does not promise a quantitive increase. Under certain conditions our providential production plans pertain to very remote periods in the future, for instance, to one hundred years hence in the case of replanting a lot of oak-forest cleared of timber having a 100 year turnover. But we never go any further than the point at which the last increase of duration is accompanied by an increase in productivity. No rational forester will extend the period of turnover beyond 200 years if the natural limit of wooded growth of his trees lies at 200.[22]

But why do we not go beyond this zone in our production plans? I am fully aware that also this question must be raised and answered. For if we do not go beyond merely because we are fundamentally prevented by another of my three reasons, then Bortkiewicz's expectation may still have some justification. Its formulation, indeed, would still be erroneous, but some problems would remain unclarified.

The situation is quite different, however. We refrain from expanding our reasonable production plans beyond the zone of advantageous production lengthenings *not only* because one of my other reasons would fundamentally prevent it, that is, because psychological reasons make us disregard or at least discount future wants, or because as I indicated earlier in my distinction between the 'first' and 'third reason' on page 278 of *Positive Theory of Capital*, 'differences in the situations of supply on account of *other causes*' would force us to limit our productive provisions exclusively to immediate want periods. But on page 277 ff. of *Positive Theory of Capital* I endeavoured to demonstrate by way of a countertest that even if the two other reasons were not effective the fact of higher productivity of longer roundabout methods would bring about such changes in the hitherto existing evenness of supply, in valuations and adaptations of production decisions to the new situation, that this alone would lead to the value supremacy of present goods over future goods. This is a test that, in my belief, entitles me to maintain that my third reason borrows its validity neither from the psychological causes of lower valuation of future wants, nor from 'differences in the situations of supply on account of *other causes*' (first reason).

I shall analyze all this with the greatest possible accuracy further below in a different connection. Essentially the same objection returns with Irving Fisher. But in line with his straight and comprehensible train of thought it is better elaborated and less tarnished by irrelevant dialectic admixtures which often and annoyingly bar Bortkiewicz's way to truth. Thus we shall again encounter the most interesting kernel of the dispute in an environment that is more suited to its clarification. In the meanwhile I shall just proceed to cut my way through some dialectic underwood in which Bortkiewicz has entangled the main problem.

In his polemics described above, Bortkiewicz maintained that 'we are free' to conduct the schematic comparison differently, *namely declining by diagonals*.[23] Then we will always arrive at equal product quantities which, however, mature in different periods. Certainly 'we are free' to do this as Bortkiewicz states with rather obscure logic. For why would we not compare the dates of the diagonals? But it is also certain that we are *not* free to compare the diagonals *only* if the purpose is a *value* examination. Then we must compare diagonal *and* horizontal lines. For the diagonal line merely shows the results which the units of producers' goods available in different periods of time and whose values we compare may yield at *identical technical employment*. The diagonal line showing 350, for instance, in Bortkiewicz's scheme merely indicates the yields which the compared labour months would have in a three-year production period at identical technical employment. The diagonal line of 500 indicates the seven-year yield at identical technical employment. But according to the basic supposition which undoubtedly concurs with everyday life the units of producers' goods permit different ways of utilization. If we 'interrupt' our example at the 7th year, for instance, every labour month permits at least eight different ways of utilization, that is, production for the present, for one year hence, two years hence, etc., up through seven years hence. Now the value of a good that can be employed in different ways is derived from the most valuable possibility of all employments.[24] If we want to compare the value of several such goods, we must make sure that we compare the most valuable employment to which the good can be allocated. The 'diagonal' comparison by no means assures this, though it *may* do it *by coincidence* provided all compared goods find utilization in the same one of eight possible ways of employment. But this is neither inevitable nor even probable.[25] In order to conduct the comparison on a correct and safe basis we must proceed the way I did on pp. 275–77 of my *Positive Theory of Capital*. First we must determine which one of the possible employments is the most valuable one for each good compared. Then we must compare these various most valuable employments with each other. The coherence of this procedure requires that we conduct the comparison on horizontal as well as diagonal lines.

We can demonstrate in still another way, perhaps even more drastically, that a value comparison on 'diagonal' lines only is not permissible. Bortkiewicz undoubtedly agrees with me that value always results from the relationship between the state of demand and supply. And we hardly need mention that we must compare wants and supplies as they actually relate to each other, without arbitrary additions or deletions on the part of one or the other. It is obvious that it would signify a falsification of facts and results if we were to compare all the wants with, let us say, *half* the supply, or vice versa. We can neither omit a want that actually belongs to those demanding gratifications, nor add one that does not belong to them. And on the side of supply we can neither ignore a satisfaction offered by it, nor add one. But it can be readily seen that this very error is committed in a 'diagonal' value comparison. Indeed it is committed one-sidedly, irrelevantly, and to the detriment of one of the two quantities of means of production whose values we compare.

For example, let us compare the value of a labour month from 1888 with that of a month from 1889 according to the 'diagonal method.' As Bortkiewicz correctly remarked, we will always arrive at the same figure, for instance at 470 on both sides, or 500 on both sides. But how do we arrive at 470 on both sides? We arrive at this result when we consider not only the yield of 470, which a labour month invested in 1889 will have in 1895 after a six-year production period, but also the wants of 1895. Thus we assume that the valuing individual includes the wants of 1895 in his sphere of economic consideration. But if we assume this, how can we make him interrupt his comparative valuation of the labour month of 1888 at the wants of 1894 and the production figure 470 which the 1888 month can yield in a six-year production period? Either . . . or! Either the wants of 1895 find consideration and influence our valuation and thus are a part in the decisive 'state of wants' – or they are not. If they are included then they naturally must also be included for the valuation of a labour month from 1888. And we may not overlook that a labour month from 1888 may yield a product of 500 in a seven-year production period, which is *more* than the yield of the 1889 labour month. Or they are not included. But then they cannot be included for the labour month from 1889. Then also the yield of 470, which this labour month can have merely for a period from which no economic wants are considered, will be out of the question. If the last wants finding economic consideration are those of 1894, then the greatest possible yield of the 1889 labour month for the wants of 1894 is 440 obtainable from a five-year production period. We may take any class of wants as the last one being included in our valuation and economic calculation, but it always must be *one* 'final' class, and not two different classes simultaneously. The 'diagonal' comparison, however, illogically and contradictorily includes two different ultimate classes.[26]

Bortkiewicz advances still another syllogism aimed at refuting my belief in the independent efficacy of my 'third reason.' He states the following:[27]

'Böhm-Bawerk leads us back especially to the 'first reason' of interest. And that this 'first' reason instead of his 'third' is concerned can best be seen from a consideration of a special case the peculiarity of which consists of the fact that we cannot choose the length of the production period. Let us assume, for instance, that in Böhm-Bawerk's table a seven-year production period is given by the state of technology. Then all the returns that are smaller than 500 must be replaced by zero. A comparison, for instance, between an 1888 and an 1889 labour month would show zero up to the economic period 1894, and for 1895 500 on one side and zero on the other, and 500 on both sides for all later periods.'

'Now if we conduct the comparison with Böhm-Bawerk in a fallacious manner, i.e. if we disregard the years 1896, 1897, etc., then also in this special case, which is also the marginal case, the value supremacy of an older means of production arises entirely independently of the supposition that longer production periods are more productive. This very applicability of Böhm-Bawerk's reasoning to this special case, from which everything connected with various lengths of the production period has been eliminated, offers cogent proof that his chain of reasoning cannot be as complete as it is supposed to be according to Böhm-Bawerk.'[28]

This rather perplexing and obviously twisted train of thought is probably based on the following notion: My table is to demonstrate that the higher productivity of longer roundabout methods lends value supremacy to older (present) means of production over new (future) means. As opposed to this Bortkiewicz wants to demonstrate with an 'example' that according to my table the same result is obtained[29] even if the length of the production period is definitely given by the state of technology, consequently if every influence of selection of various method lengths is completely eliminated. From this he infers that the higher productivity of longer roundabout methods of production to which I appeal cannot be the true cause of higher value.

First, the 'example' construed by Bortkiewicz – for he says, 'let us assume for example,' – in reality is *no example*, but the carefully sought for *only* case that does not contradict outright his argumentation. *Every* other figure selected to demonstrate the peculiarity of absence of choice would have failed immediately. In every case of given production length of *less* or *more* than seven years the compared labour months of 1888 and 1889 would have yielded equal returns. That is to say, in the case of shorter duration they would have yielded equal effective returns (e.g. 200 units in a one-year production period, 470 units in a six-year period), and in the case of more than seven years, zero. Thus every figure other than 7, which Bortkiewicz claims to take as an 'example,' would have revealed the *relevance* of my third reason. If we include the third reason in our supposition or the freedom of choice between production periods of various lengths and productivities respectively, the value supremacy of older means of production emerges as demonstrated in my table. If we eliminate it, equality instead of supremacy will result.

Secondly, it depends on what kind of requirements Bortkiewicz's syllogism makes on its logical premises: In order to demonstrate the insignificance of my third reason does it suffice to show a few 'negative instances' in which the value supremacy of present goods emerges even without my third reason? This indeed would be the same logic as if we were to maintain that rain has nothing to do with the streets getting wet, for there are cases when the streets get wet without rain, such as the department of sanitation seeing that they are washed.

My thesis does not propose that my third reason is the *only* feasible reason for the value supremacy of present goods, in which case a single negative instance indeed would suffice for its refutation. But it offers three independent reasons for this value supremacy. Therefore it is self evident that one of the two other reasons can bring about this supremacy without any cooperation of the third reason. Bortkiewicz did not need to take the pains to construe this artificial 'special case' to seek a case of this kind. In my own text he could have found the frequent acknowledgment that there are numerous cases of this kind. Indeed I named a great number of typical situations, which by no means exhaust the case, but which have in common that the higher value of present goods may emerge without the cooperation of my third reason.[30] Therefore it is not at all surprising, according to my own theory, that in a concrete case value supremacy of older labour months results even after the elimination of the third reason from the actual suppositions, provided of course the case is such that the older month yields 500 product units for its respective wants, and the new month *nothing*. In order to deduce correctly the irrelevance of my third reason Bortkiewicz would have to maintain and prove another more exacting premise. That is to say, he would have to prove that the allegedly irrelevant cooperation of the third reason is superfluous not only in this or that case in which the value supremacy of present goods is assured by other qualities of the case; but he would have to prove that it can be eliminated in *all* cases without affecting the result. Such an analysis, however, would prove the opposite as I demonstrated above.

Thus Bortkiewicz fundamentally misjudged the logical requirements of his syllogism. And I think I am justified in saying that he could hardly have hidden the fallaciousness of his reasoning from himself if he had attempted to describe his train of thought in clear and straight expressions. In plain language he would never have dared maintain that a single case of value supremacy without the cooperation of my third reason would justify the conclusion that the third reason cannot bring about such a value supremacy. All the ambiguity of a 'special case' presented as an 'example' and the obscurity of his phrases such as the 'applicability' of my train of thought 'that cannot render the service which it is supposed to render according to Böhm-Bawerk's theory,' probably was needed in order to present his syllogism merely with the appearance of cogency.

I should like to remark only in passing that Bortkiewicz erroneously considers it a basic supposition in my theory that different methods with different degrees of productivity *must be applied* simultaneously.[31] I merely postulated that different methods are *available for selection*. The fact that they are simultaneously applied by various producers is irrelevant for me. In economic life it indeed is inconceivable that a method that is better for changed circumstances is adopted simultaneously by all producers. But this is no necessary assumption for my conclusions. Bortkiewicz could hardly have overlooked this fact if he had borne in mind my expositions on pp. 414–24 of the second edition,[32] for instance, where Table III and the supplementary contents assume and illustrate the adoption of a *single* production method as the best. Table IV, however, not only assumes the existence of two different methods, but even requires them. But Table IV is clearly described as pertaining to the peculiarity of a special situation.

Finally, in a long polemic, Bortkiewicz turns against the 'thesis of chronic capital scarcity' which he ascribes to me.[33] He indulges in a great many speculations on what I could *not* have meant with this phrase, what I actually meant, and what I *should* have meant. I reject summarily both polemics and speculations. For it is strange that Bortkiewicz deletes the very meaning I gave to the term with, in my belief, unmistakable clarity and explicitness. As far as the term 'scarcity of capital' is concerned it is no exact term coined for my own theory, as Bortkiewicz seems to assume.[34] On the contrary, I declared repeatedly that this is a common term of everyday language which is not entirely correct. For in all those problems where this term plays a role it is not capital in the technological sense that matters, but the *means of subsistence*.[35] But this formal difference which Bortkiewicz probably overlooked,[36] or at least ignored, is not so important because true capital constitutes a part, indeed a very important part, of the supply of subsistence as I precisely pointed out in my *Positive Theory of Capital (pp. 96 ff.)*. Therefore after I had questioned the correctness of the term in everyday language I could use it myself wherever nothing depended on its minute exactness.

Regarding our subject, I understood 'capital scarcity' to mean a state of affairs in which the *supply of subsistence* in an economy does not suffice for a realization of all available technically advantageous production lengthenings. Thus we must select the most productive from the great number of productive ways of utilization. This selection then leads to an agio on present goods. Like a red thread this thought goes through the whole book which makes concrete references almost superfluous. But I should like to point out expressly the anticipating remark in Note 9 to Book II, Chapter II, and the successive later full discussion of the 'market of general means and subsistence' in my *Positive Theory of Capital (pp. 336–56 of the 2nd edition, pp. 525–44 of 3rd edition, pp. 391–405 of 4th edition, and pp. 310–20 of this edition).* Furthermore, I should like to point out the detailed presentation in my 'Strittige Fragen,' especially p. 25 ff. As Bortkiewicz's polemics do not include my true opinion it is of little use to enter upon it in detail. I merely should like to emphasize that I must reject any association with, in my belief, neither fortunate, nor intelligible thoughts presented by Bortkiewicz on pp. 966–70 of his essay on 'capital scarcity' which he assumes must or ought to concur 'reasonably' with my own.

B. Irving Fisher

Fisher builds his critique in an orderly sequence of points that greatly enhances the clarity and perspicuity of argumentation.[37] I enjoy following his example all the more because there are various closely related trains of thought that often overlap but never coincide and thus invite confusion. The best safeguard against this seems to be to limit oneself to an exhaustive analysis of separate trains of thought, instead of trying to cope with everything at once.

Fisher presents his critique of my theory in four approximations, each dealt with in a section (*sections 4–7*) of Chapter IV of 'Böhm-Bawerk's Theory.' First I should like to follow him in these approximations and then in my fifth approximation I shall endeavour to pursue the matter positively, especially clarifying the significance of both our thoughts in a supplementary critique of Fisher's attempt at solution.

1. Fisher's section 4 and mathematical appendix

Like Bortkiewicz, Fisher begins his critique with my tables on pp. 275–7 (*pp. 281–5 of the second edition*). He concedes that the result is correct but believes that 'Böhm-Bawerk is mistaken in ascribing any part of the result to the fact that the longer processes are the more productive.' For in my tables I allegedly assume the existence of one or both of the *other* two factors (relative overprovision for the future or undervaluation of the future). But it can be demonstrated, according to Fisher, that it is *these* factors, and they alone, that bring about the value advantage of present goods demonstrated by the tables. Emphatically repeating this thought he states that 'the result does not at all follow from the single assumption that longer methods of production lead generally to a greater output. It has nothing whatever to do with that assumption.'[38]

In his evidence for this statement he presents the following arguments which I readily admit are entirely correct. If only the figures of the fourth column of my tables ('reduced marginal utility') demonstrate a given tendency to decline (5, 3.8, 3, 2.2), the value advantage of older labour months must emerge as the final result of the tabular comparison, no matter what the return figures of the second column may be. The same result would follow even if the productivity of the longer processes does not increase, but declines, and even if productivity increases initially and then declines (e.g. 100, 200, 230, 200, 100, etc.). In an appendix called 'Mathematical Refutation of Böhm-Bawerk's Claim as to Ground of Preference for Present over Future Investment Labor' he gives his demonstration the following general algebraic formulation:[39]

'Let the products obtainable by processes of 1, 2, 3, etc. years be p_1, p_2, p_3, etc., and the "marginal utilities reduced in perspective" beginning in 1888 be u_1, u_2, u_3, etc. Then,

A Month's Labour Available

		in 1888 yields			in 1889 yields	
For the economic period	Units of product	Marginal utility reduced in persp.	Amount of value of entire product	Units	Marg. utility	Value
1888	p_1	u_1	$p_1\ u_1$	—	u_1	—
1889	p_2	u_2	$p_2\ u_2$	p_1	u_2	$p_1\ u_2$
1890	p_3	u_3	$p_3\ u_3$	p_2	u_3	$p_2\ u_3$
1891	p_4	u_4	$p_4\ u_4$	p_3	u_4	$p_3\ u_4$
etc.	etc.	etc.	etc.	etc.	etc.	etc.

'We shall show that the labour available in 1888 is more valuable than that in 1889, provided only $u_1 > u_2 > u_3 > u_4$, etc.; that is, that the maximum of the first series of pu's, relating to 1888, is greater than the maximum of the second series, relating to 1889 (assuming of course that maxima exist). To prove this, select the maximum of the second series. Suppose it to be p_3u_4. This is necessarily less than p_3u_3 in the first series; for since $u_4 < u_3$ by hypothesis, it follows that $p_3u_4 < p_3u_3$. That is, there necessarily exists in the first series a term greater than the greatest term in the second series. A fortiori must the greatest term in the first series exceed the greatest in the second series. In other words, the value for 1888 exceeds that for 1889, provided only the marginal utilities descend, whether or not the productivities ascend.'

I am not at all surprised that this splendid argumentation impressed not only its author but also many readers as being quite compelling and cogent.[40] And yet it has its weakness.

I shall first demonstrate this summarily at the result and then explain it in detail by additional comments. I should like to reverse Fisher's logical procedure against me and claim it fully for myself. Applying the very algebraic analysis which, according to Fisher, demonstrates so cogently the fallaciousness of my theory of the cause of higher valuation of older labour months I shall demonstrate its very correctness. I shall use Fisher's own words, numbers, formulas, and trains of thought, and merely change the premise of his hypothesis. I shall make no assumption regarding the rank of marginal utility (u_1, u_2, etc.) and merely assume that (in accordance with my thesis) the yield of a longer production period is always greater than that of a shorter period. In other words, $p_2 > p_1$, $p_3 > p_2$, $p_4 > p_3$, etc. Let me cite Fisher's conclusion in his own words: 'Select the maximum of the second series. Suppose it to be p_3u_4. This is necessarily less than p_4u_4 in the first series; for since $p_3 < p_4$ by hypothesis, it follows that $p_3u_4 < p_4u_4$. That is, there necessarily exists in the first series a term greater than the greatest term in the second series. A *fortiori* must the *greatest* term in the first series exceed the greatest in the second series. In other words, the value for 1888 exceeds that for 1889, provided only the productivities ascend, whether or not the marginal utilities descend.'

Thus the conclusion literally proves the correctness of my thesis.

Let me comment on this perhaps rather surprising result. Fisher erred regarding the scope of his premises. He erred asserting that the conclusions drawn from his premises refute my evidence and even the content of my theory. In reality, in spite of its forceful impression, it merely forces an open door. His correct train of argumentation proves nothing more nor less than a self-evident fact which has never been denied and which surprises nobody. This is the fact that in all cases where one of two other reasons for the value advantage of present goods is effective, the emergence of the advantage is assured regardless of whether the third reason does or does not play a role. If u continually increases in rank because of the first or second or both reasons, higher valuation of present goods naturally must take place no matter whether or not, in accordance with the third reason, the return figures of longer production methods increase, like the pavement getting wet when it is sprinkled no matter whether or not it rains.

But what is the significance of this conclusion which is as correct as it is self-evident?

Fisher could have maintained justifiably that examples of such a nature are unsuited, or at least not suited without further ado, to test affirmatively the independent efficacy of the third reason. I readily admit that emergence of the value advantage under such assumptions leading to higher valuation already on account of other causes constitutes no cogent proof for the asserted influence of higher productivity, at least so long as we do not methodologically elaborate or refine the test.[41] If Fisher had been satisfied with objecting that my presentation, as far as its premise assumes the efficacy of the first and second reasons, is not conclusive for an independent influence of the third reason, I could but fullheartedly agree with him.

But that a certain contention is not proven affirmatively by a certain analysis (actually by a certain part of an analysis), or that the contention itself is fallacious and proven to be so are two different things. Fisher's train of thought in the first approximation, and especially in his mathematical appendix, does not contain anything that could support a conclusion of the latter. For the fact that a certain circumstance (in our case the higher productivity of longer production methods) can be an independent cause of a certain result is neither proven nor disproven if the result can come about also without this certain circumstance provided other sufficient causes of the same result are involved. (The assertion that rain wets the pavement is certainly not refuted by evidence of the pavement getting wet also without rain.) But we must test whether or not the effect sets in while all other possible causes are eliminated.

Fisher's first approximation does not even deal with this test. Instead of carefully clarifying the much narrower scope of his first approximation, Fisher throws in some remarks that are bound to create the impression that he considers already this part a refutation of my theory. He expressly gives his appendix the presumptuous title of 'mathematical refutation' of my thesis on the cause of higher valuation of present labour. It cannot be surprising therefore that his readers also gain the strong but fallacious impression that his irrefutable logic actually explodes a contention of mine. In reality, he presents an inoffensive truth which both of us readily acknowledge.

But if Fisher's first approximation does not explode my actual contention, does it not refute something I said in behalf of its verification? This, too, is not the case. The attentive reader will notice the following. Above all I did not only appeal to this *one* schematic example for the numerical verification of my thesis which I presented and proved at first in general terms (*p. 277 ff. of second edition, p. 272 ff. of this edition*) and against which Fisher objects that I presuppose the two other reasons of higher valuation. Repeatedly and explicitly I appealed to the fact (*pp. 280, 283*) that the schematic comparison must lead us to the same result 'at every conceivable state of subjective valuation' and 'at every possible numerical assumption of product quantity and unit value during the various years.' And I asked the reader to vary at random the numerical assumptions (*p. 280*). My present experience with Fisher, however, shows that it would have been more prudent on my part if I had conducted the demonstration in detail with figures, instead of offering evidence merely in general terms. I should have included also those cases in which the marginal utility does not decline continuously, but is assumed to rise or vary. This would undoubtedly have exploded Fisher's objection right from the outset. But, of course, it does not change the matter how and in what detail I have presented the thought appealed to in the text. The presentation becomes broader, but the logic does not change or improve when the numerical examples I offer as evidence are actually produced in all detail. It is decisive however, whether or not they show the result claimed by the author when analyzed in detail. And this is actually the case as we shall clearly see a little further below.

Besides, I introduced the cooperation of the 'first two reasons,' against which Fisher objects, merely at the very outset (*pp. 281–283*). But throughout the presentation (*beginning with page 284 of the second edition*) I successively eliminated it. I explicitly offered reasons for this procedure. At the beginning I introduced the cooperation of the first two reasons in order to make the illustration rather 'true to life' (*p. 284*). Because in real life the first and second reason are always operative, I allowed for their cooperation in the figures representing marginal utility which in our example forms a declining series. I thus made *this initial part* of my numerical analysis very illustrative, but not cogent. I was fully aware of this circumstance and the fact that I had assumed the efficacy of the two other causes of higher valuation (*p. 284*). Actual proof therefore that the 'third reason' acts independently of the two other reasons was offered merely in the concluding part of my presentation where I finally eliminated the cooperation of the two other reasons from my assumptions (*pp. 284–286*). That part of my presentation against which Fisher raises his objections of his 'first approximation' was supposed to offer no evidence at all.[42]

In order to remove all possibility of doubt let us demonstrate a few numerical examples. In Table 1 I should like to illustrate the effect of a continuous *increase* of the marginal utility from 5 to 5.7. In the next table I shall demonstrate the effect of its *initial increase* from 5 to 8 and *later successive decline* to 4.

As must be expected both tables, in spite of their diverging assumptions of the state and trend of marginal utility show greater value maxima emphasized by boldface for the older 1888 labour month than for the 1889 month: 2850 and 2800 as compared with 2679 and 2450.

TABLE I
A MONTH'S LABOUR AVAILABLE

For the economic period	Product units	Marginal utility	Value	Product Units	Marginal utility	Value
		in 1888 yields			*in 1889 yields*	
1888	100	5.0	500	—	5.0	—
1889	200	5.1	1020	100	5.1	510
1890	280	5.2	1456	200	5.2	1040
1891	350	5.3	1855	280	5.3	1484
1892	400	5.4	2160	350	5.4	1890
1893	440	5.5	2420	400	5.5	2200
1894	470	5.6	2632	440	5.6	2464
1895	500	5.7	**2850**	470	5.7	**2679**

TABLE II
A MONTH'S LABOUR AVAILABLE

For the economic period	Product units	Marginal utility	Value	Product Units	Marginal utility	Value
		in 1888 yields			*in 1889 yields*	
1888	100	5	500	—	5	—
1889	200	6	1200	100	6	600
1890	280	7	1960	200	7	1400
1891	350	8	**2800**	280	8	2240
1892	400	7	**2800**	350	7	**2450**
1893	440	6	2640	400	6	2400
1894	470	5	2350	440	5	2200
1895	500	4	2000	470	4	1800

And now a third analytical example. It deals with the following variation: marginal utility tends to decline on the whole; however it does not
decline evenly, but rather moves *with leaps*. Let us assume, for example,
that the marginal utility for the first two years amounts to 5, for the
following two years to 4, and then in the fifth year falls to zero. This
variation roughly reflects the effect which in my *Positive Theory of
Capital*,[43] I ascribe to our consideration of the uncertainty of life. In the
immediate future this consideration does not yet exert a value-depressing
influence; in the next remote period it decreases the value somewhat, and
in a third remoter period being beyond our life expectancy it eliminates
value entirely. The number of years representing these three periods and

the number and sequence of leaps naturally is without significance for our general analysis.

TABLE III
A MONTH'S LABOUR AVAILABLE

For the economic period	in 1888 yields			in 1889 yields		
	Product units	Marginal utility	Value	Product Units	Marginal utility	Value
1888	100	5	500	—	5	—
1889	200	5	1000	100	5	500
1890	280	4	1120	200	4	800
1891	350	4	**1400**	280	4	**1120**
1892	400	0	—	350	0	—
1893	440	0	—	400	0	—
1894	470	0	—	440	0	—
1895	500	0	—	470	0	—

Let us now compare the value tables of this type. In order to make the countertest to Fisher's complete, I shall follow his example and take into consideration all those circumstances that can affect the productivity of longer production processes. That is to say, I shall analyze the case of *rising productivity* (according to my usual model, Table III), the case of *stable* productivity (e.g. 300 product units per labour month; Table IV), the case of *declining* productivity (e.g. from 100 product units at the present to 90 in one-year production, 80 in two years, etc., down to 30 in 7 years; Table V), and finally the case of initially rising and then declining productivity (the series 100, 200, 300, 200, 100, etc.; Table VI).

TABLE IV
A MONTH'S LABOUR AVAILABLE

For the economic period	in 1888 yields			in 1889 yields		
	Product units	Marginal utility	Value	Product Units	Marginal utility	Value
1888	300	5	**1500**	—	5	—
1889	300	5	**1500**	300	5	**1500**
1890	300	4	1200	300	4	1200
1891	300	4	1200	300	4	1200
1892	300	0	—	300	0	—
1893	300	0	—	300	0	—
1894	300	0	—	300	0	—
1895	300	0	—	300	0	—

TABLE V
A MONTH'S LABOUR AVAILABLE

For the economic period	*in 1888 yields*			*in 1889 yields*		
	Product units	Marginal utility	Value	Product Units	Marginal utility	Value
1888	100	5	**500**	—	5	—
1889	90	5	450	100	5	**500**
1890	80	4	320	90	4	360
1891	70	4	280	80	4	320
1892	60	0	0	70	0	0
1893	50	0	0	60	0	0
1894	40	0	0	50	0	0
1895	30	0	0	40	0	0

What do these tables demonstrate? They demonstrate that the value maxima (emphasizing by boldface) of the compared 1888 and 1889 labour months *differ*, that is, that of the 1888 labour month exceeds that of the 1889 month in the first table only (Table III). In all other tables they are *equal*. This means that under identical assumptions of the rank of marginal utility the value advantage of older labour months always emerges when we assume higher productivity of longer production methods. It does not emerge where we eliminate higher productivity from our assumptions. In other words, the tables prove precisely what Fisher endeavoured to demonstrate away through reasoning based on faulty premises. They prove the relevance of my third reason for the emergence of the value advantage.[44]

TABLE VI
A MONTH'S LABOUR AVAILABLE

For the economic period	*in 1888 yields*			*in 1889 yields*		
	Product units	Marginal utility	Value	Product Units	Marginal utility	Value
1888	100	5	500	—	5	—
1889	200	5	1000	100	5	500
1890	300	4	**1200**	200	4	800
1891	200	4	800	300	4	**1200**
1892	100	0	—	200	0	0
1893	100	0	—	100	0	0
1894	100	0	—	100	0	0
1895	100	0	—	100	0	0

I could construe many more tables with numerical variations proving the correctness of my thesis. But there is a shorter and simpler way. This is the algebraic method which Fisher himself showed me by his example. I dealt with it at the very outset; but I have occasion, after all these explanations and special investigations, to return to it now. In general formulation it demonstrates that no matter what the marginal utilities (u) may be, the older labour month must always yield greater product value than the newer month provided merely the yield (p) of longer production methods continues to increase.

I know, of course, that Fisher raises objections other than those in his 'first approximation' against many of my present and earlier statements. And I know that he will especially have a counterargument against the foregoing reversal of his algebraic test, which will lead us deep into the last subtleties of a problem that by itself is rather difficult and subtle. But this concerns his other late approximations which we will have to analyze in proper sequence and at the proper place. At this point I am mainly concerned with repelling, as it were, a logical surprisal which the first approximation seems to attempt in a hasty anticipating conclusion.[45]

2. Fisher's Section 5

In this 'second approximation' Fisher uses the following method of refutation or inference. He eliminates entirely the efficacy of *both* other reasons from the assumptions of my tables. He does this by taking 5 as the figure of the 'reduced marginal utility' for all years throughout. Thus he arrives at the following table:

TABLE VII
A MONTH'S LABOUR AVAILABLE

For the economic period	*in 1888 yields*			*in 1889 yields*		
	Product units	Marginal utility	Value	Product Units	Marginal utility	Value
1888	100	5	500	—	5	—
1889	200	5	1000	100	5	500
1890	280	5	1400	200	5	1000
1891	350	5	1750	280	5	1400
1892	400	5	2000	350	5	1750
1893	440	5	2200	400	5	2000
1894	470	5	2350	440	5	2200
1895	500	5	2500	470	5	2350
						2500

167

Fisher then adds the following comment: 'The figures in the value columns for 1888 and 1889 are here absolutely alike; hence the maximum of the former, if there be a maximum, must be identical with the maximum of the latter.'

In a numerical supplement which is as interesting as it is correct with respect to facts, he remarks correctly that also according to my thesis of the higher productivity of longer production methods the yield of a labour unit never increases to infinity, but at the utmost can asymptotically approach a definite maximum.[46]

If this definite maximum amounts to 1000 product units, for instance, then according to Fisher 'a month's labour, whether available in 1888 or 1889, will now have the same maximum value, exactly 1000,[47] and there will be no 'technical superiority' in present over future goods whatever.'[48]

How does this reasoning refute my thesis that the higher productivity of capitalist production methods constitutes an independent third reason for the higher valuation of present goods? Fisher apparently believes that it does. But as in his 'first approximation' he depends on a general impression for lending conviction. He takes no pains to join, pedantically, link after link of his syllogism until the last link clearly collides and conflicts with my thesis. Indeed, a little pedantry would have been very useful.

Let us attempt to complete the syllogistic chain which Fisher merely indicates through his final conclusion instead of elaborating it carefully. It obviously assumes the following intermediary step: If my third reason cannot bring about the value advantage of present goods when the two other reasons are absent, this proves that it is no independent reason in addition to them. The effect must then *solely* be ascribed to the two other reasons.[49] In other words, Fisher postulates the logical equivalence of 'not without me' and 'only through me,' which is a fallacy based on an insufficient premise. It is a false conclusion similar to the one we often meet in the negligent manner of thought and speech of everyday life, which nevertheless constitutes negligent incorrect thinking.

First, an example. On his first stroll out a convalescent passes a house from whose pediment a piece breaks off and injures him fatally. Certainly the man would not have been killed if he had postponed his first stroll, which perhaps was too early also from the point of view of his recovery. Nothing is more common in popular thought and expression than to make the following comment: 'The man died only because of his obstinancy. If he had postponed his walk, which everybody advised him to do, he would still be alive.' Of course, this comment is wrong materially and logically with respect to the word 'only.' In dialectic exaggeration it substitutes for the circumstance that the early stroll exerted an influence indispensable for the fatal effect the entirely different circumstance that the early stroll *alone* exerted the whole influence. It is obvious that the indispensability of one reason (the early stroll) for the fatal accident offers no satisfactory logical basis for denying at least the position of an equal independent reason to the fall of the pediment besides the early stroll. The falling stone is certainly not only 'the early stroll in disguise.'

The same dialectic exaggeration with the same logical leap underlies Fisher's argumentation. Let me demonstrate this by using a second example whose nature is even more closely related to our case. By means of charges of black powder siege artillery hurls explosive shells filled with melinite at enemy bastions. The landing shells explode and have a considerable effect. What are the causes of this effect? Nobody will doubt that the melinite filling of the shell is an independent part-cause of the total effect of the shot in addition to the powder charge propelling the shell which would have caused some damage even without filling. An enumeration of the part-causes obviously would be incorrect and incomplete if we were to mention only the powder charge of the gun. Certainly nobody will allow himself to be confused by the dialectic objection that without the powder charge the shell would not have reached the enemy bastion and caused some damage. And nobody will maintain that we, therefore, must ascribe the whole effect to the powder charge *alone* and that the alleged second independent cause 'melinite filling' merely is 'the first cause in disguise.'

Fisher's premise is equally insufficient and deceptive for the conclusion he draws from it. Let us assume for a moment that my third reason really is ineffective without the simultaneous or preceding operating of the first two reasons – which we will have to discuss in detail in connection with Fisher's 'fourth approximation.' We can by no means infer from this assumption that my third reason is no 'independent cause' of the value advantage of present goods. We cannot infer that we can omit it from a complete enumeration of all causes of the phenomenon. But Fisher drew these very inferences. At the utmost we could arrive at the indispensability of the first two reasons, by no means at the lack of influence of the third reason, which can be as effective and independent as the two other reasons. In the death of our convalescent the falling pediment, too, was an independent part-cause of the accident besides his early stroll, as the melinite filling of the shell was an independent part-cause of the damage besides the powder charge that propelled the shell.

I am truly surprised that Fisher in his endeavour to test the correctness of my thesis again and again conducts faulty and irrelevant analyses. But he did not come upon the nearest and really pertinent test. This is the test whether or not addition of my third reason to a given case, or its removal from it, affects the emergence or degree of the value advantage of present goods.

Now let us conduct an analysis of an example that is cleared of all possible sources of errror. Let us assume that 'the first and second reasons' are such that they result in a stable marginal utility of 5 per product unit during the first four years 1888–1891, a marginal utility of 8 in 1892, and then again of 5 in the following years. This assumption perhaps corresponds to the situation of somebody enjoying a steady income and stable demand. But in one year of the series his income for once suffers a considerable decline because, for instance, an old debt falls due. Let us also assume that his steady income merely amounts to a minimum for subsistence. We thus exclude that during the better-provided years he may save towards payment of his debt and thus level out his provision during the normal years and that of the exceptional year. This would stabilize the marginal utilities of product units. We thus avoid that, on the one hand, our initial supposition is eliminated again and, on the other, the primary effect is disturbed and obscured through the introduction of secondary effects which invites the danger that *effects* resulting from the process are mistaken for its *causes*. This very error seems to have portentously influenced Fisher's opinion on our subject.

Now what happens if the first two reasons are assumed to be constant, but the data pertaining to the 'third reason' are variable? In Table I I assume higher productivity fo longer production methods and completely free choice with respect to the production period. In Table II I exclude the higher productivity, but maintain the freedom of choice between production methods of different lengths (through the assumption of a product of 300 units that remains unchanged for every production period). In Table III, finally, I also exclude freedom of choice (in accordance with a suggestion by Bortkiewicz[50]) but assume adoption of a certain, e.g., 5-year, production period with a return fo 300 as ultimately given by technical conditions.

TABLE I

A MONTH'S LABOUR AVAILABLE

For the economic period	in 1888 yields			in 1889 yields		
	Product units	Marginal utility	Value	Product Units	Marginal utility	Value
1888	100	5	500	—	5	—
1889	200	5	1000	100	5	500
1890	280	5	1400	200	5	1000
1891	350	5	1750	280	5	1400
1892	400	8	**3200**	350	8	**2800**
1893	440	5	2200	400	5	2000
1894	470	5	2350	440	5	2200
1895	500	5	2500	470	5	2350

Let us now vary the assumptions for Table III. Let us assume a 3- or 4-year production period, instead of a 5-year period. Then (at a return of 300) in the case of a 3-year period the 1888 labour month yields a value figure of 1500, and the 1889 labour month a value of 2400. In the case of a 4-year period, we arrive inversely at a value figure of 2400 for the 1888 labour month and at 1500 for the 1889 labour month, which can be readily seen without special tables.

TABLE II
A MONTH'S LABOUR AVAILABLE

For the economic period	*in 1888 yields*			*in 1889 yields*		
	Product units	Marginal utility	Value	Product Units	Marginal utility	Value
1888	300	5	1500	—	5	—
1889	300	5	1500	300	5	1500
1890	300	5	1500	300	5	1500
1891	300	5	1500	300	5	1500
1892	300	8	**2400**	300	8	**2400**
1893	300	5	1500	300	5	1500
1894	300	5	1500	300	5	1500
1895	300	5	1500	300	5	1500

TABLE III
A MONTH'S LABOUR AVAILABLE

For the economic period	*in 1888 yields*			*in 1889 yields*		
	Product units	Marginal utility	Value	Product Units	Marginal utility	Value
1888	—	5	—	—	5	—
1889	—	5	—	—	5	—
1890	—	5	—	—	5	—
1891	—	5	—	—	5	—
1892	—	8	—	—	8	—
1893	300	5	1500	—	5	—
1894	—	5	—	300	5	1500
1895	—	5	—	—	5	—

Thus while the first two reasons remain unchanged we observe *value advantage* of the present (older) labour month in Table I. Under the

171

assumptions of Table II we observe *value equality*, and under those of Table III value equality or value advantage of the older labour month, or even of the newer month, depending on our assumption as to the duration of the ultimately given production period. In my belief, the fact that under the assumptions of Table I value advantage of present means emerges, proves the efficacy of my third reason. We do not owe this value advantage to the first two reasons which we assumed to have remained unchanged. They cannot bring it about, or at least cannot do so constantly, or under certain circumstances can even bring about the opposite effect, that is, value advantage of newer means of production.

The number of these tests can be increased at will. But instead of adding more examples – my analyses in Tables III to VI on pp. 165 ff. also serve as such – I should like to return to my general algebraic test presented above (*p. 160*). It leads me to the conclusion that at any state of the first two reasons (of the marginal utility u) the higher valuation of older labour months must emerge provided merely p (the returns of longer production methods) increases continuously. At my first presentation of this material I mentioned a reservation because of an eventual objection by Fisher.[51] Let us now analyze this objection in detail. For it is materially identical with Fisher's objection raised in his 'second approximation' which, as we have seen in the meantime, is fallacious.

My algebraic test shows that the maximum of the second series (values for the 1889 labour year), no matter where it may lie, must be exceeded by the maximum of the first series (values of the 1888 labour year). This is so because in accordance with our assumption the first series contains a magnitude that is the product of an equal u and a greater p. In accordance with Fisher's line of thought the following objection can now be raised. With p continuously increasing, the second series can only have a maximum, that is, an earlier magnitude of the series can be greater than later following magnitudes, if u declines from a certain point on. The term p_3u_4 of the second series, for instance, indeed can constitute a maximum, that is, can be greater than the following term p_4u_5 of the same series, if u_5 is *smaller* than u_4, for the other magnitude of the compared product, i.e., p_4 is greater than p_3. Thus the existence of a definite maximum in the second series allegedly assumes a decline of u. This means, one of the two 'first reasons' is present which is said to be proof that the emergence of a value advantage must *not* be ascribed to the higher productivity of longer production methods, but rather to the first two reasons alone.[52]

This is identical with the fallacy of tracing back the death of our convalescent solely to his early walk, or the damage by the melinite shell to the powder charge of the gun. It is to mistake 'only through me' for 'not without me.' Or to express it for once in proper scientific terms, it is a confusion of a simple antithesis with a contradictory antithesis. There are not only the two possibilities that an effect is brought about either entirely without a certain circumstance or through this circumstance alone. It is true if this were the case, we must assume emergence of the latter when the former does not take place. But there is still a third possibility. An effect cannot be brought about without a certain circumstance, and not with it alone, but with it in cooperation with other circumstances. Fisher carelessly overlooks this third possibility.

I want to encounter the abstract dialectics employed by my excellent opponent not only with more abstract dialectics – which I hope is more nearly correct – but I also should like to illustrate my point of view in readily understood concrete language. I am offered a bill of exchange – let us call it bill A – that entitles me to receive at option either 300 lbs. of wheat on a certain Argentine farm or 200 lbs. in my home town, Vienna. I am also offered another bill of exchange, called B, that entitles me to receive 300 lbs. of wheat in Vienna. There cannot be any doubt that I shall value bill B higher than bill A. Why? At first I shall answer this question with intentionally one-sided fallacious dialectics, that is, consecutively with the same syllogism in opposite ways.

First answer: Only because I prefer Vienna as the *place of settlement*. For if it would make no difference whether I received 300 lbs. in Vienna or Argentina, I would ascribe equal value to both bills of exchange.

Second answer: Only because bill B on Vienna entitles me to a *larger quantity* than bill A and because I prefer the larger quantity. For if both bills of exchange on Vienna entitle me to the same quantity, if for instance, bill B covers only 200 lbs., or bill A 300 lbs. to be delivered in Vienna, or if for any reason I would not prefer the larger quantity because, for instance, I absolutely need no more than 200 lbs. in Vienna and 100 additional pounds would be useless to me, I would again ascribe equal value to both bills in spite of my preference for Vienna as the place of settlement.

Both conclusions are false because of their one-sided dialectics. The obvious truth is that the higher valuation of bill B arises from *both* the reasons, my preference of Vienna as a place of settlement and the fact that bill B entitles me to more than A does in Vienna. This is similar to our other examples in which the stroll and falling pediment, or the powder charge of the gun and the melinite filling of the shell, constituted equal causes for the corresponding effects. Depending on the occasion for our inquiry, either one or the other of the two reasons may stand in the foreground and appear as the 'decisive reason' in the case. For instance, if I should prefer the first of the two choices offered by bill A, that is, if I would value 300 lbs. delivered in Argentina higher than 200 lbs. delivered in Vienna, the decisive reason for my higher valuation of bill B would then be my preference of Vienna as *place of settlement*. In other words, I prefer B because I value 300 lbs. in Vienna higher than 300 lbs. in Argentina which I would have chosen and received with bill A. On the other hand, if I would value 200 lbs. in Vienna higher than 300 lbs. in Argentina, the *quantitative advantage* of bill B on Vienna would then constitute the decisive reason for my choice. I prefer B because its 300 lbs. delivered in Vienna are worth more to me than 200 lbs. delivered in Vienna which I would have chosen and received with bill A. I hope that this is sufficiently clear.

Precisely comparable to the difference of location on the one hand and the higher quantity at the preferred location on the other, is our case regarding pure time preference on the one hand and the greater product quantity for the preferred period. Why do we value a forest that is 100 years old higher than one that is only 80 years old? We certainly would not value it higher if we were indifferent about receiving the wood of the 100-year old forest today or only twenty years hence when the now 80-year old forest would also be 100 years old. And we certainly do not value it any higher if it does not yield more wood than the younger forest, that is, if it is not 'technically superior' through its greater quantity of wood with respect to its possible employment in an earlier period, e.g., in the present. Similarly, we cannot deny the influence which the fact that older wine is better than young wine exerts on our higher valuation of the older wine. Indeed, the dissolution of the technical superiority of older means of production into other factors of causation as attempted by Fisher is a dialectic illusion.

3. Fisher's Section 6

In this section Fisher attempts to demonstrate even more clearly his alleged refutation. He does this by changing one point in the actual assumption of my tables to which he resorts rather frequently. He thinks he may change this point to coincide with real life. He maintains that beyond a certain limit the product quantity obtainable by a further lengthening of the production period sometimes decreases again. With this assumption he arrives at the following table:

YIELD OF A LABOUR MONTH AVAILABLE IN THE YEARS 1888 TO 1892,
STATED IN PRODUCT UNITS

For the economic period	1888	1889	1890	1891	1892
1888	100	—	—	—	—
1889	200	100	—	—	—
1890	280	200	100	—	—
1891	350	280	200	100	—
1892	400	350	280	200	100
1893	440	400	350	280	200
1894	470	440	400	350	280
1895	**500**	470	440	400	350
1896	490	**500**	470	440	400
1897	480	490	**500**	470	440
1898	460	480	490	**500**	470
1899	430	460	480	490	**500**
1900	410	430	460	480	490

In the preceding section we eliminated the efficacy of the first two reasons by taking the constant figure 5 as the marginal utility of the product unit. If we do this now we arrive at a table whose 'value figures' throughout are five times greater than those in the preceding table. The value maxima for all five labour months from 1888 to 1892 will be 2500. Fisher comments on this result as follows:

'Our conclusion is that if we eliminate the 'other two circumstances' (relative underestimate of, and overprovision for, the future), we eliminate entirely the superiority of present over future goods, and the supposed third circumstance of 'technical superiority' therefore turns out to be non-existent.'[53]

I should like to make the following comment:

First, I do not believe that Fisher has reason to appeal to everyday life regarding his statement that the yield per unit of production good tends positively to decline again when the production period is lengthened beyond a certain point.[54] But I shall attach no importance to this statement as it suffices for Fisher's conclusions that the growth of productivity ceases somewhere. I basically admit this possibility although I believe it to be very remote.[55]

In an illustration we certainly can make the assumption that the marginal or turning point is so near that it is reached in a 7-year production period and at a yield of 500 units. But Fisher further assumes that our 1888 production plans underlying 'present value in 1888'[56] include effective

175

dispositions for the years until 1899, that is, for years far beyond the 7-year zone. He thus assumes that all available productive resources can be invested in the longest production processes still leading to higher productivity. But I did not maintain the efficacy of my third reason for such an assumption which has never been realized but is merely 'conceivable.'

I completely agree with Fisher that if we make these factual assumptions perfect value equality between the 1888 and 1889 labour months will exist. But this does not prove that my 'third reason' basically cannot constitute an independent reason besides the two other reasons. It merely proves that it is not operative under these assumptions.[57] Again Fisher deduces the principle 'through the first two reasons alone' from the other principle 'not without the first two reasons.' Thus his present conclusion is as fallacious as that of his reasoning in the preceding section. We can best lead it *ad absurdum* in Fisher's own words. Applying his syllogism to our example of the convalescent we arrive at the following statement: 'Our conclusion is that if we eliminate the early stroll of the convalescent we eliminate also his fatal accident, and the supposed second circumstance of the falling pediment therefore turns out to be non-existent.' Who wants to repeat this conclusion of Fisher?

The reflections with which Fisher concludes his section 6 and embarks upon a blunder already committed by Bortkiewicz[58] suffer from the same logical shortcoming.

'The fact is that the only reason anyone can prefer the product of a month's labour invested today to the product of a month's labour invested next year is that today's investment will mature earlier than next year's investment. If a fruit tree is planted today which will bear fruit in four years, the labour available today for planting it is preferred rather than the same amount of labour available next year; because, if the planting is deferred until next year, the fruit will likewise be deferred a year, maturing in five instead of four years from the present. It does not alter this essential fact to speak of the possibility of a number of different investments. A month's labour today may, it is true, be spent in planting slow-growing or fast-growing trees; but so may a month's labour invested next year. It is from the preference for the early over the late fruition of *any* productive process that the so-called 'technical superiority of present over future goods' derives all its force. The imagined 'third circumstance' producing a superiority in present goods is only the first two circumstances in disguise.'[59]

I merely ask: is it or is it not true that in Fisher's example and in actual life the earlier labour month affords us the choice of obtaining for ourselves the same yield for an earlier period or a greater yield for the same period? If we have this choice, in the name of what law of logic are we to stare at the first alternative only and close our eyes to the second one as if it did not exist? Fisher would be right if there were a law that forces us to employ our resources of the various years always in precisely identical ways. He would be right indeed if we could choose freely according to Mephisto's motto in Goethe's *Faust*: 'Man is free to choose the first but shall be slave to the following.' If we choose whether we want to employ a labour month in production for the present, or in a 1, 2, or 3-year method, etc., but having decided in favour of a certain utilization, e.g., taking three years, we must decide for the same employment also with respect to next year's labour month. If in such a case the present labour month evidences greater value than next year's labour month, we must ascribe it to the 'sole reason' that we prefer the *earlier* enjoyment (of the same product quantity) over *later* enjoyment.

But our freedom of choice goes much further. We need not choose in a parallel way, we may also choose divergingly or convergingly. We can employ our means of production available in different years for the *same purpose*, that is, for the satisfaction of wants of one and the same period. Of course, we must then employ different methods of utilization. The 1888 labour month must be employed in a 4-year method, the 1889 month in a 3-year method in order to satisfy wants in 1892. Such converging choices in favour of a single purpose are very frequent in actual life. As the best open possibilities they play a role in our valuations. We readily perceive in them the 'technical superiority' of older over newer productive forces which no dialectics can deny.[60] And the influence which this superiority exerts on the valuation of 'older' means is by no means merely dialectic, but very real. When a timber dealer simultaneously clears a 100-year old and an 80-year old forest, he will value the older forest higher simply because it actually yields more timber. And when we drink 'old' and young wine, we value the older wine higher simply because it is superior in quality. Is this or is this not a real technical superiority?

Fisher may raise the objection that the convergence of our choices merely constitutes the effect of the first two reasons. He may object that we regard the investment of the 1889 labour month in a 3-year production for our 1892 wants as the best possible utilization only if we value the smaller product quantity obtainable in 1892 higher than a larger quantity obtainable in 1893. We have encountered this objection and recognized its deceptive dialectics before. It is again the confusion of 'not without me' and 'only through me.' I readily admit, although we shall have to return to it in our following section, that resources invested in different periods will find their 'economic point of gravity' in the same class of wants only if the first two reasons move the point of gravity closer to the present. But they merely provide the opportunity for the 'technical superiority' to exert its own influence on valuation. They themselves do not exert this influence. They compare with the early stroll of our convalescent that provided the occasion for the falling pediment to strike him on the head. The causative effect of the falling pediment nevertheless cannot be dissolved entirely in the effect of the stroll. I endeavoured to demonstrate above through an unobjectionable schematic test that a certain independent effect of the 'technical superiority' remains.[61]

4. Fisher's Section 7

I also examined the 'independence' of my third reason from the two other reasons by assuming a situation in which the effectiveness of the latter was entirely excluded from the outset. Now if only the third reason is effective, it brings about a 'divergency of provision for wants.' From this I thought I could infer that the third reason 'is far removed from a necessity of borrowing strength and effectiveness from any difference arising out of other sources in the situation relating to provision for wants. So far removed is it, in fact, that *this cause itself* is capable of creating such a difference, should that become necessary.'[62]

Fisher cites my exposition in literal or sometimes rather free translation. He raises no objection against my description of the actual state of affairs. But he adds the following critical comment to my conclusion therefrom: my reasoning allegedly demonstrates that if the two other interest-creating circumstances are temporarily absent, they reappear through our choice of roundabout methods. 'In other words, the "technical superiority of present goods" produces interest by restoring the "other two circumstances." But this is tantamount to the admission that "technical superiority" actually depends for its force on these "other two circumstances" and is not "independent".'[63]

First it seems to me that Fisher is indulging in a play of words. He places and interprets my words differently from the way my presentation places and interprets them. Thus he misplaces the subject of our controversy. He ignores the wording of my argument cited above in which I proclaim the indubitable independence of my third cause 'from any difference *arising out of other sources* in the situation relating to provision for wants.' To refute my argument phrased like this would have been simply impossible. Fisher certainly does not want to maintain that under my stated conditions the effectiveness of my third reason further 'depends' on the presence or addition of a divergency resulting from *other* causes. For instance, he does not want to maintain that it depends on the presence or addition of typical cases of momentary emergency enumerated under the heading 'first reason' (such as crop failure, fire loss, unemployment, etc.) or on cases of an 'advancing career' (for instance, of beginners in a scientific or artistic profession). Thus Fisher in a polemic voice replies to something other than what I maintained above. He could miss the precise wording of my thesis in spite of his great and laudable conscientiousness because in an otherwise literal translation he unfortunately cited the decisive phrase in rather free translation whereby the significant words were deleted.[64]

But Fisher seems to be playing with words even if we do not consider the relationship of the third reason to a divergency in the provision for wants resulting from *other* sources, which I had discussed, but rather consider the divergency resulting from *the third reason* itself. He seems to shift the customary meaning of the word 'dependent' when in his causal chain he ascribes the role of 'dependent' factor to the 'third reason.' Does the cause depend on its effect, or the effect on its cause? In my terminology does the cause 'borrow' its effectiveness from its effect, or does the effect not rather derive its own existence and thus also all its concomitant effects from its cause? Does the striking cue 'borrow' its force from the billiard-ball, or does the latter not inversely borrow its force from the striking cue? In my argumentation I endeavoured in fact to exclude a thought which I anticipated could be made to serve as an objection against my preceding schematic presentation. As a matter of fact, this objection was then raised especially by Fisher who advanced it with forceful explicitness. He maintained that my preceding tables show a value advantage of present means of production only because I had already introduced the first two reasons, or at least one of them, 'as being effective.' But I endeavoured to demonstrate, and I hope I actually succeeded in showing that the *presence* of the other circumstances treated under the heading 'first' and 'second reason' is not required to assure the effectiveness of the third reason. In this sense I certainly was justified in maintaining the 'independence' of my third reason.

This may seem like arguing about words, which it actually is to a certain degree. Let us therefore follow the controversy to its innermost kernel where there can be no evading or playing with words, where truth or error will be revealed. Let us adopt the same presumptuous interpretation to which Fisher now limits the term 'independent.' I maintain also in this sense my third reason is an 'independent' reason. It is independent of the first and all the more of the second reason insofar as its effect of value advantage need not necessarily traverse supply divergencies brought about by it. This is the point to which Fisher's further counter-arguments lead us. I proceed by citing this passage.

'The essential fact is that its presence does not produce interest when

179

the other two are absent. In short, the "technical superiority" of present goods is a delusion, and the *only* way in which the existence of long processes of production acts on interest is by *overendowing the future and underendowing the present,* thus creating a "scarcity value" of present goods."[65]

This is a material error. I shall demonstrate that, on the contrary, the 'technical superiority' of present goods can bring forth a value advantage, that is, interest, also if the state of demand and supply in present and future is *constant.* From this follows *ipso facto* that the interest-creating force of the technical superiority even in Fisher's sense does not 'depend' on the underendowment of the present brought about as intermediary effect.

Let us form an example suitable for this demonstration. It must necessarily be somewhat casuistical. The higher productivity of longer production methods naturally always tends, in case of correct economic behaviour, to lead to a more plentiful provision for remoter periods in which its yields will be higher.[66] But in order nevertheless to assume constancy of the states of provision we must introduce a casuistic assumption that offsets this tendency as to kind and degree. If it should then become apparent that the higher productivity of longer production methods leads us to a value advantage of older means of production in spite of the constancy in the states of provision, this would prove that the otherwise more plentiful provision for the future merely is a secondary effect, and not, as Fisher asserts, the indispensable *cause* of higher valuation.

Let us take up the example used on pp. 170 ff. and elaborate it a little for the present purpose. Let us imagine a man living on a minimum for existence. His demand generally is constant. He acquires his minimum for existence of 2,400 product units through application of his labour in a one-year production method which his resources permit. The yield of his labour is supposed to be 200 product units per labour month and the marginal utility of a product unit a constant five. Now this constancy of provision is endangered in a single period, let us say, 1892, because during this period his demand increases by 960 product units. This may be the case because, for instance, a debt of this amount falls due or because of the anticipated necessity to support temporarily a disabled member of his family who up to then had lived on another income, or because of any other reason. In such cases his income remains unchanged at 2,400 product units, but the marginal utility rises from 5 to 8. Let us suppose that in this situation a neighbour makes him the welcome offer of exchanging a future labour year for a present year. The neighbour proposes working for our family head during the year 1890 under the condition that he will work for the neighbour in 1891. This offer presents the following possibility. Our supporter would have applied his 1891 labour in a one-year production for the 1892 wants. This provision will now be lacking because he is to work for the neighbour in 1891. But if he therefore asks his neighbour in 1890 to work for his wants in 1892, his labour can be employed in 2-year production methods with a return of 280 product units per month or a return of 3,360 units for the labour year. In this way even after provision for the extraordinary demand of 960 units the normal demand of 2,400 units could be satisfied and the marginal utility of the unit would result again in 5.[67]

What does this prove for our question? Let us accompany our family head in his deliberation on whether or not he should accept the offer. He certainly will accept it readily, for he will value the older labour year offered to him more highly than the later year he must give in exchange. Why? No dialectic evasion is possible: he does so for no other reason than its 'technical superiority.' It yields more for the 1892 wants which both compared labour years are to satisfy. It yields 3,360 product units as compared with 2,400 units which the 1891 labour yield can provide. And this value advantage of the older labour year is brought about by its technical superiority. No divergency in the provision for wants during the various periods, no 'overendowment' of remoter periods and 'underendowment' of earlier periods need cause this effect. For the supply situation finding reflection in the marginal utility and value of a product unit has remained unchanged: the marginal utility was constant at 5. This proves again that the underendowment of the present is not the 'only way,' as Fisher asserts, by which the higher productivity of longer production methods can lead to a value advantage of present goods. It proves that the more plentiful supply for future periods which, it is true, higher productivity usually tends to bring about, merely is another concomitant effect of the same cause. It itself is not the real cause of higher valuation.

More than that! The tendency toward a more plentiful supply for the future, and consequently a decline of the corresponding marginal utility, affects also our example. It merely is counteracted by the opposite tendency resulting from the assumed increase of demand. This counter-tendency prevents it from lowering the marginal utility of the unit in the 1892 economic period *below the level of 5* which it otherwise would. It now effects that the marginal utility of 8, which a unit would attain without the higher productivity of the longer production period, is lowered to the *level of 5*.

Now let us assume for a moment that this lowering effect would not be exerted and that the marginal utility would remain at 8 on account of the greater demand. What would happen to the value advantage of the earlier labour year? It would not only remain, but emerge to an even greater degree. Naturally 3,360 units of a value of 8 per unit represents a greater value total than 3,360 units of a value of 5 per unit.[68] And similarly the older labour year as the source of the greater value total is valued higher than the source of the smaller total. If the value of the source of the smaller total already exceeded that of the following labour year, its value total advantage would merely increase if it were valued as the source of the greater value total. But this reveals that the improvement in the provisions for later peiods, which also the higher productivity of longer production periods tends to bring about, is so far removed from constituting the real *cause* of higher valuation that it even *counteracts* this higher valuation. Thus, Fisher, like Carver, in a similar situation,[69] not only took a mere accompanying phenomenon for the cause, but even presented erroneously a phenomenon that *counteracts* and weakens the specific effect of value advantage as its actually effective cause.[70]

But all this becomes even clearer and more readily intelligible when in the following section I compare Fisher's own attempt at interpreting the coherence of the facts leading to higher valuation with my own.

5. Fisher's own Arrangement of the Causes of Higher Valuation

Fisher's exposition of his own interest theory comprises several hundred pages of his keen and profound work on 'The Rate of Interest.' To prepare an excerpt therefrom which is both short and pertinent is extremely difficult. This is due partially to the organization of his presentation in approximations[71] and partially because it is *not* organized according to the fundamental causes of interest and the rate of interest. Consequently we must search for many principles within the specific presentation of the rate of interest which characteristically also constitutes the title of Fisher's work. It is so difficult finally because in many cases he has formulated a peculiar original terminology whose employment in a short survey would require lengthy explanations, especially since Fisher sometimes gives customary technical terms unusual meanings.[72] I am therefore presenting a summary of what appears to be the gist of his interest theory, a summary that differs from his order of presentation as well as from his terminology. I only hope that I shall escape misunderstandings and inaccuracies, at least as to the main point, although they are difficult to avoid in these cases.

If I understand Fisher correctly he groups differently and by way of a different generalization the same facts to which I appeal in my explanation of the interest phenomenon. He agrees with me in that he places the higher valuation of present goods, which he calls 'time preference,' in the center of his interest theory.[73] But he actually amalgamates my three causes of higher valuation in a single cause: the divergency of provisions, that is, the comparatively scarce provision for the present (or the period closer to the present). He does this by way of the following train of thought.

His starting point is the well-known sentence that the higher valuation of present goods over future goods can actually be dissolved in a preference for earlier over later use services (according to Fisher's terminology, 'income').[74]

Whether or not such a preference can emerge depends on 'the whole future income stream' of a person, that is, on the size and temporal distribution of the anticipated income, on its relative abundance in early or distant periods. If his income during a distant period will be especially high, he will want to exchange a large part of it against a relatively small amount of present income (p. 92). As Fisher remarks correctly, this sentence corresponds to that of the general price theory according to which the marginal utility of every good depends on its quantity. Fisher also observed correctly at another place (p. 98) that it corresponds basically to my 'first reason.'[75] Indeed he also basically accepts the facts of my 'second reason' (anticipation, self-control, brevity and uncertainty of life). But he describes their influence with the rather mysterious formula that they merely affect the 'form of function,' which is said to express the dependency of time-preference on income (p. 103). Everyone's time-preference essentially depends on his income; only the form of this dependency varies according to the aforementioned circumstances (p. 109). What Fisher materially means herewith can, I believe, be expressed more simply and naturally as follows: the great time-preference of the thoughtless spendthrift results because he undervalues his future wants on account of lack of foresight or willpower. He deems his future want and supply situation more favourable than it actually will be. Thus he imagines an erroneous overendowment of the future and underendowment of the present.[76] Through this construction Fisher groups also my second reason under the general heading of diverging provisions for present and future.

But the temporal distribution of the whole available income stream, on which time-preference mainly depends, is influenced considerably by the individual's *own way of action*. The temporal distribution of income which his available stock of wealth can yield is not dictated to him rigidly and irrevocably. He always can choose between various ways of utilization. He can choose between a great number of 'options.' He may borrow or lend, buy or sell, and generally change the utilization of available goods. He can choose between 'spending' and investing,' and again between investing for a shorter or longer period, and between various production methods that will yield their returns in different periods.[77] Whoever, for instance, possesses goods that by their very nature yield nothing in the immediate future but much in later years (for example, a young forest) can level out this irregular income stream by borrowing during the earlier years and repaying during the later years.

In fact, we choose among the various possible income streams according to 'the maximum desirability.' Our choice of the 'most desirable' stream must agree with the principles governing the rate of interest.[78] That is to say, we always choose the income that represents the maximum present value calculated at the market rate of interest.[79] Fisher emphasizes through italics that this choice 'depends on the rate of interest.'[80]

Realization of this principle effects among others that the degree of 'time-preference,' which originally may differ greatly with every individual, is harmonized on one level for all individuals, that is, on the market rate of interest. If a person's individual rate of 'time-preference' differs from the market rate because of the initial 'time-shape' of his income, his individual degree of foresight, self-control, etc., he will adjust the time-shape of his income through borrowing, lending, or the execution of his available 'options' in such a way that his 'preference rate' harmonizes with the market 'interest rate.' Persons who initially have a higher individual preference rate (e.g. 10% while the market rate stands at 5%) will sell a part of their relatively high future income in order to improve the relatively meager present income. This will cause a rise in the value of the future income and a decline in that of the present income. And this process continues to the point at which the individual preference rate will coincide with the market rate. 'In other words, a person whose preference rate exceeds the current rate of interest will borrow up to the point which will make the two rates equal.'[81] The market rate is established at the point at which there is equilibrium, this means, where loans and borrowings offset each other.[82]

So much by Fisher. Now where in this line of reasoning is the logical chain of explanation that, according to Fisher, is to explain not only the rate of interest but also its existence?[83]

The time-preference which present goods attain over future goods on the market is to be explained. Fisher very affirmatively states that this rate is causatively determined by the individual rates of time-preference. It is true, the market rate is relatively fixed, a given fact for every individual. While he adapts his rate to that of the market the latter indeed appears as cause, his individual rate as effect. But for society in general the sequence of cause and effect is the reverse. The preference-rates of individuals determine the interest rate.[84]

The personal rate of preference, according to Fisher, depends on the nature of his income-stream 'as finally modified and determined by the *very act of borrowing or lending, buying or selling.*'[85] Thus if we apply what Fisher said about the 'character of the income-stream' at the beginning[86] he explains in final analysis the existence of interest from the relatively poor endowment of the present and the relatively rich endowment of the future *as it appears with each individual after completion of all offsetting operations required by the concurrence of the individual rates of time-preference with the market rate of interest.*[87]

In my belief, this way of connecting the facts leading to the value advantage of present goods is untenable for several important reasons.

At first glance it appears impressively simple to reduce all reasons of higher valuation to the single reason of diverging demand and supply situations. It is both ingenious and logical, in spite of its paradoxical appearance, to explain also squandering, for instance, by referring to a scarcity of present supply even though it may be only imaginary. But at second glance this impressively simple thought proves to be too simple to satisfy us completely. For it tells us either too much or too little. It tells us too little if we appeal to it merely in general terms, without determining exactly the concrete form in which this 'relationship of demand and supply' makes its appearance. It is true but meaningless, and an empty truism. For it is self-evident for everybody who deduces the value of goods from the relationship of demand and supply, that value *differences* assume differences of demand and supply. The explanation of value differences, however, hardly advances a step by pointing out that the value differences between present and future goods in general are connected with differences in demand and supply. Neither does it advance by remarking that the very circumstance that affects the value ratios between present and future goods must also affect in some way the demand and supply situations.

At any rate, our investigation into the causes of the value advantage of present goods is not yet completed. Behind this first general presentation, which merely constitutes a restatement of the problem, there arises the question of concrete reasons that influence the demand and supply situation in such a way that the preference for present goods always results. At this point the unity, which in the end must emerge again, is dispersed in a multiplicity of concrete part-reasons.

Or, the sentence tells us more than this foregone conclusion. It may want to designate a certain demand and supply situation as the only possible one from which the higher value of present goods can emerge. In fact, this is the very meaning which Fisher has given his sentence. According to him, the *relatively scarce provision for the present* is the only feasible demand and supply situation from which the value advantage of present goods can emerge. But such an appeal goes much too far. It is materially wrong. And Fisher asserts that this scarce provision for the present results from an execution of the levelling 'options.' Therefore we must raise the further objections that he confuses cause and effect and that he argues in a vicious circle.

Let us explain this step by step.

First I maintain that, in spite of his correct recognition that every value difference must result from diverging demand and supply situations, Fisher draws too one-sided a picture of this relationship. He believes that a higher valuation of present goods requires apodictically that the present supply is scarcer and consequently the marginal utility higher in the present than in the future. But this is actually wrong. I have proven this with some examples presented on another occasion.[88] Nevertheless I should like to explain also here why Fisher's picture is one-sided and which of the other possibilities it deletes.

One hundred pounds of grain in a year with a good crop usually will be worth less than one hundred pounds in a year with a bad crop. Why? According to Fisher's understanding this is so because the supply during the latter year is scarce and therefore the marginal utility of a hundred-weight high. Two hundredweights of grain in a year with a good harvest probably will be worth more than one hundredweight in a year with a bad harvest. Why? Fisher's picture obviously does not explain the value difference. In this case the greater value does not result from the side of scarce provision and high marginal utility of the product unit, but from the opposite side of plentiful provision and the undoubtedly lower value unit 'hundredweight of grain.' The reason obviously lies with an entirely different 'want and supply situation.' It lies with the fact that two hundredweights of grain constitute a greater supply for the existing demand for grain than one hundredweight: the total utility of two hundredweight in fact is greater than that of one hundredweight. In our first comparison the value difference is all the *greater* the more the supply situations and marginal utilities of a unit vary; in our second case, however, the value advantage of 'two hundredweights' is all the greater the *less* the supply situations and marginal utilities of a unit vary. The two hundredweights will all the more surpass the one hundredweight in value, the less the improvement of provision brought about by the greater supply and the decline in marginal utility lower the total value of two hundredweights. For instance, if the marginal utility of one hundredweight belonging to a scarce supply amounts to 3, the two hundredweights of the latter will surpass in value the one hundredweight of the former by a ratio of 6 to 5. If the supply differences are smaller and the marginal utility of a unit of the more plentiful supply is merely lowered to 4.5, two hundredweights of the latter will surpass in value one hundredweight of the former by a ratio of 9 to 5.[89] This proves that in cases of such a nature 'abundance' as used by Fisher is no *cause*, but rather a counterforce to the emerging value difference.

Now the road to the higher value of present means of production on account of higher productivity of longer production methods does not lead via the reasons by which one hundredweight of a scarce supply is more valuable than one hundredweight of a more plentiful supply. It leads via the other reasons by which two hundredweights are more valuable than one. If an 1888 labour month by way of a three-year production process can be transformed to 350 product units for 1891, and an 1889 labour month can be transformed to only 280 product units for the same 1891 wants, assuming the best methods are used in both instances, then the value advantage of the older labour month results from the fact that it yields more product units for the 1891 wants than the later labour month – 350 instead of 280 units. The fact that the marginal utility of one of 350 units may be smaller than that of one of 280 units is an accidental circumstance that not only is unessential for the existence of higher value, but also rather suited to lessen and reduce it. Thus this case can hardly be made to fit Fisher's picture in which a circumstance that obviously can here merely reduce the value advantage, must constitute its cause.

Fisher nevertheless attempted to fit this case into his picture. But he does this by way of a justification that earned him my second objection: *to have confounded cause and effect.*

The fact that we can at will transform a present good to a greater number of future product units through execution of one of the many possible 'options' brings about certain secondary effects of a levelling nature. Fisher observed and described this very well. Among the several or many possibilities of utilization of an available good we rationally choose that one yielding the *most valuable return*. Let us assume that the product unit of a later period maintains so high a value that the larger number of future product units attainable through an option is worth more than the smaller number of units attainable in production for the present or nearer future. In this case we tend to extend the option further in the future. That is to say, of all our available resources we tend to withdraw more and more product units from production for the present and near future where they merely yield a smaller number of units with a smaller value total. We then employ them in production for the remote future where they can yield a greater number of units with a still greater value total. But the successive decrease of present supply and increase of future supply naturally increases the marginal utility and value of a product unit belonging to the former, and lowers the marginal utility and value of one belonging to the latter. Finally the point is reached where the smaller number of units with the higher marginal utility and the larger number of units with the smaller marginal utility and unit value represent the same value total. At this point the options for the present will reach equilibrium with those for the future.

Thus there emerges a difference between present and future supply situations that is connected with a different marginal utility and value of a product unit. And this finally leads to the situation assumed by Fisher in his explanation. But the process of higher valuation of present production goods *does not begin* here, it *ends* here. The value advantage was already in existence. It had to be present before the levelling dispositions which it brought forth could lead to this development. The motivating force that managed to lead the options for the future beyond the point of equal marginal utility and that had already created the value advantage of present goods stems from a heterogeneous source. This is the fact that two product units are worth more than one, 350 more than 280. Consequently a good that can be converted to 350 units must be worth more than a good that can be converted to only 280 product units.

Two tests can here be made that prove that my presentation of the causal chain corresponds to the facts. In my example on p. 180 I introduced the assumption that the provision for the present and near future amounts to a minimum for subsistence. Thus I excluded the execution of levelling options between present and future, for the present has nothing to spare for the future. The result was that the value advantage of present goods was by no means eliminated, it still prevailed. It even was compatible with marginal utility equality in present and future.[90] This proves that the absent factors cannot constitute the cause of higher valuation.

A second test seems to invite also the following observation. What then is the nature of the aforementioned 'options' by which we reduce the present supply in order to obtain a more plentiful 'income' in the future? They are true *savings*. The further we extend these options, the greater will be the savings, that is, the product quantity withdrawn from the present and transferred to the future. Now everybody will agree that abundance of savings is a factor that certainly does not tend to increase the rate of interest or even bring forth its very existence, but rather tends to lower it. According to Fisher's line of thought, however, the situation is reversed. Savings are said to constitute a source of interest because they allocate present goods for future use services. An increase of savings is said to bring about a greater value difference between present and future goods, that is, an increase of the rate of interest, because it means greater withdrawals from or 'underendowment' of the present.

Of course, this is not the case, and cannot be so. Fisher knowingly repeated an error committed already by Carver. He misunderstands the causal relationship between two series of facts that actually are interdependent causatively. A certain value advantage of present goods and the interest phenomenon is assumed to be given. Then people save and, assuming exact calculation and economical behaviour, will continue to save until with increasing wealth the marginal utility of the product unit in both present and future declines. This is described in detail on p. 372 of my *Positive Theory of Capital*. And the higher the interest rate is assumed to be, the more will be saved provided people act perfectly economically. Actual accumulation, however, then counteracts and moderates the interest phenomenon. This indeed is a well-known fact of experience which my theory adequately explains.[91]

Carver and Fisher allowed themselves to be deceived on the causal relationship by the inseparable interdependence of both facts. They erroneously took an effect of interest, indeed an *attenuating* effect, as the cause of interest. With Carver I illustrated this, I believe, in detail and clearly enough.[92] What I said about him is also valid regarding Fisher. But I believe the following can in addition be said about both. Their common mistake is of a logical nature that compares with an explanation of the causes of local price differences with arbitrage transactions resulting therefrom. Both phenomena always appear together. Where local price differences appear, there will be arbitrage transactions. And the greater the price differences, the more lively will be the arbitrage business. Of course, it would be entirely fallacious to explain this coexistence in such a way that the arbitrage transactions constitute the cause of the price differences and that the liveliness of the arbitrage business is the cause of the extent of price differences. But it can here easily be seen that the price difference is the cause, the appearance of arbitrage transactions the effect which retrospectively results in a diminution of the causative phenomenon, but never the entire elimination of it. The same is true in our field. Interest as an existing fact calls forth savings dispositions proceeding even beyond the point of equal marginal utility in present and future. They do this by withdrawing supply from the present until the value of a smaller present sum of goods equals the value of a sum of future goods enhanced by the rate of interest. Continuous accumulation then tends retrospectively to diminish the rate of interest, that is, the initial value difference between present and future goods. But it can never eliminate it entirely. As can be seen, Fisher and Carver err in their explanation of the origin of this difference. They appeal to factors that inversely work towards its elimination, but can never entirely achieve it.

With this obscurity on the actual causal relationship it cannot be surprising that Fisher's line of thought finally leads to a *vicious circle of explanation*, which is my third reproach. For he is moving in a vicious circle when he maintains the following: society's rate of interest is determined by the individual rates of time-preference (*e.g. p. 131*). These are said to 'depend' on the nature of the income stream' as it results *after execution* of the options of borrowing and lending, buying, and selling (*p. 132*), which bring about an 'adjustment' of the time-shape of the income stream in such a way that the individual preference rates coincide with the interest rate (*p. 118*). Thus Fisher presents interest to us as a resultant from that character of its factors which these adopted *after* their adjustment to the resultant. But this means nothing else than explaining the resultant from itself.

Fisher sensed very well that this explanation almost provokes the objection of a vicious circle. Therefore he took great pains to defend himself against it in advance (*Section 5, Chapter VIII*), in my belief, without success! On the contrary, his defense reveals very dubious notions on the nature of an explanation to which he was led by his mathematic train of thought and approach.

Fisher freely admits that according to his explanation 'it is perfectly true that the rate of interest depends on a series of factors which finally depend on the rate of interest.' Yet this series, according to Fisher, is not the vicious circle it seems, 'for the last step is not the inverse of the first.'[93] Fisher therefore wants to demonstrate mathematically the difference between a truly vicious circle and one that merely seems so. We want to determine the height of a father of whom we know that he is three times taller than his child. We also need some knowledge of the height of the child. Now if we are merely told that the height of the child differs from that of its father by double the child's height, the problem indeed is 'circular and insoluble.' For the second sentence leads back to the first; it is merely the inverse of the former in disguise. But if we are told that the height of the child differs from that of its father by 'four times its height minus four feet,' this merely seems as if we explain circularly the height of the father from that of his child and that of the child from that of its father. In reality the question permits full determination, the father is six feet tall, the child two. 'The mere fact that each of these magnitudes is specified in terms of the other does not constitute a vicious circle.'

According to Fisher the same is true with his explanation of the interest rate. He deems the problem sufficiently determined because there are as many 'independent determining factors' as there are unknown quantities. In a lengthy exposition he shows correctly and cogently that there is always a single interest rate that fulfills both conditions: all individuals adjust to it their options for certain income streams, and the demand for and the offer of loans are in equilibrium. To every interest rate there corresponds a certain state of 'options,' in which supply of and demand for loans are in perfect equilibrium. This, according to Fisher, is 'the particular rate of interest, which will solve the problem.' At an interest rate of 5% for instance, the options called forth may be such that the demand for loans is smaller than the supply. An interest rate of 4% may call forth options that result in the supply of loans being smaller than their demand. Only at a certain medium interest rate, let us say 4½%, can both concur. The options called forth by this interest rate then have the further quality of 'clearing' the market.

This all would be rather nice if mathematical and causal 'solutions' of problems were the same or even similar. But *to find* a certain quantity that matches other given assumptions and *to explain* this quantity are two entirely different things. In Fisher's example of father and child the 'solution of the problem' consists in the information that the father is six feet tall. We do not get the slightest information on why he is so tall. Neither is there any causal relationship between the height of the father and that of the child. Or let us take a case where there is causal interdependence. A mathematical solution always proceeds from known to unknown quantities, either from effect to cause or from cause to effect. If I know the capacity of a reservoir and the number of days that are required for filling it, I can compute the flow of the water supply. It is 'unequivocally determined' by the given data. The magnitude of the cause is clearly determined by the data on the effect. Inversely, if the flow of water supply and the filling time are given, I can compute the capacity of the reservoir, that is, I can compute the magnitude of effect from that of its cause. Mathematical determination is neutral with regard to the question of causality. It has nothing to do with it.

'Unequivocal determination' of a problem thus by no means comprises a causal solution. By no means does it protect us from vicious circle explanations. As a matter of fact, we can continue to move in circles with problems that have been determined mathematically. It seems to me that Fisher committed this very error. Certainly a single interest rate corresponds to the state of options that 'clears' the market; the problem is solved mathematically. But this mathematical determination fails to inform us on the sequence of causality between the facts. Therefore causal interpretation must accompany mathematical determination. In the case of father and child there was no causal relation between their heights. In the case of water supply and reservoir we saw a perfect mathematical interdependence between the three factors, flow of water supply, filling time, and capacity of the reservoir. We easily recognized that the flow of the water supply was the cause, the filling of the reservoir the effect.

The same is true in our case. Although the interest rate is unequivocally determined at a certain state of options where the market is 'cleared' we

191

must still explain the cause and effect relationship. This task unfortunately leaves ample room for errors of interpretation, and especially for vicious circles. 'Unequivocal determination' does not protect us from them, as Fisher seems to assume. Fisher himself falls prey to one when he does not explain the interest rate as a resultant from the originary preference rates of individuals, but rather from preference rates that are adjusted to the interest rate. This in fact means to explain the establishment of the interest rate from the established interest rate, or the resultant from the resultant.[94]

But still another peculiar feature of Fisher's approach may have contributed to obscuring all these relations. Fisher differs from me in that he does not separate his explanation of the *origin* of interest from that of its *rate*. He rejects intentionally and expressly such a separation and limits his presentation to the determining factors of the interest rate. According to him, 'to determine the rate of interest will include the determination of whether the rate must necessarily always be greater than zero.'[95]

Properly understood this is indeed correct. But this method renders a clear elaboration of the sources of interest more difficult, which are by no means identical with the determining factors of its rate. All interest-originating causes undoubtedly are also determining factors for the actual rate. But not all rate-determining factors are also interest-creating causes; they may also be *obstacles* that have been overcome. When we inquire into the causes of a flood we certainly cannot cite the dams and reservoirs built to prevent or at least mitigate inundations. But they are a determining factor for the actual water-mark of the flood. They check the flooding of the river's banks or, in case they cannot prevent this entirely, tend to mitigate the extent of the flood. Similarly, there are other circumstances besides the actual interest-creating causes that bring about or enhance the value advantage of present goods over future goods. There are circumstances that tend inversely to counteract this advantage but are too weak to eliminate it entirely. They undoubtedly are determining factors for the rate of interest, but undoubtedly are not originating causes of it. They stand to its existence as do arbitrage transactions to local price differences, or as a watch's escapement regulating its motion to the movement of its works.

In his presentation Fisher did not clearly separate the originating forces from the determining forces. Consequently it could easily escape him that an undubitably determining factor, which interest calls forth in the form of saving[96] and which tends to mitigate the interest phenomenon, actually is no *originating* cause.

I had to cast serious doubts on a line of thought that deserves respect

192

because of its compactness and profoundness. I consider Fisher's theory one of the most remarkable performances in the field of interest. It is an interesting attempt at presenting the facts upon which my 'agio theory' rests in another even simpler generalization. But on grounds of the reasons elaborated above I cannot regard his attempt as successful. In my belief my theory deserves at least relative preference.

And now a final remark.

I could easily have passed over this controversy raised by Fisher and Bortkiewicz as a mere trifle. For formally it merely pertains to the question whether or not my 'third reason' whose actual effect on interest is not, or at least not expressly denied,[97] constitutes an independent reason *besides* the 'first reason,' or whether or not it merely constitutes a partial reason *within* the 'first reason.' Seen in this light it merely deals with a question of proper arrangement.

I could easily have taken the position that such a question is of minor importance. I could have stated that at the very beginning I admitted that this question is open for discussion because the arrangement of reasons can be changed in such a way that the first and third reasons stand combined.[98] I could have maintained that I am correct at least formally in my own arrangement because my third reason indubitably differs from my first reason insofar as I defined the latter as supply divergencies resulting 'from other sources.' Both my opponents seem to have overlooked this.[99]

But such a formalistic treatment of the controversy would have diverted our attention and discussion from the more far-reaching fundamental disagreement on the motivation underlying our formal points of view. Once having intruded our economic thought, these material disagreements sooner or later undoubtedly would have emerged also in more significant deductions. Therefore I preferred to take them up at my first opportunity and present them for consideration by those colleagues who are interested in the ultimate theoretical foundation of interest. Our case is similar to certain legal cases in which a trifle is at stake, but important fundamental judicial decisions are made. Indeed it is a trifle whether the 'third reason' outwardly is independent or must be grouped under the main heading 'first reason.' It is of utmost importance, however, for the future development of economic thought and the problem of interest whether the causal relationship between the facts surrounding the interest phenomenon proceeds the way my opponents believe it to proceed, or the way I am inclined to believe. This is why I did not evade a discussion which, if it was to occur at all, had to grow almost to a book within a book. I know very well that only very few readers will be grateful for its insertion.

NOTES

1. A further explanation of 'Present and Future in Economic Life' as presented in *Positive Theory of Capital*, p. 271 ff.
2. Cf. Marshall's 'productiveness and prospectiveness' of capital.
3. Rodbertus, *Soziale Frage*, pp. 77 ff., *Das Kapital*, pp. 236 ff.
4. Cf., for instance, Landry: '...enfin il est *trop évident* qui'il faut que la productivité du capital tienne une place dans une théorie de l'intérêt.' (*L'intérêt du capital*, p. 85, note 1.)
5. With the rather obscure position of Fisher on my thesis of the higher productivity of longer roundabout methods of production I dealt in detail in 'Essay IV'. At any rate Fisher does not deny the fact, although he ascribes its 'regularity' to a different origin. Unfortunately in many other questions Bortkiewicz is irresolute as to the facts. He wavers between semi-recognition and semi-denial, but finally states expressly that in the development of his objection he wants to 'assume as correct' the facts asserted by me. ('Der Kardinalfehler der Böhm-Bawerkschen Zinstheorie' in Schmoller's *Jahrbuch*, vol. xxx (1906), p. 951).
6. Ibid., p. 951.
7. *Rate of Interest*, p. 62.
8. Bortkiewicz, op. cit., p. 958.
9. Preface to the third edition of *Positive Theory of Capital*, p. 388.
10. 'Der Kardinalfehler der Böhm-Bawerkschen Zinstheorie' in Schmoller's *Jahrbuch*, vol. xxx (1906), pp. 951 ff.
11. It concurs materially with the expositions on foregoing pp. 271 ff.
12. Italics added.
13. *Positive Theory of Capital*, pp. 273–5.
14. 'But for one and the same person at one and the same point of time, the larger quantity always has the greater value. No matter what the absolute value of a bushel or of a pound may be, one thing is certain, and that is, that for me *two pounds or two bushels that I have today* are worth more than one pound or one bushel that I have today.' *Positive Theory of Capital*, p. 273
15. Bortkiewicz, op. cit., p. 953.
16. E.g., op. cit., pp. 953 ff., 959 ff.
17. They are identical with the passage beginning on p. 272 of this edition of *Positive Theory of Capital*: 'If we translate the language ...' and ending on p. 273 with '... which variant of our example is chosen.'
18. Bortkiewicz obviously is even thinking of a physical impossibility for lengthening the production roundaboutness, for he makes zero the

product of an eight-year production period. For our problem, however, it is merely important whether seven years constitute the limit of *higher* productivity of further production lengthenings, which at any rate still lies before the physical impossibility. Bortkiewicz's broader assumption naturally includes the narrower one. In the following passage which is no longer included in the foregoing quotation he himself demonstrates this. He takes 500 as the product, which is the yield of the longest production period (7 years) leading to greater productivity, instead of zero (p. 955). But for our problem it is irrelevant whether we take 500 or zero: it is most important whether we assume that the productivity is increased beyond the seventh year.

19. *Positive Theory of Capital*, pp. 319 ff.; cf. also my later very explicit explanations and illustrations in 'Einige strittige Fragen,' especially pp. 25 ff., and 40 ff.; and in 'Essay I', pp. 10 f. of this volume.

20. Besides, Bortkiewicz returns to this rather strange methodological postulate a second time further below. As the touchstone of the correctness of a theory that does not conceive interest as a 'momentary extra gain' but, like my theory, as an 'income of permanent nature,' he demands that it must be conclusive even 'where the length of the production period seems to be given *without choice between different methods*' (op. cit., pp. 970 ff.). This again is the expectation that the fact of various productivities of methods of various lengths to which I refer is to maintain its interest-creating power even where it does not exist, and only a single method with a single length is technically feasible. But I readily admit that Bortkiewicz made this later remark in connection with his opinion, already known to us, that simultaneous knowledge of several production methods of various productivities conflicts with the assumption of a 'stationary' state of society in which alone a static income can exist. From the standpoint of this premise his postulate indeed is correct; but of course, the premise is fallacious! (cf. my 'Essay I', note 39).

21. I chose this expression in order to avoid a mistaken objection which could be deduced from the fact that some of our economic actions *benefit also* periods that certainly lie beyond the zone of productivity. If I build a stone bench in my garden today, perhaps it may last 2,000 years and still serve wants of the fourth millenium after Christ. But I did not build it *for the sake of these wants*. Its extension of services to these remote wants is irrelevant for my own economic calculation. Neither does it induce me to designate a production plan, nor does it affect one. Of course here we are merely concerned with the question of whether we ever employ means of production for purposes lying clearly beyond the zone of higher productivity.

22. Perhaps it is not wholly superfluous to remark further that the *average* length of a production period comprises merely a modest number of years. On p. 319 of *Positive Theory of Capital* I estimated the average in case of 'enormous national wealth' at only ten years. But this average, I pointed out at several places in the text (e.g., pp. 105, 365 ff.) comprises special periods of very different lengths which the various branches of production require according to their special circumstances. And I pointed out that even these special production periods rarely if ever are 'uniformly distributed' (cf. *Positive Theory*, p. 87). In case of uneven distribution of successive investments even at a modest average, a considerable interval between single investments and the first want satisfaction may result. Thus single investments for very remote want satisfactions (e.g., many decades or even a century removed) may still belong to a process lying within the zone of higher productivity. Perhaps if Bortkiewicz had borne this clearly in mind he would have hesitated to allow producers to 'calculate' with returns obtainable only beyond the outer limit for efficiency of method lengthenings (ibid., p. 954). In this respect the numerically low assumption under which Bortkiewicz already reached this limit after seven years has perhaps left its harmful work in spite of its nature of mere example.

23. Cf. p. 149 in the foregoing text and the diagram modified according to Bortkiewicz.

24. I explained this rule and defined it against possible misunderstandings on pp. 156 ff. of *Positive Theory of Capital*.

25. On account of a faulty syllogism, Bortkiewicz fails to recognize even this fact. On page 955 he asserts the following: 'According to the marginal utility theory producers' goods receive their value from consumers' goods in the production of which they serve. If producers' goods from various investment periods are concerned, we may assume that value differences can arise only insofar as their consumers' goods are produced in different periods.' But this 'may perhaps be assumed' provided we are not free to vary the length of the production period and thus also the quality of the obtainable consumers' goods. Only when the production period is inflexibly given, may we distinguish the consumers' goods flowing from producers' goods that are available in different periods. The only criterion of distinction is the fact 'that they come to completion in different periods.' Cf. also in the following text my expositions on Fisher who repeats Bortkiewicz's error.

26. This part of Bortkiewicz's argumentation apparently suffers from the strange imputation to which I referred above. This is the imputation that my diagrams compare the valuation of various producers. If

valuations of various persons were actually concerned it would indeed not be unfeasible *a priori* that everyone takes a different year as the 'last' one to be considered for his valuations. Bortkiewicz should have noticed this contradiction if he had clearly realized that value comparisons of one and the same person are concerned.

27. I am sorry I must quote again in all detail because, as will soon be seen, the whole conclusion hinges on words.

28. Bortkiewicz, op. cit., p. 956.

29. This is probably what Bortkiewicz meant with the words 'applicability of Böhm-Bawerk's reasoning' to the example.

30. Cf. *Positive Theory of Capital*, pp. 263 ff. The capacity of the first two reasons to lead to the higher value of present goods without the cooperation of the third reason is presented especially cogently on pp. 266 and 281.

31. Bortkiewicz, op. cit., pp. 960, 964, 970.

32. They correspond to pp. 354–61 of this edition.

33. Bortkiewicz, op. cit., pp. 964–70.

34. Ibid., pp. 965 ff.

35. Cf., for instance, *Positive Theory of Capital*, 2nd edn, p. 92, note 1, pp. 100 ff., 429; 'Einige strittige Fragen', p. 25, note 1. Occasionally I expressed my personal reservations towards a name which I consider not quite correct by the repeated use of quotation marks in my own expositions (e.g. *Positive Theory of Capital*, 2nd edn, p. 429 and 'Einige strittige Fragen,' p. 25).

36. He could not otherwise have connected his critique with the remark that 'to him' capital means nothing but those goods serving *continuous production.*' For in the following he repeatedly contrasts the *factor of production* capital and the two other factors, use of land and labour. And he could not have sincerely disregarded my reservation mentioned above which certainly is not irrelevant for an interpretation of my opinion on 'capital scarcity.'

37. *Rate of Interest* (New York, 1907).

38. Ibid., pp. 61 ff.

39. Ibid., appendix to chapter 4, section 4, pp. 354 ff.

40. Sanger, for instance, in a review of Fisher's work writes the following: 'It is doubtful how far this theory (meaning my theory) has been held by economists; *but the refutation of this in a very short appendix is very forcible*' (*Economic Journal* (March, 1908), p. 67).

41. For instance, through an examination of differences of value advantage resulting from an addition of the third reason to the two other reasons, etc.

42. I therefore did not alter materially my presentation in this fourth

edition of my book although it would have been easy to counter Fisher's objection discussed above through another numerical example. Only through a few stylistic changes of presentation did I endeavor to avoid the impression – in case it ever arose – that that part of my numerical illustration assuming declining marginal utility on account of *other* reasons not merely illustrates my contentions but rather offers new important proof.

43. Pp. 268 ff.

44. Someone may believe that the figures of this example represent an exceptional case artificially prepared for this occasion. This is a mistake. It is not the concrete figures that are important, but the type. The type of a marginal utility, however, that is stationary for some time and declining in later periods is as frequent as it is important. With all people who save their wealth for the future the motives of the first and second reasons intermingle and compensate each other. Consequently as far as these two reasons are concerned *value equivalence* of present and future goods results with respect to the near future in which these people expect to live. I explained this in my *Positive Theory of Capital*, note 23 to book iv, chapter i, and on p. 307. Only the appearance of the third reason induces them to value present goods higher than future goods.

45. In spite of its different circumstances and altered dialectic appearance the attentive reader will easily recognize the same logical error which we discovered in Bortkiewicz (cf. foregoing p. 155 ff.).

46. Cf. 'Essay I', foregoing pp. 11 f., and note 27 to 'Essay I'.

47. When speaking of 'the same maximum *value*' Fisher obviously should have taken 5,000 instead of 1,000 (1,000 product units at a reduced marginal utility of 5). But this is irrelevant for the general train of thought.

48. Fisher, op. cit., pp. 66 f.

49. Throughout all his approximations Fisher repeatedly and very clearly described his unchanging subject of evidence as follows: '. . . that these elements, *and these alone*, produce the advantage of present over future goods' (p. 62); 'the fact is that the *only* reason (for the value advantage of present labour months) is that today's investment will mature earlier . . .' (pp. 70–1); the so-called technical supremacy 'derives all its force' from the advantage of an earlier over a later enjoyment; the alleged third reason '*is only the first two* circumstances in disguise' (p. 71).

50. Op. cit., p. 956.

51. Cf. foregoing p. 169.

52. In his publications Fisher did not expound this objection in detail. But he frequently hinted at it with the clause '*if there be a maximum*

(op. cit., p. 66), or *'assuming of course that maxima exist'* (p. 355), which is clear enough for the expert. Besides, Professor Fisher was kind enough to inform me regarding this opinion of his through an occasional letter (cf. note 11 to 'Essay IV').

53. Ibid., pp. 69–70.
54. On this point cf. my 'Essay I', p. 12.
55. Cf. my 'Essay I', pp. 11 f. also on this point.
56. Fisher, op. cit., p. 70.
57. If we assume the subsistence fund to be insufficient, we arrive at the variation discussed by Fisher in section 7 in which the value advantage of the older labour month immediately emerges. Cf. the following text.
58. Cf. note 25 to 'Essay XII'.
59. Fisher, pp. 70–1. In a very fascinating way Fisher repeats this fallacy in his positive presentation. On pp. 89 ff. he demonstrates that the 'time preference' of an older capital good is based on the fact that the 'income' therefrom (which is Fisher's term for the final *use services* of the capital good) are available earlier. Also this sentence, in spite of its apparent axiomatic certainty, must be read *cum grano salis*. Similar to my foregoing exposition we must not overlook that the older capital good must not yield *earlier* use services. Through method lengthenings it may also yield *other* and *more* services for the *same point of time*. 'Time-preference' can be based also on this possibility.
60. Fisher calls this technical superiority a 'delusion' (p. 72).
61. Someone whose thought is not confused by artificial subtleties could never have doubted that 'to get *more*' is another reason for preference than 'to get it earlier.' Each one of these cases could very well occur without the other (e.g., if we *must* always choose 'convergingly,' or never *can* choose so). Absence of one of these possibilities always exerts a considerable influence on the scope and degree of our actual preferences. This should suffice to convince everybody whose sight is not dimmed by wrong dialectical glasses that absence of the alternative 'getting more' deprives the case of something not present in the alternative 'getting earlier.' It must therefore have been present as an 'independent cause.' The shortest and easiest refutation of Fisher thus seems to lie in the simple *argumentum ad hominem* to which I referred at the beginning of this controversy. I referred to the argument that the phenomenon of interest in its present scope and magnitude would no longer exist if longer production processes would no longer lead to higher productivity.

So far my task merely consisted in proving positively and in detail that the dialectical glasses through which Bortkiewicz and Fisher urge us to view the facts are badly selected. The alleged logical force leading to their point of view, in final analysis, springs from a fallacy. I hope I have created this ease of mind to all those who view naturally.

But to all those readers who have not yet found it I should like to recommend the following two examples for their analytical consideration. They are taken from a great number of analogous cases at which we can observe a similar amalgamation of really independent reasons for preference. A new engine for ships is invented that in comparison with the customary engines offers a choice of one of two advantages. It permits either greater speed with the same fuel consumption, or the same speed with less consumption. It is likely that express liners will prefer the new engine for the first reason, and freighters for the second reason. Now can the second reason, savings of fuel, be dissolved entirely in the first reason, greater speed? If speed is entirely irrelevant does also the second reason, savings, play no role? Would the more economical engines not be used, but only sails? Another example: Laying siege to a fortress the sieging army endeavours to advance its batteries successively because the most advanced batteries are most valuable from the point of view of siege technique. Why? Because they afford the choice either to reach important distant targets that lie in the interior of the sieged territory and that cannot be reached by batteries further back, or to bombard more effectively nearer targets that lie already within reach of the rear batteries. Now can this second advantage, which in a real siege is often decisive, be converted to the first by arguing with Fisher as follows: since the only difference between the advanced and rear batteries consists in the advanced position of the former, that is, in preference as to territory, the only reason for their greater value can be the preference as to territory, that is, the circumstance that they reach more distant targets than rear batteries?

62. Cf. *Positive Theory of Capital*, 2nd edn, pp. 285 ff. The same exposition is now on pp. 277 ff. of this edition. The reader may reread it there.

63. Fisher, op. cit., p. 72.

64. Fisher namely translated my words 'from any difference arising out of other sources' with the words 'from any *such* difference' which coincides with the former neither in wording nor meaning.

65. Fisher, op. cit., p. 72.

66. By the way, this whole strange controversy on the independence of the third reason could never have arisen if in reality the two other reasons would not also exert certain effects on the supply situation, that is, on facts of the 'first reason.' Consequently empirical reality

always reveals the coexistence of facts and effects of all three reasons. It further follows that this frustrates the simplest and most self-evident test of independence. This test would reveal that in actual life and empirical experiment the third reason brings about the said effect when all facts pertaining to the first and second reason are excluded completely and indubitably. But unfortunately our explanation of existing causal relations is crowded off the path of a clear empirical examination, which would leave no room for differences of opinion, and is forced on the road of dialectical evidence, which unfortunately often leaves ample room for obscurities and confusion. Here it must bear the further burden in order to furnish its weary proof that the very road that is closest to the empirical examination, which I should like to call the road of mental experiment, forces us to construct artificial and involved assumptions. For in order to abstract clearly the effectiveness of the third reason, the ever-present influence of the two other reasons must be artificially offset, and eliminated through special assumptions. This is the reason for the casuistic nature of the example offered in the text and of other similar examples I have given.

67. Essentially the same result is achieved if the neighbour's offer would not pertain to an exchange of the 1891 labour year for his 1890 labour, but rather to an exchange of 2,400 product units completed in 1892 for 2,400 units maturing in 1891. In this case our family in 1891 could live on the borrowed 1891 products. This would set our supporter's 1890 labour free which could now be invested in a *two-year* production yielding 3,360 units for the wants of 1892. In 1892 he could repay the loan of 2,400 units and with the rest of 960 units satisfy the extraordinary demand. The normal demand of 2,400 units could be satisfied with the yield of his 1891 labour which would be invested as before in a one-year production process.

Probably no reader will object that in this fundamental investigation I neglect the technical difficulties resulting from such adaptations of the production process and especially from the correct definition of whole labour years because of the necessary 'process continuation.' To take them into consideration would mean to render the example unwieldy and unintelligible. It would not alter the principle involved.

68. In the text of my *Positive Theory of Capital*, note 32 to book iv, chapter i, I discussed the question of whether or not a mere multiplication of the number of units and marginal utility is proper for this comparison. At any rate, the first total exceeds the second total even if we use no multiplication, but rather add the terms of a series that rises from the basis 8, which is more suitable for arriving at the total value of a uniform supply.

69. Cf. my *History and Critique of Interest Theories*, pp. 393 ff., especially pp. 397 ff.

70. I need hardly remark for the benefit of attentive readers of pp. 281 ff. of my *Positive Theory of Capital* that it is no contradiction to ascribe a weakening effect on another heterogeneous cause of higher valuation to a circumstance that by itself is capable of constituting a cause of higher valuation.

71. He presents it by way of increasingly involved assumptions as 'first,' 'second,' and 'third' approximation.

72. For instance, the term 'income.' Entirely new are Fisher's terms 'size' and 'time-shape' of the income stream.

73. 'This 'time preference' (namely the preference for present over future goods) is the central fact in the theory of interest,' *Rate of Interest*, p. 88. Because of this identity of fundamental thought and our far-reaching concurrence also as to the facts on which we both in final analysis base the explanation of interest, Fisher himself calls his 'presentation of the interest theory' a 'form' of my 'agio theory.' The difference, according to him, mainly lies in his elimination of the 'technical superiority of present goods' and his express introduction of the concept of 'income' (pp. 87 ff.). In a small later publication which I received when this work had already gone to press, Fisher introduces the term 'impatience theory' for his own theory. But he continues to characterize it as a mere 'modification of Böhm-Bawerk's agio theory' (The 'Impatience Theory of Interest,' reprint from the journal *Scientia, Rivista di Scienza*, vol. ix (1911), p. 386). As to its content, also this publication entirely represents the point of view of his older main work, *The Rate of Interest*.

74. Fisher, op. cit., p. 89.

75. It is true, Fisher mentions this identification only in connection with the influence of 'time-shape,' that is, the temporal distribution of income, besides which he also mentions absolute 'size,' 'composition,' and 'probability' of income as the determinants of 'time-preference.' But the former is so decisive because the indirect effectiveness of the other determinants necessarily must act through it that I think I can neglect the latter in this presentation aimed at the gist of the problem.

76. Fisher hints at this construction, for instance, on p. 103, note 2. This may perhaps explain an apparent contradiction. On p. 88 Fisher declares that time-preference is almost identical with my 'perspective undervaluation of the future.' On p. 98, however, he declares that the dependency of time-preference on the temporal distribution of income is practically identical with my *first reason*.

77. Fisher illustrates this principle with the example of the owner of a

parcel of land, who has the choice of using it for mining, farming, or foresting. Let us assume that he chooses the first alternative and that the iron ore is readily accessible and the richest vein closest to the surface. In this case he would reap the highest income in the beginning. Later when the vein is increasingly near exhaustion he will receive an ever smaller income until finally, when the bed is completely empty, his income will cease altogether. In case he should farm the land he would enjoy an even income throughout. Finally, if he should employ his land for foresting he would receive no income whatever in the first years after the planting, but a rising income in later years. This is obviously the point at which Fisher takes into consideration, and incorporates in his theoretical system, the facts pertaining to the difference in the length of the production period, that is, my 'third reason.'

78. Fisher, op. cit., p. 139.
79. '... the choice among the options will simply depend on the one which gives the maximum present value reckoned at the market rate of interest,' ibid., p. 140.
80. Ibid., p. 145
81. Ibid., p. 119; also pp. 117 ff. with detailed illustration.
82. Ibid., pp. 131, 133 paragraph 3, 150 paragraph 5. Fisher presents a complete point-by-point summary for his 'first approximation' on pp. 132 ff. for the 'second approximation' on p. 150. The 'third approximation,' which merely also considers the 'uncertainty' of income, is of no fundamental importance for our question. As a matter of fact, I have also deleted all details of Fisher's first two approximations that do not affect the main principles of explanation.
83. Ibid., p. 93
84. Ibid., pp. 130 ff.
85. Ibid., p. 132.
86. 'The time-preference depends on the relative abundance of the early and remote incomes or what we may call the time-shape of the income stream' (p. 92; cf. also p. 183 of this Essay).
87. When he sums up the 'second approximation' he no longer emphasizes that abundance *after completion of all offsetting operations* is decisive for individual time preference. He simply says 'each individual's preference rate depends on *his* income-stream' (p. 150, paragraph 2). But the whole context leaves no doubt that he is thinking also here of this definite income-stream that is left after having executed his options.
88. Cf. pp. 100 ff. of this Essay.
89. On the exactness of figures and the use of multiplication in the value

determination of larger quantities cf. my several reservations, for instance, on pp. 182 ff. of this Essay and p. 274 of *Positive Theory of Capital*, together with note 32 to book iv, chapter i.

90. Cf. pp. 181 ff. in the foregoing text. Of course, we would arrive at a similar result also if it is not the lowering of the minimum of existence that prevents the shifting of use services between the present and the future, but also any other reason of factual nature.

91. The increasing supplies for subsistence enlarged by every saving permit application of productive method lengthenings up to an ever lower point on the declining scale of productivity increases. Cf. *Positive Theory of Capital*, pp. 370 ff.

92. *History and Critique of Interest Theories*, pp. 400 ff.

93. Fisher, op. cit., p. 147.

94. Fisher's own illustration contains some features that make the actual situation almost self-evident. He demonstrates (p. 148, cf. pp. 190 f. in the foregoing text) that at a given state of originary factors (initial income streams and individual preference-rates) the interest rate of 5% cannot be the one at which the market arrives at equilibrium. What then are the forces that lower the definitely unfeasible rate to the definitely feasible and obligatory rate of 4½%? Is it not obvious that only the originary equilibrium-seeking forces can bring about this necessary change, and not the ultimately resulting state of forces after the adjustment is completed? A state that follows the completion of adjustment never can constitute the cause of the adjustment.

Fisher's position on our question offers an instructive example of the methodological dangers connected with an adoption of the mathematical formalistic approach and especially with the predilection for the 'concept of function' instead of that of 'causality.' It entices us to an early relaxation as soon as we arrive at an 'unequivocally determined interdependence,' and weakens our alertness towards lurking errors in the causal interpretation of interrelated facts. Cf. on this point note 10 to 'Essay VIII'.

95. Ibid., p. 93

96. Or that part of saving that is called forth by the existence of interest. Another part would be accumulated also without interest, which has been pointed out again and again (e.g., by Carver and Landry).

97. Cf. p. 146 in the foregoing text, and especially note 5 to 'Essay XII'.

98. Cf. note 36 to book iv, chapter i of *Positive Theory of Capital* which appeared already in the first two editions.

99. *Positive Theory of Capital*, 2nd German edn, p. 286; cf. also pp. 178 f. of this Essay.

Friedrich von Wieser, 'Ueber das Verhältnis der Kosten zum Wert' (1876), in F. von Wieser, *Gesammelte Abhandlungen* (Tübingen: J. C. B. Mohr, 1929), pp. 377–404.

This paper by Friedrich von Wieser (1851–1926) was first published in the original German in *Gesammelte Abhandlungen*, the posthumous collection of his essays edited by F. A. Hayek. It is the earliest piece of work we have by Wieser, a member of the 'founding triumvirate' of the Austrian School with Carl Menger and Eugen von Böhm-Bawerk, and the one with the longest teaching career. Written by Wieser while he was a student, as a contribution to Karl Knies's seminar at Heidelberg, the paper contains many of the ideas which Wieser was to pursue in his better-known 1884 monograph, *Ursprung und Hauptgesetze des Wirtschaftlichen Wertes*, and has considerable historical significance. F. A. Hayek (ibid.) noted that this paper establishes Wieser's claim to priority in the development of the opportunity-cost notion. It has been translated into English especially for this volume.

8

On the Relationship of Costs to Value

FRIEDRICH von WIESER

Translated by
WILLIAM KIRBY

I

The purpose of the following exposition is to examine the relationship of costs to value or, in other words, to demonstrate the influence which the use of economic goods of a higher order to produce goods of a lower order has on the value of the latter.

In our examination, let us proceed from the simplest form in which the economic process to be observed can be presented.

Let us imagine an isolated subject engaging in economic activity who, while being amply supplied with all other goods, is dependent with regard to the satisfaction of particular needs on goods which are not immediately available but which first have to be obtained by production. All the goods required for production would be at hand in sufficient quantity apart from one, through, for example, all the relevant means of production being available in abundance, but the expenditure of labour which our subject is capable of not being sufficient to produce the said goods in the desired quantity. Accordingly, a single economic good is assumed to be available, which is used for manufacturing in conjunction with other, non-economic, goods. Let us assume that this economic good is only used as a second-order good, i.e. is directly used to produce the first-order goods which are consumed.

To simplify still further the case which we are to observe, let us first make the further assumption that the productive economic good is only available during a specific period, within which production must be completed and the requirements for the entire subsequent period must be procured. Therefore we present the case thus: the productive good is available once and for all in a specific period for production and for procuring the requirements and afterwards further production is not possible.

Let us now assume that our subject is able to produce many different kinds of first-order goods from the entire productive good, but not all with the same expenditure of quantities of the productive goods. While, in order to produce a unit of the first good, he needs a quantity of the productive good which we shall call a unit, a unit of the second first-order good requires two, a unit of the third three and a unit of the fourth four such quantities for their production. Let us designate the first-order goods by the Roman numerals I-IV according to the number of units of the productive good required for their production.

Finally, let us assume that the subject we are observing has at his disposal a total of 30 units of the second-order economic good, a quantity which is insufficient to produce all the first-order goods required to fully satisfy his needs. He is therefore obliged to proceed in an economic manner in using this good, that is, to use all available quantities thereof in a way which achieves the principal need-satisfactions which are dependent on this good. Since, however, the productive good cannot be directly used for need-satisfaction but is to be used to produce goods for consumption, the general rule regarding the use of economic goods is modified and for our subject says that with the productive good available in limited quantity he should produce those first-order goods which procure for him the greatest possible need-satisfaction. Thus, before commencing production, he will have to examine the relative importance of the needs in question and of the first-order goods to be directly used to satisfy them.

In the course of this examination, he now finds that the need which is satisfied by the goods of category I is of such an intensity that the first available good of this kind acquires the greatest importance that any good can have, in that the preservation of his life depends on this good being available. Let us assign to this importance the number 10. Each subsequent good of the same type would have an importance diminished by 1 with regard to his welfare. For the goods of category II, it is assumed that the intensity of need is such that the first available good acquires an importance which gives rise to an importance of 9 for each of the two quantities of the productive good which are contained therein. This is to say that the importance of this good is such that for each unit of the productive good that it contains, the same importance results as if it were used to produce a category I good with an importance of 9. Therefore the first category II good has the same importance of two category I goods, if each of them had an importance of 9. Here again, it is assumed that for

208

each subsequent good the importance, that is, in respect of the unit of the productive good that is used, is diminished by 1.

However, it would clearly not correspond to conditions in real life if we were to assume such a smooth gradation of the importance of the individual acts of need-satisfaction for various categories of need. It may be that a good which procures for us the satisfaction of the most important needs, on the presence of which our existence depends, nevertheless very quickly declines in importance for our economic awareness as soon as the available quantity of this good exceeds a particular limited measure, in that the next quantities available over and above this measure would at most allow us a certain degree of freedom in the use of the good and would relieve us of our concern to satisfy such a pressing need, and any further quantities would no longer have any importance at all, as we would be unable to satisfy any needs with them.

For a Canadian hunter, for instance, the first clothing made from animal skins which protects him from the rigours of the weather and ensures the preservation of his life has the highest importance attributed by him to any good. A second set of clothing might appear useful to him as a spare in case the first becomes spoiled. However, he would be unable to use or value a third set. Or let us imagine a person living by simple habits; a certain supply of food preserves his life and a further supply affords him full satiation; however, as he has fully satisfied his need for food and he despises finer culinary delights, further supplies of food of whatever quality would be of no further use or importance to him.

In contrast, other goods which are intended to satisfy needs which are by no means as urgent retain their importance even if their quantity continues to increase; in fact, their importance scarcely appears to decline. A collector of rare objects or the owner of an art gallery obtains, with every new acquisition, a barely diminished feeling of satisfied collectors' desire. Between these extremes, we may observe goods which pass through all the grades of value which take their justification from the whole range of our feelings from concern for preservation of one's life to the desire to brighten one's life.

The gradual decrease in the importance of the individual types of good, which can be perceived for every kind of good, may therefore be uneven for different kinds of good; in fact, it may vary for the same kind of good, being sometimes faster and sometimes slower, even almost imperceptible.

In line with this observation, our subject finds in category III that in the case of the first available good, for each of the three unit quantities of the productive good that are required for its production an importance of 8 results, while for the second good it is 6, for the third 2 and for the fourth 1, as can be seen from the chart below. In category IV, in the same way

209

the numbers in the chart should be understood as expressing the importance of a unit of the productive good.

For a unit of the productive good, the importance is:	In category			
	I.	II.	III.	IV.
for the 1st available good	10	9	8	7
„ „ 2nd „ „	9	8	6	5
„ „ 3rd „ „	8	7	2	3
„ „ 4th „ „	7	6	1	1
„ „ 5th „ „	6	5	0	0
„ „ 6th „ „	5	4		
„ „ 7th „ „	4	3		
„ „ 8th „ „	3	2		
„ „ 9th „ „	2	1		
„ „ 10th „ „	1	0		

A simple calculation now tells the subject that of the 30 quantities of the productive good that are available to him, he must use 6 to produce 6 category I goods, 10 to produce 5 category II goods, 6 to produce 2 category III goods and 8 to produce 2 category IV goods, because with this selection he can procure the maximum attainable enjoyment of goods. If he proceeded differently, e.g. if he produced only 4 category II goods and used the two quantities of the productive good thus saved to produce two extra category I goods, he would deprive himself of the possibility of satisfying a need, the importance of which is equivalent to the importance of two acts of need-satisfaction in category I with an intensity of 5, and would find only an imperfect substitute for this in securing satisfaction of needs, of which one has an importance of 4 and the other an importance of 3.

By therefore following the rule prescribed to him by his concern for his well-being that he should not produce any good which would only be capable of supplying a less important need provided that one can be produced, the use of which is able to give him greater enjoyment, he is bound to a specific sequence of production which he may only deviate from to his disadvantage, if we assume his needs to be fixed.

Let us now imagine that production according to the schedule developed above has been undertaken and completed, and let us examine the value of the goods. Let us ask three questions and try to answer them.

1. What was the value of the productive good?

2. What is the value of the first-order good in the different categories of goods?

3. What influence do these two values have on each other?

1. The value of the unit of the productive good depends on the magnitude of the need which would have to remain unsatisfied if the quantity of the productive good were reduced by 1. If our subject had not 30 but 29 goods at his disposal, it is clear that the way to use them most economically would have been to use the same quantity for production in the categories II-IV but to only produce 5 goods of category I. For our subject, therefore, the good in question has the same importance as the 6th category I good, namely 5.

2. According to the same general rule of the magnitude of the value of goods, the value of a unit of category I goods is 5. In category II, there depends on the availability of the unit of the good a need-satisfaction, the importance of which we have equated above with two acts of need-satisfaction with an intensity of 5. Let us express this as 2 times 5, as in our scale the number 10 has already acquired a different meaning. The value of a unit of category II goods is therefore equal to 2 times 5, while in category III it is equal to 3 times 6 and in category IV, 4 times 5.

3. Leaving aside category III, the special circumstances of which we will discuss later, we accordingly find a congruence between the value of the second-order good and the first-order goods which appears to be a law and can be expressed as follows: the value of the first-order goods is equal to the value of the quantity of the productive good required for their manufacture. The category I good, for the production of which one quantity is sufficient, has the same value as this quantity; the value of the category II good, for the production of which two quantities were used, is equal to the value of these two quantities, and so on. If we compare the first-order goods with each other (again leaving aside category III), the value is in direct proportion to the quantities of the higher-order good that are used.

If we look for the reason for this phenomenon, we may first be led to suppose that it is the value of the productive good which determines the value of the product and, as it occurs to the same extent in all products, is the consequence of the proportionality between the value and the quantity used of the productive good. This assumption, however, is immediately proved wrong if we imagine that production was not undertaken in the economic manner we have described. If the subject, instead of producing two category IV goods, had produced only one and had used the productive goods thus saved to produce another four category I goods, the value of a good of this category, the manufacture of which required one unit of the productive good, would be equal to 1 and the value of this single category IV good produced, which contains four units, would be equal to 4 times 7, which would not be compatible with that assumption. If one were to maintain, taking the facts into account, that while the productive good could not transfer its value to the product regardless of the use, this

211

result would definitely be achieved if the use were an economic one, this explains nothing. For after all, the limitation 'if the use were an economic one' means nothing more than 'if it were one in which the need-satisfaction were the most complete possible'.

So another solution must be looked for, which can only be found if the nature and measure of the value are correctly recognised. Before proceeding to the solution of this problem, therefore, we will describe the nature and measure of the value, in the relationship of the first-order goods to the need-satisfactions, where they can be most directly grasped. This relationship will also give us a full analogy with that existing between first-order and second-order goods, and we will therefore have to also take it as a basis for preparing the solution to the main question concerning us.

The importance to us of the individual acts of need-satisfaction is rooted in our nature, in that some secure for us the preservation of our life while others give us greater or lesser enjoyment. It is therefore completely independent of the value of the goods. Even where we make use of the non-economic goods which are available in excess, we precisely distinguish the importance of the individual acts of use, take pains to ensure that everything which is intended to assist the preservation of our life by means of such goods actually happens, and are aware of the greater or lesser enjoyment afforded by their consumption. But the care which we denote as economic, which proceeds from the circumstances of failure to satisfy the demand, is far from all our minds. We are able to satisfy all our needs right down to the least, and we therefore need not distinguish between those which may still be economically satisfied and those which must remain unsatisfied. The goods will therefore doubtless seem to us to be the causes of our welfare, but no individual good will be in a causal relationship with the satisfaction of a need which is crucial for success; each one individually may fall away without our suffering a loss of our enjoyment. In such circumstances the value of the goods does not manifest itself. Let us imagine that although sufficient quantities of goods are available to fully satisfy our demand, an external force prevents us from performing more than a certain number of acts of need-satisfaction. Here too, we will not care about the quantity of goods available provided there are enough of them to ensure that the number of acts of enjoyment in question can be performed. Moreover, even if goods are added or lost, this will be neither to our advantage nor our disadvantage. Even the individual good which we have taken possession of in order to consume it may be destroyed or lost before it can be consumed without our consumption suffering thereby. The value of the goods is irrelevant. On the other hand, if we perceive our interests differently, we will be concerned to make a choice as to what act of need-satisfaction we should perform. We will make this choice according to the importance of the individual acts for our life-preservation and welfare, and in this connection strive to satisfy those that are more important and leave the less important ones unsatisfied.

The same compulsion which we have assumed to proceed from an external force, namely, that we can only perform a certain number of acts of need-satisfaction, will be imposed on us by the goods themselves if they are available in limited quantity compared with the demand. Then, however, the goods take on a completely different importance for our economic awareness. They no longer seem to us to be causes of need-satisfactions which can be replaced by others without our losing out; it is no longer all the same to us what use the individual good is put to; instead, we see in the goods available to us the sole requirement for achieving the need-satisfactions which are most important for our life and welfare and are only possible through goods of this kind, the number of need-satisfactions being determined by the quantity of goods. The goods appear to us as requirements, as the sole causes of these most important need-satisfactions, which means that if we do not obtain them, we do not obtain the need-satisfactions; but if we do obtain them, it is self-evident to us that provided no external influences are brought to bear, we will also obtain the need-satisfactions. The availability or otherwise of the goods therefore means that we are able or unable to obtain the most important need-satisfactions, and the whole importance which the latter have for us is necessarily transferred to their requirements, the goods. This is how the value of goods arises.

Thus there must be a relative rarity on the part of the goods for them to acquire a value. The importance of the needs exists as soon as needs arise. However, the importance of the needs is only communicated to the goods when they acquire a further characteristic: the rarity which binds, as it were, the otherwise diffuse importance of the need to the goods. The entire content of our concept of value is thus drawn from the existence of needs, but the fact of its having been drawn therefrom and the extent to which it was drawn is the effect of a factor which is inherent in the goods.

The larger the available quantity, all other things being equal, provided that it does not satisfy the demand, the larger is the value of the entire quantities of goods, as the larger is the number of acts of enjoyment to be attained, but the smaller is the value of a unit. For in the same way that the whole quantity of the goods appears to us as the requirement for the most important need-satisfactions achievable, an individual good is to be regarded as the requirement for the least important act of satisfaction in the group thus determined. If, however, we speak of the value of goods, our concept is always based on the quantities of goods which normally apply in economic life. These, though, are not the entire quantities, but only parts of them, which we regard as their units as we are used to seeing and using in real life.

If we understand the nature and measure of the value of goods in this way, what is the consequence for the use of goods in general? This is essentially the same question as that which we have to answer with regard to the use of higher-order goods in production. Thus we only have to apply to it the solution worked out here.

Based on the preceding exposition, it is clear that the value of a good – as is found if the situation is correctly understood – has not the slightest influence on the importance which the use of the good has for us. The importance of an act of need-satisfaction is based solely on the nature of the needs. Only the performance of the act is dependent on the use of the good. But even the way in which a good is used is not directly and inevitably determined by its value. It is entirely possible for a good which had obtained its importance in value from the fact that it was the requirement for a particular, indeed the most important achievable, need-satisfaction to be wasted unused; for us to allow it to spoil or to use it for a less important need-satisfaction instead of it being used according to its value to obtain that most important need-satisfaction.

If a good is used below its value, this does not mean that our judgement of its value was incorrect. By means of value we make a judgement on the highest importance of the goods for us. This importance is not an arbitrary one, but one which necessarily arises from the given conditions of economic life. Our judgement of value was only incorrect if we were mistaken about the conditions or drew the wrong conclusions from them; if we either misjudged the importance of the needs or erroneously attributed to the good an importance which in reality it did not possess, as we saw it as the sole cause of need-satisfactions which it was unable to bring about either at all or to the exclusion of other goods. However, the fact that that most important act which could and should have been achieved by the good was in reality not achieved, either due to our own deliberately economic course of action or due to the intervention of external circumstances, does not mean that our value judgement was incorrect. The value of goods is determined not by their actual use but by their economically appropriate use as far as we are able to discern it. Therefore, if I use an economic good to satisfy not the most important need attributed to it but a lesser need, I have used it below its value, and if it has been wasted unused, its value has been wasted. In the same way, therefore, that the importance of the need-satisfaction actually provided is independent of the value of the good, which is based on the importance of the need-satisfaction which ought to be brought about, the value of the goods – the importance of the act that ought to occur – is entirely independent of the importance of the act that was actually brought about.

However, the concern for our welfare which causes us to discern the value of goods also impels us to use the goods in accordance with their value; to produce just those acts of enjoyment as the conditions of which they had acquired value for us and the importance of which we had transferred to them. If the importance of a good to us thus reappears in the importance which its use has for us, this stems from the fact that the same concern for our welfare guides our economic understanding and actions.

We have therefore achieved the following results with regard to the general relationship between the value of goods and their use:

1. The importance of the act of need-satisfaction is rooted in human nature and is thus basically entirely independent of the value of the good used.

2. Furthermore, the value of goods as the importance of economic goods due to their being used in the most beneficial way possible is independent of the use which actually occurs.

3. However, man's concern for economic well-being impels him to use goods in accordance with their value and to actually bring about the need-satisfactions which he recognizes as the most important that can be produced by them.

Let us apply these principles to the relationship between a productive good and its products, which offers a full analogy with the relationship of a good to the needs for it. As needs determine the value of the first-order goods, this value is, for the value of the second-order goods, the source from which the content of the value flows. In the same way, however, that it was not enough for us to have needs and goods, but the latter had to be available in limited quantity, the value of the first-order goods is only communicated to the second-order goods if they are insufficient in quantity to satisfy the demand. In both cases the value arises from the same source: the – direct or indirect – dependence of our need-satisfaction on goods which appear to be the requirements for it. From the fact that an available quantity of higher-order goods is unable to satisfy a demand for first-order goods and consequently the resulting demand for higher-order goods as well, not only the existence but also the magnitude of the value of the productive goods follows in the nature of a law; the available quantities of the productive goods and the probable value of the products create the economic circumstances which give rise to the magnitude of the value of the productive goods. However, of the many products which can be produced from the available quantity of higher-order goods, the ones which appear to our understanding as guided by our economic concern to be of prime importance and to determine value are those which are themselves the most valuable. We communicate to the productive goods the importance of the most valuable products which can be produced from the available quantity of them or, respectively, the importance of the greatest need-satisfactions which are dependent on them. The value of a unit of the productive good is in turn ultimately determined by the importance of the need-satisfaction which is dependent on the availability of this unit or, if we imagine the economic situation in its simplest form, by the value of the least valuable of all the products which can be produced from the unit of the productive good. Thus (within the entire economic situation) the value of the last product that can still be produced economically determines the value of the higher-order good. In our example, the matter is complicated by the fact that one and the same second-order good may and will be used to produce various kinds of first-order goods which meet various needs. Thus, when determining the products whose value is to be used as the basis for the value of the productive good, we have to take account both of the categories of first-order goods and of the quantity in each category. There is no category, even if the first available good in this category has the greatest value for us, where an increase in the stock of goods will seem desirable to us as long as in another category products of a higher value can be produced with the same expenditure of productive goods. The general rule that we transfer the importance of the most valuable products to the productive goods is thus valid in this case too, but it should be noted that it depends on the category of products and the quantity in each category which goods are to be considered the most valuable in a particular case. The least valuable product in the group of products thus determined which can still be produced with the unit of the productive good determines the value of this unit. Products with this least value need not be capable of being produced in every category of goods. In our example we have created a category of goods (III) where this is not the case.

This said, let us return to our question: What influence does the value of the productive good have on the value of the products made from it? If we apply the results we have obtained with regard to the relationship of the value of goods to the use of the goods in general, it follows that:

1. The existence of a productive good does not necessarily mean that any particular product will be produced. Productive goods can just as easily go to waste as give the greatest utility in production. It is even less the case, however, that the value of the productive good determines the value of the product. Even if the product we desire has been made from the productive good, its value is in no way derived from that of the productive good, but is based completely independently on its relationship to needs. In fact, the value of the productive good was derived from the probable value of the product.

216

Thus the value of the product is completely independent of the value of the productive good, and if we perceive a congruence between the two, this cannot be caused by the value of the higher-order good being transferred to the lower-order good.

2. Inasmuch as the value of the productive good is the transferred importance of the lower-order good which should be produced in an economic manner, it is in turn completely independent of the value of the product that was produced. If we observe a congruence between the two, it does not simply follow from this that the former derives from the latter.

3. Our concern for the greatest possible satisfaction of our needs demands, however, that we actually produce those products whose probable value had become decisive for determining the value of the productive good. In every act of production we destroy a good which for us was the cause of a specific – the most important achievable – need-satisfaction due to the fact that the good capable of directly satisfying the need was produced. Recognition of this possibility caused us to transfer the value of the product to the productive resource. Our economic awareness demands that as a replacement for a good of such value, a product of the same value be produced. Our economic insight (in the value judgement) has a determining effect on our economic actions (in production). We establish equilibrium between the value of the productive good and that of the product by regulating, as far as we are able, the categories of goods produced and the quantities of each category through our intervention in the production process.

Therefore we may state the following as the final result:

1. Our insight into the value of the productive goods gives rise to a rule of production: that production should be organised in such a way that we use the productive goods according to their value by using them to produce the products for which the productive goods had appeared to us to be requirements and whose value was therefore transferred to the productive goods.

2. If we have organised production in this way and it has been completed in accordance with our intentions, the value of the products will be equal to that of the productive goods – not as a direct consequence thereof but indirectly caused by the congruence between our economic understanding and our economic actions, both of which are guided by the same concern for our welfare. I first transfer the (probable) product value to the productive good, thus determining its value, and then actually use that good in production, thus bringing about the congruence of value.

3. This principle cannot be applied to products whose value determines the value of the productive good indirectly, inasmuch as it contributed to the economic situation as a whole, but not decisively – products such as we

find in category III. On the other hand, it will apply without limitation to categories I, II and IV.

If these three categories of goods all required the same quantities of the productive good for their production, the latter would have to be organised in such a way that goods of identical value are produced in all categories. Any other arrangement would be uneconomic. However, as they use different quantities, production of goods must be organised in such a way that the values only differ from one another to the extent that the quantities of the productive good used differ.

II

Let us now drop the restriction we have placed on our observations so far: that the higher-order goods were only available for production on a single occasion and that the required consumer goods had to be procured once and for all, and examine the case which we constantly perceive in real life: that new higher-order goods are available for production over and over again, and in the same way that man's demand is continual, production of the goods for consumption to satisfy this demand goes on all the time.

Let us again present this case in its simplest form. Therefore we will change none of our previous assumptions except that what was previously established once and for all will now be repeated on a regular basis. The same available quantity of the productive good and the same demand which was previously taken as a single instance will now recur over specific periods of identical length. During a certain period, thought of as a unit, the same demand is asserted again and again with, on the opposite side, the same quantity of goods available for production to satisfy it.

The boundary between one such period and the next is in no way imagined such that at this time the entire stock of both second-order and first-order goods is exhausted. As any production takes time, this would result in a shortage of goods for consumption and a suspension of consumption for the whole duration of the subsequent production. People engaging in economic activity avoid this problem by laying in stocks of goods for consumption with which they supply themselves until fresh production has produced fresh goods for consumption.

The situation is therefore changed to the extent that means of production and products are available simultaneously, that continuous production takes place alongside continuous consumption and that as our stock of goods is depleted by consumption, replacements are available through the production going on simultaneously.

In the changed situation, too, the rule of production which we established for the previous state of affairs, that productive goods should be used for production according to their value, will remain valid. We now have to examine whether the principles of value determination have remained the same.

1. We had determined the value of the productive good in advance by comparing the available quantity of this good with the demand and established, taking both into account, which first-order goods should be produced in an economic manner and equated the value of a unit of the productive good with the value of the good to be produced with it which had the least value in the series of goods thus determined. Here again, our subject will proceed exactly according to this rule, but with the modification, following from the circumstances, that he will compare the available quantity and the demand with reference to the periods in which they occur. He may not simply relate the quantity now available to the demand which is asserted in the next period, but (1) he has to ascertain what quantities of goods will become available to him in the entire period over which his economic provision extends and at what intervals this will happen, and (2) he has to determine the demand in the same way. By assigning available quantities of goods to be used for satisfying the demand in a future period in which they may meet stronger needs or by postponing need-satisfactions which cannot take place now to a future period, depending on the results of this study, he establishes for each period which productive goods are to be used for production and what needs are to be satisfied thereby. This forms the basis for the determination of value.

We must always imagine economic provision as seeking to smooth out differences between the individual periods. It will always be concerned to compare the value of the goods in one period with their probable value in the next and to achieve a certain regularity in the value of the goods or (which comes to the same thing) in the extent of the need-satisfactions by saving up the surplus stock of goods or postponing consumption.

If we look at such a period by itself, our subject does not carry out the determination of the value of the productive good and the organisation of the related production at the beginning of the period alone, but continuously. The value of the productive good and the organisation of production, provided that its modification is acceptable, will therefore not be established once and for all but will be continuously regulated according to the economic situation. Any change in the latter produces a change in value.

However, let us assume for the time being that changes in the economic situation which would lead to variations in the value do not occur. The value of the productive good will therefore appear to us to be constant; it will always be equal to 5.

2. Since, in the first case which we examined, the first-order goods were only assumed to be available after the productive good had been used in production and consumed, their value in relation to the productive good could only be influenced to the extent that the latter influenced the organisation of production. Once production had been completed, the values of the goods for consumption in each category were determined solely according to the quantity produced and still available and the intensity of the needs which depended on that quantity. The consequence was that even if we assume that production proceeds in a completely normal manner and subsequently did not allow any changes to occur in the economic situation, it could happen that a unit of the productive good which was tied to one category of goods for consumption received a higher value than those tied to other categories. In category III we found that the value of the productive good was 6, whereas in all other categories it was only 5. This relationship perfectly satisfied the law that each good receives the importance of the need of which it is a requirement.

Under the changed circumstances as we now assume them to be, no more category III goods are produced in the period of time which we are taking as a unit than before, namely 2. However, as before, the importance of the need which the first of these goods satisfies will be 3 times 8 and that of the second 3 times 6. But the economic situation which previously existed, that a good in this category is not merely the cause of a need-satisfaction equalling 3 times 6 but a requirement thereof no longer applies. Productive goods are now available all the time, and if a good of this category is lost, they can economically justifiably be used for its restoration. For since the value of the productive good with regard to all other uses is equal to 5, our subject would have no reason to produce a third category III good (intended for consumption within the same period) which would give an importance of only 2 for the productive good; on the other hand, concern for his welfare cannot but cause him to use the productive good to produce another category III good if the second good already produced has been lost.He will rather do without one good in each of categories I and II and thus cause a loss in his consumption which he puts at 3 times 5 than leave a need unsatisfied which has an importance for him of 3 times 6. He will therefore try to modify his production in such a way that to replace the second category III good which has been lost, he produces a further category III good with the productive resources which he would otherwise have used to produce a sixth category I good and a fifth category II good.

Of course, every production operation takes time. If we have productive goods available in the present, this means that we do not yet have products available with which we could satisfy our present needs. Moreover, it is

220

not possible to postpone the need-satisfactions at will, just as they cannot be undertaken before the needs assert themselves. Instead, they are tied to a longer or shorter period of time which stems from the nature of the needs. The need-satisfactions must be undertaken within these periods if the needs are to be satisfied at all. Postponement of the satisfaction beyond this time is annulment thereof. If our subject is unable to modify his production in such a way that he supplies his needs within the period of time established by their nature, he has not supplied them, and we should not take the fact that he subsequently acquires the resources which previously would have produced a certain intensity of need-satisfaction as indicating that this can also be achieved now.

Therefore everything depends – and only then does the train of thought which we embarked on above have the force of evidence – on whether it is possible within the period of time set by the nature of the needs of category III to replace the category III good which has been lost by category I and II goods in the manner indicated. Simple conversion of the latter to category III goods is not possible; modification of the production already in progress is only possible if the latter is not yet so advanced that the productive goods are tied to one or the other category of goods. Then there would be nothing for it but to wait for the next production operation while postponing the need-satisfaction to the latest possible time at which it can still be undertaken.

We noted earlier, however, that people engaging in economic activity never organise their production of goods and their consumption in such a way that at the very time that a production operation is completed and fresh goods for consumption become available, the entire stock of goods for consumption is used up; instead, they accumulate stocks of goods so that they do not suffer any loss of need-satisfaction if losses of goods occur, production fails or unexpected demand occurs. Unless an entirely unforeseen change in conditions takes place, they are thus able, from these stocks, to fully satisfy the stronger demand of the present and are furthermore able to modify their production so as to achieve an increase in the products which satisfy the more important needs in question against a decrease in those which satisfy the least important needs. They will increase the former by an amount sufficient to restore the stock of goods to its former level and decrease the latter by the amount necessitated by the withdrawal of productive resources which this causes.

Depending on the circumstances, therefore, the loss suffered by a subject due to the loss of a more valuable product may be compensated as fully as possible, in that ultimately only the least valuable good which can be produced with the same number of productive goods is lost, or it may be only partly possible or even impossible to compensate the loss. It can be assumed, however, that provided no more serious losses have occurred, the worst economic disadvantage can be avoided and instead the least disadvantage is obtained.

Provided that our subject is able, for one of the stated reasons, to produce another category III good from the productive good with the effect that the need it was intended to satisfy can be satisfied without unacceptable delay or a feeling of want, and provided that this replacement is enabled by his producing fewer goods of categories I and II, the deprivation which he suffers due to the loss of a category III good will not be equal to the level of the need which he was able to satisfy with this good (3 times 6); instead, he receives its importance from those needs which are the very least for which he still undertakes productive acts in order to supply them, and which can be supplied with the same quantity of productive goods. A category III good is therefore the cause of an enjoyment measured at 3 times 6, but is a requirement only in respect of one which he puts at 3 times 5. This will also be the magnitude of the importance which it receives in his economic awareness, that is, its value.

With the aforementioned proviso, therefore, the value of a category III good will be determined from the number of units of the productive good that are required for its production and from the value of the unit of the productive good under the general economic conditions. Thus the category of goods III also complies with the rule which we have established in respect of the other goods: that its value in absolute terms is equal to the value of the unit of the productive good multiplied by the number of units required for production – and that its value in relation to the value of other products behaves like the units used of the common productive good.

This congruence, however, is an accident which stems from the fact that in our example, the expenditure when the category III good was manufactured for the first time is equal to that required for its restoration.

We can perhaps formulate what has just been expounded by disregarding our example and stating a general version: the value of goods which can be produced from other goods is not determined by the relationship of the immediately available stock of goods to demand to the extent that higher-order goods are available by means of which they can be (economically) restored with full effectiveness in satisfying the needs. Now, if the higher-order goods are only used to produce these products or are also used to produce goods of other categories, their value, which is determined by the quantity in which they are available and by the quantity of the products already in existence in relation to the needs, will always influence the production of the products in question and the possibility of production will always influence the value of the products.

We have developed these principles in harmony with those which we

222

established in Section I. However, they may equally well contrast with the latter if the cost of production differs from the cost of repeat production. The former was related to the influence of the production actually completed, while the latter relate to that of the possible production of new goods. We have therefore determined a second cause, due to which the value of the productive good may influence that of the product.

Even here, we do not discern any exception from the general law of value, but instead its confirmation. For here again, the measure of the magnitude of the value lies in the need whose satisfaction depended on the availability of the good in question. However, as the theory of value shows that it is not the need-satisfaction which was caused but that which is at stake which determines the value, here again it was not the need-satisfaction which was directly produced but that which was ultimately dependent which was decisive for our subject.

The only curious thing about our example (which we will refer to in the following; the general application causes no further problems) was that the 'dependent' need-satisfaction does not occur in the category of goods in question but in a different one. For the productive good and the production produce a link between the categories of goods, as a result of which a lack in the available quantity of the one leads to a lack in the need-satisfactions which are dependent on the other. If we assume that production is continuous and the first-order goods can be produced from the higher-order good again and again, the former appear to us, as it were, as manifestations of the same good in different forms, which in economic terms can only have a different importance if they contain different quantities of the one good. If a single first-order good is considered, it is not a question of the need-satisfaction for which it was originally intended but that which is the least that can be satisfied with an equal number of units of the productive good.

If we have 10 goods of the same category at our disposal which are intended to procure 10 acts of need-satisfaction, of which the first has an importance equal to 10 and each subsequent one has an importance decreased by 1, so that the importance of the last is equal to 1, and if we also assume that we had discovered which acts of satisfaction were to be performed with each individual good, and the good with which we have intended to perform the act of satisfaction with an importance of 10 ceases to be available, we know that the loss we suffer is nevertheless only 1, because the 10th good, which we intended to use to perform an act of enjoyment with an importance of 1, is just as appropriate for satisfying our most intensive need as the first good which is no longer available, as it is of the same kind and can fully replace it, and because our concern to satisfy our needs as fully as possible causes us to use this good to perform not the last but the first act of need-satisfaction. We therefore attribute to the first good a value of only 1, although we had intended to use it to procure a need-satisfaction equal to 10, because the need-satisfaction which depended on the availability of this good has only this lower importance.

In our example, however, no category of goods is able to replace another, but the productive goods which are not yet tied to a particular category in production may equally be used to produce any of the categories of goods, and guided by our concern for the greatest possible enjoyment of the goods, we will always use them in such a way that the first-order good which by dint of the nature of its category and the available quantity is intended to satisfy a more important need is produced before that which is required to satisfy a less important need. If a category I good ceases to exist, it will be replaced by production and instead in the latter as many units fewer of the productive good will be used and consequently fewer products will be produced as are required for this production.

Thus the value of the products continues to be determined by the needs which are dependent on it and, as before, it is determined, on the basis of available quantities and demand, which these needs are; but the comparison of quantity and demand in each category of goods is superseded by a more comprehensive comparison of the overall demand for products made from a higher-order good and the total quantity of this good. From the value of the last product to be produced in each category of goods, the value of the productive good is determined, which is then reflected in all the other categories of goods. The need, which is the deciding factor in the value of the product, may thus be something which is initially completely foreign to it and is only related to it by the agency of the productive good, which binds all its products into a whole.

If we look back over everything we have expounded so far and now examine an opinion such as the following: 'It is not the needs which we use the goods to satisfy that regulate their value (or, although they influence the value, they do so only in that they establish the upper limit which it cannot exceed), but the costs, i.e. the value, of the higher-order goods which are required for their production or repeat production; we value goods according to what they cost us', we realise that such an opinion is unable to discover the true final reason for the value of either the higher-order or the first-order goods; as it does not take in the entire complex of the phenomena which combine to form an economic unit and stops at the individual, it is incomplete and incorrect. It should therefore be rejected, even if it does not claim to be a general, permanent rule.

III

So far we have considered the economic situation as calm and not subject to variations. We still need to examine how the principles we have established behave if changes in economic conditions occur.

As value is in no way something which attaches to the goods per se but is rooted in a relationship of the goods to needs which is subject to change, no determination of value, not even that which stemmed from the relationship of the productive goods to the products, can be preserved permanently. The value of the products at the time of completion of production will change independently of all other conditions in force at this time as soon as, in a subsequent period, different conditions for determination of value have occurred on the part of the goods or the needs.

This will indisputably be the case where any effect on the part of the productive good due to new production is ruled out; that is, in all cases where production has taken place on a once-only basis, in cases where the changes in the conditions for determination of value have occurred so quickly that a remedy cannot be obtained by reorganising production, and lastly, wherever the influence of production on the available quantity of goods for consumption is ruled out due to the particular circumstances of the location or in another way.

What effect will the change in the economic situation have on production?

The changes which may occur are many and varied. They may occur with regard to the goods or the needs; they may relate to the productive good or the products, to the quantity or the composition of the goods; they may affect all categories of goods to the same extent or solely or mainly affect individual ones. Those that concern all categories of goods would include: changes, increases or decreases in the available quantity of the productive good, uniform improvement of production in all sectors, uniform growth or decline of the entire sphere of need. The changes in the individual categories of goods include progress in the production of the particular category, changes in the particular sphere of need, etc.

Whatever form the changes may take, the organisation of production has to be modified along with them. Our examination will be facilitated if we assume at the outset that the new economic situation will in turn be permanent and that any further change is therefore ruled out. It is this probably continuing economic situation which now determines our subject's production schedule. He would have a poor understanding of his interests if he continued to use the same quantities of the productive good as before to produce the individual categories of the first-order goods. For the conditions which justified the former organisation of the production of goods, the probable value of the products and the ensuing value of the productive good, have changed. The probable value of the products, with regard to each quantity of them that is produced, is different; the value of the productive good, determined with regard to the most advantageous production, is different.

If our economic subject follows the rule which his interests compel him to follow, namely, to use the productive good in accordance with its value, he will restrict the quantity of some products and increase the quantity of others. Therefore he will (1) expand his production and use a larger quantity of the productive good wherever use of the quantity previously required would lead to the full benefit which could be gained from production not actually being attained. Wherever according to the former organisation of production the probable value of the products, reduced to the unit of the productive good, would be greater than the newly determined value of the latter, and where at the same time an expansion of production is possible without the value of the products falling below that of the productive good,[1] he has the opportunity, by sacrificing his productive good that he cannot immediately enjoy, to gain goods for consumption of greater, or at least the same, value. As a subject engaging in economic activity, he will exploit this opportunity and expand production to the limit at which the value of the product becomes equal to that of the productive good.

(2) On the other hand, he will restrict production wherever the use of the former quantity of productive goods would produce a quantity of products whose value reduced to the unit of the productive good would be lower than the value of the productive good. The possibility afforded by the productive good of satisfying needs of a certain level, which possibility has become the basis of the value, would not be fully exploited if he continued to produce products of a lower value. He will therefore cut production back to the limit at which the value of the product corresponds to that of the productive good.

If he has assessed the economic conditions correctly and if production has turned out in accordance with his intentions, on the changed basis there will again be a congruence between the value of the product and that of the productive good. The value which has thus been determined afresh will also be transferred to all the products which are left over from former production runs (the quantity of which should be taken into account when organising production). Provided that their composition is otherwise the same, their value will be identical to the value of the newly produced goods as determined on the basis of the new circumstances. The fact that they were produced under circumstances in which a different appraisal of

226

the value of the first-order and second-order goods guided the action of our subject has not the slightest influence on their present value. Their value is equal to that of the products of the same category and has fallen or risen with it.

If, in particular, we observe not the goods' absolute value but their value relative to one another, it will have remained completely unchanged if all the first-order goods require the same number of units of the productive good or a uniformly changed number for their production. However, it will have fallen for one category of goods if a smaller number of these units is required, and will have risen for all other categories. The value of the goods from previous production runs which were produced at a higher cost will nevertheless have fallen, in that it adjusts to the level of all goods in the same category.

We have thus seen that people are caused by their economic interests to restore the equilibrium in the value of the higher-order and first-order goods which has been disturbed by the change in the economic situation by restricting production here and expanding it there. However, it is possible to conceive of a case in which restoration of equilibrium has become impossible. This happens wherever production of one category of goods has become impossible. This may be caused in various ways. The importance of the needs which are dependent on a certain category of goods may have fallen or the value of the productive good as determined on the basis of other categories of goods may have risen to such an extent that the production of goods of the category in question from this productive good is no longer acceptable in economic terms. Or production of a certain quantity would be acceptable, but the quantity already in existence would be greater than this. Production of this good must be suspended. It cannot be resumed until the value of the productive good or the demand for this good changes or the existing quantity has fallen so far due to use that a resumption of production is economically justified. If, however, the products are durable in nature or if the changed economic circumstances persist, it may come about that production is no longer possible at all and that we use those previously produced goods to satisfy our needs, production of which at the present time we would see as mismanagement or waste.

IV

Before we proceed to the conclusion, it is necessary to explain, albeit in only a few words, what application the principles we have expounded have for the conditions of exchange transactions.

If we move from the simple circumstances on which our observations have so far been based to the complicated conditions of developed exchange transactions, our uniform picture disintegrates into a multiplicity of phenomena, within which we have to regain unity in a different way.

The needs which we have hitherto imagined as a uniform class exist in a whole range of people and in a very large diversity of intensities and gradations. The productive goods which were hitherto in the hands of a single subject are distributed among many persons who are in turn different from those who we recognised as subjects of the needs. The production which was guided by a single schedule is undertaken by many people. The estimation of value which until now has emanated from a single consciousness may now be fundamentally different for all individuals, and certainly for two groups: producers and consumers. The situation is made even more complicated by the fact that a new good appears: the productive good and the products are joined by the price good, in which the prices are given and which is in turn subject to very diverse estimations of value. Its value and that of the products associate with each other in a wide variety of combinations, the final result of which is the price of the products.

The principles we have developed therefore cannot be applied to this situation until the theory of prices has been expounded in full. This, however, would go far beyond the narrow bounds which my essay must keep to. So I will make only a rather cursory attempt to explain how I imagine the principles established so far to be modified in exchange transactions between people. I will limit myself to a very brief exposition of the main points.

In doing so, let us for the sake of clarity use the framework established earlier, although we will have to attribute a changed importance to the figures. Thus we would again have a single economic productive good which would be available in a certain quantity and used to produce the four categories of goods I-IV mentioned previously. We will now let the numbers which previously expressed the importance of each first-order good to the economic awareness of our isolated subject be the prices which could be obtained in exchange transactions depending on the number of units of first-order goods which are brought to market (reduced to the unit of the productive good), in that they indicate the average of the price limits established by the estimations of value of producers and consumers. In line with the broadened situation, however, each subsequent price may apply not to a single good newly put on the market but only to a larger quantity of goods which we think of as a unit and which we may assume to be any desired size.

What way of organising production will now be the most beneficial?

The concern which induced the isolated subject to secure the greatest possible need-satisfactions by means of the goods produced by him is no longer decisive, as the producers no longer use their products for the direct satisfaction of their needs, but instead for the exchange of goods, and it is only through their agency that the goods with which they intend to perform the need-satisfactions come into their possession. But even if concern to achieve the greatest possible need-satisfaction does not directly influence production, it influences it indirectly. It is now no less the ultimate goal of economic action than it was before. Now as before, the success of production will be judged according to whether or not the greatest possible need-satisfaction has been secured. Now, however, it will be secured when the highest price is obtained for the products, as this then creates the greatest opportunity to purchase those goods which the producers intend to use directly.

The rule of production now reads: Production should be organised in such a way that the sale of the products results in the highest obtainable price being received. The value of the productive good will now be determined with reference to this price; now as before, therefore, production should be organised in accordance with the value of the productive good, but the latter is now determined by the highest obtainable price of the products.

From this point onwards, all the motives which we have discussed in connection with the production undertaken by our isolated subject will take effect. Consequently, in production for exchange too people will be concerned to protect their interests, and will achieve this goal by organising the production of the goods according to the value of the productive resources. Every change in the situation, which probably leads to a change in the prices, will thus as far as possible entail changes in the organisation of production because the value of the productive good has changed, all of which in turn have the goal of finding remuneration for the value of the productive good in the price of the products.

However, it will never be possible to demonstrate such an exact congruence between the value of the higher-order good and the price of the products in the way that an exact congruence of the values could be demonstrated. Prices are never as sharply defined by an economic situation as the value of the goods. In any economic situation there are only certain limits within which price formation must take place. Within these limits, the individual prices that are actually paid and received in the marketplace will doubtless approach one another but will not strictly coincide. The current price is an average of the actual prices which vary upwards and downwards.

If, however, we leave this aside and assume that production is undertaken

229

according to our example, the productive good proved to have the value attributed to it and the products had obtained the very prices which had become the basis of this value – then the following would apply to the magnitude of the prices and values.

1. Prices. In the case of the goods in categories I, II and IV, congruence between the price of the lower-order good and the value of the higher-order good would immediately become established. The prices of the products will behave in relation to one another like the quantities of the productive good used in production.

But there can be no exception for the goods in category III either; for them, too, the price in respect of a unit of the productive good will be not 6 but 5. For we were nevertheless permitted to assume that in the case of an isolated economic subject the estimation of the value of a good could be significantly influenced by whether one unit more or less of the good was available. In people's exchange transactions, however, whether a single good more or less is put on the market generally has not the slightest influence on the market. It takes a larger quantity of units of the good to change the price only a little. Within the price limit, therefore, there will be no price which could not be achieved by controlling production and supply accordingly. Thus the scale in our framework no longer completely fits the vast majority of cases. In a case such as exists in category III, further production will take place over and above the quantity at which a price of 6 appeared to be more likely, but not in the full quantity which we considered as a unit in the scale, because a price of 2 would otherwise be the average price. But there is no compulsion to produce this amount more, as there was previously in the isolated economy where the unit of a good was indivisible. However, even where circumstances are different from those we have just established, it should be borne in mind that the price 6 is the probable average but not the only possible price. Every price within the limits set by the estimations of value of consumers and producers is equally possible, including, therefore, a price of 5, and in the long run (and we are assuming only steady-state conditions) this price alone will be paid and accepted in the marketplace, because it is only at this price that equilibrium in this production sector can be maintained against the others.

In the same way that we spoke of a congruence between the value of the productive good and that of the products, we can also speak of a congruence, albeit not with the same exactness, between the value of the productive good and the price of the products.

2. How, though, will the value of the products behave in relation to that of the productive good under the conditions of exchange transactions? For the price is neither the value pure and simple nor an individual

manifestation of the value. Let us make a distinction here and discuss first the products' value for the producers and then their value for the consumers.

a) The products' value for the producers. The value to be considered in economic terms for the producers is the value in exchange; this, however, depends on the prices. For each individual producer, therefore, the products will behave in relation to one another in terms of their value in the same way as their prices. If the latter behave in the same way as the quantities of the productive good that are required for production, the values of the products will also be in this relationship.

b) The value of the products for the consumers. While the price is the same in the entire market, the consumers' estimation of value which influenced the formation of the market price differs widely. To this extent it will be impossible to demonstrate that a relationship exists between value and price. However, if, as we have assumed, production and demand continue on a regular basis and every consumer therefore has the certainty of again obtaining any good on the market at the same price which he paid for it previously, his estimation of the value of the goods must become different from what it was originally. The good which originally appeared as the requirement for a particular need-satisfaction no longer has this function. This good may cease to exist without the need-satisfaction in question having to be foregone. For it can of course now be secured by the consumer acquiring another good of the same category in the marketplace on payment of the market price. Provided that he is able to have disposal of the necessary quantity of the price good, that is, if he not only possesses it but it is available to him for satisfying the need in question, for purchasing this good, by the fact that he would have otherwise intended to use it to purchase a good which he proposed to satisfy a lesser need, he will now, if he is guided by a concern to use his goods in the most economic manner, use the price good to buy not the good for which it was originally intended but to purchase another good of the first-named category which we have assumed to have become lost.

Each good will therefore no longer have the importance for him which it had before the price formation and due to the need that was to be directly satisfied, but instead the importance attributable to the number of goods for exchange which are to be handed over as the price. Each good will therefore have the same value for him as its price.

Two things follow from this: 1. For the consumer, the cost of the goods is their price; this is known as the cost of purchase. Under the stated conditions, therefore, for him the values of his goods will behave like their price, the cost of purchase. 2. If, however, the prices depend on the number of units of the productive good that are used to produce the goods, for the consumer too the values of the products will be relative to the latter, the cost of production.

This in no way means, however, that the price is the final basis of the value. The opposite is true; the value is the final basis of the price. But in the same way that in our earlier examples of isolated economic activity the possibility of producing a good from its productive good, the value of which is kept at a certain level by the general economic situation, retroactively influenced the value of this good, the possibility of obtaining a good at a certain price in the marketplace will modify its value, whereas, however, the price of the good that is formed in the marketplace is itself the result of the estimation of the values of the good for purchase and the price good which is made by producers and consumers.

Lastly, we must very briefly refer to a phenomenon which only occurs under social conditions and is not possible under conditions of isolated economic activity: monopoly.

If one of the four production sectors which we have here were monopolised and the monopolist's interest lay in his limiting the quantity of products in order to raise their price, the prices which he receives for his products will no longer behave relative to the prices of the other products made from the same productive good in the same way as the quantities of the productive good that are required for production, but will be higher than they would be according to this relationship. Everything we have concluded, on the basis of the price, about the relationship between the cost of production and the value of the goods for consumers will cease to apply. For the monopoly producer himself, however, the basis of the products' value will not be the price at which he sells them but the price for which he buys the productive good (together with the other producers), which is of necessity lower.

V

Summarising, we have arrived at the following results:

The same concern which governs any economic actions of people governs them in production as well and causes us to use the productive goods in the most beneficial manner in production. This, however, is achieved only when by this means those categories and quantities of the products are produced, the probable value of which determined the value of the productive goods. For some of the first-order goods, organising production in this way would directly result in their value being congruent with that of the productive good, namely for all goods whose value directly determined the value of the latter. However, the same drive to achieve the most beneficial production produced this congruence for the other goods as well, insofar as their restoration was possible at the expense of the other products. In this we have the phenomenon of a second influence of the value of the productive good on the value of the product, which we tried to put in more general terms. For while (1) the value of the productive good prescribed a certain initial organisation of production and the production completed according to this plan governed the value of the products, we found (2) that in the relationship of the value of the productive good to that of the product may be contained a constant support for the renewal of production, and this possibility of repeat production itself influences the value of the product.

Finally, we have seen that with every change in the economic situation, the drive to produce in the most beneficial manner repeatedly asserts itself and causes constant changes in the organisation of production in the direction of restoring congruence between the value of the productive good and the products made from it.

We then briefly reviewed the broader conditions of exchange transactions.

The only thing that has proved to be permanent under all circumstances is people's efforts, in production as in their other economic affairs, to safeguard their interests as far as possible, which they achieve by directing their efforts in each case towards realising the value of the productive goods in that of the products.

For these efforts to bear fruit, however, certain requirements apply, namely:

1. That the probable value of the products and, with it, that of the productive good are correctly determined. This will depend on the probable demand for products and the extent and intensity of the needs to be satisfied being correctly identified and no mistake being made with regard to the available quantity and the quality of higher-order and first-order goods.

2. That the economic activity, production, takes place in line with economic understanding. Mistakes and carelessness or clumsiness are thus obstacles to bringing these efforts to fruition.

3. That the success of production, insofar as it depends on external factors, meets these requirements.

However, the value of the products determined in this way has no claim to permanency, any more than any other determination of value, or to validity in all circumstances.

Therefore, if a rule is to be formulated on the value of products in relation to the productive goods, it will not be worded 'It is' but 'It should', and it can only claim validity to the extent that the conditions under which it was made apply and persist.

233

We find the economic process which we have just observed in a simple form and in isolation combined with the many other phenomena of economic life, in a wide variety of applications. We find not just one good but a whole range of goods as productive goods, and not just used as second-order goods but at a much higher order, and often used at the same time as first-order goods. If they are used in an economic manner, no kind of use may be performed in which they would have a lower value than they might receive in a different use. Thus their value constantly regulates production and each productive good forms around it a group of lower-order goods, the extent and direction of which is constantly redetermined due to people's efforts. Continually changing conditions lead to continually changing behaviour.

But how, in the infinite diversity and complexity of human economic life, can mistakes or mismanagement fail to have an influence? Who wants to guarantee the success of the riskiest undertakings? How, in a process of continual change, can what appeared to be true yesterday be regarded as true today? Can judgements survive beyond their grounds?

However, the principles which we have conditionally developed for the value of products from the motives for production have been made out to be the bedrock on which the theory of value and price must be founded. An attempt has been made to give them the most far-reaching significance by incorrectly declaring a small number of goods to be goods of the highest order which are contained in all others. These principles have been seen as the ultimate explanation of value and price, and various phenomena of life where unexplained randomness prevails have had to be made out to be exceptions. In doing so, the fact has been overlooked that what was understood as the rule and what was understood as the exception exhibit the same law-like unity. In the end, not even the rule that was formulated could be definitively justified. It was possible to explain the value of the products but not that of the highest-order goods, and in this way the ultimate explanation of value has been pushed back from the line of the lower-order goods to that of the highest-order goods, yet has not been solved there.

NOTE

1. The German text actually says '. . . without the value of the products falling below that of the *product*', which does not make sense. The original text should probably read '. . ., ohne dass der Wert der Produkte unter den des Produktivgutes herabsänke'; my translation assumes this to be correct. [*Trans. note*].

Friedrich von Wieser, 'The Austrian School and the Theory of Value',
Economic Journal, March, 1891, pp. 108–21.

This paper by Wieser was first published as an English-language
contribution to the first volume of *Economic Journal* in March
1891. It offered British readers an outline of the newly-emergent
'Austrian School' and its doctrines.

9

The Austrian School and the Theory of Value

FRIEDRICH von WIESER

I

The historical school of political economists in Germany, and the Austrian, or as it is frequently termed, the abstract school are more nearly related than is at first sight apparent. Both follow the spirit of the age in rejecting speculative theory and in seeking their highest laurels on the field of observation. In art, as in science, naturalism must be distinguished from truth to nature, and we Austrians, while we have certainly no wish to be disciples of naturalism, are wholly set on being experientialists. This is what I would remark in the first place to the readers of this Journal, in complying with the Editor's kind invitation to give some account of our theories. And on this point the method we employ must not be suffered to mislead. M. Leon Walras says very happily of this method, which he himself employs, that it idealizes. It does not copy nature, but gives us a simplified representation of it, which is no misrepresentation, but such as sharpens our vision in view of the complexities of reality, – like the ideal picture which the geographer draws in his map, as a means not to deception but to more effective guidance, he meanwhile assuming, that they who are to profit by the map will know how to read it, *i.e.*, to interpret it in accordance with nature.

The investigations of the Austrian school have not been restricted to the subject of value, but embrace the most comprehensive theories on economy in general. Accordingly I must confine myself to as brief a survey as may be of our views on value. I could not do justice even to this task in the space kindly allotted to me, were it not that I can find resource in referring English readers to Jevons. Thus I can omit a good deal from Prof. Menger's theories, which, while to us they are fundamental principles, are

237

in England known in substance through Jevons's 'theory of utility' and 'theory of exchange.' I can further refer my readers to Dr Bonar's excellent essay on 'The Austrian Economists' in the *Quarterly Journal of Economics*, October, 1888. An account of the Austrian school by Dr Böhm-Bawerk has appeared in the *Annals of the American Academy*. I regret that I have no space for the numerous comparisons which might be drawn between our views and the remarkable developments of the theory of value in England since Jevons.

The works to which I shall chiefly refer in what follows are Professor Menger's *Grundsätze der Volkswirthschaftslehre* (1871); Dr Böhm-Bawerk's *Capital und Capitalzins*, vol. i (1884), vol. ii (1889) (of which the first volume has been recently translated by Mr Smart and the second volume is about to follow); also by the same author, 'Grundzüge der Theorie des wirthschaftlichen Güterwerths' in the *Conrad'sche Jahrbücher* (1886); and Professor Sax's *Grundlegung der theoretischen Staatswirthschaft* (1887). Besides these my own works, *Ueber den Ursprung und die Hauptgesetze des wirthschaftlichen Werthes* (1884), and *Der natürliche Werth* (1889). The *Untersuchungen über die Theorie des Preises* by MM. Auspitz and Lieben is on Jevonian lines.

II

The value of commodities is derived wholly from their utility, but the utility they afford is not wholly convertible into value. Commodities which may be had freely in abundance are of no value, however much utility they may afford. But those commodities too, which, because they are not to be had in sufficient quantity, are valuable for the sake of their utility, acquire a value which as a rule is less than their utility. The harvest, to which a nation owes the maintenance of so many millions of lives during a whole year, has a value which is no approximate expression of the service rendered. Nor ought it to be; the value should express not the total utility, but only a part of it; 'the final degree of utility,' as Jevons said, the 'marginal utility' (*Grenznutzen*) as we say. The value of the harvest is reckoned by multiplying the supply, the quantity of in-gathered harvest-units, by the marginal utility. All the utility above the margin, all 'surplus utility' (*Uebernutzen*), including precisely that which relieves necessity in the highest degree, is neglected and finds no place in value at all.

I will tarry no longer over these propositions familiar to every English student of Jevons. The Austrian school, it is true, assigns to the propositions a slightly different meaning and a slightly different basis; to this point I shall revert later. For the present I will examine by the light of this principle of value a few of its intricacies.

The agents of production, land, capital, and labour, derive their value from the value of their products, ultimately, therefore, from the utility of those products. As stock is valued by the expected dividend, so is the field by the expected crop. A simple idea; yet thereby hangs one of the weightiest problems. Land, capital, and labour yield a return only by their combined agency. Now what is the clue to the distribution amongst the separate effective factors of this joint return? The comparison with stocks and dividends is of no further use to us here, for one share in an investment is like another, while land, capital and labour are diverse. Even if labour alone be considered, the difficulty still confronts us. How are we to divide a machine, constructed by a number of labourers according to the instructions and under the direction of the inventor, so as to refer every part to its true originator?

Theorists have hitherto set down this problem as insoluble, and insoluble it is as commonly stated. It is impossible, to put it briefly, to give a reply to the question as to which part of the child is derived from the father and which from the mother. The question in itself is an absurdity. But it is just in this sense that the problem does not admit of statement, if it is to be correctly stated in the light of practical economy. What is required in economy is, not physical division of the product amongst all its creative factors, but the practical *imputation* of it, imputation in the sense used by a magistrate in speaking of a legal 'charge'. A sophist might maintain the impossibility of determining, amongst the thousand conditions, without the conjunction of which a murder could not have been effected, what share in the deed fell on the murderer; the judge, unperplexed by such scruples, sifts those thousand causes solely to get at the responsible author, and charges him with the whole of the deed. Who would accuse him of offending nature and logic thereby? And as he is concerned with the responsible author, so in economy, it is always amongst the thousand implicated causes with the practically determining factor that we have to do.

A field cultivated with the same expenditure of capital and labour as another field of greater fertility yields a larger return. This surplus crop is by no means produced by the field alone, capital and labour as well are wrought into it; nevertheless every agriculturist will rightly charge not the capital nor the labour with the crop, but, simply and solely, the better field, the value of which is raised by just the amount of the surplus. Such a judgment, so far from being illogical, embodies a great practical truth. In imputing the return by this method, I am enabled to find the correct adjustment of the economic measurement, which has to be carried out in the case of the commodities of production. It would, for example, be impossible for me to decide whether to purchase a machine and what price

239

to consent to give for it, if I did not know how to calculate the work it would do for me, *i.e.*, what share in the total return to my undertaking should be imputed to it in particular. Without the art of imputation there would be no business calculations, no economic method, no economy, just as without the system of criminal charge, there could be no society. Fortunately the practice of it is universal, everyone, be he never so stupid and inexperienced, applying it though with varying degrees of acuteness.

These rules of economic imputation as used in practical life the Austrian school has endeavoured to connect by way of theory. The principle under which it formulates them points back to its general principle for estimating value. If I say, 'free commodities have no value for me,' this means that I do not 'charge' them with the utility which they afford. The reason for this is, that I do not feel myself to be dependent upon them; if that supply which happens to be next to hand were for some reason or other to be withdrawn from my possession, I could take any other quantity from the abundance everywhere about me and use it. I impute utility only to those commodities which are not to be had in profusion, and on which I feel myself dependent in consequence. I meanwhile reflecting, that with every portion lost from my possession I lose a definite utility not to be had without it. Now the agriculturist, in losing a cow from his yard, does not forfeit with her the whole return on his farming, but suffers only a certain diminution in it, just as in the opposite event of his introducing some improved machinery he gains a certain increase. In these diminishing and increasing returns, varying with the variations in productive combinations, the principle of imputed returns finds its simplest elucidation, notwithstanding the many difficulties arising by the way. Space fails me to explain my meaning more precisely. I will only specify further, that in the particular instance account must be taken of supply, demand, circumstances of allied products, technical progress, &c., in short of all the well-known conditions, from which experts are able with so much success to infer what importance to attach now to this, now to that element in production.

The most momentous consequence of the theory of imputation is, I take it, that it is false, with the Socialists, to impute to labour alone the entire productive return. Land and Capital as well must find recognition as collaborating factors in production, from the point of view of practical economy; excepting the case of their being available in superabundant quantities, which, however, can only be true of Land. The fact of fertility alone does not constitute an adequate condition for imputing rent to land, any more than utility as such makes a commodity valuable. Productive imputation requires the conjunction of utility and scarcity. But in the case of land, if scarcity be assumed, the charge of rent arises, whatever the form of land-tenure, and whether the produce is sold in the market or not. Even in a socialistic state a surplus reaped from better soil must be taken into account as soon as inferior soils are cultivated; the occupier farming the better land will be made responsible for a larger yield in view of the nature of the soil.

A further complication of value is afforded by the cost of production. Experience shows, that in very many cases the value of products is less than equivalent to the utility they bestow, because it is adjusted to the measure of the expense required for their production. Hence a great many theorists have concluded that value is not derived from utility, but is governed by another principle, viz., cost of production. But what is the cost, and how is it measured? The readiest way of expressing in figures the expenditure of materials and labour required to produce any article is to give the supplies to be consumed, the number of working days, the number of tons of coal, the time during which machinery is at work, the figure of each of the infinite number of items used in the production, and so on. This runs up a long list, but the items are incapable of being added up; these magnitudes are as mere bulk incomparable, incommensurable, and cannot be concentrated in one term. To sum them, every item must be put down in terms of value – but how is this to be determined? We can tell at once. The value of the productive elements is determined on the ground of utility as afforded by the products, and this holds good of the labour no less than of the coals, the machinery, and all the other means of production. To insist then on cost of production is ultimately to insist on some utility. There is no new principle to be discovered, none save utility.

Estimation of cost shows us in each particular case what utility the productive elements would confer if they were consumed otherwise than in turning out the produce desired. It shows us, for example, that the utility of the materials and labour, by the aid of which an important telegraphic communication is set up, would have amounted to very much less in those other uses, from which they have been withdrawn in order to do this. From this however it follows, that it is impossible to estimate the value of the communication as highly as its own high utility would absolutely warrant, since it can only be, – and precisely if it can be, – set up at the much smaller sacrifice of that utility which is involved in the cost of production. This extraneous utility is in this case the 'marginal utility' which affords a measure for the value. To value a product by its cost means then to impute as much utility to it as is to be *imputed to all its productive elements taken together*. Taken thus, products present themselves not merely according to their sources, but according to their value as well, as *the syntheses of their productive elements*. That product which requires them in greater quantity has the greater value. Consequently cost

241

of production determines the *relative* value of produce, while the *absolute* value of the commodities consumed in the cost is determined by the value of the forthcoming produce.

Labour, like land and capital, owes the reward imputed to it not only to its productiveness, but also to its scarcity, *i.e.*, to the fact that it is not to be had in free abundance. Labour, however, has yet another motive force in itself, by which it can influence the estimation of value. Everyone is personally concerned to evade the toils and perils of labour. Value may accrue to products from this consideration, inasmuch as the man who possesses them is spared the toils and dangers of acquiring them. This is Ricardo's fundamental idea, and on its development he lavished all the keenness of his intellect. The Austrian school has not passed carelessly over this motive force and its theoretic expositions, but has devoted a very thorough-going attention to them. On this occasion I shall limit myself to a single comment. If Ricardo's idea were correct, and commodities were, in the strict sense of the word, of no importance to us, except that the possession of them saved us labour, which we should otherwise have to apply elsewhere, then the difference between rich and poor would perforce be quite other than what it unfortunately is. The rich man's privileges would consist only in possessing those things which the poor man will also possess, but which he must first give himself the trouble of acquiring; his prerogative would lie, not in greater enjoyment or a more secure existence, but in greater ease. What nation would not eagerly exchange the facts of life for this Utopia!

Finally there are further complications involved in the nature of land and capital. The first problem confronting us here is that of the rent of the soil, and it is not the most difficult. Ricardo's theory of rent is nothing else than the application of the theory of imputation, and that to the simplest-conceivable case. Ricardo discloses the reasons why certain differences occurring in the returns from the cultivation of land must be imputed to just those portions of the soil in relation to which they arise, as constituting *their* share of reward, as rent. The value of the soil presents a much harder problem: the same is true of interest and the value of capital. Concerning these I shall say nothing, for special reasons, till the next section.

By our investing a certain amount of capital during a certain time in a certain product, we deprive ourselves of the interest which some other investment of our capital would fetch. The sacrifice of utility which we make in production consists therefore not only in the consumption of capital, but also in the sacrifice of interest, which is larger in proportion as the capital is larger and the period of investment longer. Accordingly, the current interest for the given interval of time is to be reckoned in the cost of production, and determines, together with the other elements of cost, the value of the products. I will not touch now on the knotty question, whether rent, too, is to be reckoned in the cost of production.

It has been objected that interest is a surplus of profit over expenditure, that it is conditioned by the value of the products and cannot, therefore, itself determine the value of the products. But is not the value of the productive commodities also conditioned by the value of the produce? And yet we say that it, as cost value, itself jointly determines the same. Equally are we entitled to say the same of interest. The value of iron depends on the value of iron products, but the relative value of the iron products is determined by the mass of iron required. The rate of interest depends upon the value of the goods, but the relative value of the goods is determined by the quantity of capital required and by the length of time during which it is invested.

III

We have asserted that the value of capital is based on the value of the produce into which capital is transposed. Experience does not wholly verify this theory. The sum of 105 gulden, which I am entitled to demand after a year's interval, constitutes the base on which its capital value is reckoned, but that value is not an equivalent amount. It is reckoned as somewhat less, deduction being made for interest. How is this deduction justified? In this way does the Austrian school state the problem of interest, the solution of which is essential to the complete solution of the problem of the value of capital.

The problem of the value of land moreover stands in connection with it. A piece of land contains for its owner the promise of rent for an indefinite number of years, and therefore its value ought to be equal to the sum of this whole series of years, which might even be taken as infinite. Actually, however, the value of land is rated much lower, viz., as the product of the annual rent multiplied by twenty, thirty, or some such shorter term of years.

The Austrian school does not maintain its unanimity over the theory of interest. As it is impossible for me to set forth here all our attempts to explain it, the reader will forgive me if I merely set forth my own. I can the more readily venture on such a course in that our several theories, although they do not thoroughly harmonize, are nevertheless mutually related like variations on the same, or similar themes: while the theory of Dr Böhm-Bawerk and that of his opponent Prof. Menger are accessible to the English public in the translation of 'Capital and Interest' by Mr Smart.

I start from the notion of imputation. A portion of the product must be assigned to capital. But of this share we must first replace as much of the capital as was consumed. Now experience shows that this being done, the

243

reward of capital as a rule is not exhausted, a surplus of clear profit remaining over. That capital is in this sense productive is just as truly a fact of experience as that the soil always brings forth fresh produce.

I ask the reader to note that hitherto I have spoken only of produce in kind, and not yet of its value. The aggregate gross income of capital, considered in kind, contains in itself the replacement of capital in kind, besides a surplus produce, viz. net profit. If the total capital $= x$ and the net profit $= 5$, then, assuming that all the capital is consumed, the total gross produce is $x + 5$. But if this is so, if the total produce is greater than was the total capital, then its *value* must also be greater, and that by just the amount of net profit. The value of 100 items must be less than that of 105, just as that of the field cleared of its harvest must be less than the value of field *plus* crop. The difference between the value of capital and the value of gross profits can only disappear if capital ceases to be productive and yield profit.[1]

From these consideration the following conclusions emerge: –

1. – The value of circulating capital is found by *discounting, i.e.,* by deduction of interest from gross income.

2. – If a capital of 100 can after a year be converted into 105, then is a sum of 100 which can only be claimed after a year, of less value than 100. Future goods have, therefore, less value than present goods.

3. – The capital value of a perpetual rental may be found by summing the several instalments, but only after their future value has been reduced to present value by continuous discounting. An abbreviated method for arriving at the same result is that of *capitalization, i.e.,* the multiplication of the yearly rental by a figure, the key to which is derived from the current rate of interest, *e.g.*, if this be 5 per. cent., multiply by 20. This abbreviated procedure yields mathematically the same result as the longer method of discounting interest and compound interest.

This gives us, besides, the rule for reckoning the value of land.

4. – The value of fixed capital is reckoned by corresponding combinations, either through discounting or capitalizing, attention being given to the principle of amortization or sinking fund.

IV

Value is, in the first instance, estimated by every one from a personal standpoint as 'value in use.' In the exchange of commodities, however, these individual estimates join issue, and thence arises price or 'value in exchange.' Prof. Sax explains price as the average of individual estimates of value; in the opinion of the other Austrian economists it obeys another law.

The maximum price which the consumer can ever afford to give does not exceed what he, according to his own estimate of money, looks upon as the full equivalent of the value in use which the commodities he is buying will have for him. And if he wishes to buy several items of the same commodity he measures the value of an item by marginal utility. A wealthier purchaser therefore, whose need is equally insistent, will be able to afford a higher price, since he in his pecuniary estimates will equate with the same value in use a larger sum of money. In practice, however, even the wealthiest of purchasers will consent to this higher price only if he must do so in order to keep off less wealthy bidders, who else could take the goods out of the market. Yet if so much of the commodity is offered, that even for lower bidders something is left over, the price must be adjusted to their estimates, in order that everything may find a sale; and then, since the price in the same market is the same for all buyers, the bidders of greater purchasing power pay less than what they by their estimates of money and goods were ready to give. The more goods there are, the deeper must be the strata of population having lower money-estimates of goods, who are thereby admitted to purchase. That money-equivalent, which obtains with the last group of buyers thus admitted for the last item bought (viz., of a commodity of which a number is always bought), and which determines the price, we may call the marginal equivalent.

Thus we see exchange value and price following the law of margins like value in use, with this qualification, that they are determined directly, not by marginal utility but by marginal equivalence, in which, not only supply and demand, but also the wealth of the purchasers is taken into account. Rare articles of luxury, e.g., precious stones, fetch very high prices, because the rich contend for them with the poor and the richest with the rich. Stock goods supplied for imperative needs command very low prices, corresponding to the purchasing power of the lowest strata of the population. According to the economic stratification of any given nation, we may reproduce in terms of money, the marginal utility of stock commodities by a very low equivalent, and that of articles of luxury by a very high equivalent. Hence from prices as such we can draw no inference whatever as to the national economic significance implied by commodities, in virtue of the relation of their supply to need as such; the picture they reveal is distorted, because it is unequally projected. Prices cannot be taken without qualification as the social expression of the valuation of commodities; they are the results of a conflict waged over those commodities; in which power besides need and more than need, has decided the issue.

Production follows prices. That which can be sold dear is produced more eagerly at greater cost in larger quantities. To this extent is our production diverted from its purely economic aim, to minister to wants as such and allay them as far as possible. Those misshapen prices which are engendered by monopolies may be abolished by the suppression of monopolies, and those which, especially in the matter of wages, arise from the distress in the position of the labourer, may be removed by a general coalition of labourers; but those which result from inequality in the means of purchasers are, I take it, inextricably bound up with our economic *régime*.

V

Value in use and value in exchange, understood in the sense we have employed hitherto, are to be distinguished not only in extension but also in intension. Value in use is not only particular but also subjective: value in exchange is not only general but also objective. There is no doubt a subjective exchange-value as well, which plays an extremely important part in economy, but for brevity's sake there shall be no mention of that here.

If value is understood as subjective, then the question, why commodities are valuable, becomes equivalent to, why do men prize commodities? The phenomena requiring explanation is, the love of men for material goods, *auri sacra fames*, side by side with the love of men for men, and their love for moral goods. The Austrian school, while indicating utility as the root and measure of that love, seeks to establish this principle in the sphere of material objects, as the utilitarians do in estimating moral values. And yet how complicated even in the material world is the calculus of self-interest! We value commodities for the sake of their utility, yet we do not value utility when it is coupled with abundance; in other commodities we value as a rule not the total, but only the marginal utility; in the cost of production we value, instead of the utility of the product itself, the utility of other extraneous products; and finally through it all runs the difficulty of imputing the reward of production.

What on the other hand is the nature of value in exchange as objective? It informs us respecting the ratio of the prices of commodities, telling us that such a commodity has such a price, while it brings it into comparison with the prices other commodities are commanding at the same time. It is concerned only with the relations between commodities, nowhere with those between men. There is no definition under which we may combine both conceptions of value, the subjective and the objective. We must be content with showing their mutual relation.

In economy both find application. Every decision arrived at by any one respecting a commodity is based upon his subjective judgment of value. Price and exchange-value on the other hand furnish the general principles of exchange and of the calculus of production.

Theory has to examine both phenomena. I will restrict myself to showing why it may not neglect subjective values. The reason is, that it would thereby leave unexplained all individual decisions in economic matters, *e.g.* it would not even explain why any one buys. For by objective standards wares and prices have the same value; by objective standards we give equals for equals, for which we should have no motive. But further, exchange-value itself, considered objectively, can only find its explanation in the laws of subjective value, obeyed by buyer and seller in concluding a bargain. If commodities which are to be had in abundance fetch no price, this can only be owing to the fact that they have subjectively no value for anyone. The law, that in the same market equal portions of the same commodity are equal in price, could not hold, did not every owner always assign equal value to equal portions. Price follows marginal equivalent because subjective value follows marginal utility; it only adjusts itself to cost of production, because every producer subjectively for himself assigns a value to products as syntheses of their productive elements. Rent is paid for land, interest for capital, wages for labour, because in subjective valuation a share of the aggregate return is imputed to land, a share to capital, a share to labour; nor could any more precisely quantitative expression be found for price, were it not that subjective value, by its bearing on supply, number, and cost of production, already admitted of computation. Motives it is true are ever coming into play through the conflict of price, which are wanting in the personal calculus; on the other hand monopoly suppresses the effect of the influence of cost, and other such differences; nevertheless without the subjective influences of the estimation of values, no dealings in price would ultimately be conceivable, nor could the law of price be maintained.

I must abstain from any complete demonstration of this governing idea, and will pursue it a little further in one direction only. In reply to a passage in my book on *Natural Value*, Prof. Edgeworth[2] has said that the difference between the valuations under an Economic and those under a Socialistic *régime* is most briefly and appropriately expressed by the statement that in the former case the tendency to maximum utility is, while in the latter case it is not, subject to the condition 'that there should be only one rate of exchange in a market.' With the same request as he then made, that my forced brevity may not be taken for want of courtesy, I remark that in my judgment, of course, not 'one rate of exchange,' but nevertheless 'one rate of value' would still obtain under socialism. If a million tons of grain are lying ready for distribution among the citizens, each ton, assuming it is of equal quality, will have to be held equal in value to any other. In consumption the several tons will not afford equal degrees of utility, but equal utility will be imputed to them as their value. I admit that, when goods are not sold to citizens, but distributed among them, equal prices will not come to be paid for equal items, nevertheless equality in judgments on value would manifest itself in many other directions, chiefly in the calculus of production. Thus, to take as example a simple, though comparatively unimportant case, the effective capacity of two machines would be judged by the quantity of products they yielded, in which it would not occur to any one to assume the value of those products, equal quality being assumed, as other than equal. If it were not essentially required in economic procedure, that we should regard a number of commodities, similar in quality but affording different degrees of utility, as economically equal, the fact of their being held as equal in price would be an offence against economic procedure, detrimental to either buyer, or seller, or both. If there were no better explanation of this fact than competition, if its foundation did not lie deep in the nature of each individual economic subject, economy would go astray wherever and whenever it proceeded on the principle of prices reckoned in this manner.

I touch at this point of the difference, alluded to at the outset, which exists between Jevons and the Austrian school respecting the conception of value and the principle of the law of value. For us, Jevons holds too closely to the narrower view, which sees in price the only manifestation of value. We conform to an idea always firmly maintained in Germany, when we say that in economy value decides everything, not only the price of the bargain, but also what amount of consumption, productive employment, and outlay entering into it is permissible. But while the older German school suffers this general function of value to depend ultimately on bare usefulness, to which it gives the empty name of value-in-use (*Gebrauchswerth*), we explain the determining cause as value in its true, complete meaning, value with all the principal laws revealing themselves in price; value as following the law of margins and the cost of production; value as demanding productive imputation, rent and interest. But precisely on this ground do we hold the view that the current mode of reckoning in economy by exchange-value is not a dictum of the market, but, in spite of many peculiarities conditioned by the market, a dictum of economy itself.

The exposition I have given here has permitted but scanty recognition of these more intimate lines of thought in the Austrian school. I have not been without fear, that our special language might, in so condensed an exposition, sound strange overmuch.

VI

The guiding principle in devoting commodities to public purposes, as in consumption generally, should be the consideration of their value. The scale of state-consumption and state-mechanism, which each citizen will wish to see, must vary in proportion to his own valuation of commodities. It is only reasonable that the rich man, who retains, after covering his most pressing personal outgoings, a surplus of goods for any other purposes, should desire a more expanded public expenditure than the poor man. A just system of taxation will take account of these variations in the valuations made by different classes of people, and adjust the fiscal burdens to the citizens by covering the costs of state-administration with contributions graduated accordingly.

It would take me too far were I to show how Prof. Sax, starting from this idea, has carried out the theory of value in a system of progressive taxation. I should like to point out a remarkable political phenomenon. The state, in taxing citizens unequally, suffers itself to be paid unequally, for its equal services, – and we find this equitable. In the market every purchaser, from the richest to the poorest, pays the same price for the same service, the millionaire paying for what he buys in common with the beggar by the beggar's standard, – and this we find natural. How shall we interpret these inconsistencies?

Prague, February 1891   F. WIESER

NOTES

1. This explanation of interest is valid only in the case of 'producer's capital.' Interest on emergency-loans or on principal lent to the spendthrift require to be otherwise explained. Here we have the debtor, by reason of distress or carelessness, setting more store by the goods of the present than by those of the future, and utterly regardless of any expected net profit; hence his promising for a certain supply of present cash, a larger supply of future cash.
2. 'Address to the Economic Science and Statistics Section of the British Association' (Newcastle-upon-Tyne, 1889), p. 26.

Friedrich von Wieser, 'The Theory of Urban Ground Rent' (1909);
Louise Sommer (ed.) *Essays in European Economic Thought* (Princeton,
NJ: Van Nostrand, 1960), pp. 39–80.

Wieser's 'Theory of Urban Ground Rent' was first published in
German as the introduction to a book (*Mietzinse und Bodenwerte
in Prag*) by W. Mildschuh (Vienna and Leipzig: Carl Deuticke,
1909). It was republished in F. A. Hayek (ed.), Wieser: *Gesammelte Abhandlungen* (Tübingen: J. C. B. Mohr, 1929), pp. 126–
63.

10

The Theory of Urban
Ground Rent

FRIEDRICH von WIESER

Preface

The theory of urban ground rent, which I here submit to the public in a separate reprint, appears at the same time as an introduction to a detailed study made by Dr W. Mildschuh entitled 'Residential Rents and Land Values in Prague,' recently issued as Part 1 of Volume IX of the Wiener Staatswissenschaftliche Studien. Although I occasionally refer in a few places in the text to figures arrived at by Dr Mildschuh, my presentation is nevertheless complete in itself, and I therefore feel justified in publishing it independently in the hope that in this form it may be of interest to readers seeking an explanation of the theory. A few words are needed to clarify the relationship between my work and Dr Mildschuh's.

The paper was inspired by a discussion of the theory of urban ground rent which I conducted about six years ago in my seminar in economics at the German University of Prague. With a view to verifying the theory there developed, Dr Mildschuh, one of the participants in the seminar, declared himself willing to make a study of the data available for Prague and its suburbs. The assessment of the Austrian tax on residential rents, being calculated on the basis of an official register in which all the rents paid in a municipality are scrupulously recorded year by year and dwelling by dwelling, furnishes the scientific investigator with a wealth of data such as no researcher, no matter how diligent, could succeed in assembling elsewhere. Dr Mildschuh has earnestly and judiciously sifted through this entire mass of material on tax assessment, as well as all the available information offered by the official registers of landed property, mortgage records, and other sources. He has, in fact, expanded the scope of his original project in all the directions in which theoretical interest extends. Every student of the theory of urban ground rent will benefit from the completeness and clarity with which he has placed before the reader the actual conditions bringing about an increase in rent in a town which, in the period under examination, was going through the transition to a large modern city.

Originally I intended to supplement Dr Mildschuh's work with a comprehensive theoretical dissertation. Unfortunately, lack of time prevented me from doing so, and I have had to limit myself to an introductory essay confined to the exposition of only what is absolutely essential for the understanding of the statistics he presents. I have had to set aside any consideration of their wider implications and in particular to abstain from discussing the extensive literature concerning this subject. Nor have I been able to enter into the related problem – so important for Austria – of the shift in the incidence of our taxes on residential rents. I refer in this connection to the official minutes of the inquiry conducted by the Austrian Ministry of Finance in the fall of 1902 into the question of revising the tax rates on inhabited dwellings. On that occasion I presented a detailed statement of my position on the subject. In regard to this problem Dr Mildschuh likewise provides comprehensive data, and I think one is warranted in assuming that his documentation will not fail to impress the reader even in the absence of any theoretical commentary. I could not very well have provided such a commentary at this time without entering deeply into polemical discussions, but I reserve the right to publish it independently.

The theory of urban ground rent that I propose to expound here I already presented on the occasion of the aforementioned inquiry, although only in a condensed form. Even at that time I was able to refer for corroboration to certain results obtained by Dr Mildschuh in his treatment of the data from Prague. I trust I am not wrong in assuming that his work, now submitted to the public in its completed form, will provide the theory set forth here with a broad empirical verification.

The Theory of Urban Ground Rent

Every theory of urban ground rent has to begin with an exposition of the Ricardo-Thünen theory of agricultural ground rent. Today we have become so unfamiliar with the ideas which gave rise to that theory that it seems advisable first to discuss Ricardo's personality as a scientific investigator. This can be done in a few words. Ricardo is generally considered as hyperabstract. Indeed, he is often described as the most resolute opponent of empirical inquiry. In fact, however, his chief limitation seems to have been his incapacity to detach himself sufficiently from reality. He lacks the ability to analyze complex phenomena into their elements; he is wanting in depth of penetration; and even his exceptionally keen perspicacity is at bottom but the shrewdness of a businessman schooled in the practical affairs of life. His very insistence on simplification, on which he is so emphatic, is just the practical man's way of disregarding everything but the actual results and of ignoring all the factors in the background that may have played a role in the shaping of events. He thus makes it impossible for himself to arrive at a true explanation. That is the reason why he had to resort to artificial explanations that appear to us today as unempirical abstractions. The fact is that his formulas are ultimately drawn from the large stock of popularly accepted beliefs, of which he was a remarkably observant student. It is understandable that science in its early stages, as long as it had to be content with only half the truth, should have admired these surprisingly concise formulations as complete solutions. Only recently has it been realized that they block access to the other half of the truth and that one has to accomplish the difficult feat of freeing oneself from their seductive charm and of trying new paths if one wishes to discover the whole truth.

Today this work has been achieved in great part, and as a result many of Ricardo's theories have finally been found to be untenable. Others are on the point of being discredited and are still held only in outward form until the right theory, of which we are already on the track, is fully established. It is his theory of ground rent that has best withstood the corrosive influence of critical examination. This is easily understandable. The explanation of agricultural ground rent does not require very deep scientific penetration. There are only certain prominent peaks of value that have to be illuminated, if one may be permitted the metaphor, while the whole complex network of other value phenomena, with all their interconnections, may be left in darkness. Even if one is unable to explain the formation of prices or the essential nature of costs, it is relatively easy to demonstrate that pieces of land that are exceptionally well favoured or soil that is especially fertile, since they keep costs low, yield the owner a surplus above the price of his produce. Here was a problem that challenged Ricardo's best scientific abilities. Yet even here he failed to achieve a definitive formulation: his theory is lacking in certain refinements, and for all its apparent precision it conceals intrinsic contradictions that have to be winnowed out. However, as it doubtless provides a faithful representation of most of the phenomena involved, Ricardo's theory of ground rent is, in view of the nature of the problem, assured of lasting value. Whatever it still lacks in theoretical completeness is added of itself once it is fitted into the framework of a completed theory of value and price formation.

The problem of urban rent seems to be closely related to that of agricultural rent. In both cases what we have to deal with is a differential rent that can be regarded as the peculiar benefit deriving from the permanent advantages that certain especially favoured pieces of land offer the proprietor. In both cases, too, these advantages are due to favourable location. And in both cases it is the scarcity in the amount of such land that exerts an influence upon the formation of rent. If conditions in both cases correspond in so many respects – and still others could be mentioned – then there must follow a certain correspondence in the result. Nevertheless, there is no feasible way of effecting a transition from Ricardo's theory to a theory of urban rent. The advantage to the agricultural producer offered by relatively favourable land or by soil that is exceptionally fertile consists in the fact that they keep his costs of production comparatively low. This, at least, is the only advantage investigated by Ricardo, and quite rightly, since the other advantage that is offered, namely, that better land also yields better crops, is of no special theoretical interest. For urban land, however, the contrary is true: here it is of no theoretical interest that in certain cases the conditions of the subsoil help to keep the costs of construction comparatively low; the theory of urban rent is concerned exclusively with those advantages that are provided, directly or indirectly, by location. But location, as such, has nothing to do with the costs of construction. It will not do to assert that central locations are more favourable because they serve to keep these costs comparatively low and that the graduation in rents that one finds as one passes from the centre of town to outlying areas is to be accounted for by the difference in these costs. Hence, the theory of agricultural ground rent has to start, as Pantaleoni rightly observes, from the fact that for fruits of the soil produced at unequal costs equal prices are obtained; whereas the theory of urban rent must be based on the fact that with equal costs unequal prices are obtained.

This contrast goes even deeper. We have already observed that the basic idea of Ricardo's theory of ground rent can be understood without entering into the subtleties of the theory of price formation. Indeed, one has no need to refer to the latter theory at all: agricultural ground rent, in its primary form, does not presuppose a market. Even in the self-sufficient domestic economy of the rural household the surplus obtained will be imputed, as its rent, to the more fertile land, which produces the same quantity at lower cost. Urban rent, on the other hand, is entirely a phenomenon of the market. To explain it one needs a fully perfected theory of the formation of prices, and, what is more, one has to adjust this general theory very precisely to the special peculiarities of the market in urban rents and to develop it farther in this direction.

This is what we shall attempt to do in what follows. But first it is necessary once again to revert to the matter of savings in costs. So far we have spoken only of the costs of construction, but apart from these perhaps other costs might come into question too. A tenant, if he lives in a relatively unfavourable location, has, under the circumstances, to make daily use of means of transportation that, in the long run, put him to considerable expense. There is hardly anybody who would not be willing to pay correspondingly more for a dwelling place so situated as to save him 'costs' of this kind. Should it not be possible to derive from these facts a law of urban rent that, in essence, would coincide with Ricardo's law? Ricardo speaks, to be sure, of savings in costs on the side of supply, which do not appear in the price, whereas we are concerned with savings in costs on the side of demand, which would raise the price; but both really amount to the same thing. One must start from the fact that the total outlay for rent plus the 'costs' of transportation occasioned by the location of one's place of residence will amount to a certain sum for each level of income. Thus, as in the case studied by Ricardo, prices (the total outlay) would be equal, while 'costs' would be unequal. Hence the owner of a dwelling so situated as to save transportation costs would receive a higher rental for it; in other words, he would earn a differential rent in the strictly economic sense of Ricardo's theory.

There can be no doubt that such calculations are actually made quite often and that they are one source of urban rent. But only a small part of the rents actually received come from this source. It would be quite erroneous to assume that everybody who lives in the outlying areas has to go into the centre of town every day. Most of the families who live on the outskirts describe the more or less narrow orbit of their daily lives within the area of the outer reaches themselves. Nor can costs of transportation alone explain either the range or the number of the actual differences that exist between the rents paid in different localities. The gradations in the fares charged for different distances on the mass transportation lines, even in a very large city, are generally small and few in number, and then only for long distances. But what a difference there is between residential rents within each of these transportation zones and, even more, between one zone and another! The greatest disparities are to be found in the central sectors over very short distances – so short, indeed, that no means of transportation is needed at all. It is clear, therefore, that a tenant's appraisement of the advantages of any particular location is, in the main, determined by considerations of a quite different kind.

The theory of urban ground rent has to discover what these are and what role they play in determining rental values on the market. For this purpose it is advisable to begin by assuming the case of a town with a relatively stable or slowly increasing population. A large modern city springs up so rapidly that many of the connections between the different factors involved are too confused to be easily analyzed. Therefore, the discussion of the special case of the market in residential rents in a large modern city, with particular reference to the related question of speculation in land, will be reserved for our conclusion, since it can be more readily understood once one has grasped the law governing more stable phenomena.

The case we propose to take up first is, in fact, approximately that of the towns of Austria up to 1848 and even into the eighteen-sixties, the years of economic upswing. Let us consider the case of a town that has already outgrown its medieval walls and is now spreading out quite freely, but, for the time being, only very slowly, into the surrounding countryside. The predominant type of dwelling is the rented house; the privately owned home is becoming less common. (As long as the latter is still the prevailing type, a market in residential rents has not yet fully developed.) We shall assume a situation like that which prevails generally in Germany and Austria, where, contrary to the English custom, several families share the same floor of an apartment house. Although the theory of urban ground rent is essentially the same in either case as long as the market in residential rents is sufficiently extensive, its treatment is greatly facilitated if it is confined to one definite type, and we shall therefore make use of this helpful procedure.

In a town with a slowly growing population, residential rents will, in the long run, have to cover at least the cost of production if the supply of buildings is to keep pace with the demand. These costs are divisible into two types. The first consists of the original investment and comprises construction costs proper, including the average profit of the builder as well as the capital expended for the acquisition of the building lot itself, which, however, in this calculation of minimum costs, is to be reckoned only at the value of arable land. The second comprises current expenditures annually required for the house, namely, taxes, costs of administration and maintenance, and amortization of the invested capital. The rentals received should exceed these annual costs by an amount such that the customary interest on the still unamortized capital invested in the building can be paid from the remaining surplus. Ground rent is always included in the lowest residential rental paid. This is evidently true at least of agricultural ground rent, which is capitalized in the value of arable land; but it is also true of urban rent, for if one wishes to acquire property for urban construction, one must bid more than its value as arable land.

Urban ground rent, however, comprises only a very small part of the lowest residential rental paid and will not be really high even in proportion to the value of the property as arable land; for under our provisional assumption of a slowly growing population, the market will favour a tendency toward the acquisition of new land for urban construction. Under the conditions we have assumed, we do not yet have to reckon with speculation in land, since urban demand is directly met by rural supply. The builder will be willing to pay the value of the property as arable land plus a certain premium, since this expenditure, when added to his others, is still not very great. Only a small premium will be required to induce some one of the many rural proprietors to sell his land. There is still plenty of agricultural land surrounding the town, much in excess of the demand (which we assume as rather limited) for new urban construction. Property on the outskirts of the town, in high demand for agricultural purposes, is available in abundance if viewed from the standpoint of urban demand.

As long as this remains the case, not more than the lowest residential rental, calculated on the basis described above, will, as a rule, have to be paid for the poorest urban locations. The situation is quite different, however, in the better sections of town. Since they are limited in number, only some of those seeking accommodations will find them there, and competition will therefore have to decide who these tenants are to be. The theory of price formation teaches us what the result of competition is: only those tenants will be admitted who combine the most urgent need with the greatest ability to pay. But to attain their end they have to make their superior ability to pay effectual by so decisively outbidding their weaker rivals as to eliminate them entirely. To the first relatively small premium which the builder has to be willing to pay in order to outbid those who wish to use the land for agricultural purposes must now be added ever-increasing increments in view of the competition within the town itself; and the more desirable and limited is the space available, and the more affluent the class of those who have to outbid, the higher this premium becomes. It is from this kind of bidding that urban ground rent is built up: it is that part of the residential rental which is offered as a premium, over and above the basic cost, for comparatively favourable locations.

This is a simple idea – as simple, indeed, as the idea that agricultural rent originates from savings in costs, and equally important. To appreciate its importance fully one has to make clear to what extent the urban market in residential rents demands this kind of competitive bidding, just as in the theory of agricultural rent everything depends on the extent to which savings in costs actually occur. The theory of urban rent has no other task than to determine the cost basis of the lowest residential rental paid and then to demonstrate the system of competitive bidding that is erected over and above this foundation.

In the market in residential rents this competitive bidding is carried on in some cases differently from the way it is in the market in business rents. We shall have to examine separately the manner in which prices are formed in each of these markets. We propose to begin with the market in residential rents, as it is the one that is the more important for the mass of the population.

The market in residential rents is divided into a greater or smaller number of sites graded according to their relative desirability. In towns built on the older pattern there is generally a nucleus that forms the hub of all municipal life. It is here that we find the town hall, the main church, the residences of the prince's court, the government buildings, and the cathedral. Here too we find concentrated all the other buildings that are representative of the town. Here all the objects of historical or touristic interest are collected; here all the pageantry of the town is displayed; here pulse the main arteries of its political, ecclesiastical, commercial, and social life. All of those who play a role in civic affairs, all the people who want to see and to be seen, endeavour to dwell in this area. It is not always the geometrical centre; it may even be situated on the periphery – for example, on the ocean or extending along one of the banks of a river. (One has only to think of Venice or Hamburg.) But wherever it may be, it is always from here that one measures distances in determining the relative desirability of different sites, even though distance alone is not decisive, for many other factors may also be of importance and may lead to all kinds of irregular configurations in the pattern of residential rents. Nevertheless, we shall provisionally assume a thoroughly regular town plan, arranged in concentric rings around a central section, although we are fully aware of the fact that in doing so we are idealizing the irregular phenomena actually encountered in reality. Idealization is a most useful expedient of which all the exact sciences take advantage. So, for instance, geometry starts with perfectly regular figures, although it is well understood that these are pure abstractions.

In our case the assumption of a concentric town plan faithfully represents the two most important facts characterizing the towns of the pre-revolutionary period preceding March, 1848. The elucidation of the theoretical significance of this arrangement must be our first task, and apart from that everything else must be relegated to the background. The first fact is that most, if not all, of the poorer quarters were situated near the town border; and the other is that the better quarters, being densely concentrated in the interior part of the town, were in shorter supply according as they were more favourably located. What gives the urban

258

market in residential rents its peculiar character is precisely the fact that the scarcity of the supply increases in proportion to the favourableness of the location. In this market the demand does not consist of parties who enter into competition all at once and just for once, but rather of groups competing successively and frequently in the whole graded series of rings surrounding the heart of the town. After the weakest bidders have been pushed into the outermost ring by their stronger competitors, the next higher stratum of tenants will be composed of the second weakest, who will be prevented from advancing further in than the second ring from the last by their inability to pay the rent (now raised higher by the renewed competition of the remaining bidders) demanded in the third ring; and so, by virtue of this continually renewed competitive bidding at every level, residential rents form themselves into a graded series comprising as many different steps as there are major residential sections, together with their respective subdivisions, until the highest rents include a premium that may well equal or even exceed the basic cost. If I may revert to an example that I used at the Austrian inquiry into tax rates on inhabited dwellings, the highest residential rentals paid on the Stephansplatz in Vienna form one end of an unbroken chain that extends as far as the lowest rentals paid in the outermost suburbs, the whole of which, in the last analysis, is based on competitive bidding.

The major residential areas or quarters are quite different from one another in the character of their buildings. What a contrast there is between the streets and houses of the elegant districts and those in the poorer sections of town! In fact, if one were to judge from the outward impression that one receives even more from the older type of town plan than from that of the modern city, one would think that every district was sharply defined and demarcated from every other, i.e., not only fixed immovably to a definite location, but, above all, constituted as a residential area restricted exclusively to a certain class, in very much the same way as, in the strictest sense, the old Jewish quarter, the ghetto, indeed was.

If this were really the case, then, as soon as demand became more urgent, that pitiless law of residential rents which has recently been called 'the brass law of rents' could in fact become operative; that is, the urgent demand for a supply that cannot be increased could be exploited in every dwelling, including the good and the best ones, so that tenants of every income level, even the middle and the highest, would be obliged to strain their resources to the utmost in order to secure a place to live. However, the market in residential rents should not be conceived in this way, still less the partial markets into which it is divided, for the connections among all of them are quite fluid.

Nevertheless, the picture that we have given of these connections as forming a concentric pattern is not altogether clear; at least it needs a more precise interpretation, perhaps even a correction, in order to avoid misunderstanding. For the town plan that we have taken as our model gives undue prominence to distance from the centre as the one factor determining the relative desirability of different locations. Distance from the centre is a given quantity whose economic consequences can, at best, be mitigated by an improvement in the means of transportation, but which, in all other respects, is fixed. The subdivisions in the market in residential rents, on the other hand, are by no means fixed in relation to one another, for in reality distance plays only a secondary role in tenants' appraisal of the relative desirability of different locations.

The primary factor is of social origin and one whose theoretical significance has thus far been neglected. Indeed, the whole theory of price formation has, in general, been treated up to now with far too little consideration to social influences. Choosing a place to live is like deciding whether one is going to travel first, second or third class on the railway: both decisions reflect one's sense of one's own social status, which is in turn affected by the pressure of conventional opinion. In these days of democracy, when all classes wear very much the same kind of clothing, the location of one's home serves more than anything else to indicate the social status that one claims for oneself, especially as one generally lives in the same place for some length of time and the reputation of the neighbourhood is a matter of public knowledge. 'Tell me the neighbourhood you live in, and I'll tell you what you are.' This is more or less the feeling that actuates tenants in choosing a place to live. Whether a location is good or bad is determined by the social class of the people who have settled there – even though, as we shall see later, people of different social classes may be found stacked, as it were, above one another on different floors of the same house. If, for instance, the sections in which the middle classes have settled are less highly regarded than the most elegant neighbourhoods, the decisive reason is not that the former are further from the centre of town, for this is not always the case, but that they are not occupied by people of distinction. One must add, however, that, as a rule, the less fashionable neighbourhoods will be found at a greater distance from the centre of town precisely because the central locations have been taken by the social elite.

Hence we may draw the important theoretical conclusion that the spatial extension of any neighbourhood will, in the long run, always accommodate itself to the size of the social class or the number of people of a given income level who live in it. In the concentrically arranged urban community which we have imagined, one must always assume that there are as many major residential zones as there are major levels in the town's social hierarchy. These large zones are divided into smaller ones corresponding to the finer gradations within each income level and are again still further subdivided according to their distance from the centre of town. If the ranks of a particular social class increase, the neighbourhood that it occupies will in the long run also expand by the construction, sooner or later, of streets and of houses built in its characteristic style of architecture, at the expense of the people of lower income level inhabiting contiguous areas. When Wallenstein erected his palace in the 'Kleinseite' of Prague, he provided the space he needed by buying some sixty houses from poor people in the area and razing them. Thus, the example of the powerful Duke of Friedland served to widen the zone whose residents could pass as elegant.

To summarize: the subdivisions of the total urban market in residential rents are as freely extensible in relation to one another as the latter is in relation to arable land. These partial markets, in both the area of their extension and the architectural style of the buildings within them, express the specific stratification of urban society, as determined not only by income distribution, but also by conventional views regarding the type of accommodation required by each social class. The upper class feel obliged to maintain a certain standard of living suitable to their position, while those in more modest circumstances find it necessary to live in more densely populated areas and even to sublet their apartments or take in lodgers.

The well-known distinction made in the German textbooks on economics between goods of which the supply can be increased at will and goods of which the supply can be increased only at higher costs of production needs to be supplemented, if we are to understand the urban market in residential rents, by a third category, for we can consider dwelling places as goods of which the supply can be increased by the payment of a premium. The condition required by the 'brass law of residential rents,' namely, that of rigidly restricted partial markets, is absent here. The different social classes are not confined to specific zones of fixed extension and therefore do not find it necessary to strain their resources to the utmost in an exhausting competitive struggle within each zone. Competition in this case is confined to outbidding weaker rivals living in contiguous areas by just enough to force them to release the desired ground.

The rich enjoy less of an advantage in bidding for a place to live than they do in buying staple foods, for which they need to pay only what the poorest classes can afford. But, on the other hand, they are in a better position in the market in residential rents than they are in the market for diamonds, which they bid up to luxury prices by competition among themselves. The market in residential rents thus stands somewhere in between: the rich have to strain their resources, but only as far as is required to outbid weaker competitors of lower income level living in contiguous areas, who, for their part, have already had to overcome the competition of still weaker bidders, This statement is in full accord with the well-known empirical fact that the proportion of income allotted to the payment of rent decreases with increasing income, even though the need for a place to live could in this case be more richly satisfied.

Here we have found a first point of vantage from which we can look back at Ricardo's theory of prices. According to Ricardo, there can be a law of price formation only for goods that can be regularly reproduced, because their prices have to adjust themselves to given costs. However, the price of goods having scarcity value, such as precious stocks of wine, do not conform to any law, but depend upon the whims of the consumers and the ups and downs of their financial circumstances. They are, if one may say so, capricious prices. So far Ricardo.

Now the rents paid for the most desirable urban locations form a graduated scale no less closely integrated than that which is exhibited in the formation of the prices of commodities produced in branches of production operating with the utmost regularity. Dwelling places are no doubt scarce in every town, but they are goods of which the supply can be increased by the payment of a premium, and they therefore faithfully reflect, in the rents paid for them, the economic stratification of the townsfolk. Urban residential rents are in no sense capricious prices. Just as their gross amount conforms to a stringent law, so likewise does their net yield over and above costs, which constitutes ground rent in the strict sense of the term. Urban ground rent also conforms to the economic stratification of the people of the town and shifts only gradually with it. The modern theory takes full cognizance of the fact that the 'objectively' given costs of production have their basis in subjective valuation. The constancy in the cost of the goods and the labour most widely needed in production is attributable to the fact that they are objects of demand for mass consumption. The law of urban ground rent and the law explaining the formation of commodity prices ultimately coincide in that they both rest on the solid ground of mass social phenomena.

The market in business rents is likewise composed of several independent subdivisions. For the wholesale trade this market is to be found in a central location, the best being in the vicinity of the Exchange. Separately situated we find the highest governmental and municipal offices, the houses of parliament, and the like, generally, however, in buildings of their own and only under exceptional circumstances in rented quarters. They too seek to be centrally situated, but they are not all together in a district restricted exclusively to them. Finally, there is a rent market for retail business. The following observations refer to this type of market.

Like the market in residential rents, it is composed of partial markets among which the connections are quite fluid. However, the market in business rents is much more restricted than the market in residential rents. The only commercially important sites and streets are those in which traffic is relatively dense, in particular the hub of the town, into which all roads lead and from which they radiate in all directions, and then too, of course, the large arterial avenues themselves. It is not necessary to elaborate any further on a phenomenon so well known, but one fact not usually discussed needs to be emphasized, namely, that such a location represents one of the most effective means of advertising. Since the partial markets in rents for retail business follow the major traffic lanes and expand only along with them, their range is less extensible than that of the partial markets in residential rents, and therefore the competitive struggle for desirable business locations is correspondingly much keener.

Even more important from the theoretical point of view is a second difference. The increased profits obtained from businesses situated in advantageous locations increase the fund available for competitive bidding, and since this is true for all enterprises that can be carried on within a given area, competition on the side of demand increases in intensity. The amount of the premium that one has to pay in order to secure a favourable location for one's business is determined not only by the lower profits that weaker competitors, after having been squeezed out, will make outside the preferred area, but also from the higher profits that they had hoped to realize if they had succeeded in finding a location within it.

Nevertheless, the opinion so often heard that the urban businessman works only for his landlord is incorrect. The general law of marginal utility that governs the formation of commodity prices applies also to the market in business rents to the extent that the conditions that it presupposes are in fact given, since the problem is almost never that of 'the only possible site,' but, as a rule, involves a certain choice among different locations. At least the more successful entrepreneurs in a given part of the market can afford to pay a premium that is not within the reach of competitors still left in the area who are operating at a lower profit. Yet business rents always do rise higher than residential rents, and in the most desirable locations they stand considerably higher. The same holds true for the central market in wholesale business. The graduated scale of residential rents may be likened to a vault that arches upward from the border of the town to its centre. Above this, in the area of the main arteries of commerce that radiate from the centre, the highest business rents rise still further upward, like the ribs of the vault and the central steeple over the dome.

So far we have been concerned only with what may be called the rent of location. One must also raise the question whether the architectural plan of urban construction does not, like agricultural management, give rise to a rent of intensity. The question can be easily answered. Such a rent of intensity does indeed arise. But, just as the rent of intensity from agricultural land is always only the enhancement that higher fertility and greater proximity to the market add to an original rent, so the rent of intensity on urban land is only an enhancement of the original rent of location. In the favourable locations the builders have a chance to increase the rent by increasing the capital invested in construction; and the better the location, the greater the opportunity for an increase in rent. Here an increase in capital enables one to build in a narrower space, to a greater height, and with greater luxury, and by thus increasing horizontal, vertical and qualitative intensity, to earn a higher rent in all these directions. But it is obvious that this rent will always remain a rent of location.

The town of our fathers and grandfathers exhibits, as we proceed from the border to the centre, a gradual transition in architectural styles, starting with houses of still half-rustic construction, with a wide courtyard and garden consisting of a ground floor only, or of a single story of very simple structure. The more we proceed inward, the fewer become the gardens, and the more narrow the courtyards, owing to the construction of outbuildings in response to the demand for them; the fewer become the additional subsidiary rooms as the predominant consideration of tenants in outbidding one another becomes the turning of all available space to immediate use for living quarters; the more floors are superimposed upon one another, since they help to increase the rent by multiplying the land's capacity to accommodate occupants; the more costly the materials used in construction, the more artistic the labour employed, and the more luxurious the fixtures and installations, since it is with these that one hopes to satisfy the pretentions of – and thereby to attract – the class of tenants both ready and able to pay the highest rent. So manifold are the ways of increasing intensity by way of construction, so simple is, in general, their theoretical interrelationship, that only a few additional remarks are required.

As far as horizontal intensity is concerned, it will be opposed in the richer neighbourhoods by a counterpressure in the direction of qualitative intensity, that is, toward greater comfort and, in addition to other luxuries, the luxury of more room for each family. Needless to say, this has to be paid for at higher cost, since the provision of more space where ground is already so precious requires a great increase in capital investment. If, on behalf of the wealthier classes, building regulations are demanded for such areas prohibiting the full utilization of the available space for apartment houses and requiring houses with gardens, the influence that these classes have on the administrative authorities will tend to be used to their own advantage. They will want the government to take measures to restrain the vexatious competition occasioned by an excessively heavy demand for space, to prevent the increase in the price of land brought about by crowded construction, and to make possible, precisely in this part of the town, a spacious style of building at lower cost.

As for qualitative intensity, it must be noted that landlords seek to earn not only interest at the prevailing rate on the capital invested in construction, but, even more, the highest rentals obtainable from competitive bidding in any area. Hence they will decide in favour of a relatively expensive type of construction only if the entire capital investment offers the prospect of yielding a return, over and above interest at the prevailing rate, that is at least equal to the differential rent deriving from the advantages offered by a favourable location; otherwise they could utilize the same amount of capital more profitably by a more extensive investment spread out over a wider area. By attracting the richest tenants, among whom competitive bidding must, of necessity, reach the greatest heights, they can even expect a further increase in differential rent.

Of the greatest theoretical interest is the increase in intensity obtained by vertical construction. We have to begin by considering how tenants appraise the different floors of the same building. For a retail shop, location on the ground floor is preferred. Certain other business establishments may be situated to equal, or perhaps even greater, advantage on higher floors. The installation of elevators, however, has brought about important changes in these respects. In urban areas that are built up, ground-floor apartments are considered less desirable, the main floor being greatly preferred. Some tenants even have a preference for still higher locations, where there is better light, purer air, and less noise from the street. In general, however, most tenants above the main floor are more conscious of the disadvantages than of the advantages of living so high up, and from here upwards, therefore, apartments as well as business lofts are the less valued the higher they are situated; or, in other words, from here on up the increments in premiums offered in competitive bidding become progressively smaller. Finally, everywhere – in inferior locations at a lower point, in the better locations at a higher point – a floor must be reached above which a higher bid can no longer be obtained.

If the interests of the owner of the building were the sole deciding factor, one story would continue to be superimposed upon another until a point was reached at which the rent obtainable from any further elevation would no longer defray the cost of its construction. In such a calculation he would have to take into account the fact that every additional story would cost him proportionately less, since the ratio of the cost of the foundation and the roof to the total costs of construction will be calculated with a correspondingly larger divisor. Besides, as we have already mentioned, people of different income levels may very frequently be found above one another on different floors of the same building. In most sections of town the upper floors are inhabited by families of relatively low income, who are less sensitive to the inconveniences of living higher up and for whom, therefore, a more economical type of accommodation suffices, so that the builder saves money on them and can still have a surplus in spite of the fact that he charges them less.

Subject to all the reservations we have mentioned, we can formulate a rule or, if one may be permitted the expression, a 'law,' which could be called the law of diminishing returns on residential quarters. It calls to mind the law of diminishing returns on agricultural land and must be taken into account in a complete theory of urban ground rent just as its analogue is in Ricardo's theory, except that, of course, it produces different effects, depending upon the peculiar structure of the market in urban rents. In this market, as we know, price is directly determined by costs only in quarters inhabited by the very poorest tenants; the price paid for better quarters rises above costs as a result of competitive bidding. The law of diminishing returns on residential quarters makes it clear that the lowest-paying quarters are found not only in the poorest areas lying on the outskirts of town, but well within the interior. The border of the town, if the latter is conceived in the sense of a market, extends not only outward, but upward. The rising line of premiums paid as a result of competitive bidding thus curves in a double direction: horizontally, from the outskirts to the interior of the town, according to the varying character of its residential zones; and vertically, from the top to the ground floor in each house.

These two concatenated series of prices always counterbalance each other. The rent for each apartment is weighed, on the one hand, against the rents paid in other streets and neighbourhoods for the same floor (or also for higher or lower floors inhabited by the same social class) and, on the other hand, against the rents paid on higher or lower floors in the same house.

American skyscrapers show how high the border of a city can be pushed. Such gigantic buildings, to be sure, can be erected only here and there, and then only for business purposes. Nevertheless, our towns could rise much higher towards the interior if landlords were not hampered by our building regulations, which restrict the number of floors for the sake of the general welfare. Since the effect of these regulations is to broaden and flatten out the town's vertical profile, the result is that in the areas where rentals are the highest, the buildings with the greatest number of floors are generally the most remunerative, because the competition for their top floors still produces a premium over and above costs, i.e., a rent in the strictly economic sense. Only in the poorer districts might it happen that a rent can no longer be earned on the highest floor still permitted by the building regulations. And it could even happen – as is, for instance, the case in Prague – that houses in a given area are not built as high as the law permits them to be, simply because the rent that could thereby be earned would no longer cover the costs of construction. In any house in which the number of floors is kept down solely by force of law, the ground rent – that is, in a house of several stories, the sum of the premiums, over and above costs, yielded by competitive bidding on all the floors taken together – will, of course, be likewise reduced.

In spite of this reduction brought about by building regulations, the rent derived from an advantageous location will, in favoured areas, be very considerably increased by virtue of the fact that it can be made to yield a rent of intensity. It will be recalled that we concluded our earlier discussion of what we have called the rent of location by comparing residential rentals to a vault arching upward from the border of the town to its centre. This vault will soar considerably higher by virtue of the rent of intensity. Towards the interior there will be an upward gradation in the increments that competitive bidding can yield per unit of surface utilized and a consequent increase in the intensity of construction. As the space available for the construction of apartments becomes more congested, they will be arranged in superimposed levels. Finally, in the preferred locations, the more elegant style of construction will raise the basic costs above which premiums have to be offered in competitive bidding. As the rentals paid for such apartments arch upward, like a vault, over the most highly favoured locations, the ground rent included in them will also rise, and no special proof is required to show that the curve of the latter will necessarily rise more steeply than that of gross rentals paid.

And now a word about the large modern city. As a consequence of the 'lure of the city,' its circumference has increased enormously in comparison to that of earlier days. The demand for new accommodations is, as a rule, continually growing and is often even urgent. As a further consequence, the market in urban rents is fundamentally transformed in many different ways.

Let us discuss first the immediate effects brought about by the enormous extension in the area occupied by the city, and let us assume provisionally, as we have up to now, a concentric arrangement in its layout. Even on the assumption that the cost of the poorest accommodations on the outer fringes of the city remains unchanged, gross rental values, as well as ground rents, are bound to increase considerably in the favoured areas, and this applies as much to living quarters as it does to places of business. Residential rents rise because of the considerable increase in the number of concentric rings that results from the fact that the population is more widely spread out and more intensely stratified; and business rents rise because of the considerable increase in the number of business sections and, concomitantly, in the profits to be earned in the very best locations now that traffic has spread out and, at the same time, increased heavily in the most favoured areas. Between centre and border there are now located considerably more partial markets than before. The premium that one previously had to offer, over and above the rental paid at the town border, in order to secure a place further in the interior is now no longer sufficient because the whole scale of gradations in the amounts offered in competitive bidding from the border to the centre has been considerably lengthened and its height considerably increased. Where one previously had to meet the competition of bidders at twenty different levels, one now has to reckon with perhaps forty, and the premium one really has to pay in order to drive competitors from the field has to be larger because of their increased ability to pay.

In regard to this crucial point, I should like to call the reader's attention specifically to the facts that Dr Mildschuh has brought out with reference to Prague[1]. The cost of an apartment located on the outskirts of the city is today scarcely higher than it was in 1882 at what was then the border of Prague, since the increase in taxes and in the direct costs of construction has approximately been balanced by the decrease in the prevailing rate of interest. Yet in spite of this, residential rents in the interior increased considerably in this same period. No doubt one reason for this is that apartments today are more richly equipped, but the major part of the increase can be explained only by the intensification of competitive bidding. The figures adduced by Dr Mildschuh show clearly that as a town extends its borders, the whole scale of rents from border to centre gradually becomes more steeply inclined.

Although Prague has, for the most part, retained its concentric arrangement, one would by no means be justified in assuming that this is the general rule in large modern cities and in treating it theoretically as the prevailing type. With the growth of population the number of people in the upper-income brackets increased so greatly and so rapidly everywhere that they could no longer provide space for themselves in the central part of town simply by driving the poorer classes further out. Any attempt to do so would have been self-defeating, in view of the great difficulties involved in rebuilding and all the different kinds of resistance that traditional elements usually oppose to change. One had to resort to other expedients.

In Vienna, of course, a historical coincidence has made it possible to create an elegant quarter of very large extension immediately adjacent to the old central section of town. The latter was fortified, and the dismantling of the fortifications has made room for the fashionable 'Ringstrasse' and a whole network of side streets. In Prague the situation was similar, for here too there was an old fortification, which had been partly razed. This, together with other local circumstances, has made it possible to erect, immediately adjoining the old hub of the town, elegant new residential areas, which in one sector have been extended further and further out from the centre. These are the areas Dr Mildschuh has especially examined. In the other towns of Austria, following, in general, the example of the capital city, the well-to-do families have still retained their traditional preference for the interior sections. However, the rapid expansion of Vienna has led to the development of richer neighbourhoods farther out from the centre, and the city now possesses a number of suburban areas of this kind. In Berlin and other German cities this arrangement is even more popular.

Does not such a development destroy the factual basis of the law that the graduated scale of residential rents is determined by competitive bidding for favoured locations? If good apartment houses can also be built on the outskirts of the city, should one still have to pay a premium in order to get a good location? And what about cities that have stopped growing?

The formation of a city is the completion of a process that starts with the creation of separate islands consisting of good neighbourhoods located on the outskirts. The distance of these residential sections from the centre of the city increases as soon as it becomes the general practice of those in business or the professions to arrange their hours of work in such a way as to require them to leave home but once a day. Thus, the connection between one's place of work and the location of one's own home becomes less important, so that even if all of one's work always has to be carried on in the downtown areas, it is still possible to take up residence farther away, where a wide variety of advantages are offered that could not be provided in the central part of the city for even the richest people. All that then remains on the most expensive sites in the city are public buildings, the offices of big business, and monuments of historical or tourist interest, The residential sections, including even the most fashionable neighbourhoods, are all situated as far outside the downtown area as the constantly improving means of transportation make it possible to be.

However, it should not be supposed that proximity to the centre of the city and the convenience of the transit facilities to and from it are no longer considered as advantages. Other things being equal, these factors will still play a decisive role, but it will often happen that they will be outweighed by other advantages even more highly valued. A theory of urban rent that would make everything dependent exclusively upon proximity to the centre would be applicable only to a rather limited extent to the large modern city. It would, of course, explain why rents are higher within the city and along the main arteries of traffic, but in regard to the residential sections it would take into account only one of the motives for competitive bidding – and one that, moreover, is becoming less and less significant. Besides, such a theory would have to meet the objection that it completely fails to account for the existence of good residential areas located well outside the city, right next to vacant land. Hence, it is important to observe, as we have already seen in the case of the old town, that proximity to the centre is only a secondary consideration and that the primary factor is that of social stratification.

Consequently, we do not need to seek for any new theory in dealing with the large modern city. Today as in the past each social class will be in possession of just so much ground as befits its status in relation to all the others, and it will succeed in gaining possession of this ground for itself only by outbidding the less solvent classes. There will never be an abundant supply of vacant land at the disposal of the great majority of the inhabitants of a city, unless we suppose that its centripetal force will be compensated by a corresponding flight from the city and that the congested masses of houses existing today will be completely broken up and dispersed over a wider area like little villages.

Apart from proximity to the centre there will always be some other characteristics – however indifferent some of them may seem – that determine the valuation, and the rich will always tend to occupy the necessarily limited areas offering the greatest advantages, whatever these may be. Today as in the past the primary factor is social prestige. The neighbourhoods in which one can live 'suitably,' that is, in a manner befitting one's social position, will always be limited in number since one always wishes to live where other, 'better' families have already settled. Even if the suburban areas sought out for the better quarters were not, for a variety of other reasons, already rather limited, they would in any case be restricted in order to protect them from the encroachment of the proletariat. The number of people energetic enough to liberate themselves from social prejudices and to choose their places of residence independently is very small – quite as small, indeed, as the number of independently acting individuals has always been within the memory of man – and only such a minority will take advantage of the possibility of settling down where rents have not yet been raised by the competitive bidding of their social peers.

It cannot be denied that the irregular layout of the modern large city possesses, under present circumstances, very obvious advantages over the concentric arrangement of earlier days. By reducing the social prestige of proximity to the centre, the existing arrangement will no doubt help to lower residential rental values as well as ground rents. But it cannot altogether break down the system of graduated competitive bidding in the market in residential rents, even if we disregard the fact that, in the case of business rents, proximity to the centre becomes the more important the greater the number of people for whom transportation through the centre is the shortest route. It will be recalled that in describing conditions in the town of earlier days we represented residential rental values and ground rents as forming a kind of vault with a central dome and ascending ribs. In the modern large city this image is applicable only to the business districts. In regard to the residential sections, the pattern that we should have to draw today is highly irregular, with a number of larger or smaller domes, each spanning some local centre, and yet all oriented, to some extent, towards the heart of the city and the chief centres of business.

We can bring this part of our discussion to a conclusion with the observation that the market in residential rents in a large city, although far more spread out and less easily surveyed, basically conforms to the same law of a graduated scale of competitive bids as the more limited, but at the same time more regular, market in the small town of earlier days. But we have not yet finished. The supply of and the demand for apartments will less easily adjust themselves to each other when the town is growing rapidly than when its population remains relatively stable. As a general rule, demand will take the lead, but sometimes supply will do so. The latter situation occurred in many Austrian towns and elsewhere on a large scale in the troubled times around 1873. Dr Mildschuh devotes a thorough investigation to the effects that the crisis of that year had in Prague, thereby bringing to our attention facts that deserve a more precise theoretical interpretation. Many workers' families at that time were forced to leave town, the income of those remaining behind was sharply reduced, and in the outlying districts inhabited by the working class residential rents and land values declined considerably. It is very interesting to note that in the better sections of town rents and land values declined only moderately, and in the best neighbourhoods least of all.

These facts would seem to constitute a powerful argument in favour of the opinion we have opposed here, namely, that the partial markets in residential rents are quite independent of one another. But if one examines the matter more closely, nothing more is proved than that the partial markets are, as their name indicates, merely parts of a large market in which prices are formed to a certain extent independently, without, however, completely losing their connection with one another. The different residential sections of the city are so sharply separated from one

271

another that the available supply of accommodations in any given neighbourhood does not easily find outside buyers of a different income level, nor does the demand for accommodations find it easy to penetrate into alien neighbourhoods. This explains, among other things, why landlords in the better quarters are reluctant, even when vacancies occur, to accept the lower rent that poorer tenants, of whom there is always an abundance, are able to offer.

After the crisis of 1873, which in Prague affected the middle classes less than it did the industrial workers, the relationship between demand and supply did not change much in the better neighbourhoods. There was no reason for the families residing in these sections to move out and establish themselves in the quarters formerly occupied by the workers, where inexpensive apartments were now available, nor could they have so very easily without lowering their social status. Considerations of this kind play a role in determining the valuation placed on any given dwelling, and the great majority of tenants submit to this sort of social constraint even though it costs them dear. However, there is no doubt that if the emigration of workers from Prague had continued longer, residential rents would have declined even in the good neighbourhoods as the pressure to outbid people of lower income level gradually diminished.

When the demand outstrips the supply, a whole chain of consequences of the greatest practical importance is produced, but these can only be touched upon in a theoretical investigation such as ours, which is oriented primarily towards the treatment of general principles. And so we wish merely to call attention briefly to the fact that the people who are at present moving into the city belong to a different social class from that of the residents who are already established there. As a result of increasing industrialization, the influx of proletarians into the large cities is today much heavier than it ever was. Thus, an ever-increasing class of needy and economically helpless workers, living on extremely low and insecure daily wages, makes its appearance in the market in residential rents. Districts of a pronouncedly proletarian character come into being, which are separated from the rest of this market far more sharply than is any other partial market, and a supply of a peculiar nature adapts itself to their condition. In the large cities rents are everywhere as high as they can be pushed as a result of the increase in the costs of construction and competitive bidding. In the proletarian sections, because of the impotence of demand in the face of the overwhelming power of those in control of the supply, housing conditions are very likely to be extremely wretched and rents exorbitant. This is a matter of the utmost importance for the municipal authorities, but it is of no special significance for the theory of urban ground rent, since these well-nigh isolated markets have as little effect on rents in other parts of the city as the usury market in emergency loans made to the improvident or to those in dire need has on the interest rates of gilt-edged securities and first mortgages.

Another set of problems of equal administrative importance – and hence naturally lending themselves also to literary treatment – but of no great theoretical significance, results from the fact that even outside the entirely proletarian districts there are markets in which the demand sometimes outstrips the supply. In such cases, speculators in building contracts, without business experience, moral integrity, capital, or credit may enter the field; and it is they who are responsible for usurious practices in the building trades, the overburdening of mortgages with abnormally heavy interest rates, and unsound and costly modes of construction. The more widespread is the activity of such promotors, the more disastrous its effect. It might even bring about a general rise in the minimum costs of construction and thereby, to that extent at least, finally affect the entire market.

A problem of considerable theoretical importance is presented by land speculation, another phenomenon prevalent in the real-estate market of a large city. This indeed needs to be discussed, but before doing so we must emphasize, in view of our immediately preceding remarks, that usury in all its many different forms will definitely be excluded from this inquiry.

There can be no doubt as to the origin of speculation in urban real estate. It began with the whirlwind growth of modern cities, which increased, in rapid sequence, gross residential rentals and the ground rents included in them, and, with these, real-estate values as calculated by the capitalization of ground rents. The speculator who purchases land at the right time can make big profits if only he guesses correctly the tendency of the market. Speculation has turned, by preference, towards vacant land on the outskirts of the city. Increases in real-estate values, reckoned per unit of surface area, are much greater in their gross amount in the good neighbourhoods inside the city; but relatively, i.e., in proportion to the land values hitherto prevailing, they are greater outside the city, where, as Dr Mildschuh, taking Prague as an example, demonstrates statistically, the capital invested yields a higher rate of profit. Besides, speculation inside the city is rendered difficult wherever buildings have already been erected because these buildings have to be purchased, with an investment of additional capital, as well as the land they occupy.

We have to distinguish sharply between speculation in land and usurious practices in the rental of land or of buildings. To be sure, the speculator too is lured by the expectation of inordinate profits, but he has to gain them by other means. The speculator endeavours to employ his superior knowledge of the market solely for the purpose of choosing the right moment to make his purchase and then biding his time until the right moment comes when the land can again be disposed of. Moreover, he operates in a free market, accessible in principle to everyone, even though not everyone speculates. The usurer, on the other hand, operates in a virtually isolated market which is shunned by any businessman jealous of his good reputation and which can therefore be more easily dominated. That is why profits from land speculation will not, on the average, be usuriously high. Adolf Weber has shown this to be true for a number of cities, and Dr Mildschuh has done the same for Prague. He demonstrates that profits were exceptionally high only for such persons as possessed real estate that they had purchased at first hand or had acquired at approximately the value of arable land. Speculative purchasers entering the market at a later time must, as a result of their mutual competition, more or less anticipate in their purchase price the expected increase in value.

In characterizing the urban real-estate market as a free market, in which competition exerts its effect, we have to some extent already pointed to its most important distinguishing characteristic. There are many writers today who attribute a monopolistic power to land speculation. And does not this charge seem well founded? Can one resist the impression that the natural development of the large modern city is being stunted by an overwhelmingly powerful force, such as a private businessman could acquire only by monopoly? The town of our fathers and grandfathers presents the picture of natural transition from the village beyond its borders, its towering and massive buildings quite naturally supplanting the simple rural houses of the countryside. The modern city, on the other hand, in many places builds its tenement houses right out to the very border. How else can the existence of these 'rented barracks' in the outermost reaches of the city be explained if not only by a 'prohibition on building' dictated by a monopoly that crowds tenants together within narrow walls and refuses to release new land for building until demand is so hard pressed that it is prepared to pay ground rent for new tenements?

For the theory of urban rent, as we have developed it, tenements erected on the outskirts of the city present a problem of particular importance. We have declared that ground rent arises from the fact that in the better locations one has to pay a premium over and above the lowest rental paid in the poorest location. Is there an even worse location than that of the slums on the outskirts? For it now appears that here too there is not only an urban rent in general, but, corresponding to the extensive capital investment involved in such a large project, even a comparatively high rent of intensity. We have explained urban rent – in agreement with Ricardo in this respect – as differential rent. But where can one find a worse place by comparison with which the slums on the farthermost outskirts of the city would be considered as worth such a differential?

Conditions in Prague may help us to see in what direction the answer lies. According to Dr Mildschuh's report, land speculation in Prague started in the boom years preceding the crisis of 1873. Consequently, in certain sections on the outskirts of modern Prague, as in other large cities, multiple dwellings are to be found advancing right into the surrounding countryside. And yet, as Dr Mildschuh reports, there is not the slightest trace of a monopolistic organization in the Prague realty market. It must therefore be possible to explain the existence of big apartment houses on the outskirts, directly adjacent to a zone of vacant land, without any reference to monopoly.

But first we have to clarify the concept of monopoly. Monopoly is the domination of supply or demand by a single party, whether by a physical person or by some overt association of a few or many persons. Limited competition should not be confused with monopoly. However limited competition may be, its power over the market is never as great as that of a true monopoly, since only the latter admits of a policy of unrestrained ruthlessness. The confounding of monopoly with scarcity has unfortunately become quite common since the founding of classical economics, although no less confusion is involved in speaking, on the other hand, of absolutely free competition, since there is nothing whatsoever in the economy the supply of which could be increased 'at will.'

In the same way, it is permissible to speak of a natural or actual monopoly only in connection with a completely isolated economic event. The possession of urban real-estate does not in the least constitute a natural monopoly. In every large city there are thousands and thousands of separately owned pieces of land, and even in any particular neighbourhood there is usually a considerable number. Besides, as we have seen, the differently situated sections of the city should in no way be thought of as partial markets that are rigidly separated from one another. Let us not forget that the supply of even the best locations can be increased by the payment of a premium, and all the more easily in a modern city, where less social prestige attaches to a central location. Still less can one speak of a natural monopoly at the border of the city, where the extended radius increases the circumference of the zones, since the supply is by nature less restricted here than in any other location. As long as speculation in land does not interfere, new urban property can, in general, be acquired at the expense of arable land, without requiring more than a small premium over and above the value of the latter.

Here, however, the emergence of land speculation has caused a change. Instead of the value of arable land, a higher value is fixed on tracts of land spreading over a rather wide area, corresponding to the anticipated extent of urban construction and the time it is expected to take. The anticipated urban ground rent will be capitalized, and from the capital value will be deducted the sum of the rentals not receivable during the intervening period of time up to the completion of the building program.

What degree of intensity of construction is here presumed? That is the decisive question. Evidently the speculator is faced with several possibilities. The longer he waits to start building, the more intensive will the demand have become, the greater will be the intensity of construction, and the higher the future gross rentals, the future ground rent, and the future value of the land will be; on the other hand, however, the greater also becomes the discount that has to be deducted from the future value of the land in calculating its present value. It is in the self-interest of the speculator to select from all the given possibilities those which, according to his appraisal, yield the highest present value.

What these will be will depend essentially upon the anticipated rapidity of the increase in population. On those points along the periphery where experience shows that the city is expanding but slowly, builders will immediately start extensive construction, in order not to lose the rents that can be garnered in the interim, as soon as there is any demand at all. The case is different, however, on those points along the periphery where the working-class quarters are expanding most rapidly. As long as the demand here is not yet sufficient to pay the prevailing rent for all the space available in houses customarily for rent in this area, the speculator will find it temporarily unprofitable to erect a big tenement house. But neither will he find it advantageous, under these circumstances, to build extensively, since he thereby forfeits the prospect of realizing, within a reasonable time, the high rental values that could otherwise be derived from construction on an intensive scale, unless he razes the buildings of simpler construction that he first erected and proceeds, in spite of temporary losses, to build tenement houses in their place.

If we take Prague as an example, the statistics presented by Dr Mildschuh are very instructive in this respect. In front of the town gate of Strahow, in a slowly growing working-class neighbourhood there has developed during recent years the village of Tejnka. Its houses are built in a semirural style. The construction of a tenement house here would not have paid, nor would there have been any advantage in postponing construction entirely. The suburb of Weinberge, on the other hand, which lies in the direction of rapidly advancing development, pushes forward with the construction of big apartment houses right into the fields, which at the same time are held free for the building of still more apartment houses. In both cases it is considerations of self-interest that determine the decision of the speculator in land, as he adjusts his conduct to the demand in the market. Everything is accomplished without monopoly or concerted arrangement, simply in the interest of each individual speculator, which, in turn, is guided by the conditions of the market.

No entrepreneur could proceed any differently in his calculations. The so-called 'prohibition on construction' allegedly dictated by speculators enjoying monopolistic advantages proves to be nothing more than a decision of business policy that the urgency of the demand forces upon competitors on the side of supply. Perhaps an administrative agency, working on behalf of the entire community in the interest of social welfare, could find more economical ways and means of meeting this urgent demand than private industry does with its tenement houses. But the study of such questions, important as they are, lies beyond the goal of our theoretical investigation, which has to confine itself to the explanation of given market phenomena. And the conclusion that we have reached may be formulated thus: tenement houses situated on the outskirts, beyond a zone of vacant land, are the product of the free market of a large, rapidly growing city. Supply in the hands of private owners obeys in its way the will of urgent demand. This demand generates the centripetal force which, since the time the city was founded, has been crowding its inhabitants together and which still continues to do so even more than ever in the rapidly growing city of the present day. Just as coming events cast their shadows before them, so, in the light of present tendencies, we must expect that future residential areas will be even more crowded than they are today.

This relationship is much easier to understand if one clearly realizes that the so-called 'border' of the large modern city is not in fact its border at all. Beyond the zone in which there are no buildings and opposite which tenement houses have not yet been constructed there is much other land on which an urban population has settled. Strictly speaking, the inhabitants of the area are also part of the city's population, since large numbers of able-bodied men, and perhaps even women and children, go into the city to work everyday. Separated from what may be called the inner periphery of the city by a zone of vacant land there lies still farther out an 'ultraperiphery.' In criticizing my theory of a graduated scale of competitive bids, Mr Auspitz, one of the experts called in the inquiry into the tax rates on inhabited dwellings, used this term half-ironically, but we can adopt it quite seriously. Such an 'ultraperiphery' does indeed exist.

Naturally, however, it should not be thought of as forming part of a regularly developing concentric arrangement. The large modern city radiates differently in different directions, in one place nearer to the centre, and in another farther out. Just as an ever-increasing number of the most fashionable people choose to settle on the outskirts, so also do certain members of the very humblest classes. They find it too expensive to live in tenement houses, and they go to work on foot or use the cheapest means of transportation. They live in a number of dispersed hamlets or in growing villages that gradually adopt urban characteristics, or even in real towns, nearer in or farther out, depending upon the facilities for transportation.

Just as the town of our fathers and grandfathers gradually overflowed into rural settlements, so, as we now see, does the large modern city, except that, in view of the enormously greater scale of the whole operation, the transitional zone is correspondingly very much larger and hence no longer lends itself as readily to a synoptic survey. Like a great fortress with its surrounding out-works, a large city is encompassed by all kinds of outlying suburbs. The entire population is by no means crowded together in the very heart of the city. Only after having first traversed a rather wide zone of urban settlements outside the city proper does one come upon the tenement houses of the inner periphery. If these yield their owners a rent of intensity, this is entirely the result of their location, which possesses the advantage most highly appreciated by the mass of tenants, viz., immediate access to the centre of the city and its numerous administrative buildings. In the most modest dwellings situated farther out one pays the lowest rent; for apartments located on the inner periphery, one already has to pay a differential rent.

This development of the inner periphery is anticipated by the speculator. Taking into consideration the expected increase in future value to be produced by more intensive construction, he fixes a higher present value on land in this area. This very expectation of being able to proceed, within a relatively short time, to construction on a more intensive scale, acts, as long as it prevails, as a deterrent to more extensive construction. If, however, the development of the city comes to a standstill or slows down too much or spreads in other directions, the speculator has miscalculated and has at best to be satisfied with the lower rents to be derived from more extensive construction on land for which he has already paid a high price; at the worst, he has to forgo construction entirely. Under no circumstances does he have any power whatsoever to compel the construction of tenement houses, nor has he any claim to reimbursement for the money he has invested.

Obviously, the demand for accommodations in a particular place must, if it is to be satisfied, always cover the necessary costs, but these include only so much of the cost of acquiring the building lot as is equal to its value as mere arable land, for only to this extent is the amount paid by the speculator an already given quantity, fixed by the relatively alien market in agricultural land. Whatever he chooses to pay over and above this amount for land to be used for construction is a matter of his own speculation and risk; it does not figure as one of the necessary costs. If the speculation fails, this is the amount that, in the reckoning of accounts, has first to be written off as a loss. The speculator is never in a position to extort a higher rent just because he paid too much in the first place in purchasing his building lots; on the contrary, the rent that the demand is finally willing to pay is the measure of what it would have been more reasonable for him to have paid originally in acquiring them.

This line of reasoning is in accord with the interpretation advocated by Voigt. Dr Mildschuh is an adherent of the opposite opinion, which he supports in a very interesting way.[2] He has found by means of carefully compiled statistics, that in Prague, during the years 1870 to 1875, residential rents rose to an extent which cannot be explained by the increase in costs proper, and which evidently was related to the speculative increase in land values that began to occur at this time. As Dr Mildschuh interprets this relationship, this speculative increase in land values raised the costs of building houses.

In reality, however, the connection between the rise in rents and the increase in land values has to be interpreted quite differently. The development of the 'ultraperiphery' of which we have spoken was a concomitant of the speculation in land and was, indeed, brought about by the same cause, namely, the rapid growth of the city. The inner periphery had ceased to be the real border and became a preferred location, to which tenants could find admittance only by the payment of a premium in competitive bidding. Once residential rents increased on the inner periphery, all the other rents further in toward the centre also increased, as a necessary consequence of the raising of the lower limit above which a premium had to be bid. Nor should one overlook the fact that during the boom the old bourgeois population living in the interior had grown rapidly in numbers and wealth and had become stratified into a diversity of social classes, the members of which had to outbid one another in the ensuing competition for dwelling space.

In concluding, let us once again revert to the distinction between agricultural rent and urban rent. The former springs from a productive process, the latter is a market phenomenon, and these two facts constituted our original starting point. Now that we know more precisely in what sense urban rent is a market phenomenon, we are in a position to determine its character definitively and to distinguish it from agricultural ground rent.

Regardless of whether a piece of land is fertile or not, extensively or intensively cultivated, or nearer to or farther from the market, its crop commands the same price in the market. From the price as such, therefore, we cannot tell how high a rent is left over for the owner of the land or even whether it yields a rent at all. In order to answer these questions, we first have to go behind the price and to take into account the elements that entered into its formation, namely, the processes of agricultural production and transportation. The calculation to be made for this purpose is theoretically very simple: it depends on the amount of the crop and its cost. In practice, however, even in the simplest cases, this calculation can be performed only very inexactly. In the process of production, which is repeated every year anew, the performance of the soil is so thoroughly bound up with that of capital and labour that we can make a clear and distinct separation among these three factors only in theory. This applies especially to the substance of the soil, which only in theory can be isolated and separated from the capital connected with it. We define it as the 'indestructible' powers of the soil, but in practice who can separate these from the other powers of the soil?

Under the circumstances, the widespread notion that agricultural rent accrues undeservedly to the owner of that land stands in need of some qualification. Whatever one may say against the big landowner who reaps a profit from the toil of tenant farmers or of hired overseers and day labourers, the case is quite different with the farmer who tills his own land and himself participates in the process of agricultural production, wresting from the soil, by a difficult effort, sheaf by sheaf and fruit by fruit, what economic theory calls 'rent,' but what is, in practice, indistinguishable from the rest of the yield. The advantage of owning productive property which the free farmer enjoys and the proletarian lacks is not absolute. Everything depends essentially upon the distribution of the property, and generally this is such that the farmer is perfectly right in considering his agricultural 'rent' as a well-deserved reward for his hard work. It is something he has to count on, and when he does not get it, his expectations are cruelly disappointed, since all his labour is oriented towards the hope of receiving a rent. For the big landowner, on the other hand, who manages his own estate, agricultural rent is combined with an entrepreneurial profit, at least in those places where modern law has freed landed property of restrictions on ownership and alienation and rewards more intensive cultivation by permitting the landowner to retain his title to the increased returns.

The case is different with urban rent. It is not concealed by an outer covering of uniform costs from which it has to be removed in order to be visible at all; it presents itself quite openly as a market phenomenon. The line of gross rental values ascending from the worst residential areas to the best makes clearly apparent the proportionate magnitude of urban ground rent. It is true that the prices charged for the use of urban land are likewise not quite clearly presented in the market, since gross residential rentals always include a considerable quota that has to be imputed to the capital invested in construction. This second factor, however, must be sharply distinguished, not only theoretically, but also practically, from the premium paid for location. Unlike the prices paid for agricultural land, those of vacant lots intended to be used for urban construction also contain capitalized ground rent quite independently, without any alien admixture whatsoever. These prices express, with the fluctuations brought about by the ups and downs of speculative expectation, nothing but land values, inasmuch as speculation derives them from the expected future rents. An entrepreneurial profit is earned only once during the lifetime of a house: at the time of its construction, or, to be altogether precise, also in smaller measure on later occasions when various additions to the building are made. It is only during the comparatively short period while the house is being built that entrepreneurial activity takes place. Its most important task consists in determining the admissible degree of intensity of construction. Throughout the decades that follow, all that is needed is simple day-to-day administration, which the landlord can very well leave to an agent.

The rights of private ownership, which we so emphatically demand in the case of agricultural land for the sake of the increased returns it makes possible, are not such an imperative necessity in the case of the urban house. Urban rent is therefore not only more clearly evident and more amenable to calculation than agricultural rent, but also very much less affected by economic policy. And to all this we must finally add the important fact that under present conditions it is far more capable of a rapid increase. In the large cities it rises steeply toward the major centres, and its ascent becomes even steeper with the unceasing growth in population. The resulting increases in rent accrue to the landlord undeservedly; for, if one rightly understands them, they are unexpected, in the sense that, once the construction is completed, it is no longer his economic activity that is oriented toward the future, but at best only his speculative expectations.

Consequently, urban rent is in fact that undeserved income from rent which the followers of Ricardo speak of in connection with ground rent. Without the necessity of any further effort on his part, the urban landlord is assured of a continual rise in rent in the better locations, which are always in scarce supply, simply by virtue of the law of graduated competitive bidding and the increase in the number of bidders brought about by the natural growth of the population.

There is still another important difference. All purchasers in the same market pay the same price for the same fruits of the soil, and hence all purchasers of the same produce bear an equal share of the burden of agricultural ground rent included in its price. The curve of urban rent, on the other hand, rises in such a way as to burden tenants according to their ability to pay. The premium paid for preferred locations amounts to a kind of tax that the tenants impose on themselves according to principles which, at least in regard to residential rents, exactly correspond to the requirements of justice in taxation. By the inherent process of its formation, urban rent readily lends itself to taxation by the community. However, in a theoretical dissertation such as ours, whose task is to explain how phenomena come into being, we cannot enter more deeply into this aspect of the question.

We must likewise leave for separate treatment the discussion of the great problems involved in a policy of municipal housing, contenting ourselves here with a brief summary of the conclusions that can be drawn in this respect from the theory of urban rent.

Only those who attribute all the hardships and inconveniences associated with urban housing, and especially the rise in rents, to a monopoly in urban land can indulge in the illusion that everything will be better when private monopoly is replaced by a more considerate and perhaps also more economical policy on the part of the public authorities. The explanation we have given of urban rent shows that it is demand, the pressure of competitive bidding on the part of the tenants, that is really responsible for the hardships involved. Most of the tenants are not satisfied to live in the same general locality; they attach great importance to living close together, since they wish to work together, to trade with one another, and to enjoy together the comforts and conveniences of urban life. Supply merely serves demand, executing the will of the latter over a given area, though naturally only in so far as doing so is within its power and serves its own interests. The enormous urgency of the demand that has crowded our cities so densely and raised them up so high cannot be mitigated simply by changing in one way or another the organization of supply.

No doubt a reasonable exercise of public authority could remove many of the evils now existing. Certainly far too little has so far been done in this direction. But the pressure of the demand sets a clearly evident limit on what can be accomplished by intervention on the part of the municipality. Building regulations may be able to set a limit on how high walls can be constructed, but they will not thereby succeed in setting any limit on how high ground rents can rise. In order to do so, one would have to find some means not only of discouraging people from living close together in crowded quarters, but also of equalizing the incomes of the different social classes as well as the relative advantages of different locations, since these are the factors that find expression in the graduated scale of rentals paid for accommodation in various parts of the city. Only if the factor of distance from the centre could be entirely eliminated by advances in methods of transportation and if all class distinctions among the citizens could be abolished could urban residential rents be equalized and reduced to the insignificant premium that in any case has to be offered over and above the value of arable land.

NOTES

1. See specifically pp. 120 and 125.
2. See especially pp. 74–5 and pp. 145–6 of his report.

Friedrich von Wieser, 'Das Wesen und der Hauptinhalt der Theoretischen Nationalökonomie', *Gesammelte Abhandlungen* (Tübingen: J. C. B. Mohr, 1929), pp. 10–34.

This paper was first published in the German in *Jahrbuch für Gesetzgebung, Verwaltung und Volkswirtschaft im Deutschen Reich*, xxxv, no. 2 (1911). The paper's importance consists in its being Wieser's review essay of Schumpeter's first book, published in 1908 under the above title.

Joseph A. Schumpeter (1883–1950) was a brilliant young Viennese economist, a leading participant in Böhm-Bawerk's seminar (but whose later credentials as a member of the Austrian School have aroused spirited debate). His book was a methodological challenge to his teachers, partly derived from the positivist doctrines developing at that time in Vienna under the influence of Ernst Mach. In this paper Wieser expresses a carefully modulated critique of the work of this *enfant terrible* of the Austrian School. It has been translated into English especially for this volume.

11

The Nature and Substance
of Theoretical Economics

FRIEDRICH von WIESER

Translated by

WILLIAM KIRBY

CRITICAL COMMENTS[1]

Contents

Schumpeter's book has already been subjected to a number of very thorough discussions which take many different directions, and this fact alone testifies to its value, even though there has been no lack of decisive opposition in the reviews. It proves the great interest with which the richness of its content has been received.

In my discussion, I will refrain from dealing with the details of the book's content and will in this connection simply make the brief comment that the individual sections seem to me to succeed to varying degrees, but the book as a whole entirely accomplishes the task announced in its title of describing the substance of theoretical economics; I have reservations in only one respect, which I will return to in detail later. The way in which Schumpeter accomplishes this task deserves the highest praise. He does not give us a dry review of the literature, and in fact mentions very few names at all, but his book indeed contains, as announced in the preface, most of the ideas which make up modern pure economics. In particular, Schumpeter also achieves his further goal of giving the German academic world an understanding of the theories prevailing in other countries. Moreover, he also proves his knowledge and versatility beyond the bounds of his subject, for however strictly he attempts to keep within them, one recognises, at every point where he interrupts the study, his widely educated, diversely trained mind, which is open to all the intellectual currents of the day, and one becomes eager to see the author active in other fields too. He has an unusually good command of language, and his discourse combines scientific precision with artistic freedom.

According to the author's intention, the book has a second purpose to fulfil: it is also intended to teach us the nature of theoretical economics, and this is his main intention, as its initial position in the title indicates. He is interested, he says, not so much in the individual theorems per se but in their nature and their position in the system of the science. He develops the theorems in order to clearly understand the methodology from working with them, and from this clarity regarding the methodological principles he in turn wishes to achieve certainty in solving the specific problems. Thus he regards general discussions of methodology as unproductive; their study, he claims, cannot be divorced from the study of the actual problems and they only make sense with regard to the latter; one should not construct for oneself the methodological concept a priori but must always do whatever leads furthest, uninfluenced by all considerations. Schumpeter nevertheless believes at the end that he can attain a unifying methodological way of thinking – 'Methodology must not be the first but the last chapter of a system' – and he confidently expects that from his way of working 'something like an epistemology of economics or a contribution thereto' will develop. Does he fulfil this ambitious promise?

It is with this question alone that my discussion will be concerned. I have a special reason for this; for through the criticism that I make, I also have to conduct my defence. It is true that Schumpeter's views are very close to the theoretical school of thought to which I belong, and in particular he names me as one of the authors to which he feels closest; but I am obliged to say that in fact, he only agrees with this school of thought with regard to the results, whereas he entirely rejects its psychological method. He believes that the only way he can rescue our results is to substitute his new method for ours. After careful consideration of what he says, and while willingly admitting that I have received many suggestions from his methodological discussions, I believe that I must remain an adherent of the psychological method. Anyone who accepts our results must also accept our method; they cannot be divorced from one another. So I do not believe that Schumpeter's methodology has really grown out of the material in the way that he says, for surely, from that point of view, he would have had to accept as proven the method whose results he acknowledges? In reality he brings in, without knowing it, his methodological concept ready-made from outside; he is under the spell of the epistemology which has recently been developed by the exact natural sciences; this, in his words, is 'the latest thing, which in this case is the best'. Far be it from me to make any judgment of my own about this epistemology, but I think I can say that the way in which Schumpeter applies it to our science does not grow out of its material but instead does violence to it. Blinded by the success of the exact natural sciences, he takes their way of thinking as a model even where it in no way suits our material and thus constructs an artificial method with which he would never have achieved the results which he wishes to adopt from his forerunners. Indeed, he is not even able to fully convey these results in the language he uses. This is the point which I referred to earlier; here his view of the nature of theoretical economics prevents him from fully portraying its substance. His methodological concept infringes the psychological foundations of our results. If Schumpeter were correct in his methodology, I and the entire school of thought to which I belong would be wrong in what we regard as our most important achievement.

I will have to speak in some detail. The subject-matter is difficult, and Schumpeter has not only dealt with it cleverly but has penetrated into the heart of it in order to firmly establish his position. But I have to remember that his views emanate from a great intellectual movement which, led by high-ranking thinkers, is backed by the entire vast power with which the natural sciences influence our modern way of thinking and threaten to restrict the individuality of the arts. Finally, Schumpeter's attack is not the only one directed against the psychological method. This time, of course, I cannot oppose the manifold other objections, but I would nevertheless like to clarify the psychological method as regards its provisos to the extent that from it the direction of the answer which I would have to give to the other opponents can be deduced.

The most striking change which Schumpeter makes to the traditional substance of economic theory for the sake of his method concerns the interest on capital, which he eliminates from the system as he does not recognise it as a static segment of income; he relegates it to the dynamic side. I do not wish to go into detail about this; it would not be possible without a detailed discussion of the interest problem, and anyway, this innovation of Schumpeter's affects not only the psychological school of thought but opposes all the schools which are intent on explaining the interest on capital; it shakes the foundations of the traditional system. I would like to point out by means of a single word that it is already evident here how Schumpeter carries opinions from the world of the exact natural sciences into our field, regardless of whether they can be combined with our material. Does the physical concept of 'statics' automatically fit into economics – or should it perhaps be refashioned accordingly? Should not any theory which accepts interest on capital at all be formulated in such a way that it explains it at the same time? Does not our entire system begin to totter, and can, especially, wages and the ground rent still be thought of as in equilibrium if the interest on capital with which it is so closely linked is not thought of in this way? If Schumpeter is unwilling to recognise interest as a static branch of income, he is, I believe, required to refashion the concept of statics which he brings in from the natural sciences for our discipline in such a way that it can encompass interest on capital. But I will let this point rest.

In other respects too, I will try to restrict the discussion as far as possible; I will not follow Schumpeter wherever he goes. He is over-sensitive in his epistemological scrupulousness. For instance, he criticises the conventional definition of goods as 'things of the external world'; he finds this 'expression which strongly reminds one of metaphysics' questionable (p. 65); nor does he wish to be forced 'to make the hypothesis that the judgment processes of everyone else operate in the same way as mine' (p. 67). I do not know how far Schumpeter intends to go with these statements, but I for my part wish to state very clearly my decision in respect of the two schools of thought. The assumption of a physical world which differs from my psychological world and the further assumption of another self which differs from mine but nevertheless resembles it belong to the essential prerequisites of sound thinking and communication of thoughts. As far as I can see, the new epistemology of the natural sciences also accepts both assumptions; this, at least, is the opinion of Mach, who is nevertheless one of its most extreme representatives. From a condensed explanation of his theory which he recently published ('Die Leitgedanken meiner naturwissenschaftlichen Erkenntnislehre', *Scientia, Rivista di Scienza*, vol. vii (1910), pp. 234–5) I have taken the following sentences: 'The simplest experiences are sufficient to justify the assumption of a world that is common to all and another self apart from one's own, which assumptions...prove to be advantageous for both theoretical and practical behaviour' and preceding this: 'Observation of other people leads, due to an irresistible analogy, to the assumption that they make observations that are very similar to mine...' He explicitly warns against monstrous idealistic and solipsistic systems and demands that all perceptions which are not conveyed by healthy sensory organs should be corrected by other persons 'if it is a question of a judgment that is intended to have scientific and therefore social value'. The purpose of every scientific discussion is to produce judgments with a scientific and therefore social value. A writer who tries to present his best reasons as proof of his claims thus tacitly admits that these best reasons must also be considered as conclusive by the readers whose agreement he is trying to obtain, and that 'the judgment processes of others operate in the same way as his'. That which he assumes of the scientific judgment process, he cannot easily deny of the economic judgment process.

I also have no reason to discuss a further range of Schumpeter's reservations, because I consider them to be fully justified, with the result that they do not affect the psychological school of thought as I – and, by the way, not just I – understand it: at least, as I understand it today, having learnt to formulate many things more carefully that in the stormy days of my scientific beginnings. Schumpeter fears that by the psychological method he will be led into areas which are foreign to us as economists, namely psychology and physiology (p. 64); in particular, he is afraid of being pushed towards the problem of free will and will per se and being forced to adopt a particular position which may have certain metaphysical prerequisites (pp. 66, 67). He therefore seeks starting-points for his ideas which are entirely independent of psychological justification from the point of view of both the theory of will and the theory of feelings, which are not identical with Weber's Law, do not depend on it and cannot be affected by the objections to it; he wants economics to make its assumptions with regard to human action entirely independently and in no way to discuss the science to which they belong (p. 542). I agree with him completely in all these respects. The psychological school of thought of economics must distinguish its territory very clearly from that of scientific psychology. Its tasks are not our tasks. It would help us if it had progressed further beyond its beginnings and were less caught up in controversy; we would undoubtedly see many things more clearly if it were already clearer about itself, but we do not seek any direct help from it, nor could we find any, for our tasks are entirely foreign to it. Perhaps our method would be less misunderstood if it had not been called 'psychological' but 'emotional', but this name too would be open to misunderstandings. Our subject-matter is simply the consciousness of a person engaging in economic activity with his treasure-house of universal experience, that is, the experience possessed by every practitioner and which every theoretician finds ready in him as a practitioner without his first needing to gather it by means of special scientific methods. Our task is to scientifically analyse and interpret the rich experiential content of common economic understanding; in this we are interested in the internal and external facts which we find assembled here, and the connection (I will return to this word) which is made between them in people's understanding, without wanting in any way to fundamentally investigate the processes which take place in the mind in this regard. We too want to be independent of psychological grounds in the direction of the theory of will or the theory of feelings or in any other direction; we do not wish to be associated with Weber's Law either, we want to be totally independent of psychology. We in no way become involved in its analyses of people's basic psychological make-up, but search for insights which remain valid no matter what basic psychological make-ups are established by scientific psychology. You could say that we are laymen where psychology is concerned and want to remain so. We are entirely uninterested in physiology; it is a natural science with which we have no connection at all with regard to methodology. When we deal with needs, we concern ourselves with certain phenomena, partly physiologically based, which arise in a person's consciousness and from which economic actions follow; but we simply establish them as we find them in people's consciousness and also establish what reactions follow from them in consequence of their appearance, and in no way ask what are the reasons for them, why they arise, or what underlying processes cause economic actions to follow from them.

I have rather more reservations about Schumpeter's comments which are based on the concept of 'cause'. He wants to eliminate this concept from economic theory, just as scientific epistemology has eliminated it, and, following this example, wishes to replace it and the related concept of 'effect' by the more absolute concept of 'function' (pp. 58 and XVI). Referring to Kirchhoff's famous definition of mechanics (p. 38), which says that its purpose is to describe movements as fully and simply as possible, he claims that we too can contribute nothing to the explanation of economic phenomena but their description (p. 37). Even with regard to these thoughts I, and doubtless other proponents of the psychological school of thought as well, come much closer to Schumpeter than he thinks, but I have to make certain reservations. First of all, I will leave aside the things we agree on and highlight the things on which we part company.

The opposing positions can be put in a nutshell. Schumpeter wants to observe economic facts from outside alone, just as natural scientists do with phenomena, whereas the psychological method observes them above all from inside one's consciousness. It does so because from there it can observe incomparably more and in more depth than from outside. We can only observe nature from outside, but we can observe ourselves from

290

inside as well, and why should we forego this opportunity when we can do it? The best method will always be the one which yields the most knowledge; here, however, it is the psychological method, because it uses the most favourable observation post. In the store of common economic experience, it finds all the most important facts of economics assembled, and why should it not draw on them at the source? It finds that certain acts are performed in the consciousness with the feeling of need, and why should it try to formulate a law by means of long induction series while every one of us clearly hears the voice of the law in himself? What an enormous advantage it would be for the natural scientist if the voices of the organic and inorganic worlds proclaimed their laws so clearly – and yet we should forego such an aid? It finds that certain series of consecutive acts are sensible, that is, they are performed with an understanding of their internal relationship, whereas other acts are seen as unrelated, mistaken or senseless and therefore incapable of reasonable performance – and yet it should not try to make its series of observations by entrusting itself to the guidance of practical sense which distinguishes so precisely? Of course, the psychological method has its own special difficulties; it is much easier to make series of observations from outside than to clearly interpret the inner sense of an economic act, because this can only succeed if one fully grasps the enormous entirety of economic connections in their interrelationships, and so clearly that one is able to lift out the common features from the confusing jumble of details. However, someone who knows how to apply the method successfully will have the satisfaction of convincing his listeners in their innermost being, for he will arouse the same sense in all of them, they will recognise themselves and their nature from his portrayal and will confirm from their own experience that he has hit the nail on the head.

As to whether such a convincing portrayal may use the concepts of cause and effect or whether it ought to replace them by the more absolute concept of function, and whether it is an explanation or a description, these are questions which, I believe, can also be answered by the psychological method in such a way that one comes very close to Schumpeter's way of thinking or perhaps even adopts it. For the fact that one makes the sense of an action clear may of course not fully explain the action; the 'why?' with which this clarification contents itself may not be a final 'why?'. My answer to the question of the final 'why?', the question of how it is that I think and do so according to certain rules may ultimately have to be, with Lichtenberg, 'it thinks'. The mind works unconsciously and cannot give an account of why the facts appear and disappear in it; there is something more under the threshold of consciousness on which this depends, which we do not control and which is as foreign to our sense as external nature.

291

From this point of view, any explanation of the sense of our actions is only description after all, and the theoretical pronouncements which we make about this sense are not final explanations but mere statements of facts, of internal and external facts or, to be more precise, of perceptions of external facts which are accompanied by ideas of their sense and, by forming connections, give rise to other ideas or other psychological acts which in turn have an effect on external facts. One could say that our theoretical pronouncements are morsels of wisdom on the operation of certain psychologically imparted series, supplied by people who feel called to make such pronouncements in the expectation of being confirmed by general agreement and in this way receiving social and therefore scientific value. With such an interpretation, I would only differ from Schumpeter in that he wishes to limit himself entirely to observing external facts, whereas I am concerned above all with internal facts, but I would agree with him that the internal facts can always only be observed in a descriptive manner. Would this not remove the metaphysical reservations which frighten him? It should not be forgotten that external observations have a metaphysical background too, and just as the natural scientist overcomes it, we can do so too with regard to internal observation; and to correct the mistakes we are liable to make in internal observation, we need use no more dubious means than those that are used to correct the mistakes that are also unavoidable in external observation and to give the asserted judgments scientific value. Would this not bring me to Schumpeter's epistemological standpoint? You see, the transition to his way of thinking is not very difficult, and I would not hesitate for a moment to make it if I were not – an economist. As such, I believe that I must keep within the boundaries of my science and must avoid making epistemological claims or even couching my testimony on the substance of economic understanding in terms which are foreign to common experience. I believe it would be best for me to speak of 'cause and effect' and to claim to give 'explanations', because I believe that in this way I can best reproduce the sense of economic actions; I fear that I can only reproduce it in a distorted manner if I put it in words which are foreign to the common understanding. If my remarks are then epistemologically revised by the thinkers who are competent to do so, I am ready for it. I believe that it is of more use to epistemological work if I give it my material in its original form than if I were myself to try and adapt it for their work, which I as an economist have no mastery of and in which I would run the risk of mutilating the material. In short, I think that an economist remains more philosophical if he does not philosophise, and in this I set myself apart from Schumpeter, who wants to make a contribution to epistemology. I believe that in doing so he transgresses the boundaries of our science, which he otherwise guards so strictly and successfully. He is mistaken about the nature of theoretical economics and the consequence is that he is inevitably liable to make mistakes about its substance.

This means that he has not avoided the risk of mutilating the substance of economic theory either. However, he personally comes off better than would be expected from his methodology due to the fact that, as already mentioned, he adopts the existing ready-made scientific results, but because he has to take this methodology into account, he only adopts the results with qualifications which reduce their value. Moreover, in order that he can only adopt them with qualifications, he must first build a bridge which allows him to pass from his standpoint of external observation to the results of internal observation. Even though he uses a great deal of astuteness to do so, he fails in his attempt. Let me now show why. Here again, I have to criticise for the sake of self-defence, for the building blocks which Schumpeter uses to construct his crossing are partly taken from the psychological research method, and I have to point out that he uses them differently from the way we intend them to be used. For us they are aids to empirical research, but the way he uses them obscures this character, and therefore I am concerned to make their correct use clear.

What I am talking about is the aid afforded by assumptions. Schumpeter makes use of them to introduce the results which we obtain by the simple means of internal observation by a roundabout way. I will explain his method later by reference to examples and begin by describing it in general terms. This, though, is not easy, because he does not express himself clearly on this subject, and I therefore have to limit myself to characterising its intention. The starting point is that he rejects internal observation and permits only the external kind. On the other hand, he does not wish to establish any real induction series. Therefore, although his assumptions are based on facts, they are, he says, hypothetical, because it is of course not yet certain whether they are universally valid; he regards them as 'arbitrary' or 'formal'. Now he tests the assumptions against the results and comes to the surprising conclusion that they do indeed prove valid in a large or very large number of cases. As to how this surprising conclusion can be arrived at, he has plenty to say in ingenious turns of phrase, but he does not see the true reason; later on we will find the way to show him. By avoiding introspection, he hopes not only to steer clear of the risk of engaging in metaphysics and avoid everything of an a priori nature, but also to obtain the further great advantage of bypassing a whole range of difficult controversies with which theory has become burdened. He says in his preface (XV) that in the normal method 'there is too much use of "true" and "false" instead of "appropriate" and "inappropriate". He wants to proceed differently; he chooses his interpretations 'because it is the most practical way of obtaining our results, because thereby we make the most progress, but we shall not claim that any other interpretation is wrong' (p. 57). He contents himself with the fact that he is 'not compromised by the facts'. It can be seen that here too he follows an example from the natural sciences: his assumptions have the character of hypotheses and he calls them by this name in many places.

In contrast to Schumpeter, the assumptions which the psychological school uses are all empirical. However numerous they are, they must all be supported by facts. But why does the school use assumptions, a seemingly artificial aid, at all? To answer as briefly as possible, I do not wish to explain further the fact that other theoretical sciences, including theoretical natural science, use them too and they can no more do without them then we can, but I will just say that we depend on them because of the circumstances under which we make our observations. We can only make observations into thoughts with the aid of the visual memories of the facts which we store in our consciousness; direct observation of the working psyche is denied to us. Experimentation, too, is denied to us by the nature of our object; we cannot even attempt it to the limited extent to which it is available to scientific psychology. As with direct observation and experimentation, however, even when making observations into thoughts the facts with which one is confronted must of course be precisely established. The characteristic aid for this purpose is the assumption; it is the aid to thinking that is necessary in order to check the provisos which one records in thoughts. The theoretician needs them in his work to make attempts at the right solution; but he also needs them when he publishes his corroborated solutions as an aid to thinking for his listeners and hearers, who of course can also only make observations into thoughts. A theory which wishes to exploit the rich substance of common economic experience has to develop a whole range of assumptions in order to make its observations into thoughts, one after the other, under secure control. To ensure that the theory does not lose its empirical character, however, all these assumptions have to be drawn from experience; not only should they not have anything hypothetical about them, but they should not have anything arbitrary or formal either. Their usefulness or appropriateness depends on their truth. In this it is wholly acceptable that they do not always offer the whole truth. As the natural scientist does in experimentation, we too have to isolate when making observations into thoughts; the complex experiences cannot be interpreted as a whole, we have to split them into their elements in order to understand what they mean; only then are we in a position to deduce the overall effect by assembling the discrete units. This method requires one to deviate from the straight truth to the extent that the elements never enter one's consciousness individually; but this is surely a permissible deviation which is also justified by the constant practice of the exact natural sciences; after all, the ultimate intention is to reach full agreement with the facts, and therefore theory does not lose its empirical nature by making use of isolation. Another use which we make of assumptions appears more questionable; alongside the isolating assumptions which contain less than the whole truth, our theory makes many of an idealising nature, and it is undoubtedly these which give the most offence. In them we elevate the empirical case in thoughts to the level of the highest possible perfection. For example, we assume the existence of a model person engaging in economic activity such as has never actually existed and never can; another well-known example is Thünen's isolated state, which is incompletely described by its name, as it is not only thought of as being isolated from its surroundings but, more importantly, is also idealised through the assumption that within its borders the conditions of agriculture are evenly distributed around the focal point of the sole market; let this example also testify to the fact that it was not the psychological method which created the idealising assumption; it has been used since people begun to think scientifically. It is used, like isolation, as a temporary aid in order to deduce rules under simplified conditions which are only then applied to the complex conditions of reality. Even such idealising assumptions in no way render our theory unempirical, for they too are always only made in order to understand reality, and therefore they are only temporary assumptions which in the end have to be corrected. Of course, theory does not always make the corrections itself; it only does so if it can do so with its own resources, or if it is otherwise appropriate for it to do so itself; for example, it will no longer be appropriate if it would have to increase too far the number of possible assumptions which have to be considered. In all such cases it leaves the process of correction to other sciences or methods or even to the practical policy which has to deal with the given individual case and its special nature. The sentences with which it concludes are, it is true, unempirically phrased, but they are not unempirically intended, because, of course, they are only intended for empirical supplementation. Here theory demands the continuing work of other methods which realistically draw in the details which it itself is unable to express with its idealistically stylizing mode of presentation. This shows that it is not in opposition to these other methods, but touches and supplements them; in particular, it is clear that it, just like the other methods, is fundamentally empirical, for how else could it combine with them? Schumpeter, who has good insights into these relationships provided that he is not hindered by his epistemological prejudices, describes this relationship by saying that descriptive economics stops at cataloguing facts (this, however, is not a correct definition of its purpose) while theory undertakes a transformation with the facts, not with a particular mysterious aim but only for the sake of a clearer understanding. I think I may say that it only transforms just enough to achieve, in the spirit of Kirchhoff, the simplest description, the description of what is simplest, what is essential for a summary understanding. Only with this intention does it idealize the economic movements, in the same way that mechanics idealizes the movements of masses.

The facts drawn from experience, which are considered in isolation or transformed in an idealizing manner where necessary, offer the psychological method the substance for its assumptions, which it gradually builds up until they form a system which is advanced enough to exploit the entire wealth of common economic experience. I believe I have made it clear that Schumpeter is wrong to want to use hypotheses in our theory; hypotheses are assumptions regarding the unknown, whereas our idealizing assumptions are deliberate transformations of things that are known. Now I can repeat my earlier assertion with greater emphasis: that this whole system of assumptions must be justified by the facts and there is no room in it for hypotheses. The psychological method does not tolerate hypotheses. The natural scientist needs them to reach into areas where his process of observation fails if he expects with their help to simplify the description of the facts observed by him by reconciling them in their beginnings which are beyond his observation. Certainly, he will experience some difficulty in formulating his hypotheses and will not venture too far into the dark with them because, of course, they take him away from firm ground, but he does not have to abstain from them in principle. The psychological method, though, is fundamentally excluded from making hypotheses; for it no path leads into 'uncharted, forbidden territory'; it may not go beyond the region of the psyche and here may not even wish to see to the bottom of it. It follows the guidance of the sense of economics, and its system of assumptions must therefore stop at the point where sense ceases to build up economics.

Schumpeter wishes to avoid internal observation and therefore chooses the means of information of his 'hypotheses' based on external facts. In doing so he overlooks the fact that if he adopts our results, he owes the entire substance of his 'hypotheses' to internal observation, because our system of assumptions, which is constructed on the basis of internal experience, gives him the means of doing so; he would be helpless if he were dependent on his external observations alone. Now we can also explain why he makes the 'surprising' perception that his 'hypotheses' prove true; they prove true because they are not hypotheses at all but rest on the solid ground of internal experience. He would have to conduct the trial with his external observation alone in an area where the psychological method has not yet prepared the ground for him; then he would often enough be spared this welcome surprise. But something more needs to be added: even in such areas – provided that they fall within the boundaries of economic activity – he would not be able to relinquish the assistance of psychological participation entirely. No theoretician can divest himself of his practical awareness; he will always be guided in his speculations by consideration for the familiar meaning in practice, which will inspire him with the directions of his research, encourage him when he approaches the familiar meaning in practice by the idea that he is on the right track, and remind him to be careful if he is in danger of becoming meaningless or nonsensical. The method which Schumpeter wants to use cannot be used in a completely pure form; we cannot merely observe ourselves externally or suppress our inherent knowledge of ourselves, for we know too much about ourselves and we understand ourselves too well. Even though Schumpeter officially dismisses the psychological method, he cannot silence the psychological overtones of economic experience. There has never been a theoretical school of economics which would have worked without these psychological overtones; the psychological school differs from all the older ones only in that it has created a method from their naive process. If the psychological method were to be abandoned today, it would doubtless not be long before the need were again felt, for the sake of logical orderliness, to elevate the psychological aids from their hidden participation to the status of a deliberate method again. In the meantime, of course, the progress of theory would inevitably be halted, the necessary improvements could not be made, and some of what has already been developed would even be lost – perhaps the best part, because it is the deepest part which only discloses itself to the most insistent attentiveness. Even a portrayal such as that given by Schumpeter makes this clear. Even though he wishes to retain his forerunners' results, he is obliged, for the sake of his methodological principles, to refrain from expounding them with the full effect of their meaning, and therefore their effect on his readers cannot be completely convincing. In doing so, wherever he feels that in his own way he has too little effect on his readers he nevertheless uses all kinds of means of information which, if he were to apply his method with the greatest stringency, he ought not to allow himself to use; in such places he is happy to refer to the description given by the psychological economists, or he virtually makes use of their method of presentation, in the same way as an author otherwise uses an image. Does this not imply a tacit confession that the psychological method is indispensable? Schumpeter only attributes a heuristic value to it, but in reality its results cannot even be presented without the aid of its means of expression. It was more than the chance aid to the discovery of these results; it was necessary

– and its deliberate application will always be necessary in order to remain in control of the full results.

Although I fear I have already wearied my readers, I would still like to discuss a few individual cases with the aid of which Schumpeter develops his method. With their aid I would like to show that he is prevented by them from expressing the full substance of the results which he wants to save; his method forces him to trim them just at their finest psychological root-ends, from which they receive the sustenance of their meaning.

Schumpeter criticises the way in which the psychological economists derive Gossen's law of the satiation of needs, which says that the intensity of arousal of needs diminishes with increasing satiation (pp. 64 and 70 ff.). He claims that they have justified the law by virtue of the needs and in doing so have gone into their psychological and physiological foundations. They would probably have been able to manage with the simpler concept of 'requiring', but even this would have been going too far, for even this concept, he says, represents an attempt at a justification which is not faultless from the epistemological point of view. Schumpeter thus proposes a different method, in which he restricts himself entirely to external observation. He says that individual persons engaging in economic activity should be asked a number of questions which he formulates in such a way that they contain the main premises of Gossen's law and by means of which it is intended to find out the prices which people are willing to pay first for one and then for a further specific quantity of any good; the questions should be repeated as often as possible; the prices stated in reply should be noted *without any attempt at explanation* and the individual quantities of goods and the individual prices should plotted as the abscissae and ordinates on a two-dimensional system of coordinates. This, he claims, provides all that is necessary. The kernel that is relevant for us has been extracted from its psychological and physiological shell and the exact form of Gossen's law has been found – which, by the way, is not a law for us, even though it may be one for other sciences; for us, he says, it is an assumption based on a generalization of certain economic facts, and no psychological and physiological objections can be raised against this assumption. As such, it is in principle arbitrary; there is nothing to stop us making the opposite assumption and it could not be said to be 'wrong' to do so; in it we would have a hypothetical function, in itself unreal and in principle arbitrary, which we are led to through observation of the facts. This is what Schumpeter says. I think I am right in claiming that he himself has not adhered to the method he proposes and thus has not asked such questions himself. I also maintain that if he were to ask them, he would be very disappointed at the answers he received. People would not be able to state the specific prices he expects; they would at best be able to say that the larger the quantity of a particular good that is bought, the further the price would be reduced (to avoid any misunderstanding, I would like to emphasise that we would be dealing not with businessmen but with people who buy things for consumption), and even this limited answer would undoubtedly only be given by people who have the rather rare gift of making observations of their own thoughts. It is one thing to decide in the market place in a specific situation and another to decide in one's thoughts in this way. Schumpeter expects the practitioner to do the theoretician's work. That which can be learnt can be obtained much better by the method followed by the psychological economists. They each put the crucial questions to themselves and answer them according to their inner experience; to reveal the questions and answers to their fellow economists and to the public in a well-thought-out presentation is the only practical way of making things clear. The practitioner who reads Gossen's own masterly presentation of his law and concurs with it expresses himself in a manner which is much more valuable than anything he could say in response to direct questioning. But this is not the most important mistake that Schumpeter makes. His most serious error lies concealed in his statement that he wants the answers to be given 'without any attempt at explanation'. In this he confuses 'explanation' with internal experience and therefore rejects the latter's decisive testimony. Within us the process claimed by Gossen's law takes place with the feeling of necessity, and this testimony must not be suppressed. It is extremely important to state that the reply to this is: without induction series, by this means we obtain from the testimony of inner experience knowledge of a law which we know we can effectively take for granted in all circumstances. We obtain this knowledge – I repeat – without having to go into the psychological and physiological foundations of the law, nor do we wish to go into them; we simply wish to remain on the surface of consciousness, never to go into its remoter depths and least of all to penetrate below its threshold. Should we reject this knowledge of a universal fact which comes to us in such a simple, harmless way? Economic theory as a genuine empirical science must, after all, consider it important to demonstrate that the relationships which it describes are the real relationships of experience and that it has overlooked none of these real relationships. Surely, by recognising Gossen's law as a law, we have gained far more knowledge than we would have if we had been dealing with an 'assumption which is in principle arbitrary', 'whose opposite we could not call wrong', or with 'a hypothetical function which is in itself unreal and in principle arbitrary'?

Elsewhere (p. 57) Schumpeter talks about the well-known great debate which is going on in economic theory over whether the explanation of prices or, as we can say with him, the description of the exchange relationships should be based on the cost principle or the value principle, that is, the principle of value in use. He states that the choice between the two principles must not depend on an a priori discussion of their correctness. He says that in general he does not want to quarrel about principles, and anyway he is not interested in their correctness but in their usefulness. He will use the value principle, but only because it is the most practical way of achieving the results; on the other hand, he does not wish to maintain that all other opinions are wrong. He then goes on to list the deficiencies exhibited by the cost principle in the practice of scientific work. It fails, he claims, in the case of products which cannot be increased in quantity and in relation to monopoly prices, and it also fails in the case of the most interesting price problems, that is, those relating to labour and land; even more striking than its deficiencies in relation to markets which are absolutely quiet are those in relation to markets which are in motion, therefore necessitating a number of ancillary hypotheses. On the other hand, he states, the value principle allows a faultlessly pure system to be deduced in a completely unified manner without such hypotheses, and it would therefore be foolish to reject it. These are sufficient reasons for using it, without needing to become involved in a dispute over principles. He goes on to say that the researchers who established the value principle had had a different point of view. They had emphasised its truth rather than its productiveness and had therefore attempted to show that it contained the correct understanding of economic processes. He does not wish to join them in doing so, in order to avoid becoming caught up in discussions of an a priori nature which, 'conducted with general reasons and similes', gave little hope of reaching agreement, and also in order to avoid being pushed into the foreign territory of psychology and physiology, and finally because a theoretician is not concerned about the absolute correctness of his hypotheses; they do not form part of his results, which he has to stand by, but are simply methodological aids whose value is only apparent from their fruits and which play a purely formal role. Economic laws would gain nothing from showing that they were also truths per se.

I believe that it is not only the declared supporters of the psychological method who should oppose these statements, but that they are essentially incompatible with the views of all the theoreticians who have ever referred to facts of the mind when explaining prices, which has probably been done explicitly or tacitly by all those who have dealt with price theory up to now. If the deficiencies of the cost principle which are stated by Schumpeter are subjected to closer examination, one sees that they unanimously claim that the cost principle is 'compromised' by the facts; this, though, means that it proves to be impractical because it is incorrect. It is incorrect in respect of goods which are not obtained by production at all, to which it is actually never applied, nor can it be applied to them, and it is incorrect in respect of goods which are produced to the extent that for them too it cannot actually be applied to every instance of price formation. This nevertheless leaves very many cases to which it could be applied if only the external facts were followed and, as the history of economic doctrine teaches us, to which it has actually been applied without the ancillary hypotheses which it requires having been a deterrent. After all, consideration for the universality of the explanation is not the only deciding factor in economic theory; the guidance of the meaning takes precedence. Therefore the cost principle, despite its patchwork of ancillary hypotheses has been supported by the great majority of economists for as long as the value principle was considered nonsense, because they were unable to interpret it correctly, whereas they could see at least a certain amount of sense in the cost principle. The turning by a new and widespread school towards the value principle has occurred at the moment when this school believed it could interpret it in such a way that the facts could reasonably be explained on the basis of it. When the school then also claimed to recognize that the spirit of the cost principle was always attributable to the value principle, it was only in the latter that one had a principle which was universal and above all 'spotlessly pure', i.e. a principle which is borne out without contradiction by the facts and the sense in which people engaging in economic activity understand the facts. If there have to be difficult controversies over this, then so be it. The relationships of value estimations extend from our inner self into all essential conditions of the procurement of goods and the organisation of markets, and to deduce correctly the sense of the thoughts from such far-reaching relationships is a difficult task. Portrayals like Schumpeter's do not help in accomplishing this task, and may be an obstacle along the way, as they obscure the sense. Schumpeter himself still knows it, as he has been introduced to his understanding by his forerunners, but the pupils he introduces will no longer know it, because he withholds from them the portrayal of the extremely fine connections which only reveal themselves to inner observation. They will have to begin afresh to develop the principles as soon as they are faced with the job of having to defend them against attack or wish to succeed in making important advances.

More typical references could be listed to show how Schumpeter, in order to justify his epistemological opinions, jeopardizes the foundations of psychological economic theory whose results he wants to rescue, but I will refrain from doing so, as I would otherwise have to go too far beyond the limits of a critical discussion. On the contrary, I would like to stress at this point that Schumpeter's methodology is entirely appropriate to the subject as soon as he has passed beyond the topics closest to the psychological foundations to the great mass of problems which do not arouse in him reservations of an a priori or metaphysical nature and for which the psychological overtones of the sense is sufficient to point in the right direction. Only occasionally does his methodology lead him astray here too; as, for example, in the section on the theory of ground rent (which, by the way, is one of the most successful parts of the book and shows its best scientific qualities) when he discusses the fact that we no longer need the law of diminishing returns on land. He says that the classical economists, with their incomplete theory of prices, still needed it in order to deduce the ground rent, but the modern, complete price theory can do without it. For us this law is just a technical fact which is of course very important in practice but has ceased to be relevant to the pure theory of economics. In such a case it can again be seen that he treats our theoretical assumptions as 'hypotheses'. For him the law of diminishing returns on land is a mere hypothesis; therefore he believes that he can abandon this law without more ado if the hypothesis seems unnecessary to him. In truth, though, it is not reasons of expediency which decide what we should include in our assumptions, but the facts. We are obliged to incorporate all the important facts which are contained in people's common economic awareness into the system of our assumptions; otherwise our description would not be full, and it is a full description which we have to give according to Kirchhoff, but Schumpeter has nevertheless failed to follow him.

I have finished. I believe that Schumpeter would have described the substance of theoretical economics more fully and more simply if he had not wanted to portray its nature according to his method. At one point in his preface he says some very fine words about the importance of tradition in our science, saying that the work of those who come later grows organically out of the work of those who went before, and he declares himself all the more satisfied, the less there is in his book that comes across as new and foreign. I think that the historical context of the methods of research could have given him grounds for such a reflection which are just as good as those that are to be found in the substance of the theories. So it is by no means the psychological method alone but the theoretical method of research per se that I have had to defend against Schumpeter's theoretical innovations. But one cannot imagine the work without the tendrils of the methodological ideas which luxuriantly – sometimes almost too luxuriantly – wind around its objective statements; with their ingenious twists and turns, they are one of the attractions of the book and very much characterise the author's nature. They reveal the uncommon mental energy which he has devoted to his task and which above all lured him to the places where the difficulties are greatest. While he quickly passes over the things which he thinks have been explained clearly enough by others, he spends time on all the hard and very hard things and he, who himself began only a few years ago, can say with justifiable pride that his book is not written for beginners but requires a fairly precise knowledge of how far our science has progressed. The attempt has succeeded beyond all expectations, even though the reviewer has to say that Schumpeter has set himself too high a goal with his methodological intentions. He may realise at some time in the future that methodology should be not the first but the last enterprise of a systematist. One will certainly gain much benefit from reading the book. Through its mental energy it will also compel those who know economic theory very well to think it through again in order to decide according to all the many relationships to which Schumpeter directs one's attention. His main mistake is wanting to master too much; one feels that the author has not yet achieved his equilibrium and must learn to limit himself. Such youthful exuberance is the most praiseworthy of all errors; it is indicative of great strength.

NOTE

1. Schumpeter, Josef, *Das Wesen und der Hauptinhalt der theoretischen Nationalökonomie* (Duncker & Humblot: Leipzig, 1910).

Franz Čuhel, *Zur Lehre von den Bedürfinissen, Theoretische Untersuchungen über das Grenzgebiet der Ökonomik und der Psychologie* (Innsbruck: Wagner 'schen Universitats Buchhandlung, 1907), ch. 6, pp. 173–216.

Franz Čuhel was a Czech economist who had been a member of Eugen von Böhm-Bawerk's seminar in the years before World War I. This paper is famous as a pioneering attempt at establishing the concept of ordinal (rather than cardinal) utility. In his 1912 book *Theory of Money and Credit*, Ludwig von Mises supported Čuhel's effort in this regard, joining him in his criticism of Böhm-Bawerk's cardinalism. In his 1940 autobiography, later published as *Notes and Recollections* (South Holland, IL: Libertarian Press, 1978) Mises wrote that despite his obscurity (in 1940) 'in the end Čuhel will occupy a deservedly honoured place in the history of our science.'

This paper has been translated into English especially for this volume. References to parts of the original German text not included in this chapter have been retained. Readers wishing to follow up these references should consult the 1907 edition.

12

On the Theory of Needs

Theoretical studies of the border area between economics and psychology

FRANZ ČUHEL

Translated by

WILLIAM KIRBY

ON THE COMMENSURABILITY OF NEEDS

I. *Preliminary notions*

247. Our studies so far (cf. § 70) have taught us that in accordance with the division of labour which prevails between the individual disciplines, the task of economics only begins when it has been established by its neighbouring disciplines, whether theoretical or practical, which (i.e. relating to which means) use desires people have or are assumed to have under the respective conditions of time and place and what is or is assumed to be the intensity of these desires. With regard to use desires, however, certain characteristics and phenomena are observable which are of the utmost importance for economics, but which the relevant neighbouring disciplines, especially psychology, deal with either not at all or only superficially, with the result that the economist is unable to deduce from them the principles falling within their province which he needs to construct his theoretical framework.

A similar relationship exists between, for example, mechanics and pure physics. In the same way as the investigation of the changes which the steam enclosed in the cylinder of a steam engine undergoes during a piston stroke is assigned not to pure physics but to the special science of the theory of machines, which manifests itself as 'applied physics', it is appropriate to treat the aforementioned changes observable in the course of an individual use need as part of the field of research of that applied psychology to which, in § 84, we gave the name 'chreonomics'.

However, since these changes are only reflections of the changes which take place in the welfare needs which are caused by the relevant use needs, chreonomics needs to deal with these changes too.

Investigation of both these changes, though, requires that a comparison be made between the welfare needs and use needs in which they occur and other needs which are assumed to be constant. Therefore chreonomics also has to answer the question of the comparability (commensurability) of the needs.

248. In the case of every desire, and thus in the case of every welfare desire too, it is necessary, as we know from §§ 24–27, to distinguish, firstly, the impulse of desire or the drive for satisfaction, secondly, the idea of the increase in welfare to be achieved which is the goal of the drive for satisfaction, and thirdly, the feeling which accompanies the sensation or perception of the present state of welfare or, as the case may be, the imagined feeling which accompanies the idea of the state of welfare to be achieved or averted and the existential judgments described in detail in the aforementioned passage.

As is well known, two or more welfare desires, even if they are aimed at achieving increases in welfare of the same kind and duration, are not always equally strong; it is also known that other things being equal, the stronger of two welfare desires is generally the one which is aimed at the achievement of the more prolonged increase in welfare. Thus the welfare desire should be regarded as a two-dimensional quantity which depends on the duration of the increase in welfare which is to be achieved and the intensity of the drive for satisfaction. This quantity may be compared with the attraction which the earth exerts on the bodies on its surface and which depends firstly on the intensity of the force of gravity and secondly on the mass of the body concerned. This attraction reveals itself in the pressure which the bodies exert on the surface they rest on, the cause of which language has sought exclusively in a property of the bodies which it has termed 'weight'. In similar fashion, language has sought the cause of the fact that certain states of welfare (or their achievement) form the object of welfare desires exclusively in a property of the welfare desires in question for which it has coined the analogous terms 'importance', 'significance', 'utility' and 'value'. Economics,[1] too, has so far followed common usage and even the proponents of the theory of marginal value are no exception to this rule. For when *Menger*[2] speaks of the significance and importance of need-satisfactions, by which he means the states of welfare which occur due to the satisfaction of a need, when *Böhm-Bawerk*[3] uses the expression 'importance of the dependent need', which he says is synonymous with the importance of the dependent need-satisfaction, and speaks of the 'significance of the successive part-satisfactions', when *Wieser*[4] states: 'It is the satisfactions of needs which are primarily of value – or, as it is more commonly put, importance – to people, they are what is really desired and worthy of desire...The value of goods is derived from the value of needs', it sounds as if these authors too regard the fact that the states of welfare which occur following satisfaction of the needs are the object of our desire (the welfare desire) as a property of these states of welfare.

249. Without prejudice to the way in which the theory of goods and value was treated at the time with regard to the use of the terms 'importance', etc., I wish in this book to use a special term for the aforementioned, hitherto unnamed two-dimensional quantity, partly for methodological reasons so as to enable me to deal further with the theory of needs without having to presuppose knowledge which really belongs to the theory of goods, and partly to show that the latter theory can also be dealt with formally in a way which is appropriate to the present state of our discipline's factual knowledge concerning the problem of value.

Of all the terms at my disposal for this purpose, the word 'egence' seemed to be the most appropriate. From now on, therefore, we will take *'egence' to mean 'the two-dimensional quantity which manifests itself in the present welfare desires and is dependent on the intensity of their drive for satisfaction and on the duration of the increase in welfare which is to be achieved.'*

In formulating this definition, only the positive welfare desire was thought of at first, in consequence of which the defined term should be called *'positive egence'*. By analogy, though, *the two-dimensional quantity which manifests itself in any negative welfare desire (reluctance to achieve certain states of welfare)* may be termed *'negative egence'* or *'disegence'*.

Both definitions only take account of the welfare desires which we previously (§ 80) termed 'current welfare needs'; let us express this fact by grouping the two concepts of 'egence' discussed so far under the common name of *'current egences'* or, respectively, *'current disegences'*.

However, we also have to regard the dispositions to welfare desires, the potential or dispositional welfare needs, as a psychological quantity of the same kind, as they may of course change at any moment, immediately the attention of the person concerned is directed towards their goal, into current welfare desires endowed with a current drive for satisfaction. This would not be possible unless every disposition to a welfare desire were endowed with a disposition to the egence or disegence which accompanies the current welfare desire. We will therefore call the two dimensional quantities which manifest themselves in the potential welfare needs *'potential'* or *'dispositional'* *egences* or *disegences*.

307

In accordance with the division of needs into actual and latent needs in § 226, we also have to divide *egences* and *disegences* into *real* and *latent* egences/disegences.

250. In creating the concept of 'egence', we have hitherto only considered the psychological force which manifests itself in the welfare desires. We already know, however (cf. § 70), that under certain conditions the drive for satisfaction of a present welfare desire turns into the drive for satisfaction of a present use desire. Since the use desire also tends to be stronger or weaker, depending on whether it is directed at the use of a larger or a smaller quantity of the means of satisfaction in question and whether the drive for satisfaction which is directed at the use of the same quantity of the same means of satisfaction is more or less intensive, it also takes the form of a two-dimensional quantity which is entirely analogous to the 'egence' of the welfare desire. Therefore it is advisable to use the term 'egence' for this quantity too and to use the terms *'welfare egence'* and *'use egence'* to distinguish between the two concepts.

Jevons[5] also treats 'utility' as a two-dimensional quantity, the one dimension being the quantity of the good but the other the intensity of the effect on the consumers, i.e. the intensity of the feeling.

In a similar way, one obtains the term *'possession egence'*, which is also a two-dimensional quantity, the one dimension being the intensity of the desire for possession and the other the quantity of the means of satisfaction at which it is directed.

Accordingly, we will use the term 'use egence' where common usage and, following its example, current teachers of economics use the expression 'utility'[6] and the term 'possession egence' where they use the expression 'economic (subjective) value'.

II. *On the comparability of the egences of various present welfare, use and possession needs of one and the same person*

251. That the egences of all welfare needs, current or potential, which are simultaneously present in the consciousness of the same person are not equal may be maintained as an a priori fact; for if they were equal, then, when several needs coincide (as is the rule) no decision of will could be reached on the satisfaction of any one of them, as according to the organization of human will-power only the desire which surpasses all others existing simultaneously in one's consciousness and competing with it in such a way that only the one or the other but not all of them at the same time may be satisfied can become a person's will. Since, however, numerous decisions of will regarding the satisfaction of welfare desires are

made every day, the welfare needs or phases of need which are fulfilled must have had a larger egence than those which were not fulfilled.

252. This method of making our decisions of will is the best aid we currently have for recognizing which of two given welfare needs (phases of need) has the larger egence.[7] For one only needs to put oneself in a situation in which the satisfaction of either the one or the other of these two welfare needs but not both at once is possible, and according to which side the decision of will comes down on, that is the side with the larger egence.[8] Now and again, of course, it will not be necessary to actually put oneself in such a situation; sometimes it will be enough merely to imagine the situation. If one can then state with certainty which way one would decide if the imagined case actually happened, one also knows which of the given welfare needs (phases of need) has the larger egence.

This process is analogous to that which takes place if one places two objects on the two pans of a true beam balance; for the one which causes the pan to sink is said to have the greater weight. If neither of the pans sinks lower than the other, the two objects are considered to be of equal weight. In the same way it can be assumed that if two mutually exclusive welfare desires do not give rise to a decision of will within a certain time, the egences of both are of equal magnitude.

253. In our decisions of will, however, it is not always positive welfare needs alone but very often positive and negative needs and sometimes even negative needs alone which coincide. If, for example, one is faced with a decision whether to undergo an operation, the decision of will reached in such a case indicates whether the egence of the positive welfare need after regaining one's health is larger than the disegence of the negative welfare need caused by fear of the pain and risks associated with the operation or vice versa.

254. But the case where two negative welfare needs which are mutually exclusive coincide is not uncommon either. Let us assume that someone has a choice between two seats for a concert which are the same distance from the orchestra; thus the egences of the positive welfare needs can be assumed to be the same in both cases and can therefore be ignored when it comes to the decision of will. Suppose, however, that one of the seats is next to a person whom he detests and the other is in a draught: so he will undoubtedly have negative welfare desires with different disegences in respect of each of these two disadvantages. However, it can be concluded from the choice of one or other of the seats whether the former or the latter disegence is larger.

255. Based on what has been said in the preceding paragraphs, it will not be hard to answer the question of whether different needs are commensurable with each other. If the needs to be compared are understood

as several current welfare needs or phases of need which still await satisfaction and 'commensurability' is taken to mean the possibility of determining which of these needs or phases of need has the larger egence or disegence or whether the two egences or disegences are equal, this question definitely requires an affirmative answer.

256. However, we should not lose sight of the fact that in such comparisons, the comparison criterion is the size of the egence and not, as some outstanding teachers of economics[9] think, 'the intensity of the pleasure or displeasure which we feel'.

For *firstly*, economics (or chreonomics) requires, in order to compare the welfare desires, a criterion with reference to which they can be interpreted as positive and negative quantities. However, feelings of pleasure and pain do not contrast with each other in this way, as we have shown in §33; for they may exist simultaneously in one's consciousness without cancelling each other out, provided that the sensations, perceptions or ideas which accompany them are able to be sustained simultaneously in the consciousness's field of vision. If pleasure and pain thus coincide, we speak of 'mixed feelings'. Therefore pleasure and pain cannot be subtracted from each other.[10] With egences, though, it is quite different. For like all desires, the desires on which the size of the welfare egences depends are directed towards the maintenance of a present or the fulfilment of an imagined state of welfare or, on the other hand, the removal of a present or the non-fulfilment of an imagined state of welfare; so it is entirely appropriate to describe the former egences as 'positive' and the latter as 'negative'. Furthermore, two equally strong desires, of which one is directed at the fulfilment and the other at the non-fulfilment of one and the same state of welfare in fact cancel each other out just like two equal algebraic quantities with opposite signs.

257. *Secondly*, psychology has not yet settled the question of the relationship of the intensity of the desire to the intensity of the feeling which caused the desire or, more precisely, to the difference between the intensities of the feeling to be fulfilled and the feeling one would be aware of if the desire were absent. Remember the cases mentioned in §33, where a weaker desire was caused by a pure feeling of pleasure than by mixed feelings with a pleasure component equal in intensity to the pure feeling of pleasure.

Furthermore, probably everybody is aware, from their own experience, of numerous acts of will in everyday life where the intensity of the feelings which accompany them has declined so far that they cannot be perceived despite straining one's attentiveness.[11] For the feeling becomes deadened by repetition, whereas the desire retains the same intensity, and even tends to become stronger through practice.

In this context, mention should also be made of the loss of will power which occurs in certain mental illnesses and is known by the name *'abulia'*, in which the invalid's ability to perform acts of will is so weakened or disturbed, even though he does not lack vivid feelings, especially feelings of displeasure, that he is unable to take a decision of will through which these feelings of displeasure could be banished. A decline in will power also tends to be one of the consequences of chronic alcohol, morphine, cocaine and nicotine poisoning.[12]

Faced with these facts, one can hardly claim that the intensity of the desire is proportional to the intensity of the feeling which caused the desire or to the difference between the intensities of feeling and that it is therefore all the same whether, in comparing desires, one takes their egences or the intensity of the corresponding feelings as the criterion of comparison. As economics after all deals primarily with economic actions and economic needs of possession, its task will undoubtedly be made easier if it explains the intensity of these needs merely on the basis of the intensity of the use or welfare desires rather than having recourse to the intensity of the feelings behind these desires.

258. *Thirdly*, the significance of pleasure and pain is determined not just by their intensity or strength but also by their extensiveness in the dual form of their spread over particular areas of responsive tissue (acute and massive) and their duration. We choose not just between greater or lesser degrees of pleasure and pain, but also between more intense pleasure or pain of short duration and acute nature and less intense pleasure or pain of longer duration and massive nature.[13]

Bentham[14] claims that the size of the value of the pleasure or displeasure depends on no fewer than seven factors: 1. its intensity; 2. its duration; 3. the size of the probability or certainty of its occurrence; 4. the intervals at which it occurs; 5. its productiveness, i.e. the chance that it will be followed by other feelings of the same kind (pleasure by pleasure, pain by pain); 6. its purity, i.e. the chance that it will not be followed by feelings of the opposite quality (pleasure by pain, pain by pleasure); 7. its extension to a greater or smaller number of persons who are affected by it. But the 'value' of the pleasure means not the intensity of the latter itself but the intensity of the desire caused by it or the motivating force of the pleasure. It should also be noted that factors 3 and 4, to which factors 5 and 6 are also attributable, only apply to the possession desire caused by future use desires, as we shall see in chapter 8, while factor 7 applies only to the mutual and collective welfare desires.

259. *Fourthly*, if we wish to determine which of two feelings whose intensities or values[15] differ only slightly from each other or are entirely heterogeneous in nature, such as, for example, the pleasures afforded us

311

by a cold bath on a hot summer's day and by listening to a *Beethoven* symphony or through the satisfaction of a great hunger,[16] is stronger or has the greater value, we have no other aid than to establish which of these feelings the will decides in favour of in an actual case where only one of them is fulfillable and to conclude from this that the feeling in question has the greater intensity or value. In the same way, we can only find out which of two feelings, one of which is a feeling of pleasure and the other a feeling of pain, is stronger (has the greater value) if their intensities or values are not very far apart by drawing conclusions from the direction of the actual decision of will. Therefore, instead of the relationship of the intensities (or values) of the feelings being a tool for ascertaining the relationship of the egences of the desires caused by them, it is, on the contrary, the relationship of the quantities of the egences of these desires which in many cases is the only aid at present available to us for determining the relationship between the intensities (or values) of the associated feelings.[17]

260. However, this comparability of the egences exists not just between the welfare desires pertaining to the self alone, or exclusively between the mutual welfare desires, or just between the individual or the collective welfare desires but also in the case of welfare needs which belong to various of the categories just mentioned.

Similarly, it can be shown that the egences of use and the egences of possession are comparable with each other, and this comparability exists not just between the use egences alone or the possession egences alone, but between the use egences and the welfare egences on the one hand and the possession egences on the other. After all, cases are not uncommon in which a welfare or use desire, e.g. for a walk, and a possession desire, e.g. for a sum of money to be earned, coincide at a certain time in such a way that only one of them can be fulfilled to the exclusion of the other. There is no doubt that in such cases too, decisions of will are made where either the use desire or the possession desire gains the upper hand and becomes the person's will, suppressing the other desire. The direction of the actual decision of will shows which of the two competing desires had the larger egence, whereas if no decision of will can be made, both egences are deemed to be equal.

261. We can summarise the results so far of our study of the comparability of needs in the form of the following propositions:

Ia. Of the present phases of need of two welfare, use or possession desires of one and the same individual which await satisfaction in whole or in part and which are simultaneously present in his consciousness, the one with the larger egence is that which, when both desires compete with each other in such a way that only one of them can be fulfilled to the exclusion of the other, becomes the individual's will after overcoming the other.

312

Ib. If, in such a case, no decision of will is made after a fairly long time, the egences of the present phases of need of the two needs which await satisfaction in whole or in part are deemed to be equal.

As we are only talking about current egences at the moment, we can say that by means of this method it is possible to find out which of the two needs or phases of need being compared has the larger egence, even where there are only very small differences in egence.

As far as the logic value of the foregoing propositions is concerned, they are equivalent to the following propositions of exact physics: Two forces which if they act simultaneously and in opposite directions on one and the same material point cause no change in its motion or position are equal. However, if they cause a change in the motion or position of the material point, the greater force is that in the direction of which the motion or position of the material point changes.[18]

These are axioms of the branch of applied psychology which in § 84 we called 'chreonomics'; they are of fundamental importance to economics.

III. *On the measurability of the egences of present positive welfare, use and possession needs of the same person*

262. If we continue to pursue our comparison with a balance, we will remember that it can be used to determine not only which is the heavier of two objects but also which two objects have the same weight. If a sizeable quantity of such objects of equal weight have been found, each of them can be accepted as a unit of weight and it can be determined for the other objects to be weighed what multiple of this unit of weight their weight is equal to. In this way one moves from simply comparing weights to *measuring* them. Comparison and measurement are therefore related concepts, but comparison is the broader concept and measurement the narrower concept. If two quantities are compared, each of them serves as a measure for the other; if they are measured, the two have a third, common measure: the relevant unit of measurement or weight or a multiple thereof. In comparing two quantities which are not by chance equal, it is enough to indicate which of them is larger than the other; but the amount by which it is larger is not ascertained by the comparison; in measurement, on the other hand, it must always be numerically determined which product of the unit of measurement the quantity to be measured is equal to, for measurement, of course, means finding a number which indicates how many times a quantity accepted as a unit is contained in the quantity to be measured. Thus it is only possible to measure quantities for which there is a unit of measurement which is available in so many completely

identical and constant examples that a quantity which matches the quantity to be measured can be assembled from it.

However, it is not essential to the concept of measurement that a real yardstick can be mechanically applied to the quantity to be determined, as is done with a measuring rod and chain in measurement of lengths.[19] For firstly, the real yardstick can also be applied to a quantity other than the one to be measured if the relationship between this quantity and the quantity to be measured is known, as must be done, for example, when determining how far away the heavenly bodies are. This is *indirect measurement*, such as occurs when temperatures are determined by the length of expansion of the mercury column of a thermometer. Secondly, the quantity to be determined does not always need to be compared with a simultaneously perceived yardstick, but can also be compared with an imagined yardstick – for example, if we want to determine the height of a house but have left our measuring rod at home. Here too there is measurement, albeit of a less exact kind, as we attempt to indicate what multiple of the unit of measurement the quantity to be determined is equal to. In the latter case one speaks of *'estimating'*, but the cases previously dealt with are described as *'measurement in the narrower sense of the word'*. We will always use the term 'measurement' in the broader sense (which includes estimating).

263. Can the welfare needs or their egences be called 'commensurable' even if commensurability is taken to mean the possibility of measuring them in the sense just expounded? We will now try to give a definite answer to this question, which is a source of debate among teachers of economics.

One might think at first sight that this question could automatically be answered in the affirmative, as the method of comparing the egences of different welfare needs of one and the same person which we have described appears to be entirely analogous to the process for determining the weights of objects by means of a balance. For if one puts oneself in a situation where one can decide for either one or the other of two welfare needs or phases of need to be compared but not for both at the same time, and no decision of will is made in a particular length of time, one may assume that the egences of the two welfare needs are at least approximately the same. The fact that here we must be content with an approximate equality has little significance, for strictly speaking, even with a balance we cannot determine that two bodies are absolutely equal in weight, but we have to be happy with more or less exact approximations thereto.

It might even be thought that it is much easier to measure egences than the weights of objects, as the comparison of the egences to be measured with those serving as a yardstick takes place directly, whereas measurement of the weights of objects requires an instrument by means of which the direction of the gravity acting on the balance weights must be changed into one opposite to the direction of the gravity acting on the bodies to be weighed, whereas the directions of the egences of two welfare needs which are mutually exclusive are on the whole opposite to each other. However, this drawback of weighing is amply offset by the advantage that to ascertain the equality of the weights of the objects on the two pans of the balance, we can use our very sensitive sense of sight, whereas in determining that egences are equal in size, we have to rely on internal comparison of them.

On the whole, though, this deficiency is not an obstacle to the possibility of measuring egences. For physics too is entitled to exact measurements such as are made with a balance only in respect of quantities which are attributable to straight lines or angles, whereas when measuring intensities of sound and light, for which such methods have not yet been discovered, it has to rely on direct comparison of sensation intensities, which although its degree of precision is far less than that of weighing must be regarded as measurement in the sense previously described, as it is determined by this means how many times stronger a light or sound is than an amount of light or sound adopted as a unit.

264. However, there is another, much more serious obstacle to the possibility of measuring egences. Using the above-mentioned method, it is possible to state, for example, that the egence of the welfare need (or, as it used to be called, the intensity of the need) for an apple[20] in the case of a certain person at a certain time and place has the same intensity as the welfare egence in respect of 15 plums and the welfare egence in respect of a pear has the same intensity as the welfare egence in respect of 10 plums of the same kind and quality. Now it seems to be the most natural thing in the world to say: As the welfare egence in respect of plum P_1 in the case of the same person at the same time and place is equal to the welfare egence in respect of plum P_2 or plum P_3 or any other individual plum of the same kind and quality, the welfare egence in respect of two plums in the case of the same person at the same time and place must have an intensity equal to twice the welfare egence in respect of one plum of the same kind and quality and the welfare egence in respect of 15, or for 10 plums must have an intensity equal to 15 or 10 times the welfare egence in respect of one plum. Therefore the welfare egence in respect of one plum can serve as a unit of measurement for measuring the welfare egences in respect of one apple and one pear, in exactly the same way as the weight of one cm^3 of chemically pure water at 4 degrees Celsius serves as a unit of measurement for measuring the weight of all other solid and liquid bodies.

However plausible this reasoning may appear at first sight, it contains

315

an equally great error. For the circumstance that a cm^3 of chemically pure water at 4 degrees Celsius can be used as a unit of weight is based on the fact that it has been determined by means of infallible experiments that the weight of one cm^3 of such water at the same place is equal at all times to the weight of any other cm^3 of such water, whether it is on the balance pan alone or in the company of another one or 9 or 14 or n other cm^3, because the earth's gravity acts equally on all molecules of the water at the same point on the earth's surface under all conditions. In contrast, we know from experience – and it should be put beyond all doubt by the studies in the next chapter of this book – that for the welfare egence of the phases of need to be satisfied with a plum, it is by no means immaterial whether the consumption of this plum is desired by itself or after 9 or 14 or n other plums of the same kind and quality have been consumed, but that the welfare egence of the phases of need to be satisfied with the tenth plum (if 9 plums of the same kind and quality have already been consumed) is smaller than the welfare egence of the phases of the same welfare need that are to be satisfied with the first, second, third or ninth plum and that the welfare egence in respect of the 15th plum is smaller than the welfare egence in respect of the 10th. As to what fraction of the welfare egence in respect of the first plum the welfare egences in respect of the second, tenth, fifteenth or nth plum are equal to, this cannot be determined by experimentation. From what we have said so far, therefore, it follows that while we can say that the welfare egence in respect of two, ten, fifteen or n other plums is larger than the welfare egence in respect of one plum, and this applies to both the first and to every other of these two, ten, fifteen or n plums, we cannot say that the welfare egence in respect of two, ten, fifteen or n plums is twice, ten times, fifteen times or n times larger than the welfare egence in respect of the first plum or for any one of these n plums.

Therefore, whereas the weight of n cubic centimetres of chemically pure water at 4 degrees Celsius is equal at any time and any point on the earth's surface to the product of the weight of 1 cm^3 of the same water measured at the same time and the same point on the earth's surface times n ($G_n = ng_1$), we can only state that the welfare egence in respect of n plums is equal in intensity to the total of the n welfare egences of unequal intensity of n sections (groups of phases) of one and the same welfare need which are to be satisfied by one plum at a time ($E_n = e_1 + e_2 + e_3 + e_4 + \ldots + e_n$), about which it is known only that each preceding welfare egence is stronger than the following one ($e_1 > e_2 > e_3 > e_4 > \ldots > e_n$). However, this is quite a different equation from $G_n = ng_1$.

265. What we have shown by means of this example of the plums is true of the egence of every welfare need which is subject to *Gossen*'s first law

(cf. chapter 7). Therefore we can say that the measurement of welfare egences by the method discussed up to now is impracticable, because there is no unit of egence which would remain unchanged if one were to form multiples of any size from it.[21]

Physicists would be in the same position as economists with regard to the measurement of the weight of a body if the attraction which the earth exerts on the balance weights were paralysed to an extent not precisely determinable by the mutual attraction of the weights if there were more than one of them on the pan at once.

266. However, what has been said so far has in no way settled the question of the measurability of welfare egences. For firstly, one may object that it is necessary to measure the welfare egence in respect of an apple not with welfare egences in respect of plums which are immediately consumed one after the other but with welfare egences in respect of plums which are consumed at extended intervals of time. But this objection turns out not to hold water if one bears in mind that we have no means whatsoever of determining whether the welfare egences in respect of a plum to be consumed on various days are all equal. With this method too, the prerequisite on which all measurement depends is not fulfilled: that the unit of measurement is available in enough identical examples for a quantity to be made up from it which is equal to the quantity to be measured or to an auxiliary quantity whose dimensional relationship to the quantity to be measured is known.

267. Another method by which one might hope to measure the welfare egences is as follows: If it is desired to measure the welfare egence in respect of a good Gn, one first finds a number of goods with regard to which the welfare egences are exactly the same. If it has been found, for example, that the welfare egence in respect of a bottle of wine in the case of a particular person at a particular time and place is equal to the welfare egence in respect of a particular book, food, pipe, tie, knife or inkwell, it appears that if the welfare egence in respect of the good Gn is equal to the sum of the welfare egences in respect of these seven different goods, it must be seven times the welfare egence in respect of one of them, as here *Gossen*'s first law does not have a disruptive effect.

At first sight, this method seems to have much going for it. On closer examination, however, it too turns out to be unusable. Above all, it should be borne in mind that such a process of finding various goods consisting of only one piece which form the object of equal welfare egences is very time-consuming and that it would hardly be possible to find such a large number of such goods that one could make up egence quantities which would equal the large welfare egences which are manifested in a willingness to pay prices of several hundred thousand crowns for the goods in question.

Furthermore, one should not lose sight of the fact that any determination of the equality of egence of welfare desires for several goods can only be made consecutively and that if one compares the welfare egence in respect of the third, fourth, etc. good with that for the first, one has no guarantee that the latter still has the same quantity as it had when comparing the welfare egence in respect of the second good.

It should also be noted that the relationship between the welfare egences in respect of several goods is subject to large fluctuations and that therefore, even if one has ascertained that the welfare egences in respect of several goods at a particular time are equal, these egences may differ significantly after a few hours and perhaps even after a few minutes, as a result of which the determination of the welfare egences to be used as units of measurement would have to be constantly repeated.

Finally, it could not be avoided that many of the goods to which the egences serving as units of measurement relate might bear a substitute relationship to one another, as a result of which *Gossen*'s first law would again exercise its disruptive effects, at least in part. For instance, even if it had been found that welfare egence En for a good Gn were equal to the sum of the egences E_1 to E_{20} for each of the goods G_1 to G_{20}, each of which is of a different kind, and that each of the egences E_2 to E_{20} taken individually is equal to egence E_1 for good G_1, one could not say with certainty that the welfare egence En is twenty times as large as the welfare egence E_1, because the goods G_1 to G_{20} may of course include goods which are able to fully or at least partly substitute for each other, as a result of which the sum of the egences in respect of these goods, e.g. G_5 and G_{12}, if both are used together or straight after each other, can no longer be equated with twice the egence E_1. The larger the number of units of egence that are needed to determine an egence quantity and therefore the larger the number of goods of different kinds that are required for this purpose, the more often the substitute relationship will exercise its disruptive effect.

If anyone believes that in the modern exchange-based economy it is very easy to find goods for which there are identical welfare egences, because one only needs to find goods of one piece which are obtainable at the same price, e.g. one crown, it may be said in reply that firstly, the prices of the same goods are not the same on different markets, or on the same market at different times, and that the relationship between the prices of various goods is subject to constant variation with regard to both time and place and, secondly, that the welfare egences in respect of goods of various kinds which are obtainable for the same price, e.g. one crown, differ considerably even for one and the same person, as the welfare egences of an individual do not, of course, alone determine prices.

So we see that the measurement of welfare egences is not practicable by the method just described either because, if several egence units are taken together, their complete equality with one another cannot be verified.

268. With the proposition just expressed, we have set ourselves up in clear opposition to *Böhm-Bawerk*,[22] who very determinedly holds the view that the size of the difference between the intensity of two needs can be measured numerically. As this author, as we already know, sees the intensity of the feelings or, as he puts it, sensations as the criterion for comparing needs, his hypothesis implies that pleasure-sensation A can be judged to be, for instance, three times as great as pleasure-sensation B. *Böhm-Bawerk* attempts to prove this view by means of the following argument:

'In real life we are faced time and again with making a choice between several pleasures which are not attainable simultaneously because of the limited nature of our resources. Here it is often the case that the alternative is between one greater pleasure on the one hand and many lesser pleasures of the same kind on the other. No-one will doubt that we are capable of making a sensible decision in such cases. But it is equally clear that in order to make such a decision, the general opinion that one kind of pleasure is greater than another kind of pleasure is not sufficient, nor is the opinion that the first kind of pleasure is significantly greater than the second kind of pleasure. Instead, the opinion must be strictly concerned with *how many lesser pleasures are equivalent to one pleasure of the first kind* – in other words, *how many times greater the one pleasure is than the other*.' We shall dwell on this proposition for a moment, because in it we perceive the root of *Böhm-Bawerk*'s error. He appears to regard the two phrases printed in italics as identical; in reality, though, this is by no means always so. For example, if I say 'the price of a mansion M is equivalent to the price of five houses H_1, H_2, H_3, H_4 and H_5', this opinion is certainly not always identical with the opinion 'that the price of the mansion M is five times the price of one of these houses, e.g. H_1'. For the price of the mansion may be 1,000,000 crowns, the price of H_1 300,000 crowns, that of H_2 230,000 crowns, that of H_3 220,000 crowns, that of H_4 150,000 crowns and that of H_5 100,000 crowns. From this it is clear that the price of the mansion is not in a ratio of 5:1 to any of the prices of the houses.

We fully agree with *Böhm-Bawerk* when he says that the opinion 'must be strictly concerned with how many lesser pleasures are equivalent to one greater pleasure,' but 'how many' need not, as we have just shown, mean the sum of several equal quantities, which as everyone knows is termed the 'product', but can also mean the sum of several unequal quantities. And it is indeed quite sufficient for making correct economic decisions and for 'a sensible decision' in economic matters to know whether the sum of a larger number of lesser but unequal pleasures is larger or smaller than a single greater pleasure. An opinion as to how many times larger a greater pleasure of a particular kind is than a lesser pleasure of a different kind is therefore completely superfluous both for practitioners of economic activity and for economic theory.

269. *Böhm-Bawerk* illustrates his assertion with the following example: 'Let us imagine...a boy who wants to buy some fruit with a small coin in his possession. For it he can obtain either one apple or six plums. He will of course compare in his mind the pleasures to the palate that go with the enjoyment of the two kinds of fruit.' We readily admit that for the boy to make his decision, it is not enough for him to know 'whether apples taste better to him than plums,' but we consider it superfluous that he 'would first have to give his opinion a numerical certainty to the extent that he decides whether the pleasure of eating an apple is more or less six times greater than the pleasure of eating a plum;' it is quite enough for him to know whether or not the pleasure of eating an apple exceeds the overall pleasure of eating six plums, that is, the sum of the six unequal pleasures of eating one plum at a time.

To emphasize the situation still more, *Böhm-Bawerk* has adapted the above example as follows: 'Let us imagine two boys, one of whom has an apple and the other some plums. The latter wants to obtain the apple in a swap and offers the former some of his plums for it. He, comparing the pleasures for his palate in his mind, rejects four, five, six plums; when offered seven plums, he hesitates, and finally surrenders.the apple in exchange for eight plums.'

This behaviour, however, in no way reveals, as *Böhm-Bawerk* believes, 'the numerically defined opinion that the pleasure of eating an apple is more than seven times but less than eight times greater than the pleasure of eating a plum,' but again only confirms that the pleasure of eating an apple is greater than the overall pleasure of eating seven plums but less than the overall pleasure of eating eight plums, or, in other words, is greater than the sum of seven unequal pleasures of eating one plum at a time but less than the sum of eight unequal pleasures of eating one plum at a time. For if the seven or eight plums are consumed one after the other, the pleasure of eating each following plum is of course less than the pleasure of eating each preceding plum and therefore the pleasure of eating seven or eight plums is by no means seven or eight times greater than the pleasure of eating one of them, and especially the pleasure of eating the first one. Only if the individual plums were to be enjoyed at longer intervals, e.g. six hours, might the sum of the pleasures of eating seven or eight plums be seven or eight times greater than the pleasure of eating each individual plum.

Böhm-Bawerk now continues: 'And what the boys do in this example with apples and plums, all of us do in economic life with more serious objects. Surely everyone has been in the situation of being offered an item for sale which he considered too expensive; when the item was reduced in price, e.g. from 30 to 25 guilders, he bought it.' This behaviour, too, is not always based on the opinion that the pleasure one expects to gain from the good to be purchased is more than 25 times but less than 30 times the other pleasure which one might gain for one guilder at a time, but generally only on the opinion that the pleasure expected from the good to be purchased is less than the sum of 30 possibly unequal pleasures which can be obtained for one guilder at a time but greater than the sum of 25 such pleasures.

270. Although *Böhm-Bawerk* himself admits that the opinion 'I like an apple as much as eight plums' and the opinion 'I like an apple eight times as much as a plum' are not one and the same thing, he does not attribute to this difference the importance which I believe should be attributed to it if one wishes to reach the right conclusions. For he reasons as follows: 'It may well be that we are unable to define, for instance, the difference in magnitude between the pleasure of eating an apple and that of eating a pear numerically by direct comparison. If, however, we are able to judge that we like one apple just as much as eight plums and one pear just as much as six plums, we are also able to form, via a conclusion drawn from the first two opinions, the third opinion that we like one apple exactly one third more than one pear.' However, this reasoning is incorrect, as it is based on a fallacy. *Böhm-Bawerk*'s conclusion would only be correct if the premises were: 'I like the pleasure of eating an apple eight times as much as the pleasure of eating a plum' and 'I like the pleasure of eating a pear six times as much as the pleasure of eating a plum.' But the premises are: 'I like an apple just as much as eight plums' and 'I like a pear just as much as six plums', but this is just a sloppy way, popular in common parlance, of saying 'I like the pleasure of eating an apple just as much as the overall pleasure of eating eight plums' and 'I like the pleasure of eating a pear just as much as the overall pleasure of eating six plums'. But 'the overall pleasure of eating eight (or six) plums' means the same as 'the sum of eight (or six) unequal pleasures of eating one plum at a time' and not 'the product of the pleasure of eating one plum multiplied by eight (or six)', which is, of course, the sum of eight (or six) equal pleasures of eating one plum at a time. *Böhm-Bawerk*, being a proponent of the theory of marginal value, cannot dispute this, for he knows, of course, that if six or eight plums are consumed in quick succession, the pleasure of eating the second plum is less than that of eating the first plum, the pleasure of eating the third plum is in turn less than that of eating the second and so on, and that

therefore the pleasure of eating eight plums equals not the product of the enjoyment of eating the first plum times eight ($E_8 = 8e$) but only the sum of eight unequal pleasures of eating each one of the eight plums ($E_8 = e_1 + e_2 + e_3 + e_4 + e_5 + e_6 + e_7 + e_8$, where $e_1 > e_2 > e_3 > e_4 > e_5 > e_6 > e_7 > e_8$).

If, however, one may not say that the enjoyment of eating eight plums is a third greater than that of eating six plums, as has just been demonstrated, one is not entitled either to the conclusion drawn by *Böhm-Bawerk* that 'we like an apple exactly one-third more than a pear.' The detour *Böhm-Bawerk* has taken is therefore in no way able to lead to the proof that the size of the interval between the intensity of two needs can be determined numerically, not even if the intensities of feeling are seen as the criterion of comparison of needs.

Since, though (as we have already shown), there is no exact proportional relationship between the intensity of desires and the associated feelings, one would not have proved that welfare egences are measurable even if one had succeeded in putting the measurability of intensities of feeling beyond all doubt.

271. Everything we have said in the preceding paragraphs about the impracticability of measuring egences in the case of welfare desires also applies mutatis mutandis with regard to the use and possession desires. It will also be possible to prove the correctness of this proposition by deduction later on, when, in chapter 8, we have established the relationships between the size of the possession egence and the associated use and welfare egences.

IV. *The egence scales*

272. The determination of egences is thus not measurement if one means by measurement what is intended to be meant according to the correct definitions of it described above.[23] For the measurement of egences should not be confused with numerical determination of them. One such is, for example, the determination of the hardness of minerals by means of the *Mohs* scale of hardness, which enables us to state whether a mineral has the second, third, fourth, etc. degree of hardness or if it is harder than a mineral of the second, third, fourth, etc. degree of hardness. However, these numerical determinations of hardness cannot be termed 'measurements', as it is not possible to state what multiples of a hardness adopted as the unit of hardness the hardnesses to be measured are equal to. For in saying that talc has the first degree of hardness and gypsum the second degree of hardness, this certainly does not mean that gypsum is twice as

hard as talc, but only that it is harder to a certain extent; whether the hardness of the latter is 1½ or 2 or 2½ or 3 times as great as the hardness of the former cannot, however, be determined absolutely.[24]

Despite the numerical representation, therefore, the determination of the hardness of minerals takes the form of a simple comparison, by means of which nothing else can be established than whether the hardness to be determined is equal to or greater than another hardness adopted as a model.

273. On a par with this, despite their numerical representation, are all determinations of egences. If the egence in respect of an apple is said to be equal to the egence in respect of 15 plums and the egence in respect of a pear equal to the egence in respect of 10 plums, this does not mean that the two egences are in a ratio of 15:10. For one should not be led astray by the fact that the quantity of 15 plums and that of 10 plums are exactly in the ratio 15:10, as it is not the ratio between the two quantities of plums which we have to determine, but the ratio between the egences of the welfare, use or possession needs or phases of need which are directed at the plums. Since, however, we already know that the total egence of the phases of need for 15 plums is smaller than 15 times the egence in respect of one plum of the same kind and quality and, in the same way, the total egence of the phases of need for 10 plums is smaller than 10 times the same egence, without being able to say that it is 14 or 13 or 12 etc. times or, respectively, 9½ or 9 or 8 etc. times this egence, we certainly cannot conclude that the egences in respect of an apple and a pear are in the ratio 15:10. This ratio may indeed exist; however, the ratio may equally well be 16:10 or 14:10 or any other ratio. As to which of these ratios is correct in reality, this cannot be determined absolutely. The determination of the relationship between the egences in respect of an apple and for a pear is thus entirely analogous to the determination of the relationship between the hardnesses of two minerals. In both cases this is done by comparing the quantity to be determined with the gradations or degrees of a scale and ascertaining which of these degrees it equals or between which successive degrees it lies. Thus this process cannot be called 'measurement'; the name 'scaling' would be more appropriate. The difference between these two methods of determination is outwardly expressed by the fact that the results of measurement can be stated as cardinal numbers, but the results of scaling can only be stated as ordinal numbers,[25] for in the first case the numerical determination gives us an answer to the question 'what multiple of the unit of measurement is the quantity to be determined equal to', but in the second case it only answers the question 'which of the degrees of the scale is the quantity to be determined equal to?'

Physics would be in the same position that economics is in at present if all thermometer liquids had a decreasing ability to expand as the temperature increases and the degree of this decrease could not be determined exactly.

274. Scaling, like measurement, can be either a *real operation*, if one actually places oneself in a situation where the will has to decide between the egence to be determined and an egence serving as a degree on the scale, or merely an *estimative operation*, if one simply imagines such a situation. In the former case the degree of precision is much greater than in the latter case. Even though mistakes very often occur in determining egences in real life, this does not affect theoretical economics. For an incorrect determination of the egence necessarily results in an incorrect determination of the economic value, just as a correct determination of the egence necessarily produces a correct determination of value, and it is the task of economics to explain not only the correct but also the incorrect valuations.[26]

275. Until now, neither real life nor economics has established either a *welfare egence scale* or a *use egence scale*. Real life does not need one, as the comparison of several welfare and use desires always takes place only inside one and the same consciousness and the individual is able to recognize immediately which is the larger egence. Economics, though, cannot do without at least an *ideal use egence scale*, as it has to establish the relationships between the strength of the possession desires and the strength of the use desires and therefore must somehow indicate their various degrees of egence. Since, however, the welfare egence forms the basis of both the use egence and the possession egence, it is appropriate to first establish an *ideal welfare egence scale*.

276. The first, i.e. the lowest, degree of such a scale can be regarded as the egence of the very weakest need or phase of need that one becomes aware of. This degree of egence will, it is true, differ sightly in various people, but we do not need to worry about this, as at the moment we are only comparing egences of the same person. Let us denote this degree of egence by 1^e. The egence which is larger than the first degree of egence by a just-noticeable increment forms the second degree of our ideal egence scale and will be denoted by 2^e.

Psychology has not yet settled the question of whether the just-noticeable increments of sensation are to be regarded as increments of equal size. *Fechner* has answered this question in the affirmative[27] and this assumption, which he has considered self-evident, even forms the foundation on which the psychophysical quantitative law named after him is based. *Brentano*, however, has rightly objected that it is actually by no means automatically clear that each just-noticeable increment in sensation is equal in size, but only that it is equally noticeable. In his view, the facts which form the basis of *Fechner*'s law only permit the formulation of the principle 'If the relative increments in the psychological stimulus are equal in size, the sensation increases by equally noticeable amounts', and this law is complemented by the other law added by *Brentano*: 'If the sensation increases by equally noticeable amounts, the relative increment in the sensation is the same.' Thus one may not claim that two sensations, of which one corresponds to a just-noticeable stimulus and the other in turn differs from the first by a just-noticeable increment in stimulus, are in a ratio of 1:2.

Nor may we say of the second degree of egence, which only differs from the just-noticeable egence ε_1 by a just-noticeable increment, that it equals $2\varepsilon_1$; we have to express its quantity by the sum $\varepsilon_1 + \varepsilon_2$, where ε_2 denotes the just-noticeable increment. By analogy one obtains the third degree ($3^e = \varepsilon_1 + \varepsilon_2 + \varepsilon_3$), the fourth degree ($4^e = \varepsilon_1 + \varepsilon_2 + \varepsilon_3 + \varepsilon_4$) and so on up to the nth degree of the ideal egence scale ($n^e = \varepsilon_1 + \varepsilon_2 + \varepsilon_3 + ... + \varepsilon_n$).

It is generally not necessary, in theoretical studies, to express the degrees of egence by special figures (numbers); for this purpose the general figures (letters) a, b, $c...x$, y, z suffice. If it is agreed that each subsequent letter of the alphabet denotes a higher figure than the preceding one, the following designations are obtained for various degrees of welfare egence: $a^e < b^e < c^e < ... < x^e < y^e < z^e$, to be read as the ath, b^{th}, $c^{th} ... x^{th}$, y^{th}, z^{th} degree of egence.

277. Some teachers of economics express the various degrees of importance of actual needs and of the categories of need, i.e. the various degrees of egence of the individual phases of the same need, and the unequal maximum egences of various kinds of use desire by special figures (numbers) which they interpret as proportional numbers, i.e. as multiples of an ideal unit.[28] On the whole, it is in fact not incorrect, in theoretical studies, to imagine and express the egences of given needs as multiples of an ideal unit of egence; for there is no doubt that every given egence is in reality a multiple of an egence adopted as a unit; it is just that it is impossible to establish this relationship in numerical terms. Just as in the days before the balance was invented and the weights of all objects could only be compared by means of muscular sensations, someone who for theoretical purposes imagined and expressed the weights of given objects as multiples of a certain unit of weight would have been entirely justified in doing so even though he was unable to prove that this was so. Despite this, however, we do not consider this procedure worthy of imitation, as it is liable to give the readers the false impression that the intervals between different degrees of importance or egence can actually be established or measured numerically, i.e. as true multiples of a unit of importance or egence.[29] It would therefore be better to speak of an 'ideal scale' instead of an 'ideal yardstick'.

278. In theoretical studies, however, it is generally not a matter of numerical indications of egence values, as we have already noted, in the same way that mathematics rarely uses the special figures, but usually only the general figures (letters). If a and b are two different multiples of the numerical unit, without anything being known of the interval between them in numerical terms, two differently sized egences Ea and Eb can be regarded as products of a unit of egence and the factors a and b. The most appropriate unit of egence is the egence of the just-noticeable welfare desire ; thus the mathematical expressions for the egences Ea and Eb are a and b. If each subsequent letter of the alphabet means a higher figure than the one preceding it in the alphabet, without anything being known of the interval between them in numerical terms, for indicating different welfare egences – from the lowest to the highest degree – one obtains the following mathematical expressions: $\varepsilon < a\varepsilon < b\varepsilon < c\varepsilon < d\varepsilon < ... < x\varepsilon < y\varepsilon < z\varepsilon$, which are perfectly adequate for the actual level of our knowledge of the relationship between the egence values in question.

279. The egence scale discussed in the preceding paragraphs is just as suitable for determining use and possession egences as for determining welfare egences. But an ideal use egence scale could be also constructed by imagining a means of satisfaction of which any available quantity could be used and calling the egence of the use desire in respect of the first unit of this means of satisfaction the first degree (1^u), the egence in respect of the first two units the second degree (2^u), the egence in respect of the first three units the third degree (3^u) and so on.

280. To determine possession egences, economic relations has since time immemorial had a range of scales at its disposal, the individual steps of which are the possession egences in respect of the various multiples of a monetary unit. If the monetary unit is, for instance, one heller, the possession egence in respect of the first heller is the first degree of the possession egence scale (1^v), the possession egence in respect of the first two hellers is the second degree (2^v), the possession egence in respect of the first three hellers is the third degree (3^v) and so on. This scale thus runs: $1^v < 2^v < 3^v < 4^v < ... < n^v$, i.e. the first, second, third, fourth, ...nth degree of possession egence. It is known that of these degrees, each preceding one is weaker than the one following it, but the numerical interval between them cannot be stated, as in practice no possession egence can be proved to be a specific multiple of another possession egence adopted as a unit.

Therefore the numbers 1, 2, 3, 4 ... n are not proportional numbers, as can be seen in any case from the fact that they are expressed not by cardinal but by ordinal numbers.

It is therefore incorrect for Cassel[30] to claim that in money we have a standard of value with which 'the intensity of an individual's various needs can be measured in a way which is in principle just as satisfactory as other measurements such as e.g. the measurement of time, except that the results are sometimes not as accurate.' For even if I know that 'if need be (i.e. if I cannot obtain it more cheaply) I am prepared to pay 10 marks (but not more) for a certain good' and that 'I would go up to, say, 20 marks for a different good', I still cannot say that the second good is twice as important to me as the first. In fact, I am only entitled to say that my possession egence in respect of the first good equals my possession egence in respect of 10 marks and my possession egence in respect of the second good equals my possession egence in respect of 20 marks; these propositions are in no way identical to those expressed by Cassel.

281. As the possession egences are similar to the use and welfare egences (§ 260), the possession egence scale described above can also be used to determine welfare and use egences; this occurs very often in real modern economic life, as most people are dependent on buying and selling and each is therefore very familiar with a scale consisting of his possession egences in respect of monetary units.[31] In isolated economies, on the other hand, the size of possession egences cannot be determined by means of this scale, as the possession egences in respect of money are basically nothing more than possession egences in respect of the goods which can be exchanged for them. In such cases the egence scale established in § 276 must be used.

V. On the measurability of the negative egences of one and the same person

282. What we have said so far about the measurability of positive egences applies by analogy to the measurability of negative egences or disegences. The negative egence of a reluctance to perform a 2-, 3-, 10- or n-hour job of work[32] is not 2, 3, 10 or n times the negative egence in respect of a one-hour job because, as everyone knows, where unwillingness to do a job is concerned it is by no means immaterial whether it is a question of the first hour of work or the second, third, tenth or nth, after it has been immediately preceded by one, two, nine or $(n-1)$ hours of work. Instead, the negative egence in respect of a 2-, 3-, 10- or n-hour job of work is the sum of two, or three, or ten, or n unequal disegences in respect of each individual one-hour job of work. If we wish to avoid this difficulty and compare the disegence value to be determined with the disegence in respect of 2, 3, 4...n first hours of work to be done on different days, we again lack any means of determining that the disegence in respect of

yesterday's or tomorrow's first hour of work is equal to the disegence in respect of today's first hour of work of the same kind.

Therefore the disegence in respect of the job cannot be measured either in the true sense of the word, as there is no invariable unit of disegence of which enough completely identical examples would be available for them to make up a disegence value equal to the disegence to be determined.

Consequently, numerical determination of disegences in respect of various jobs of work is only possible by way of scaling. For theoretical purposes, we can establish an *ideal disegence scale* by analogy with the procedure we followed for positive egences by taking the just-noticeable disegence (δ), i.e. the disegence of the slightest reluctance that a person can become aware of, as the first degree of disegence (1^d). This quantity, too, will differ slightly for different people. Since, however, we are only comparing the disegences of one and the same person, we can disregard these differences. The second degree of disegence (2^d) is formed by the disegence which only differs from the first degree of disegence by a just-noticeable increment in disegence (δ_2) and thus equals the sum ($\delta_1 + \delta_2$) of the two just-noticeable disegences. By analogy one obtains the third degree ($3^d = \delta_1 + \delta_2 + \delta_3$), the fourth degree ($4^d = \delta_1 + \delta_2 + \delta_3 + \delta_4$) and so on up to the nth degree ($n^d = \delta_1 + \delta_2 + \delta_3 + ... + \delta_n$) of the ideal disegence scale.

The relationship between the negative and positive egence scales is such that the egences and disegences of the positive and negative egence degrees denoted by the same number cancel each other out ($1^e + 1^d = 0$; $2^e + 2^d = 0$; $...n^e + n^d = 0$).

By analogy with § 276, the designations $a^d < b^d < c^d < ... < x^d < y^d < z^d$ may also be used for various disegence values.

283. Some teachers of economics[33] are accustomed to expressing different disegence values by numerical multiples of an ideal unit of disegence. This, it is true, is on the whole no more incorrect than the custom discussed in § 277 of using proportional numbers for the various degrees of importance of needs; for there is no doubt that in reality every disegence is some multiple of a disegence taken as a unit, even though we have no way of ascertaining the figure by which the unit of disegence should be multiplied to obtain the disegence in question. Nevertheless, I believe it would be better to avoid such numerical representations, as they may lead to the incorrect view that we have the possibility of measuring disegence values.

On the other hand, there should be no objection to disegence values being expressed in theoretical writings as products of a unit of disegence and the general figures $a, b, c ... x, y, z$. If the egence of the just-noticeable negative welfare desire δ is taken as the unit of disegence, the various disegence values are obtained as the mathematical expressions $\delta < a\delta <$

$b\delta < c\delta < ... < x\delta < y\delta < z\delta$, of which it is known that each following one is larger than the preceding one, but not the numerical interval between them.

284. The disegence scales established in the preceding paragraphs are appropriate not only to the negative welfare desires but also to the negative use and possession desires. However, a disegence scale may also be constructed from the disegences in respect of various quantities of the same work. For example, the disegence in respect of a particular job of work in the first minute may be the first degree (1^a), the disegence in respect of the same work in the first two minutes the second degree (2^a), the disegence in respect of the same work in the first three minutes the third degree (3^a), etc., of the disegence scale.

285. As positive and negative egences are quantities of the same kind, even though they are preceded by different signs, the disegence scale may also be used indirectly to determine the size of positive egences in the same way that, for example, the power of a steam engine is measured by the resistance which it equals or which it is just able to overcome. For if one imagines a situation where the welfare or use desire whose egence is to be determined can only be fulfilled if it overcomes a negative welfare or use desire which is aimed at the same target, the egence of the positive welfare desire may be equated with the disegence of the negative desire which it is just sufficient to overcome, such that the slightest increase in the disegence of the negative desire would prevent the fulfilment of the positive desire. For example, if the positive welfare or use desire is able to overcome a negative welfare or use desire of 20^d but not one of 21^d (degree of disegence), its egence can be said to be 20^e (degree of egence). It will doubtless often suffice to make such a comparison only in the mind.[34]

If we only had positive egence scales to determine the size of egences, we would not be able to ascertain the changes which affect all the egences of a person equally, just as we cannot use a beam balance to ascertain changes in weight which occur due to a change in gravity. In the same way that the latter changes may be measured by means of a spring balance or a pendulum, the disegence scale enables an economist to recognize the simultaneous changes in all the egences of a person.

286. Since the fulfilment of all possession desires requires work whose performance is generally the object of a negative use desire associated with a disegence, the possession egences can, in view of what has just been said, also be determined indirectly by means of a work disegence scale. Here the procedure is to determine each time the highest degree of disegence that the negative use desire directed against the work in question can have without the possession desire ceasing to operate. The degree of possession egence corresponding to this degree of disegence is the degree of egence

329

we are after. These ideas are encountered in the writings of many teachers of economics, but they regard work as a measure of value, whereas here, in fact, measurement does not come into it and it is not the work itself that should be used as an aid to numerical determination of the possession egences, but the disegence in respect of performing this work.

VI. *On the commensurability of positive and negative egences of different people*

287. Now that we have adequately explained, as we presume, the comparability or measurability of both the positive and negative egences of the same person, let us examine the question of whether the welfare, use and possession needs of different people are comparable with regard to their egence. If, for example, two people A and B have use or possession needs for the same piece of meat, is it possible to determine which of them has the greater egence? Here, above all, we encounter the important fact that A's needs are not recognizable by B directly, i.e. through a sensation or perception, nor are B's needs recognizable by A, nor are both their needs recognizable in this way by anyone else. This applies not only with regard to their egence but also to their existence.[35] They can merely be imagined and discerned due to particular attendant circumstances or effects; however, such imaginings and judgements regarding the existence of welfare, use and possession needs of other people are prone to a great many errors.

288. However, if merely establishing the existence of one or both of the to-be-compared needs of different people is so difficult, the task of determining the relationship between the sizes of their egences is nothing short of impossible. For as we know from the earlier explanations, the only sure aid to determining the relationship between the egences of different needs of the same person is the actual decision of will which is made on the basis of them. When comparing the egence values of different people, we have to dispense with this aid entirely, for as everyone knows, decisions of will are only made inside one and the same consciousness and on the basis of the needs which simultaneously assert themselves as such in the consciousness of that one person. Thus a direct comparison of egence values of different people is definitely impracticable. It is possible, however, to compare two or more quantities indirectly. If I know, for instance, that one house is 15 metres tall and another 12 metres tall, I can assert with complete certainty that the first house is taller than the second without having compared them directly. A prerequisite of such indirect comparisons, however, is that the quantities concerned can be directly compared with one and the same third quantity (the standard), but this is ruled out

with egences of different people. So we have to say that these egences
cannot be compared even by indirect means.

289. Fortunately, so far there is only one case in which economics has
needed to compare different people's egences in respect of the same
specific good or for the same quantity of one and the same general good,
namely, in determining the level of the taxes, especially progressive income tax, to be paid by the individual citizens,[36] whereas it is sufficient for
an understanding of barter, for which purpose such comparisons appear to
be necessary, to know how the relationship[37] between the use and possession egences in respect of the goods to be bartered in the case of the one
side behaves in respect of the same relationship in the case of the other
side. Here, therefore, only the relationship between two egence relationships needs to be established − a relationship to the power of two, so to
speak.

If, for instance, a person A owns horses and his egence in respect of a
specific horse is as great as for 40 quintals of wheat of a particular kind and
quality, and if another person B owns wheat of this kind and quality and
his egence in respect of 50 quintals thereof is as great as for the specific
horse owned by A, it is completely immaterial for the barter transaction
between the two of them what degrees their egences in respect of the horse
in question and for 40 or 50 quintals of wheat of the kind and quality in
question actually have. The intensities of A and B's egences may both be
100^e, 200^e, 300^e or n^e, or the former may be 100^e and the latter 200^e, or
200^e and 300^e, or n^e and n_1^e (where $n_1 > n$), or the relationship may be the
other way round. The same may apply to the relationship between A's
egence and B's egence with regard to 40 and 50 quintals of wheat of the
same kind and quality, except, of course, that each person's egence in
respect of 50 quintals at the same time and place will be larger than that in
respect of 40 quintals, provided that the last phases of need are not
negative. The barter thus takes place just as if A's and B's egence in
respect of 40 or 50 quintals of wheat of the kind and quality in question
were completely identical and as if the relationship of A's egence in respect
of the horse in question to B's egence in respect of the same horse were the
same as the egence in respect of 40 quintals of wheat relative to the egence
in respect of 50 quintals. However, we certainly cannot say: as if A's
egence in respect of the horse in question to that of B in respect of the
same horse were in a ratio of 40:50, since, as we will show later, the egence
in respect of 40 or 50 quintals of wheat is certainly not 40 or 50 times
greater than the egence in respect of 1 quintal of wheat of the same kind
and quality.

If it is desired to say something about the relationship between A's
egence in respect of a horse and B's egence in respect of the same horse,

331

this is only possible on the basis of the fiction that the egences of both in respect of 40 or 50 quintals of wheat of the same kind and quality are the same.[38]

In view of the preceding statements, economics is just as entitled, in determining prices, to use a fiction of this kind as mechanics, which, in order to determine the relative positions of two bodies moving in opposite directions, is allowed to base its calculations on the fiction that one of these bodies is at rest and the other is moving at a velocity equal to the sum of both their velocities.

290. The view expressed above is contradicted by a statement by *Cassel*,[39] who says: 'The quantity of electricity which passes through a copper wire in one second cannot be measured directly, yet it is possible to measure the quantity in question: by its effect on a magnetic needle. It is just as impossible to make a direct comparison between my own needs or between these needs and those of others; yet in their economic manifestations we have a means of relatively complete measurement.' These sentences, however, contain a number of inaccuracies. Firstly, there can be no doubt, based on what we said in section II, that a direct comparison in the sense indicated in § 255 between our own needs is possible. Secondly, the economic manifestations of the use and possession desires are no more measurable than the desires themselves. For if, to satisfy a particular use desire, I will spend at most 20 crowns or do at most five hours of work of a particular kind, the economic manifestation of the use desire is the overcoming of the possession egence in respect of 20 crowns or the negative use egence in respect of the effort associated with five hours of work, and the magnitude of these two egences is no more measurable than that of the positive use egence.

The comparison with the measurement of time which *Cassel* (p. 405) uses to support the correctness of his opinion, where he claims that all the times in which the earth turns through the same angle are equal, is obviously not valid. For that the earth turns through, say, 30 degrees in the same time every day is of course not a fiction but a truth which is as objective as anything that people regard as an objective truth. With this in mind, everyone must therefore concede that all events which take the same time as the turning of the earth through 30 degrees are, from an objective point of view, of exactly the same duration. Quite a different situation applies, however, to different needs, the equality of which is expressed by way of monetary estimates. For even if I know that the use egences in respect of needs N_1 and N_2 are equal to the possession egence in respect of 20 marks, I am certainly not entitled to say that these use egences are equal to one another. If the use needs belong to different persons P_1 and P_2, I can only compare the egence of use need N_1 with person P_1's possession egence in respect of 20 marks and the egence of use need N_2 with person P_2's possession egence in respect of 20 marks. Since the possession egences of P_1 and P_2 cannot be compared with each other, the use egences cannot be compared either. But even if the latter belong to the same person but at different times, it can only be said that each at its own time is equal to the possession egence in respect of 20 marks. Since, however, we have no way of telling whether two possession egences in respect of 20 marks which apply at different times are equal to one another, nothing definite can be said about the relationship of the use egences which are equal to them at different times.

291. What we have said about the impossibility of comparing the positive egences of different people also applies, by analogy, to the impossibility of comparing the disegences of different people. In barter, however, one may likewise have recourse to the fiction that the disegences in respect of jobs of the same kind and duration are equal for different people. If, for instance, in the case of one of two bartering parties (A) his egence in respect of a good G is equal to his disegence in respect of doing a three-hour job of work of a certain kind, but in the case of the other (B) it is equal to his disegence in respect of doing a five-hour job of work of the same kind and effort, one may say, on the basis of the aforementioned fiction and in consideration of the fact that for each individual the disegence in respect of a five-hour job of work is greater than that in respect of a three-hour job of work of the same kind and effort, that for A the egence in respect of the good G is smaller than for B. One certainly may not say, though, that their egences in respect of the good G are in a ratio of $3:5$; for we know, of course, that the disegence in respect of a three-hour job is not three times greater and the disegence in respect of a five-hour job is not five times greater than the disegence in respect of a one-hour job of the same kind and effort.

292. The impossibility of comparing the egence and disegence values of different people will only cause great difficulties for economics when, at some date, it includes in its studies those communist economies in which the communally acquired product will have to be distributed among the individual members of the communist communities according to the egences of the positive use needs, while the work to be communally performed will have to be shared out according to the disegences of the negative use needs in respect of the performance of this work.

VII. *On the commensurability of future welfare and use needs*

293. In our discussion so far of the commensurability of needs, we had only considered the needs and phases of need of present welfare and use desires. However, the necessity of comparing future welfare and use

desires with present or other future ones is a phenomenon which is repeated day in, day out in real economic life. For if, for instance, a future and a present use need are dependent on the same quantity of goods in such a way that the latter can satisfy only the one or the other, a choice has to be made between these two use needs, i.e. it must become clear which of these needs is the stronger. Since such decisions very often come down in favour of the future use needs, the quantity of goods at issue being prevented from satisfying the present use need and reserved for satisfying the future need, in such cases the future use need must have a stronger motivating force than the present need at the moment of the decision of will. However, it is on the possibility of making such decisions of will that all human economic activity is based, the essence of which is that if a given stock of goods is not sufficient to satisfy all the use needs that are dependent on it, the individual needs and phases of need are satisfied not in the order of their chronological occurrence but (under certain conditions) in the order of the egence values which are inherent in the present desires.

294. We know from Chapter 2 that future use desires only exist in the present in the form of ideas linked to a definite or probable judgement with regard to their future occurrence. However, the object of such ideas is not merely the goal of the future use desire but also its drive for satisfaction. Thus future use desires have no drive for satisfaction in the present. How is it, then, that in the making of present decisions of will they nevertheless win out over present use desires which are endowed with a current drive for satisfaction? The reader may remember that in § 206 we stated that an essential characteristic of a future use desire according to the requirements of economics is the fact that through a definite or a probable judgement that the use desire in mind will be manifested at a certain time, a present use desire is created. Such a desire takes the form of a current possession egence which in making a decision of will is weighed against the egence of the competing present use desire in the same way as the egences of various present use desires.

Therefore, in speaking of the commensurability of present and future use desires, what is meant is a weighing in this way of the possession egences of present possession needs created by future use desires against the use egences of present use needs. In the same way, the commensurability of future use needs means the weighing against each other of the possession egences of present possession needs created by future use needs.

Given these facts, there is no need for a detailed discussion of the statement that future use desires may without exception be compared both with each other and with present use desires in the case of one and the same person.[40] On the other hand, there is no doubt that the future use desires can no more be measured than the current ones.

NOTES

1. In place of the expression 'utility', Gide (*Econ. politique*, pp. 46–7) has suggested the term 'désirabilité', so as to be able to use the same expression with regard to goods which are used to satisfy unreasonable needs (tobacco, opium and the like), where common parlance is reluctant to use the expression 'utility'.

2. Cf. Menger, *Volkswirtschaftslehre*, pp. 87ff., especially pp. 103f.: '...for the least important need-satisfactions, which in this case depended on that quantity of 90 measures of water, were pleasures.' Likewise p. 102.

3. See Böhm-Bawerk, *Kapital II*, pp. 148, 152 and passim.

4. See Wieser, *Nat. Wert*, p. 5.

5. Cf. Jevons, *Polit. Economy*, pp. 51 and 53.

6. Gossen (*Menschl. Verkehr*, p. 4) uses, in this sense, the expression 'the power to enjoy'.

7. Cf. Jevons, *Polit. Economy*, p. 13f.

8. Cf. Wieser, *Nat. Wert*, p. 6.

9. Cf. Böhm-Bawerk, *Güterwert*, pp. 46–51: 'It is, after all, magnitudes of feelings and sensations which have to be reckoned with according to our theory.' Also Sax (*Staatswirtschaft*, p. 176): 'All needs (in the subjective sense) have, regardless of the purposes to which they relate, a tertium comparationis in sensation and consequently exhibit a precise ranking of their strength: degrees of intensity.' However, the same author says elsewhere (p. 114): 'The relative importance of the related purposes...is reflected in the corresponding strength of the desire for satisfaction by certain external means', from which one might infer that he holds the opposite view on this point. Wieser, on the other hand, seems to share our opinion, for he says (*Nat. Wert*, p. 5): 'It is enough that we can state the symptom by which the rankings of importance are recognized. It depends on the urgency with which the accomplishment of the satisfaction is desired.'

Lexis (*Grenznutzen*, p. 425) has also correctly recognised the true facts in part, in that he says that where comparisons are concerned, it is basically not the real sensations (true feelings) themselves that are compared, but only the intensities of will produced by these pleasant or unpleasant sensations (true feelings). 'For the pleasure sensations (true feelings of pleasure) afforded to me by, for instance, eating a food or drinking a glass of wine, are essentially heterogeneous and cannot be compared.' In these sentences, we especially do not approve of the expression 'intensities of will', for it is of course not just a matter

335

of the intensities of the will, but also of the extent of the states of welfare to be accomplished; we are therefore dealing not with a one-dimensional quantity, as Lexis seems to assume, but with a two-dimensional quantity. Furthermore, we consider it incorrect for this author to look for the intensities of will in the arousals of the will which are directed at obtaining or keeping the food or wine and thus in the possession desires, instead of looking for them, as we do, in the welfare desires, for the former also depend on a number of factors which modify their size.

10. Cf. Jodl, *Psychologie*, p. 377: 'It is wrong and misleading to express and illustrate the contrast between pleasure and displeasure in any way which permits the mathematical system of positive and negative quantities to be applied to feelings. For despite their contrasting nature...both pleasure and displeasure are positive; pleasure is not the neutralization of a preceding displeasure or vice versa.... Displeasure or pain can only be termed negative in the sense that aversion and reluctance are always associated with these states of feeling.'

11. See Ehrenfels, *Werttheorie* i, pp. 15f.

12. See Höfler, *Psychologie*, p. 79.

13. See Jodl, *Psychologie*, p. 378.

14. See Bentham, 'Works I', pp. 15ff., also 'Works IV', p. 540; Kraus, *Wert*, pp. 23f.; Jevons, *Polit. Economy*, pp. 30ff.

15. Here I mean by 'value', in accordance with the process applied by psychologists, the quantity resulting from the combination of the intensity of the feeling with its duration and spread.

16. See Böhm-Bawerk, *Güterwert*, p. 47.

17. Cf. Bain, *The Emotions and the Will*, 1st edn, p. 447: 'It is only an identical proposition to affirm that the greatest of two pleasures, or what appears such, sways the resulting action; for it is this resulting action that alone determines which is the greater.' (As quoted in Jevons, *Polit. Economy*, p. 14.)

18. Cf. Fisher, *Value*, p. 12.

19. Cf. Böhm-Bawerk, *Güterwert*, p. 50.

20. If we wanted to be completely accurate, we would have to say: 'The egence of the phases of need of a welfare need for the pleasure of eating this apple which may be satisfied with an apple.' For the sake of brevity we will say from now on: 'The welfare egence in respect of an apple, a pear, etc.'

21. It is therefore not correct, or at least not accurately expressed, for Neumann (*Naturgesetz*, note to p. 443) to say that desires do not have a dimension or number because there is no unit for them; for there are units, as we have shown, even for desires, except that they

do not remain constant when a larger number of desires are taken together.

22. See Böhm-Bawerk, *Güterwert*, pp. 48ff.

23. By the way, it is not only feelings and desires but also sensations that have the peculiarity of not being measurable. Cf. Jodl, *Psychologie*, p. 212: 'It is doubtless clear from direct perception that the intensity of different sensations may be larger or smaller and that it waxes or wanes; but nobody is able to express its changing values in figures and say of two given intensities of sensation, on the basis of direct perception, that the one is twice or three times as strong as the other, or in any way to interpret the one sensation as a certain multiple of the other.'

24. Cf. Voigt, *Zahl und Maß*, p. 583.

25. Cf. Voigt, *Zahl und Maß*, pp. 583f.

26. Cf. Böhm-Bawerk, *Güterwert*, pp. 50f.

27. Cf. Kraus, *Wert*, pp. 47 ff. and Jodl, *Psychologie*, pp. 223 f.

28. See Böhm-Bawerk, *Güterwert*, pp. 510ff., and *Kapital II*, p. 265. Or else Menger, *Volkswirtschaftslehre*, pp. 93ff; Wieser, *Nat. Wert*, p. 10; and Böhm-Bawerk, *Güterwert*, pp. 25ff. and *Kapital II*, pp. 153ff.

29. Cf. Voigt (*Zahl und Maß*, p. 584), who here points out that the numbers by which the various degrees of importance are expressed are not proportional numbers. It is more correct to say that proportional numbers corresponding to these numbers cannot be proved in reality.

30. See Cassel, *Preislehre*, p. 307.

31. Cf. Marshall, *Principles*, p. 151.

32. For the sake of brevity, we will say from now on: 'Negative egence or disegence in respect of a 1-, 2-, 3- or n-hour job of work.'

33. Cf. Böhm-Bawerk (*Kapital I*, pp. 342 and 626f.), in which there are numerical indications of the size of the sacrifice (pain) entailed by the work.

34. Cf. Ehrenfels, *Werttheorie*, pp. 37–8.

35. What Jevons (*Polit. Economy*, p. 15) says about feelings, namely: 'Every mind is thus inscrutable to every other mind, and no common denominator of feeling seems to be possible', is also true of desires.

36. Cf. Cassel, *Preislehre*, p. 403.

37. Cf. Böhm-Bawerk, *Güterwert*, p. 509.

38. Cf. Cassel, *Preislehre*, pp. 397f.

39. See loc. cit., p. 399.

40. Cf. Böhm-Bawerk, *Kapital II*, p. 255.

Eugen von Böhm-Bawerk, 'On the Measurability of Sensations' [1912], E. von Böhm-Bawerk, *Capital and Interest* (South Holland IL: Libertarian Press, 1959), vol. 3, pp. 124–36; footnotes pp. 232–3.

This paper was originally the 'Exkurs X' (under the title: 'Betreffend die "Messbarkeit" von Gefühlsgrössen') in Böhm-Bawerk's volume of polemical defenses of his work. It contains Böhm-Bawerk's careful response to Franz Čuhel's criticisms (see editor's note at the head of item 12). The present version is from Hans Sennholz's translation (op. cit.) of Böhm-Bawerk's *Exkurse* volume. The reader must judge whether Ludwig von Mises was correct in his later remark that 'Böhm-Bawerk endeavoured to refute Čuhel's criticism, but did not succeed in putting forward any new considerations that could help toward a solution of the problem.' (*Theory of Money and Credit* (Indianapolis: Liberty, *Classics* 1981), p. 55 n.)

13

On the 'Measurability' of Sensations[1]

EUGEN von BÖHM-BAWERK

Recently (1907) Čuhel raised a series of objections against my exposition of this subject which I discussed in almost identical language in my *Grundzüge der Theorie des wirtschaftlichen Güterwertes* (1886). I consider his objections among the most careful and well-weighed contributions to this most difficult subject. I deem it necessary, therefore, to enter upon more detailed discussion than would have been possible in a compact footnote inserted in the text.

Čuhel objects against my example of the boy who declines to exchange his apple for less than seven plums, who hesitates when he gets an offer of seven plums, and who finally exchanges it for eight. Čuhel first remarks that, according to the law of marginal utility, the gratification of each plum in case he eats seven or eight plums one after another is not the same, but decreases with each plum consumed. Thus the gratification of the seventh and eighth plums respectively is by no means seven or eight times greater than that of one, especially the first.[2]

The kernel of this objection is correct. But its significance naturally can reach no further than the factual suppositions on which it is based. They merely pertain to a part of the cases covered by my original unqualified example. Consideration of Čuhel's objection therefore merely requires a variation in the presentation of my example. I provided for such a variation through some qualifying clauses in the text of *Positive Theory of Capital*,[3] and should now like to expound on this point with all explicitness.

Within the scope of the unqualified example of the plum exchange – as I presented it in 1886 – we can distinguish the following variations:

First case: The boy intends to eat his seven or eight plums, *one immediately after another*. He knows that in this case they render *decreasing* gratifications, a consideration he bears in mind in the valuation determining his decision. Čuhel's objection in its outer import pertains to this case. And its inner import at any rate does not lead to the conclusion that the enjoyment of an apple excels the (unequal) enjoyment of a plum by a multiple proportion. Whether its inner import goes even further we shall discuss further below.

Second case: The boy does not intend to eat the plums one immediately after another, but in such intervals that Gossen's law of decreasing utility is not operative at all. This may be so because factual circumstances condition the example. For instance, in exchange for his apple our boy may merely obtain the right to pluck one ripe plum on seven different days from the tree of his neighbour. Or it may be that he receives the seven plums all at once, but decides to forego their summary consumption and eat them in intervals. Besides, I may add that such an assumption is not at all improbable or unusual. On the contrary, every housewife who buys a 10-pound bag of coffee will not base her valuation on the assumption that the whole quantity will be consumed all at once at a dinner with an abundance of coffee enjoyment, but she will divide it into numerous small portions that again and again satisfy the ever new want for coffee at breakfast, lunch, and dinner without any decrease of enjoyment. Čuhel's objection discussed so far is not at all directed at this case.

Third case: The boy does not reflect at all whether he wants to eat the plums summarily or in intervals because he lacks the experience of 'decline of enjoyment,' or at least does not think of it. And because of this lack of distinction his naïve, although perhaps erroneous, judgment is based on the assumption that his pleasures from each one of his plums are identical. It is obvious Čuhel's objection does not cover this case either. We will have to deal with this example and its significance for the whole controversy in detail further below.

With laudable insight Čuhel anticipated this or similar counter objections. He himself elaborated one that corresponds to our 'second case' in the following words: It may be 'objected that we need not compare the desire intensity for an apple with that for plums consumed all at once, but with that for plums eaten in longer time intervals.' To refute his own counterobjection he continues: 'This objection proves to be fallacious if we bear in mind that we lack the means for *determining* whether the desire intensities for plums consumed on different days are equal. We also lack the supposition on which measurement in general depends. That is, we lack the supposition that the unit of measure *is on hand in so many equal specimens* that we arrive at a magnitude equalling the data to be measured or an auxiliary quantity whose quantitative relationship to our data is known.' (*Section 266*). I reserve my own replies to this argumentation for a later broader inquiry. At this place I am satisfied to italicize those phrases or words in Čuhel's chain of reasoning that will be relevant for a decision in the controversy.

Čuhel also presents a second counterobjection – again in correct anticipation. I intend to take up also this counterobjection, not in its wording, but in its content. He states the following: 'Another method by which we may hope to arrive at a measurement of desire intensities is the following: If we are to determine the desire intensity for good G_n, we must first find a number of goods for which the desire intensities are perfectly equal. If we have established, for instance, that the desire for a bottle of wine consumed by a certain person, at a certain time and occasion, equals the desire for a certain book, or a certain food, or a certain pipe, tie, knife, or inkstand, then it seems that in case the desire intensity for good G_n equals the sum of desire intensities for these seven different goods, the former must be seven times greater than that for any single good. Thus Gossen's first law exerts no disturbing influence.' (*Section 267*).

But Čuhel also meets this method with a number of arguments directed at making it appear 'inapplicable.' Among other things he points out that the search for goods that are the object of equal desire intensities is 'very time-consuming' and that we are hardly in the position *to find a sufficiently large number of such cases* that would enable us to 'compile' the equivalent of very considerable intensities, let us say, corresponding to a product value of several hundred thousand crowns. He points out that during the time needed for the comparison between one desire intensity and many others, the first may have changed and that we therefore lack the '*guarantee*' of its unchanged intensity. He remarks that the relationship of desire intensities among each other is subject to sudden and considerable fluctuations inasmuch as an equilibrium determined for a certain point of time may disappear a few hours later, yes, even a few minutes later. Thus a new inquiry may be required. And he sums up the effect of all these counterarguments in the words 'that measurement of desire intensities according to this method is *not feasible practically* because if several intensity units are taken together their *perfect equality* cannot *be proven*.' According to Čuhel this conclusion stands in an 'open contradiction' to my conclusion that 'the magnitude of the difference between the intensities of two desires can be determined numerically.' In his opinion it can 'not be determined absolutely' what intensities exist '*in reality*.' The numerical determinations actually taking place are said to be of quite a different nature for which the term 'measurement' is unsuitable, but to which we rather should apply the term 'scalation.' This is a process, Čuhel asserts, which we may compare with the numerical determination of the hardness of minerals by way of the famous scale of 10 degrees by Mohs. In spite of the numerical expression we merely determine whether the hardness in question equals another taken as a standard or whether it is greater.[4]

I believe that Čuhel, in spite of his great carefulness and profound reflection on this chain of reasoning, has erred at the decisive point. The error lies in the fact that he does not see clearly enough our topic of contention and that consequently he does not adhere to his own doctrine. Thus he broadens the requirements of evidence I must offer in a way that neither corresponds to the nature of the subject of evidence, nor to his own opinions uttered throughout the discussion.

The argument pertains to the kind of 'numerical determination' that is contained in our judging the differences between sensation intensities. Čuhel at first distinguishes correctly between 'measurement' and mere comparison or 'scalation.' He states that 'in a comparison of two magnitudes each serves as yardstick of the other. In a measurement both have a third common yardstick, namely the corresponding unit of measure or weight. In a comparison of two magnitudes that are not equal by chance it suffices to show which one is the greater of the two. But we do not demonstrate how much greater it is. In a measurement, however, we must determine numerically what product of the unit of measure equals the magnitude to be measured. For measurement means *finding* a number that indicates how many times a magnitude taken as unit is contained in the magnitude to be measured.' And to this first strict definition of measurement he adds an equally strict requirement for the feasibility of such measurement. He demands that 'there exists a unit of measure that is present in *so many completely equal and unchanging specimens* that we can *compose* a magnitude that equals the magnitude to be measured' (*Section 262, paragraph 1*).

In his following presentations, however, Čuhel interprets this concept of measurement quite broadly in different directions. He declares it to be 'non-essential' that we can apply mechanically a certain standard to the magnitude to be determined like we apply a yardstick or measuring tape in measuring lengths. He also admits 'indirect measurement.' He yields that the standard must not be 'perceptible simultaneously,' but that we can also measure with an 'imaginary standard' like we do when we want to measure the height of a house but have left the yardstick at home. We usually call such a procedure 'estimation' which, however, 'in its broader sense' *to which Čuhel pledges adherence*, is also true measuring. In this connection Čuhel is content with a mere 'indication,' instead of his earlier 'finding' of the multiple and renounces the requirement of 'preciseness' (*Section 262, paragraph 2*).[5] And finally Čuhel remarks expressly in a paragraph (*274*) dealing with both 'measurement' and 'scalation' that the occurrence of 'errors' does not affect the usefulness of determinations for theoretical purposes. With an entirely correct reference to a similar remark of mine he states that 'an incorrect determination of the desire intensity inevitably leads to an incorrect determination of economic value, while a correct determination of the desire leads us to a correct determination of value. Economics must explain not only correct valuations, but also erroneous ones.'

It is a matter of course that lower requirements for what we call 'measurement' must also entail lower requirements for the quality of the tools absolutely required for such 'measuring.' But it is astonishing that Čuhel did not think of drawing this inference. He does not revise his requirements originally devised for measurement in its narrow and strict sense. He does not state whether and how the individual requirements contained therein are diminished as to measurement in the broader sense. But he opposes me with his unchanged list in its strictest polemic version. Thus following his own presentation we must make the revision he omitted.

Above all, we shall have to lessen considerably our requirement that the unit of measure 'is present in so many ... specimens' that we can 'compose' a magnitude that equals the magnitude to be measured. Such a requisite can hardly be maintained literally for measurement in its strictest sense. In order to measure a pole 10 yards in length we certainly do not need 10 different yardsticks; it obviously suffices if one is available which is applied 10 times to the pole. This is especially true with regard to 'estimation' with an 'imaginary' yardstick which Čuhel correctly recognized. We undoubtedly can estimate the length of the tail of a comet or the distance of two stars by 'diameter of the moon' although this standard obviously is available only once. In our imagination we just apply the only 'available' moon as often as it is necessary. Whey should we not act similarly when we estimate intensities? Why does Čuhel insist, quite contrary to the analogy, that so many *different* goods with equal degrees of intensity really exist side by side and must be 'found' through reflection in order to compose from different factors even the greatest desire intensities, e.g., values of several hundred thousand crowns?

Furthermore, Čuhel insists that for a composition of several units of intensity their 'complete equality' must be subject to *proof*.[6] This again is much too strict. For in the case of a rough estimation, which Čuhel himself considers as true measurement, a mere approximate equality suffices. We certainly can measure the circumference of a big tree or the width of a meadow – lacking a measuring tape – with a flexible wickerwork which we may give a different tension with each application. And nothing is more commonplace than to measure distances by steps whereby the complete equality of each single step naturally cannot be 'proven' or 'guaranteed,' especially if the territory to be measured is not perfectly even, or if the steps are made by different persons. This may be the case, for instance, if in a field-practice an officer would like to measure the distance between two points that lie in opposite directions from the position of his troop and if he, in order to save time, does not order one man to walk the whole distance, but rather one for each opposite direction. Thus he obtains unprecise measures with 'margins of error' whose existence and magnitude may or may not be known to him. But the procedure undoubtedly remains a measuring and does not become a 'scaling.' As Čuhel knows very well there is, on the one hand, precise, unprecise, and approximate 'measuring,' and on the other hand, precise, unprecise, and mere approximate 'scaling.'[7] At any rate, lack of accuracy of a procedure changes measurement to scalation no less than its accuracy changes scalation to measurement. Lack of 'perfect' equality of the standard does not make every kind of measuring unfeasible, as Čuhel wants to maintain. For measurement in general we may and must be content with an 'approximate' equality of the standard employed. Of course, a deviation from the 'perfect' standard may indeed be without consequences other than that our measurement (which by its very nature it always remains) becomes rather inaccurate.

But Čuhel's repeatedly asserted requirement that a certain quality of the standard must be 'proven,' 'guaranteed,' or objectively 'determined' deserves to be considered also from another point of view. What then is the consequence if the units of measure are not equal objectively, neither completely nor approximately, but are *believed* – although erroneously – to be equal? Does such a case fall outside the scope of an endeavour 'to determine what multiple of the standard the quantity to be measured equals'?[8] Certainly not! The case stays a true measuring, a search for the multiple of the standard. It merely becomes *false* and mistaken measuring which, according to Čuhel's own remark, is as valid for the theoretical explanation as correct and exact measuring. Let us assume in our example that our officer, through gross inattention, fails to observe that one of the two distances is ascending and the other level, or that the two soldiers whom he orders to walk the distances are of very different height. Then he obviously will take the different steps that serve as units of measure as being equal. Consequently he misjudges the distances. Nevertheless, he did not 'scale' them, he 'measured' them. And this false measuring because of its incorrect instruction on the range of fire, thoroughly misses the target.

Whoever is once aware of these details and then reviews the comprehensive formula which Čuhel holds against me, must immediately perceive his straying from the subject of evidence. Measuring desire intensities, he asserts, is *practically unfeasible* because the *complete* equality of several intensity units cannot be *proven*. And it cannot be *ascertained* which one of several numerical relationships *'prevails in reality'*.[9] But this is by no means the disputed point of evidence, neither for me nor for him. We are not concerned with an ascertainment of the relationship of two actual intensities of sensations or desires, provided with all guarantees of objective correctness and precision. As Čuhel stated correctly in some sporadic remarks, we are merely concerned with an 'attempt at indication,' which may be based merely on subjective estimates or application of imaginary standards, without claiming preciseness or even correctness. And, in my belief, none of Čuhel's objections refutes such an action which I described no differently in my *Positive Theory of Capital*.

Let me illustrate it again more rigorously with the example of the zone of fire. Our officer and his troop see the enemy appear in some distance. He is no longer in the position to 'determine' objectively how far this distance is 'in reality.' He lacks all of Čuhel's strict prerequisites. He lacks a sufficient number of 'specimens' of the standard in 'proven,' 'complete' equality. He even can no longer resort to the imperfect substitute of measuring by steps. Nevertheless he must make an estimate, no matter how wrong it may be, because he must order his men to fire at the enemy and because he must order them to adjust their rifles for a distance of either 400 or 800 or 1,200 steps. In such a situation he will estimate, without guarantees and proofs, the multiple of steps by applying a merely imaginary standard, such as the distance of 100 steps each, on the separating range. Of course, he must endeavour to apply the standard equally, although it may happen that he errs rather considerably, for instance, because of an incorrect consideration of the effects of perspective. At any rate, he will form a numerical estimate of the distance. And this estimate will determine the action, in this case the firing by the soldiers. The correctness of the estimate will become evident only later in the form of result.

In economic life we constantly are in a similar situation. We, too, must always 'fire' and aim if we want to act economically and not without plan. In numberless cases when we are concerned with attainment of gratifications or removal of uneasiness – we readily admit to the anti-Hedonists that there are also ends other than the attainment of gratification and removal of uneasiness – this aiming must be directed rationally by a subjective valuation of the degree (intensity and duration) of a gratification or uneasiness. The situation may be such that a simple comparison suffices, that is, a deliberation whether two gratifications are equal, or whether one and which one is the greater. For instance, we may be concerned with the decision regarding two alternative uses for one good. But as often, or even more often, such a superficial estimate does not suffice for our practical purposes, as I endeavoured to show in my examples in *Positive Theory of Capital*. It suffices as inadequately as can our officer, for his firing instructions, be content with the conclusion that one of two visible enemy columns is further away than the other. Very often an actual situation forces us to determine our actions numerically, to add up our means of gratification or goods to certain quantities, or to compare certain multiples. And such a numerical determination of our actions, if it is not to proceed in senseless arbitrariness, demands the preceding formation of numerical judgments on the degree of intensities of desired gratifications. We need these judgments if we are to act rationally; and we form them because we need them. We form them as well as we can; and we err more often than we evaluate correctly. We form them without guaranteed objective tools of measure, merely through vague, subjective, perhaps even deceptive, estimates of the intensity of sensations which we may partially experience, but mainly reproduce in our imagination. Perhaps we give correct consideration, perhaps none at all, to factors that influence the correctness of such intensity estimates like the influence of perspective on our estimates of length or height.

Here, and not with the arguments against the impossibility of 'measurement,' I believe, belongs Čuhel's remark on the gradually decreasing gratification which the consumption of a larger number of plums can render. If our boy for whom the enjoyment of an apple equals that of seven plums does not think at all of the possibility of a different consumption because of his naïve inadvertency, he deems the gratification of the apple equal to the sum of seven equal gratifications of one plum, or sevenfold such an enjoyment. He acts like a man who wants to estimate a spruce ten yards high and who repeatedly applies in his mind a standard which he believes to be one yard without considering whether what appears to be equal actually is equal due to perspective. If our boy is aware of the possibility of decreasing utility and in his numeral estimate expressly values the enjoyment of the plums when eaten separately and wisely rationed, then he acts like the man who in his estimate of height endeavours to eliminate the deceptive effects of perspective, for instance, through a successive change of his point of observation. But if our boy values the enjoyment of an apple as highly as the enjoyment of seven plums, expressly bearing in mind that he wants to eat them together in spite of their decreasing gratifications, then he acts like a man who estimates the height under the influence of the deceptive effects of perspective, but who is fully aware of these effects and therefore corrects the result of his mere impression. For instance, he bears in mind that every higher 'yard' applied by his eye in reality is more than a yard, and that a spruce that extends seven yards of uncorrected eyesight does not equal seven identical, but rather seven consecutively increasing measures. Similarly, the material content of our boy's opinion in this case is that the gratification of one apple equals the sum of seven unequal gratifications of the plums.

I should like to emphasize expressly that such a valuation, the possibility of which is expressly admitted by Čuhel,[10] extends considerably beyond that which he wishes to concede in our point of dispute. As a matter of fact Čuhel maintains that 'all determinations of desire intensities in spite of their numerical expressions are on the same level, like the numerical determination of the hardness of minerals,' which are arrived at by way of Mohs' scale of ten degrees and which may not be called 'measurement,' but mere 'scalation.' He correctly describes the significance of this scale of hardness as that 'it enables us to indicate whether a mineral has a second, third, fourth, etc., degree of hardness, or whether it is harder than a mineral of the second, third, fourth, degree, etc. We cannot designate such numerical determinations of hardness as 'measurements' because we cannot demonstrate what multiple of a hardness used as a standard unit equals to the hardness to be measured. For if we say that talc has the first degree, gypsum the second, this by no means signifies that gypsum is twice as hard as talc; it merely indicates that it is harder by a certain degree. But it absolutely cannot be ascertained whether the latter is 1½, 2, 2½ or 3 times harder than the former.'[11]

As far as Mohs' scale of hardness is concerned, this is entirely correct. But just because the second degree of hardness constitutes neither 'double' the first degree of hardness, nor any other sure or merely probable multiple of the first degree, and because the third degree constitutes no multiple of the first, second, etc., we can by no means *sum up* the scaled hardness degrees of minerals. We can by no means maintain that a mineral of the 8th degree is as hard as three minerals of the 5th, 2nd and 1st degree together. Čuhel is completely correct in stating that we cannot say the hardness of a mineral of the 8th degree equals the sum of hardness of four equally hard minerals of the 2nd degree, for instance. Such a conclusion would be identical with the assertion justly rejected by Čuhel that the mineral of the 8th degree is four times harder than that of the second degree. But for analogous reasons we cannot maintain that the hardness of a mineral of a higher degree equals some sum of *unequal* lower degrees of other minerals. For the summation of unequal magnitudes in final analysis assumes a reference to an equal magnitude used as standard, that is, a magnitude that is embodied, or is assumed to be embodied, in the unequal magnitudes at different times. The comparative magnitudes must be ascertained or ascertainable by way of a common unit of measure in order to arrive at a sum and to be able to express ourselves on the comparative magnitude of the sum and any other magnitude. I can add the unequal magnitudes 7 and 5 and consider them equalling 12 or the sum of 8 and 4,

CLASSICS IN AUSTRIAN ECONOMICS: VOLUME I

because I compare each of these figures with the common unit '1' and measure them at 1. If there were no constant relationship between 7 and 5, we could not arrive at the point to which the sum extends. Determination of multiples, that is, multiplication, which Čuhel judged so differently, is no different, but merely a sub-case of summation; it is a summation of several equal quantities. But also in the case of summation of unequal quantities we must be able to judge the degree of inequality. And for this we also need a reference to an ultimate equal quantity serving as standard. At least we must have it before our eyes. Summation of unequal quantities presupposes, as it were, a summation of equal quantities, namely a determination of the magnitude of quantities that are unequal among themselves in comparison with the magnitude of their common unit. Where one is feasible, the other also is feasible; and where one is unfeasible, the other also is unfeasible. This is true for degrees of hardness as well as desire intensities, but with opposite results. In the case of determination of hardness, ascertainment of multiples is unfeasible; so is the summation of unequal degrees of hardness. And in the case of intensities of sensations and desires, according to Čuhel's own concession, summation of unequal quantities is feasible. Therefore summation of equal quantities or, what is the same, the determination of a multiple of a quantity, cannot be unfeasible. This is why the numerical determination of desire intensities is of different nature than scalation according to the scale of hardness. It is a kind of numerical determination that extends beyond scalation and belongs to that meaningful kind of determination which I presented in my expositions in, I believe, sufficiently careful words.[12]

One question remains to be discussed. My whole presentation assumes the following sequence in the chain of motivation to which an analogous chain of theoretical explanations corresponds: To judge the degree (intensity and duration) of a given enjoyment or uneasiness is a distinctly psychical process. The sensation intensity and duration correctly or incorrectly determined lends direction and intensity to an aroused desire; and the desire finally motivates our action. Or to follow the sequence backwards: action results from desire, and desire with its intensity results from a preceding ascertainment of the degree of sensation.

Now it is maintained frequently – and in a certain degree also Čuhel is the spokesman of this opinion – that we cannot explain desire intensities by referring to sensation intensities because we infer inversely from the intensity of the desire to the degree of sensation.

'If we want to determine,' says Čuhel,[13] 'which is the greater, more valuable one of two sensations whose intensities or degrees differ only a little or have rather heterogeneous qualities, such as the enjoyment of a cold bath on a hot summer day and listening to a Beethoven symphony, or the gratification of a great hunger, we have no means other than to determine which one of these sensations we actually would choose when only one could be satisfied. Thus we may conclude that this sensation is more intense, or has higher value. Similarly, we can conclude from an actual decision which one of two sensations – one being enjoyment, the other uneasiness – whose intensities of degrees do not differ widely is the greater. It is not the intensity of sensations that affords us recognition of desire intensities or their corresponding wants, but inversely in most cases the desire intensities are the only available means to determine the intensities of corresponding sensations.' Čuhel, who thinks he can cite Wieser, Jevons, and Bain as authorities,[14] wants to draw the conclusion that economic theory should forego the explanatory deduction of desire intensities from sensation intensities which it does not need from the point of view of its own science and which may involve it in undecided questions of the special science, psychology. Thus our explanation of the value phenomenon should go back no further than our 'desire to use goods.'[15]

I am fully aware that I am touching an obscure spot of psychology. But I shall not avoid it, as Čuhel recommends, for reasons stated at another place.[16] Though I am fully aware that I, as 'non-expert,' trespass into the field of psychology, I should like to relate some experiences and make some observations that seem to oppose Čuhel's point of view. And I should like to add that the question of dispute must be discussed as to its basic principles, and does not permit, as Čuhel seems to assume, different answers for different spheres of sensations and desires.

But first some details.

For a moment a splendid lightning illumines the nightly sky and reveals to me a natural drama that affords me great aesthetic pleasure. How am I aware that my enjoyment was 'great'? Only because and when a correspondingly intensive desire has resulted from it? And what kind of desire is it supposed to be? Is it a desire that arose in the very moment of enjoyment and was directed only at momentary pleasure? But that which we possess we cannot desire.[17] Or is it a desire that emerges after the moment of joy has passed? But then it cannot be directed at this enjoyment itself, but merely at its repetition. And repetition of pleasure rather differs from the original one and often is, as we know from experience, less gratifying. Thus the intensity of the desire for repetition is no suitable yardstick for the intensity of the original enjoyment.

How did we ever gain the knowledge so well supported by common experience that the repetition of gratifications in most cases leads to a diminution of the joy connected therewith? Are we to take the intensity of the desire for repetition that makes itself felt during the interval between the original gratification and its repetition as index for the original gratification, or its repetition?[18] If it is the latter, how could we ever experience the phenomenon of 'disappointment'? If our knowledge of the intensity of a desired gratification results exclusively from the intensity of the preceding desire, how can we ever perceive a difference between the two, which in fact is the characteristic of 'disappointment.' And what source of knowledge do we have as to the intensity of sensations not preceded at all by a desire serving as an intensity index, but that come as a surprise to us, such as the enjoyment of a song by several voices heard in the forest?

But if, in order to avoid these conclusions and in spite of my preceding remarks, the intensity of our desire for repetition is to be the intensity index for the preceding original sensation, instead of for its repetition, we will run counter to other facts. For as I pointed out, it is a notorious fact culled from experience that our intensities for repetition of enjoyments in general are smaller because of the diminished joy it affords. Thus the desire for repetition would constitute a very fallacious index for the greater original sensation. For instance, I remember very well that I enjoyed very much ascending the Matterhorn several years ago. But since then and even today I do not feel the slightest desire to repeat the ascent. The lacking or even negative intensity of desire for repetition, as the corresponding intensity index of desire for the original enjoyment, would have me deny the joy I actually experienced.

Of course the following objection could be raised: The fact that I desire no repetition of my Matterhorn ascent does not mean that I do not desire a repetition of the original pleasure. It merely means that today I can expect only a smaller pleasure because of altered circumstances for a new ascent, for instance, because of greater fatigue on account of my advanced age or because it would no longer constitute a novelty, etc. Thus I may deem the repetition not worthwhile. But I certainly would wish to repeat the sensation I experienced if it were possible. I admit this at once. But first, Čuhel and his authorities do not refer to empty platonic desires as the source of knowledge for sensation intensities, but to practically demonstrable 'actual decisions,' or even to 'actions resulting therefrom' (Bain). Second, measurement of intensity of platonic desires would encounter certainly no fewer and no other difficulties than those that induced any opponents to doubt the possibility of direct recognition of sensation intensities. And third, the train of thought just stated contains some links that presuppose a direct evaluation of sensation intensities which is not deduced from desire intensities.

To me, the hypothesis that we become aware of the intensity of our sensations only by way of the intensity of some related desire, not only does not facilitate the interpretation of these phenomena, but makes it more difficult and superfluously artificial. There seems to be an abundance of illustrative evidence of which I may mention one or two.

In a dentist's chair we often suffer great pain under the hands of the dentist. Are we to perceive the great pain only in a 'decision' to rate higher than other desires our wish to evade the pain? But what if this wish does *not* prevail, if we decide to endure the pain? We then merely perceive that the pain is *less* intensive, than, for instance, the prevailing feeling of shame, of the desire to avoid future toothaches, etc. which kept us from crying or jumping up and ending the painful procedure. But we can by no means infer from this that our feelings were 'very painful.' And yet, everybody who has lived through it can testify to it. Is it not much more plausible and simpler to assume that we can perceive and evaluate directly the intensity of our sensations which we actually experienced?

With historic objectivity, uncoloured by any intervention of desires, everyone knows from his memory whether certain sensations experienced in the past were absolutely strong or weak, and which one was the stronger. I remember very well, for instance, that a sudden attack of rheumatism which I suffered in 1894 was very painful and considerably more painful than similar attacks I suffered before and after. Where are the 'desires' the intensity of which is to indicate to me the intensity of the corresponding sensations? In my present retrospective evaluation no desire whatever plays a role. And I have completely forgotten whether and which fruitless desires to avoid those violent pains at that time competed with and prevailed over other desires. If I remember anything at all of this experience – and that I do remember it there cannot be any doubt – it is not the state and intensity of my desires, but merely the intensity of my sensations. And if my memory can reproduce these sensations and their intensities, I must have been able to ascertain them originally.

According to many psychologists[19] whose opinion my personal experience seems to corroborate, there are sensations without desires or at least conscious desires that could be compared with other desires. I can delight, for instance, in listening to sublime music in pure desireless enjoyment. Furthermore, the intensity of desire can differ essentially from the intensity of the arousing sensation. The feeling of 'resignation,' for instance, is characterized by a weakness of desire which is not necessarily accompanied by dullness of sensation.[20]

All in all, the thesis that we base our knowledge of the intensity of our own sensations[21] on subsequent practical decisions seems to be a paradoxical fancy which reverses the actual sequence of causality and lacks any foundation in fact.[22] Its attraction for some people is perhaps due to its paradoxical nature and suitability for sceptical inferences which are so fashionable today. As for me, I see no cogent reason to dispense with an entirely feasible exact justification and analysis of the train of thought

351

which the orthodox opinion on the relationship between sensation and desire intensities requires.

It may have been strange to many an expert that in this essay I avoided every reference to the well-known 'basic law of psychology' and to the voluminous literature on this subject. But it seems to me that the very interesting inquiries that led to the statement of Weber's and Fechner's laws deal with very different questions than those involved in our present inquiry. There we are concerned with the determination of *sensual stimulations and perceptions*, here with the determination of *feelings of enjoyment and uneasiness*. Although these may be released by sensual stimuli, they may proceed in different ways. As is well known, if we increase stimulations and perceptions that usually arouse feelings of enjoyment, we will experience no parallel increase of enjoyment. On the contrary, extreme degrees of stimulation always arouse feelings of disturbance. Furthermore, Fechner's investigations are concerned with the problem of *exact, objectively correct* measurement of sensual intensities. But this is out of the question with our analogous subject of intensities of feelings. I never maintained the practical realizability of exact, objectively correct measurement of such intensities, but merely the existence of processes that subjectively estimate, no matter how erroneously and unprecisely, the intensity of feelings. Facts and arguments therefore differ in both cases. And I am as little justified in citing the correctness of Fechner's law, for instance, in support of my opinion, as I am in considering objections against the correctness of that law as being directed at my different subject of evidence.

NOTES

1. A further explanation of the 'Degree of Value and Degree of Emotion' as discussed in *Positive Theory of Capital*, pp. 196 ff.
2. *Zur Lehre von den Bedürfnissen*, sects 264 and 268 ff.
3. *Positive Theory of Capital*, pp. 198 ff.
4. Čuhel, op. cit., sects 264–273.
5. Similarly also sect. 263, last paragraph, where he declares 'a far inferior degree of preciseness' to be no obstacle to describing a process as true measuring.
6. Sect. 267, last sentence. Cf. my quotation on p. 341 foregoing, also Čuhel's expression 'perfectly equal' at the beginning of sect. 267.
7. Cf. Čuhel, op cit., sect. 274.
8. Čuhel, ibid., sects 262; cf. also foregoing pp. 126 ff.

9. Čuhel, ibid., sects 267, toward the end, and 273.

10. 'We fully agree with Böhm-Bawerk when he says that attention "must be directed at the question of how many small gratifications equal one large gratification." But by the expression "how many" we need not mean a sum of several equal magnitudes which we call a product, but we may also mean the sum of several unequal magnitudes' (ibid., sect. 268).

11. Ibid., sect. 272.

12. In such a situation little depends on whether Čuhel is right with his further remark that 'it is entirely sufficient for correct economic valuations and for a "reasonable decision" in economic matters if we know whether the sum of a large number of small unequal gratifications is greater or smaller than a single large gratification.' Therefore 'the decision on how many times a larger gratification of a certain kind exceeds a smaller gratification of another kind is superfluous for the businessman as well as for the economic theorist' (section 268). I believe that also in this remark Čuhel is not entirely correct, for there may be situations – although few – that demand a valuation directly aimed at the determination of a certain multiple. In most cases however, our evaluation of the sum of unequal magnitudes may suffice as I have stated with reasons in my text. And in order to distinguish expressly direct from indirect use of multiples – the latter, in my belief, is contained in every summation – and in order to bestow as much care on the formulation as possible, I mentioned 'at least very similar' processes besides the direct estimates of multiples (cf. p. 197 of *Positive Theory of Capital*. In its main aspects I published this conclusion already in 1886 in my 'Grundzüge'). Besides also Čuhel finally arrives from this point of view at the same conclusions for the justification and scientific usefulness of the subjective value theory. But even if the 'numerical determination' of the distance between sensation intensities and desire intensities merely is a simple comparison of 'scalation' as Čuhel alleges, it would suffice, in his belief, to permit numerical valuation whose explanation is the task of the economic value theory.

13. Ibid., sect. 259.

14. Whether rightly or wrongly I do not want to discuss. On page 180, note 1 he cites the following sentence by Wieser: 'It suffices that we can indicate the symptom by which we can recognize the degree of importance. The urgency with which we desire gratification is decisive.' And on page 185, note 1, he cites Bain's remark which Jevons had taken up: 'It is only an identical proposition to affirm that the greatest of two pleasures, or what appears such, sways the resulting

action; for it is this resulting action that alone determines which is greater.'

15. Ibid., sect. 256 ff., then 68 ff.; cf. *Positive Theory of Capital*, p. 191.

16. *Positive Theory of Capital*, pp. 191–6.

17. Meinong, *Psychologisch-ethische Untersuchungen zur Wertlehre* (Graz, 1894), pp. 15 ff. He says: 'I cannot desire what I have, but only something I do not have.' Ehrenfels, *System der Werttheorie*, vol. i (1897), p. 26: 'Only a non-present state of sensation can normally be desired.'

18. To avoid misunderstandings I should like to emphasize that on my own behalf I make none of these assumptions by which the desire intensities merely are brought in correlation with the intensities of *actual* sensations. Nevertheless, I must make them in order to be able to examine the opposing argumentation which accepts desire intensities as the only source of recognition for the intensity of *actual* sensations. I shall elaborate my own views in a different connection. Cf. 'Essay XI' in the text. [The reference is to the volume of *Exkurse* in which the present Essay first appeared. – Ed.].

19. E.g. Ehrenfels, *System der Werttheorie*, vol. i, p. 13.

20. Ehrenfels, ibid., p. 14. I refrain from more illustrations and further elaborations, and from an exhaustive analysis of their significance because I as nonexpert am writing no chapter on psychology. I merely want to justify my standpoint as economist on a question that is economically relevant, but not yet finally settled by psychology. Thus I must examine the facts won by experience and available to me.

21. The fact that the desire intensities of *others* are perceptible to us only through their decisions, and that the latter can serve as criterion of perception for intensities of sensations, naturally is a different matter. It would serve as such a criterion – although not as the only one – even when an independent evaluation of the respective intensities has preceded and underlies our decision. A businessman compares the profitability of purchasing coffee from two different sources, for instance, Hamburg and Trieste. He decides to buy in Trieste. Undoubtedly this decision is an apparent indication that our businessman found the purchase in Trieste more profitable. But his decision is by no means his real or even his only source of perception for this situation, for he first gained this knowledge from his calculations.

22. It is clear that we cannot do much with the evidence which Čuhel wants to deduce for his opinion from cases in which a decision must be made between two approximately equal sensations. That a non-existing difference or one that is not observable by our organs cannot be ascertained, obviously is no counterevidence against the assumption

354

that our organs can perceive the very sensations between which the unnoticeable difference exists. If I must decide which one of two approximately equal spruces I believe to be the taller one, I may indeed be at a loss in coming to a decision on the differences by mere eyesight. And yet, it would be obviously fallacious to assume that my own subjective decision, and not my eyesight, is the source for my opinion on the height and relationship of these spruces. In careful self-observation we may perceive the following even in the cases offered by Čuhel: Either that preceding our decision we formed an opinion according to which the competing sensations are indistinguishable as to their intensities. In this case circumstances may force us to decide arbitrarily (perhaps through the popular counting of buttons); or in our consciousness there is a preceding conclusion as to a tiny difference of intensity (perhaps also a vacillating opinion whereby one may prevail in the very moment of decision) to which our decision adjusts. In none of these cases was the decision the ultimate source of recognition. Furthermore, there can be no doubt that our incapacity to detect an unnoticeable or non-existing *difference* between two sensations can be accompanied by our perfect ability to determine whether the compared sensations were absolutely strong or weak – which, too, apparently contradicts Čuhel's point of view. Of course Čuhel need not take my whole counterargumentation as being directed at him. For I am fully aware that from the failure of his inner perception of unnoticeable differences of sensations he does *not* infer the general conclusion that inner perception must fail in all cases as source of perception for sensation intensities and that we basically depend on practical decisions. But thus Čuhel arrives at a divided solution of a question that not only permits a uniform solution, as I indicated in the foregoing (pp. 349 ff.) but also seems to demand one. And this seems to be an even more serious offense against the fundamentals of research.